D1082776

788.921 Mil
The Miles Davis reader

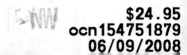

The Miles Davis Reader

DownBeat Hall of Fame Series, No. 1

The

Miles Davis

Reader

Edited and Compiled by
Frank Alkyer
Ed Enright
Jason Koransky

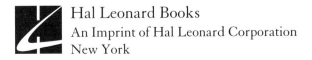
Hal Leonard Books
An Imprint of Hal Leonard Corporation
New York

Published in 2007 by Hal Leonard Books
An Imprint of Hal Leonard Corporation
19 West 21st Street, New York, NY 10010

Printed in the United States of America

Book design by Snow Creative Services

Owing to limitations of space, ackowledgments of permission to quote from previously published materials will be found on pages 355 and 356.

Library of Congress Cataloging-in-Publication Data is available upon request.

ISBN-10: 1-4234-3076-X
ISBN-13: 978-1-4234-3076-6

www.halleonard.com

CONTENTS

SECTION 2: THE *DOWNBEAT* FEATURES

PREFACE

The Miles Davis Reader from *Downbeat* serves as proof that a magazine can have a love affair with an artist. We tried to think of any other musician who has been reviewed so thoroughly, featured so often (even when he wouldn't grant an interview), or followed so closely in the pages of *DownBeat* for such a long period of time. The answer is none.

Who might come close? Charlie Parker and John Coltrane? Nope, they simply didn't live as long or record as much. Dizzy Gillespie, Duke Ellington, Count Basie, Benny Goodman, Louis Armstrong or Dave Brubeck? Maybe, but I certainly doubt it. The Miles files are just vast and voluminous.

Miles made for great copy because he was fascinating, not just musically but also personally. He was the great elusive interview, a challenge. Throughout the pages of this book, it's easy to see that *DownBeat* editors and writers earned their stripes by sitting down to interview Miles. Would he be warm, gracious, witty or ticked off and cantankerous? Could they coax a real interview out of him, just get pat answers or no answers at all? Would they get an hour with Miles, or two quick answers and the back of his jacket as he walked away? The road of music journalism is littered with quality writers who tried and failed to deliver a Miles Davis interview.

There have been plenty of artists who could talk about music. This book would not exist if Miles also didn't deliver the goods on the bandstand and in the recording studio in a way that only a select few from any musical genre ever have. He constantly changed his artistic skin. He remained restless and in search of the next musical movement right up until his death in 1991. *DownBeat* editors and writers loved every twist and turn. They were fans. But editors and writers fall in love with plenty of great artists who don't have commercial appeal. Believe me, I've seen it. I've been one of them. Luckily, the readers snapped up copies of *DownBeat* that featured Miles, making it good business, as well as good journalism, to get him into the magazine.

Miles also delivered because he lived in interesting times. I've always said that looking through the history of *DownBeat* is really looking through the history of America as told through the eyes of musicians. This book offers plenty of subtle lessons. For example, "The Slugging of Miles," a news story from 1959, tells of how New York's finest roughed up Miles for loitering outside Birdland, where he was working that night. If Miles were white, there would have been no incident.

OK, a little housekeeping before you begin to explore. The book is made up of hundreds of articles, features and reviews about Miles Davis, tons of bits and pieces cobbled together to tell his story. (It's not everything, but it includes a large portion of our Miles content). In compiling all of this information, we decided to divide the book into three broad sections: news, features and reviews. Within each section, the articles are in chronological order. It provides a real sense of going step by step through *DownBeat*'s written history of Miles. In the news section, it makes it seem as though Miles' life was one tragedy after another interspersed with one triumph after another. Maybe it was. In the features section, Miles starts out as this assured, polite young man, but develops into an assured, outspoken star, then into a revered, larger-than-life legend. In reviews, he starts with a few mentions as a sideman for Charlie Parker, but becomes an artist who is almost beyond critique. Watching these transitions develop on the printed page is fascinating.

This book was written over the course of some 60 years. That's going to create some editing issues. As a point of insider information, *DownBeat* has been a privately owned publication since its inception in 1934. The Maher family currently owns the publication, and has since 1950. It handles the business side, the editors make the product. The editors of *DownBeat* have always been, well, as independent as hogs on ice. But that's one of the reasons the magazine still exists today. The people who ran, and continue to run, the editorial side of the magazine are music people. They are serious. They have taken ownership of the work they produce. Being a *DownBeat* editor is a time-honored, sometimes turbulent tradition. Each editor brings their imagination, background, style and editorial slant to *DownBeat*. But they also bring their grammatical and linguistic quirks. Beyond that, language has simply changed during the course of 60 years. Words and phrases that were in fashion in the 1950s or the 1970s just aren't used today.

We've tried to make the style of this book as consistent as possible while keeping the language true to its time. So please don't be offended if you see the word "Negro" in articles from the 1950s. And please understand that at certain times in this magazine's history, all four-letter words were represented with a blank, like this ———. At other times, they were represented with the first and last letter with nonsense in between, like this "s#@t." And at other times, the words just appear.

The reviews chapter contains other quirks. When reading the early reviews, notice that famous songs from famous Davis albums are reviewed, each side of a single getting a star rating. The first 12-inch, 33⅓ album wasn't recorded until 1948, and we certainly didn't review everything when it came out. We catch up with the bulk of Davis' output, though, through a variety of reissues.

Finally, we owe a deep debt of gratitude to every editor and writer, designer, salesperson and circulation executive who has worked under the banner of *DownBeat*. It has been their diligence and contributions that make chronicling the great names in jazz, like Miles Davis, possible.

—Frank Alkyer,
Publisher, *DownBeat*

ACKNOWLEDGMENTS

This book could not have been compiled without the work of hundreds of writers and photographers. Those fine journalists have been credited throughout the book, and our appreciation for the work they do is endless.

It would have never gone to print without the dedication, focus and extraordinary efforts of a team of professionals who have helped pull this information into one document, edited it with an eagle eye and given up their time to see it through to completion. Kevin Maher, our president, gave this project the green light and kept the flame burning. Jeff Cagle served as a strong editorial assistant and proofreader. The same is true for Eric Bishop, who helped out in the research department. Tina Houston and Ara Tirado were of great help in the photo scanning process. And thanks to Dan Morgenstern and James "Tad" Hershorn at the Institute of Jazz Studies at Rutgers for seeking out and scanning some missing Miles covers.

Finally, big thanks to our friends at Hal Leonard. Carol Flannery and Jessica Burr stayed on us to turn this around on deadline, and Godwin Chu served as a meticulous copy editor. Keith Mardak, Larry Morton, Brad Smith and John Cerullo keep saying that we need to do more books---and, of course, they are right.

SECTION 1

Miles in the News

April 30, 1959
Miles With BMI

Trumpeter-composer Miles Davis has joined Broadcast Music, and hereafter public performances of his compositions will be licensed through BMI. Among them are: "Pent-Up," "Solar," "Blue Haze," "Valse Hot," "Donna Lee," "The Serpent's Tooth," "Take Off," "Lazy Susan" and "The Leap."

July 23, 1959
Portrait of Ira
The oldest Gershwin is still going strong.
by John Tynan

"I'm collecting all these *Porgy* albums," he announced. "It's getting to be sort of a hobby. But there are so many of them; where does it end?"

He had played the Gil Evans–Miles Davis album four times since he purchased it several days previously.

"Frankly, I didn't expect to like it at first," he confessed. "But, the more I listen to it, the more I see in it. It's certainly a worthwhile thing. What's that man's name? Miles Davis? I certainly have great respect for that man." As to Gil Evans' orchestration, Gershwin quoted praise from an unexpected quarter.

"Dimitri Tiomkin was here recently," he said, "and I played the album for him. He praised it highly. He said it was a masterly piece of work. Really, he got quite enthusiastic about it. Surprised me."

Oct. 1, 1959
The Slugging of Miles

If you go for a stroll on Broadway in the vicinity of New York's 52nd Street, you can on a normal evening spot any number of famous jazz musicians standing about, chatting, smoking cigarettes or just relaxing.

They are between sets at Birdland, and they have come upstairs for a breath of fresh air and a few minutes of comparative quiet.

On the evening of Aug. 26, the famous name standing near the curb was Miles Davis. Patrolman Gerald Kilduff, who explained later that the area is known as a trouble spot and policemen are under orders to keep crowds moving there, told Miles to move along. Said Miles, "I work here."

The officer said he told the trumpeter that in that case, he should stand near the building and not block the sidewalk. Miles—still according to the policeman's own report—said, "Lock me up."

Precisely what happened next depends on whose version of the story you hear, but within seconds, Miles was grappling with the policeman. Donald Rolker, a squad detective on night duty in plain clothes, rushed over and began beating Miles over the head with a blackjack.

Aside from the facts that (a) Miles is a fragile-built and very small man, while both the policemen were big and husky, and (b) that the skull the detective was pounding contains one of the best musical brains of our time, factors that made this incident exceptionally ugly were the following:

(1) Something close to a dozen witnesses interviewed by New York newspapers said that Det. Rolker was drunk.

(2) Almost all witnesses, including alto saxophonist Julian Adderley, made accusations of police brutality, saying that the beating was excessive and unnecessary. Said Miles later: "They beat me on the head like a tom-tom." A witness used the phrase "like a drum."

Adding to the distaste of the situation was the reaction of the Negro press. They intimated that the patrolman went for Miles because the trumpeter was seen escorting a white girl to a taxi.

Streaming blood from wounds on the head, Miles was taken to jail and his temporary cabaret card (see recent issues of *DownBeat*) was lifted. The first hint that police officials thought that Miles (admittedly known throughout the music business for arrogance, general cantankerousness and a well-developed Crow Jim attitude) might not be entirely in the wrong came the next day: He was told he could have his card restored "on demand."

Said Miles: "I don't want to work in New York anymore, especially at Birdland."

The incident should be put in social context. New York at this time is described as "like a volcano" by *DownBeat*'s New York editor George Hoefer. A number of youngsters between 14 and 20 were killed in gang rumbles within a few days. Shortly before the incident involving Miles, an attempt to arrest a drunken woman attracted a crowd of hundreds in Harlem and almost turned into a riot. Sugar Ray Robinson headed it off with a speech.

With teenage and racial troubles just at the boiling point, police are reported to be tense, worried and, in the cases of some, frightened. The same day Miles was beaten, another policeman shot a prisoner trying to escape in the parking lot at Bellevue Hospital. The prisoner was handcuffed.

Thus, the police department has been under fire. And because of the frequency of the brutality charges in the Miles Davis case, top officials of the department said a full investigation was under way.

There is a chance that, by a strange fluke, the police will hear an absolutely objective report of the incident. At the time Miles was beaten, an orchestra was in rehearsal in the studio across the street from Birdland—and taping the results. The noise outside was so bad that "we couldn't hear our own music," according to the musicians. So they decided to quit, and shoved their microphones out the window to make a record of the crowd noise.

According to the *New York Journal–American,* the four-minute tape that resulted is a complete record of the incident, including the screaming of sirens and the traffic jam that resulted on Broadway.

Meantime, while the police investigation pends, Miles was out on $1,000 bail. He was to appear Sept. 18 on a disorderly conduct charge. A simple assault charge was to be heard eventually in the Court of Special Sessions.

The trumpeter's lawyer (and personal manager), Harold Lovett, announced that he planned to sue the City of New York—for a half a million dollars.

Oct. 29, 1959

Aftermath for Miles

If the upper echelons of New York's police department have come to any conclusions in their probe of alleged brutality by two police officers against Miles Davis, they haven't said. But the investigation, made at the demand of Al Manuti, president of American Federation of Musicians Local 802, was evidently still under way.

In the meantime, the charges against the trumpeter were also pending, with this significant change: A charge of assault was reduced to one of third-degree assault. Since third-degree assault does not constitute a felony, the police thus untied their own hands to give Miles back his cabaret card, lifted on the night that a detective clobbered him over the head with a sap outside Birdland (see *DownBeat,* Oct. 1).

Now Miles faces, besides the third-degree assault charge, only a disorderly conduct charge, which was postponed to a mid-October hearing. Meanwhile, the trumpeter engaged attorneys Nathan Mitchell and William Chance to handle his end of the dispute with the New York Police Department. He was backed by a good deal of popular and press opinion, including that of the *New York Amsterdam News,* a Negro newspaper, which said he had suffered a "Georgia head whipping."

Pat Healey of the Police Legal Aid office is the attorney representing patrolman Gerald Kilduff, one of the two police officers (the other was detective Donald Rolker) involved in the slugging. Witnesses said Rolker hit the musician many times.

At the time of the incident, Miles said, "I don't want to work in New York anymore, especially in Birdland."

A couple of weeks later, his restored card in his pocket, he was again working in New York—at Birdland.

Feb. 18, 1960

Miles Exonerated

"It would be a travesty on justice to adjudge the victim of an illegal arrest guilty of the crime of assaulting the one who made the arrest."

With this acid comment, three New York justices dismissed the remaining charge, which grew out of the Birdland incident of last August, against trumpeter Miles Davis.

The justices—Benjamin Gassman, Arthur Dunaif and Evelyn Richman—considered the charges against the musician in an all-day trial at New York's Special Sessions Court. They made their statement as they cleared Miles of all charges against him.

The assault charge had grown out of an attempt by officer Gerald Kilduff to arrest the 33-year-old musician for refusing to move from in front of Birdland. Davis was working there at the time.

During the ensuing argument, Davis was struck on the head by detective Donald Rolker. Five stitches were required to close the wound. A disorderly conduct charge lodged against Davis was later dismissed in Magistrate's Court.

Commenting on the dismissal of the remaining third-degree assault charge, the three justices said, "The arresting officers may well have been guilty of misguided zeal and not a deliberate violation of law in placing the defendant under arrest."

With the dismissal of the remaining charge against Davis, his attorney, Harold Lovett, wants to file a $1 million damage suit against the City of New York. But Miles, reportedly, does not want to push the city too far, on grounds that even though he might win the damage suit, he might then become a target for the police, who might seek to nail him on any charge they could find or drum up. This could cost him his cabaret work card, issued by the New York police.

Commented Jack Whittemore, booking agent for the trumpeter, "He feels he has proved his point if he is found innocent of all the charges placed against him."

―――――――

March 31, 1960
Miles Files

Last fall, after Miles Davis was severely beaten by two cops in front of Birdland, his business manager, Harold Lovett, said he intended to sue the City of New York for $1 million.

But Miles himself evidently was not so sure about the move. He was reportedly willing to forget the whole thing if he was cleared of the third-degree assault and disorderly conduct charges—and thereby justified in his claim that the incident was unprovoked.

Later, the musician was completely cleared when judges in two courts dismissed the charges against him (*DownBeat,* Feb. 18) and, in the case of one of them, criticized the arrest of the trumpeter. Rumor in the trade had it that Miles thought the police might seek to make further trouble for him if the suit was filed.

Yet in mid-February, a court hearing was scheduled in the suit—quietly filed by Lovett last November. The grounds were false arrest, assault and battery, and malicious prosecution.

But the hearing had to be postponed. Miles was out of town—playing a gig at Chicago's Sutherland Hotel Lounge. And when he would be available in New York for a hearing was problematical, since he was scheduled to open March 21 in Paris with Norman Granz's Jazz at the Philharmonic.

Asked whether Miles was in agreement with him about filing the suit, Lovett said, "Why wouldn't he be?" Miles himself, with his legendary detachment, hadn't bothered to comment.

―――――――

March 31, 1960
Miles Davis "Approved" for Bay Concert

After much soul-searching, the management of San Francisco's Masonic Temple appears to have determined that Miles Davis fans in the Bay Area can be trusted not to beat up the ushers and tear seats apart.

The alleged proclivity to violence of Davis' admirers prompted Alvin A. Horwege, manager of the 3,200-seat auditorium, to deny the use or rental of the hall to the National Association for the Advancement of Colored People (NAACP), which plays a benefit concert there by the trumpeter in October.

Other artists similarly barred in the past from playing the temple include Nat Cole and Ray Charles. The Cole ban was in February 1960; Charles was prevented from appearing there last New Year's Eve.

In all three cases, Horwege declared his decisions were made "not because of race or color but because we had been advised the kind of audiences these artists draw could be destructive to our $7 million auditorium." In support of his nonracial reason, the manager noted that Ella Fitzgerald, Dinah Washington and Dakota Staton have played the hall at various times.

Within 30 days of the Davis ban, however, other voices apparently prevailed in straightening out temple management on the risk of a riot.

According to Al Robinson, chairman of NAACP's concert division in San Francisco, Horwege early this month reversed his decision. The temple now is available without charge for the NAACP benefit or at a fee of $650 for commercial purposes, Robinson said. He added further that future bookings there by Cole, Charles and other Negro performers would be assured without management hindrance.

All projected shows at the temple, however, will continue to be "screened" to guard against what the management termed "the wrong audiences."

Aug. 18, 1960
The Sound of Miles

Miles Davis' first music teacher in East St. Louis, Ill., was adamant on one point: He told the future jazz great, "No vibrato! You're going to get old and start shaking, so play without any vibrato." Miles was 13, and in grade school.

Twenty years later, taping a half-hour television film for CBS Films, Miles described his own playing as, "fast, light and still no vibrato."

The film, *The Sound of Miles Davis,* is one of a series of 26 on subjects ranging from drama to ballet, produced by Robert Herridge. The only other jazz film in the series is a half-hour on pianist Ahmad Jamal.

Made more than a year ago, the films are now ready for syndication to CBS outlets across the country as *The Robert Herridge Theater.* Six of the episodes, including the Davis film, are being shown during July and August on New York's WCBS-TV (non-network). The Davis film was shown July 21. It was the trumpeter's first major appearance on television.

Herridge, who appears on camera as narrator, confines his introductory remarks on Miles to a few words. The music is divided into two segments: Miles accompanied by members of his quintet, and accompanied by a 19-piece orchestra under the direction of Gil Evans.

The first nine minutes feature the quintet playing the Davis original "So What." There are short solos by tenor saxophonist John Coltrane and pianist Wynton Kelly, though most of the running time is devoted to Miles. Also on camera are bassist Paul Chambers and drummer Jimmy Cobb. (Alto saxophonist Cannonball Adderley, who at the time of the taping was a member of the Davis group, was sick and unable to make the session.)

The balance of the program—approximately 15 minutes—features three tunes played by Miles with the Evans orchestra behind him. In the larger group are Ernie Royal, Louis Mucci, John Coles, Emmett Berry and Clyde Reisinger, trumpets; Frank Rehak, Jimmy Cleveland, Bill Elton and Rod Levitt, trombones; Julius Watkins and Robert Northern, French horns; Romeo Penque, Danny Banks and Ed Caine, woodwinds; Coltrane, alto saxophone (in place of Adderley); John Barber, tuba; Chambers, bass; and Cobb, drums.

Davis, concentrating on the music in his brooding manner, is seen and heard performing "The Duke," a tribute to Duke Ellington written by Dave Brubeck; "Blues for Pablo," a ballad by Evans; and "New Rhumba," by Jamal. All are tunes from the album *Miles Ahead,* on which Davis was paired with arranger Evans.

Usually Davis hates to take a backward look at his work. He says, "You always see how you would have done it differently." Herridge feels it is significant that Miles has watched the film at least five times.

Davis, who looks and acts fiercely individualistic, has this to say: "If I play good for eight bars, it's enough for me. It's satisfaction. The only thing is, I don't tell anybody which eight bars are the good ones. That's my secret."

———

Oct. 27, 1960
Miles in the Hot Box
by George Hoefer

Once a musician is mature, he is what he plays. This simple statement was voiced by a record company executive as a personal theory regarding the jazz musician as an artist.

Miles Davis is an excellent example. There has been an image of trumpeter Davis that has been formed from the effects of his frustrations, unhappiness and problems, among other things.

This is a secondhand evaluation and not valid. It is more realistic to judge Davis upon the contributions these same factors have made to his art. After all, so much of jazz is based on the blues, and there is not a more creative, ever-seeking and expressive voice in jazz today than Miles Davis'.

Davis has been criticized (frequently by club owners) for his attitude toward listeners and for walking off the stand while not playing. He has a logical answer to the disappearing act: "I feel silly just standing around." The musical format of the Davis group, with long solos by its members, does not require the leader's constant presence.

The strange result of this conduct is that, in actuality, it is one of the most potent psychological acts of showmanship seen in a modern jazz group.

Davis is a fascinating artist to watch. His concentration, his stance and the way he handles his horn constitute an intriguing sight. It would seem that the vaudeville adage, "Leave them while they're happy," could be applied in this situation. Davis' return to the stand is looked forward to with anticipation. Miles' temporary retirement from the spotlight could also be construed as an act of courtesy to other soloists in the group.

Which all brings us to the Miles Davis press conference held recently. His new album, *Sketches of Spain,* arranged and conducted by Gil Evans, was due for release. Peter Long, assistant producer of Randall's Island Jazz Festival, arranged for the press conference to be based upon questions regarding the new album.

Everyone was aware of Davis' sensitivity and probably thinking to himself, "Miles is not going to dig this."

In fact, the conference almost blew up before it started, when Long, in order to start things off, asked a reporter if he had any questions regarding the album. The reporter answered he did not, for he had not heard the album. Miles then got up from the table and said, "That's it. Back to the bar. Nobody has heard the records, and this conference does not make sense."

Several of the questioners present had heard the work, and the conference got under way. Then came the inevitable question:

"Mr. Davis, do you feel this new work of yours is jazz?"

There was an almost imperceptible bristling visible in the Davis visage as he answered, "It's music, and I like it. I'll play anything I take a fancy to, if I feel it is possible for me to do it. Gil and I worked together on the concerto for two months in preparation for the recording."

Then Davis was asked if there was any relation between flamencan music and the blues. Miles replied, "Flamenco (Gypsy music) is the Spanish counterpart of our blues."

At this point, flamencan guitarist Augustin DiMello, who was entertaining at the party and had been on the record date, was asked to come forward. He added, "The flamenco dances and music do have the same connotation and emotional content to the Spanish people that the blues have to Americans." He also said the results obtained by Davis and Evans on the recording were authentically valid.

Davis, who was articulate as well as polite, continued, "I found the hardest parts for me were the trios, where, as I improvised, I had to watch out for the red and green lights used in recording. In the little trio part at the beginning of the concerto, it was hard for me to stay in balance with the other players. The work was originally written for guitar."

Evans mentioned at this point that they had spent three recording dates perfecting the concerto, but on the other tracks they took one take only.

When asked if this work meant he was taking on a new direction, Miles said smilingly, "If you mean am I going to Madrid to live and marry a Spanish girl, the answer is no. Gil and I are interested in doing an African ballet album. I think that will be the next direction."

Long said Davis had told him he had enjoyed the conference very much and had remarked, "Now I am a speaker."

Good. Maybe he'll start announcing the tunes.

Nov. 10, 1960
Afterthoughts
by Gene Lees

Now that Miles Davis has played England, the strange game of guessing what he is "really" like has invaded even that green and pleasant land. Ah, but England used to be such a rational nation, a land where privacy was respected and even celebrities were thought to have a right to a certain amount of it.

I've met Miles Davis exactly twice. (He was cordial enough.) Yet people expect me to speculate, on that fragile basis, about his personality. How do I know what he's "really" like? I'm not even sure what I'm like!

But more to the point, I couldn't care less what he's like. When he plays, he gives me beauty. Do most of those people we know well give half as much?

July 6, 1961
Miles Davis to Retire?

From a recent casual conversation in a San Francisco jazz club may shortly stem one of the most startling stories of jazz: the announced retirement of Miles Davis from music.

Jazz reporter Russ Wilson of the *Oakland Tribune,* covering Davis' appearance at San Francisco's Blackhawk Club, fell into conversation with the trumpeter between sets. Almost casually, Wilson reported, the 36-year-old Davis remarked he was considering giving up playing.

On further questioning, according to Wilson, Davis declared, "I'm not considering it—I'm going to retire. I've got $1,000 a week coming in now so I don't have to work. And I've been playing for 22 years—a long time."

Wilson, whose pencil now was working overtime, then asked Davis if he planned to continue recording. The answer was, "No." What would he do for musical kicks? "I'll buy records," Davis replied.

―――――

Aug. 17, 1961
Miles in Feather's Nest
by Leonard Feather

It seems that almost everyone digs Miles Davis except Uncle Sam.

Every magazine from *Jazz Echo* in Hamburg, Germany, to the Japanese edition of *DownBeat* has elected him to first place in the trumpet section of its jazz poll.

He was listed, along with Marian Anderson, Dr. Ralph Bunche and Katharine Dunham, among this country's top 10 Negroes in the international edition of *Life.* ("Why didn't they put it in the domestic edition if they believe it?" Davis asked.) He even won that best-dressed-man award from *Gentleman's Quarterly.* And if they took a poll of night-club operators, Davis would win it horns down, for he's a cinch to draw capacity business.

Despite his musical, international, sartorial and economic achievements, Miles says the U.S. State Department never has offered to subsidize a trip for his quintet, though the number of artists sent abroad on such good-will trips in the last five years has stretched into the hundreds.

"I'd rather have somebody curse me out than ignore me," he said. "Anyhow, I don't want them to send me over just because I'm a Negro, and they want to woo Africa."

Thanks to the initiative and good taste of Dr. Marshall Stearns, the State Department's jazz program started out gloriously in 1956. The first band to be sent overseas was the specially assembled interracial Dizzy Gillespie Orchestra (which enjoyed not only Stearns' blessing but also his presence as lecturer on the first tour). Later, when outside interference entered the picture, there was at least one occasion when a big jazz star was advised that the group he was to assemble on his excursion for democracy must be lily white, perhaps to placate Southern senators when fund-appropriations time drew near.

"If I ever went on one of those tours," Miles said, "they'd have to give me a badge to wear over here. A platinum badge. It would have to say on it that this man did such and such a thing for his country and his government.

"I met a man in London last fall who has something to do with sending these bands abroad. I said to him, 'Well, so you're the people that sent ———— ———— and those guys to Africa, right? Well that was the dumbest move I ever heard of in my life. An African friend of mine heard them and told me later that the Africans themselves can do better than that, so who needed it?" (Davis was talking about one of the white combos sent to Africa in recent years.)

Perhaps the State Department is not unaware that Miles, at cocktail parties in his honor overseas, would not be likely to paint the U.S. racial scene in glowing colors and that he is no more given to compromise or diplomacy in his opinions than in his music.

It is realism, not bitterness, that prompts him to comment as he does on the belated acknowledgment of jazz in its country of birth. "If Charlie Parker had been French, they'd have had a monument built for him over there," he said. "But millions of people in this country never heard of him, or just read about him when he died and then forgot him.

"They don't even publicize what they do send. Brownie McGhee went to India, and the people over here don't even know about it. Are they afraid to publish it here?

"Come to think of it, I hope the State Department does ask me to make one of those tours—just so I can have the pleasure of saying no."

Nov. 7, 1963
One Pays—Another Gets It

The hardships of paying and collecting money are well known, but few persons are confronted with the problems recently encountered by trumpeter Miles Davis and trombonist Al Grey.

Davis is paying—to the tune of $8,000. The money will be paid in installments to promoter George Woods, a disc jockey for Philadelphia's WDAS. Woods had sought $25,000 to make up for revenue he claimed he lost when Davis failed to appear at the Uptown Theater last New Year's Eve and New Year's Day, the last two days for a show that also featured organist

Jimmy Smith and singer Aretha Franklin. The penalty action was taken at a special meeting of the American Federation of Musicians' international executive board.

<hr />

Nov. 7, 1963

Gil Evans and Miles Davis Collaborate on Theater Score

Though partnered in several successful record albums (*Miles Ahead, Porgy and Bess, Sketches of Spain*), trumpeter Miles Davis and arranger Gil Evans have confined their joint efforts to records or the concert stage. Recently in Hollywood, Calif., a deal was set that changed all that. Davis and Evans, it was announced, are collaborating on the background music for a new play to open on Broadway in November.

The play, *The Time of the Barracudas,* stars Laurence Harvey and Elaine Stritch and is produced by Frederick Brisson and Roger L. Stevens. It began a tryout tour in San Francisco Oct. 21.

Harvey, it was learned, flew Evans to the coast to begin orchestrating Davis' sketches for the score. The music was recorded in Hollywood, and the taped recording is being used for the play. Evans conducted and Davis played on the tape.

<hr />

Dec. 5, 1963

Eight Men in Pit for Play Using Davis–Evans Recording

By standing union edict, a new play, *The Time of the Barracudas,* with background music recorded by Miles Davis and arranged by Gil Evans (*DB,* Nov. 7), has eight musicians in the pit who were not originally planned for by the producers. The Davis–Evans recording is played during the performance in Hollywood's Huntington Hartford Theater.

John Tranchitella, president of Los Angeles' AFM Local 47, denied the musicians constitute a stand-by band.

"Forget the word 'stand-by,'" he told *DownBeat.* "We want—and always have wanted—musicians hired who are ready, willing and able to play."

"And they will play," he added, "at least the overture."

Tranchitella pointed out that the AFM's international bylaws demand that local union permission be granted to play a pre-recorded musical tape as part of a theatrical production. The premise of this rule is that, by using such a tape, musicians are being denied work in such a production.

According to Tranchitella, Frederick Brisson, the play's producer, did not request such permission from Local 47.

The jazz background score, which is believed to mark a first for both Davis and Evans, was recorded in the Hollywood studios of Columbia Records, the label for which Davis records.

In addition to Davis and three members of his quintet—Herbie Hancock, piano; Ron Carter, bass; and Anthony Williams, drums—the recording for this play was made by top Hollywood studio musicians. Contracted by Paul Hocs, the larger group consisted of himself and Buddy Collette, flutes; Gene Cipelano, oboe; Fred Dutton, bassoon; Richard Perissi, Bill Hinshaw and Art Masbe, French horns; Dick Leith, bass trombone; and Marjorie Call, harp.

The Time of the Barracudas, a comedy starring Laurence Harvey and Elaine Stritch, is due to open on Broadway soon following break-in runs in San Francisco and Hollywood.

―――――――

Dec. 19, 1963
Davis–Evans Tape Dropped From Play

The recorded music of Miles Davis and Gil Evans struck out all the way during the Hollywood tryout run of Peter Barnes' new comedy *The Time of the Barracudas (DB,* Dec. 5, 1963).

Originally recorded by Davis and Evans for use during the play's performances at the Huntington Hartford Theater, the taped music gave rise to a dispute between AFM Local 47 and the play's producers that resulted in the elimination of the incidental score after the first week's performances.

After the initial stand taken by union officials—that the same number of musicians (eight) used on the recording would have to be paid for each performance of the play—the producers agreed, signed a contract to that effect with the union and declared they would continue to use the tape according to Max Herman, Local 47 vice president.

Fred Hebert, the play's director, told *DownBeat* he had dropped use of the tape after the first six days of the play's run.

Hebert, who declined comment on the dispute with the union, was asked why he had stopped the music. He said, "It wasn't for artistic reasons, let's say."

Herman laid the union's position on the line: "They signed a contract with us, and we're holding them to it. The musicians are reporting for work at the theater every night."

The musicians, however, were not playing because, according to Hebert, the Huntington Hartford is "not equipped" for such a live performance, either in direct conjunction with the play or as overture and exit music. During the previous run in San Francisco, he said, there was a band hired and it played.

━━━━

June 18, 1964
SF Club Owner Says Miles Goofed Gig

Art Auerbach, owner of the Jazz Workshop, and Miles Davis parted on less than friendly terms after the trumpeter's recent two-week engagement at the San Francisco club.

Auerbach said that Davis did not play a full schedule on several nights of his stay and additionally failed to appear on three other nights—once without advance notice.

During the first week, Auerbach said, Davis notified the owner he had had a tooth pulled and could not play Thursday night. The next week, Auerbach said, Davis played only one set on Tuesday night, leaving at 11 p.m.; played two sets Thursday and left at 12:30 a.m.; played three sets instead of the scheduled four on Friday night; and played four sets instead of the five scheduled for Saturday, which included a 2:30 a.m. special show.

Auerbach said Davis notified him he could not play Wednesday night of the second week, and as a result the owner kept the club closed. On Sunday night, the last of the engagement, Davis failed to appear and gave no warning of his absence, Auerbach said. As a result, the owner said, he had to close the club and refund the door charge to customers who were inside waiting.

"No other musician has ever closed my club in the seven years I've been operating it," Auerbach declared. "I feel it was inexcusable."

Because California law prohibits the presence of minors in bars, Auerbach suspended his liquor license for the Davis group's stay in order that 18-year-old drummer Tony Williams might appear with the group.

"I did this because Miles is a great musician, has an excellent group, and I wanted them to be heard in San Francisco," Auerbach said.

The club's $2 door charge and sale of soft drinks at $1.25 enabled Auerbach to make what he termed a small profit. He maintained, however, that Davis overdrew his pay by $1,000 in view of his curtailed appearances. Negotiations to settle this are under way, Auerbach said.

In between sets at New York's Village Vanguard, where he and his quintet were playing, Davis, commenting on Auerbach's charges, said, "He's made a lot of money—and he's got my horn, too."

May 20, 1965
Surgery

Trumpeter Miles Davis underwent major surgery, including bone scraping, at New York Hospital's Special Surgery Clinic April 14.

Davis had been suffering from a painful hip-bone ailment—calcium deposits in the left hip bone—for many months preceding the operation. A spokesman for Davis said the trumpeter was resting comfortably but his convalescence probably would be long.

July 1, 1965
Leg Cast Comes Off

The leg cast trumpeter Miles Davis has been wearing since his release from a New York hospital following an operation to remove calcium deposits from his hip is due to come off July 14. In the meantime, Davis is scheduled to perform at two jazz festivals, those at Pittsburgh (June 18–20) and Newport (July 1–4); if he is able to appear, he will play seated, probably in the wheelchair that has been his mode of transportation since the operation.

July 1, 1965
Rehearsals Set to Begin

Trumpeter Miles Davis was set to begin rehearsals of his quintet after several months of inactivity during which he convalesced from a hip operation. The rehearsals were to begin Aug. 10, four days before he was to play at the *DownBeat* Jazz Festival in Chicago. On Aug. 4, however, Davis fell in his New York City home and broke his leg. There has been no prediction of when Davis will be able to play in public.

Dec. 30, 1965
Miles Back in Action

Miles Davis played in public for the first time in almost eight months when he opened in mid-November at Philadelphia's Showboat Lounge. The trumpeter was operated on for calcium deposits in his hip last April, and in August he fell and broke his leg.

After the Philadelphia job, Davis took his quintet to Detroit for a one-week stand at the Grand Bar and from there to New York's Village Vanguard for a Thanksgiving-week engagement, followed by a stint at the Bohemian Caverns in Washington, D.C.

With Davis on all the gigs were tenor saxophonist Wayne Shorter, pianist Herbie Hancock and drummer Tony Williams. The bass position was filled in Philadelphia and New York by Gary Peacock and in Detroit by Reggie Workman.

In addition to future engagements in this country, there is a possibility that Davis will do a world tour under the auspices of entrepreneur George Wein.

March 24, 1966
Hospitalized Again

Miles Davis, who underwent surgery for a hip ailment last April and who broke his leg in August, was hospitalized again Jan. 31, this time for inflammation of the liver. He was confined at University Hospital in New York City until Feb. 14, when he was allowed to go home for a two-week convalescence. Davis' agents said the trumpeter was expected to resume work in early March.

Nov. 14, 1968
Miles Davis Takes New Bride of Many Talents

Betty Mabry Davis, 23, has a lot of things going for her. She wrote "Uptown" (recorded by the Chambers Brothers), has signed as a singer with Columbia Records, has appeared on the *Dating Game* TV show, been a pin-up in *Jet* magazine, operated the Celler teen club in New York and studied fashion design.

And now trumpet star Miles Davis has taken her as his spouse.

The couple was married in Gary, Ind., on the last day of September, following Davis' engagement at Chicago's Plugged Nickel. Only the trumpeter's closest friends knew of his plans, but Davis was obviously in excellent spirits throughout his stay at the Nickel.

The new Mrs. Davis, a 5-foot-7-inch beauty from Homestead, Pa., first saw Miles two years ago at a concert in New York. She says, "We were introduced, but nothing came of it until six months ago." Engaged five days before the marriage, she said: "He called me from Chicago and said, 'Sweetcakes, get your stuff together and come to Chicago, we're getting married.'" (Davis was divorced last February from Frances Taylor.)

Obviously happy in her new role, Mrs. Davis said, "One of the sexiest men alive is Miles Dewey Davis. We're going to be married forever, because I'm in love, and Mr. Davis can do no wrong as far as I'm concerned. He's experienced all facets of life, has terrific taste in everything, loves only the best and has taught me many things."

Mrs. Davis added that she has "never really been a jazz fan, because I lean mostly to R&B and pop, but Miles' *Sketches of Spain* and *Kind of Blue* really sock it to me. But Miles is the teacher, so I'm going to be cool, stay in the background and back up my man . . ."

Feb. 20, 1969

Japanese Wreck Tour by Miles Davis Group

Miles Davis and the members of his quintet were packed and ready to leave for a scheduled 13-concert tour of Japan when the bad news came: No visas would be granted.

"They had us on tenterhooks right up to the end," said Davis' personal manager, Jack Whittemore. "The Japanese promoters kept cabling us that things looked 'favorable,' but the visas never came through. When we got the final refusal, the only explanation given was 'personal reasons.' All 2,400 seats for the opening concert in Tokyo Jan. 6 were sold out."

Japanese reluctance to admit U.S. jazzmen is nothing new—the policy has been more than stringent since the arrests and convictions for narcotics offenses of several touring drummers in 1967. Up to now, however, certain unofficial guideposts seemed to exist, making it clear that no musician with a record of convictions—no matter how old or how minor—would be admitted.

It was for this reason that Davis had engaged drummer Jack DeJohnette for the tour, since regular quintet member Tony Williams had been in trouble in Japan. This was to no avail, however. Davis himself has never been convicted of any offense, but the fact that he has an old arrest record (including one for traffic tickets) leads Whittemore to suspect that the Japanese policy of exclusion has been broadened to include simple arrest without conviction.

This hypothesis is bolstered by the fact that drummer Sunny Murray was denied a visa last year, though his only scrape with the law has been an arrest for trespassing when he was a teenager. Also, the tour of a famous jazz ensemble was cancelled last fall when a visa was denied to a member of the group with an ancient narcotics arrest on his record. On the other hand, a famous drummer who was refused admission in 1967 was granted a visa in 1968.

"The policy is mystifying," Whittemore says. "Miles is terribly disappointed." And so, one might surmise, are his thousands of Japanese fans. Considering the great popularity of American jazz in Japan, the government's discriminatory policy toward its foremost practitioners appears to go beyond the normal boundaries of inscrutability.

Nov. 13, 1969
Miles Davis Shot in N.Y. Extortion Plot

Miles Davis was shot and wounded in the hip by unknown assailants in the early morning of Oct. 9 as he sat in a parked car with a friend in New York's East Village.

The injury was not serious, and Davis was treated at a hospital and released.

The trumpeter, who was appearing at the Blue Coronet in Brooklyn, told police that he had been warned four days prior to the assault not to appear at the club, located in Bedford-Stuyvesant, unless he paid part of his salary to the unidentified man making the threats.

After finishing the night's work, Davis drove a woman friend to her home. They were sitting in the car when a gypsy cab carrying three men drove up. One of the men got out and fired four shots, after which all three fled. Davis' passenger was not hit.

According to police, an unspecified quantity of marijuana was found in the car Davis was driving. He was booked on charges of possession, but these were dropped when it was established that the car had recently been driven from California and that it could not be proved how or when the grass had been placed in the car.

Davis offered a $5,000 reward for information leading to the identification and/or arrest of his assailants. He said he would never again play at the club.

April 16, 1970
Days in the Lives of Our Jazz Superstars

On March 3, Miles Davis was sitting in his $17,000 red Ferrari, stopped in a no-standing zone on Central Park South near Fifth Avenue in New York.

A patrolman went to the car to ask Davis to move, noted that it had no inspection sticker and asked the trumpeter for his license and registration.

Davis, clad in an outfit including a turban, white sheepskin coat and snakeskin pants, searched for the papers in his mod shoulder-strap handbag. A set of brass knuckles fell from the bag.

Under New York state law, brass knuckles are classified as a deadly weapon, and though Davis insisted he was carrying them for self-protection (not long ago, he was shot at, again while sitting in a parked car in Manhattan), he was booked on a weapons charge and for driving an unlicensed, unregistered and uninspected vehicle.

The next day, Davis was cleared of all charges except that of being an unlicensed driver, for which he was fined $100.

Dec. 7, 1972
Miles Breaks Both Legs in Car Crash

Miles Davis, who loves sports cars, crashed his latest into an island on Manhattan's treacherous West Side Highway about 8 a.m. on Oct. 19, having decided to take a morning drive because he felt restless.

Both the trumpeter's legs were broken, and he also suffered facial cuts requiring 12 stitches. Confined in New York Hospital, he will probably be laid up at least until mid-December.

"I'm all right," Miles told a reporter a day after the accident. "I'll just have to stop buying those little cars."

Miles and his new band had been scheduled to open at Harlem's Apollo Theater Oct. 24—an unusual booking which hopefully will be rescheduled.

March 1, 1973
Miles Back in Action; Liebman Joins Group
by Dan Morgenstern

Fully recovered from the Oct. 19 auto accident in which he broke both ankles, Miles Davis returned to action Jan. 12–13 at the Village East (formerly Fillmore East) in New York.

With the exception of soprano saxophonist Dave Liebman in place of Carlos Garnett, the group led by the newly mustachioed trumpeter was the same as last fall (Reggie Lucas, guitar; Cedric Lawson, organ and synthesizer; Bala Krishna, sitar; Mike Henderson, bass; Badal Roy, tabla; Mtume, congas; Al Foster, drums), but it sounded much more vital and together than when we last heard it at Philharmonic Hall.

Davis, exuding energy, was less fixated on his wah-wah pedal. The hour-long set on Saturday night emphasized a blues-based music of great rhythmic power, anchored in Henderson's rock-steady and huge-toned bass, Foster's agile, dancing drums and Mtume's strong conga accents. There was a surprising interlude in which Davis—in an entirely new way—recaptured the lyrical mood of the past. And throughout, Miles was in the forefront, laying out only for occasional solo spots by others, mainly Liebman, who sounded more into the group than his predecessors . . . and this is group music, no doubt about that.

From New York, the group went on to Montreal's Place Des Arts (Jan. 24), Michigan State University (Jan. 26), Minneapolis' Guthrie Theater (Jan. 28) and East Michigan University (Feb. 10). On Feb. 23, they'll be at the Music Hall in Dallas, and at the Coliseum in Houston on Feb. 26.

Before leaving New York, Miles put a new album in the can. Meanwhile, since his latest release, *On the Corner,* was brought out entirely without personnel data, we thought we'd give you this collective lineup, courtesy of Columbia: Carlos Garnett, saxophones; Herbie Hancock, Harold J. Williams, keyboards; David Creamer, guitar; Mike Henderson, bass; Colin Walcott, sitar; Badal Roy, tabla; Jack DeJohnette, Billy Hart, drums; Mtume, percussion.

April 26, 1973
At Last: Correct *On the Corner* Personnel

As everyone knows by now, Miles Davis' *On the Corner* was issued without any personnel information. Not long after the album's release, we ran into Teo Macero, Miles' producer. Teo didn't tell us why the personnel had been omitted, but did say we should call his office—they had the information handy in anticipation of requests from the press.

We called, reported the personnel in a recent news story and again used it with the review of the record. Since then, however, we've had a nice letter from Dave Liebman, Miles' saxophonist, informing us that the personnel Macero gave out is "a bit incorrect" and supplying the accurate one:

Bennie Maupin, bass clarinet; David Liebman, soprano sax (1st side only); Carlos Garnett, soprano and tenor sax (2nd side); Chick Corea, Herbie Hancock, Harold Williams, piano, electric piano, synthesizer; John McLaughlin, guitar; Colin Walcott, sitar; Michael Henderson, bass; Jack DeJohnette, drums; Billy Hart, drums, percussion, bongos; Don Alias, Mtume, congas; Badal Roy, tabla—and, of course, Miles Davis, trumpet.

To Liebman, many thanks. Miles' next we hear will be a live recording of his 1972 Philharmonic Hall concert, with the personnel a matter of record. Even so, we hope to see it listed accurately on the album somewhere, not just for the sake of interested listeners and potential buyers, but for the sake of the players, too.

April 20, 1978
Miles Cuts New Sides

It happened totally unexpectedly, catching everybody off guard. One day recently, Teo Macero received a phone call from the ever-mysterious Miles Davis. Miles, in his customary laconic fashion, said, "I'm ready" to Teo. The next day saw Davis and assembled crew in a New York studio laying down fresh material.

The latest Davis sessions feature Larry Coryell, guitar; Masabumi Kikuchi and George Paulis, keyboards; T.M. Stevens, electric bass; Al Foster, drums; and Bobby Scott, horn charts.

An observer has described the music as a cross between "late-'60s free and late-'70s disco."

February 1982
Miles Tyson the Knot

Miles Davis and Cicely Tyson celebrated their on-again/off-again 10-year romance in a silent way with Thanksgiving nuptials (his third, her second) at Shelbourne, Mass.; Bill Cosby was best man and the Rev. Andy Young, Atlanta's mayor-elect, officiated. Only a day later Miles was back onstage in Ft. Lauderdale, Fla.

―――

April 1982
Eighteen-Wheelin' Miles

Often in the forefront of crossover music, Miles Davis was caught hobnobbin' with Willie Nelson backstage at Caesar's Palace during the latter's recent gig in Las Vegas.

Rumor has it that they penned a tune called "Expect Me Around."

Miles sported a Willie Nelson hat on his recent tours, recorded a cut, "Willie Nelson," on his *Directions* LP and both are Columbia artists, so can a country-jazz duo album be in the cards?

―――

September 1982
Kool Road for Miles

Miles Davis and band appeared in Washington, D.C.'s Kennedy Center at the opening of a 20-city '82 Kool Jazz Festival tour. The first event ever to fill all four of the center's theaters also featured—at the same time on a neighboring stage—fellow trumpeters Dizzy Gillespie and Wynton Marsalis jamming with Miles' '60s rhythm team of Herbie Hancock, Ron Carter and Tony Williams.

―――

February 1994
Miles Davis Movie Projected for '96
by Ed Enright

Jazz enthusiasts can expect to see Miles Davis, as portrayed by actor Wesley Snipes, on the silver screen sometime in 1996, according to an independent, three-man movie-production team.

Former CBS Records chairman Walter Yetnikoff will finance the entire Miles Davis Project, which will be produced by Preston Holmes and Fernando Suluchin, associate producers of Spike Lee's *Malcolm X*. The three men conceived of the project and began negotiating movie rights from the Miles Davis Estate in late 1992.

Holmes and Suluchin stressed the importance of keeping the project independent as long as possible to preserve its classiness and artistic merit. "When you're going to the big box, you need to make a deal with someone," Suluchin said. "We don't want any creative input, other than the talent, because we want to make an A-plus movie."

"We want to have a script that we're happy with in hand before involving anyone else in the creative process," added Holmes.

The movie's screenplay will be provided by Charles Fuller, who won a Pulitzer Prize for *A Soldier's Play,* which later became the film *A Soldier's Story,* starring Denzel Washington.

So, can we expect something along the lines of *Bird, 'Round Midnight* or even *The Glenn Miller Story?* "I can't say that there are any other [jazz] films that have done what we hope to do here," Holmes said. "In fact, we don't see many similarities. If there are any models, we're looking at films like *Raging Bull* or *Amadeus.*"

The movie's title hasn't been decided on, either, but both Homes and Suluchin want simply to call it *Miles.* "To Miles and for Miles," Suluchin said. "That's our motto."

SECTION 2

The *DownBeat* Features

Jan. 27, 1950

Nothing But Bop? "Stupid," Says Miles

Editor's note: This is DownBeat's *first interview with Miles Davis.*

by Pat Harris

"I don't like to hear someone put down Dixieland. Those people who say there's no music but bop are just stupid; it just shows how much they don't know." This was Miles Davis speaking, and he rose to defend the universality of jazz, while decrying the much less than universal respect given the jazz musician.

Miles, whose definitely modern trumpet has been heard for the last month at the Hi-Note here, is a mild, modest, quiet young man of 23, and he has a lot of respect for his elders.

"Sidney Bechet—we played opposite him at the Paris jazz festival last year—played some of the things Charlie Parker plays, particularly a riff on 'Ko-Ko.' We talked to Bechet for some time over there, and asked him where he had gotten the riff. He told us it was from an old march, and had been transposed from a flute or clarinet part. I've heard Parker do a lot of things that show a Bechet influence, and Johnny Hodges, too.

"No, I've never played Dixieland myself. When I was growing up I played like Roy Eldridge, Harry James, Freddie Webster and anyone else I admired. You've got to start way back there before you can play bop. You've got to have a foundation."

When Miles went to New York and to Juilliard in 1945, 52nd Street was in its heyday. Coleman Hawkins was working on the street, and Joe Guy was with him on trumpet. But half the time Guy didn't show up, so Miles sat in. He was working pretty steadily, without pay, and going to school all day. Then his wife (he married at 17) came to New York, and Miles had to look around for a job that would include a paycheck.

First one he found was at the Spotlite, with tenorist Eddie Davis; Rudy Williams, alto; Ernie Washington, piano; Leonard Gaskin, bass; and Eddie Nicholson, drums. He had been playing there anyhow on the nights Guy did show up for Hawkins, so he just moved in on a business basis. This job lasted a month.

Most of the bands Miles has worked with were similar units, and the jobs were none too steady. He ruefully describes his life as months of no work, interspersed every quarter year or so with a two-week job.

"I've worked so little," Miles says, "I could probably tell you where I was playing any night in the last three years."

It doesn't seem to bother him very much, though. He likes to play what he believes is non-commercial bop; a middle-register horn, subdued and soft, with a many-noted complexity few other trumpeters can match.

"I play high when I work with a big band," Miles says, "but prefer not to. A lot of trumpeters, Gillespie is one, have trouble controlling their tone when they play low. I don't want to have that trouble."

Davis worked at Minton's with Sir Charles [Charlie Parker] and a drummer for a short time, and also played, for pay this time, with Coleman Hawkins. Then, two years after he went to New York, Miles quit school and went home to East St. Louis, Ill.

Benny Carter was playing the Riviera in St. Louis, and Miles joined him for the trip to the West Coast. Parker was on the coast then. Miles and Charlie are very close friends, Charlie having lived with the Davises for a while in New York in 1945. Miles says that when he plays with Parker or with Lee Konitz, "it sounds like one horn."

When the Royal Roost opened, Miles went in with Allen Eager, Kai Winding, Tadd Dameron, Max Roach and Curley Russell. His second date at the Roost was with a 10-piece band, including Konitz, Gerry Mulligan, Roach, Al McKibbon, John Lewis, Junior Collins, trombonist Ted Kelly and Bill Barber on tuba. Pancho Hagood sang with the unit. The first Roost date lasted eight weeks; the second, two.

The Capitol recording contract followed, with eight sides cut. Those issued already are "Move/Budo," Godchild/Jeru" and "Boplicity/Israel." The fourth release, "Venus de Milo/Rouge," will be out soon. On Miles' first recording, a blues with Herbie Fields, he says, "I couldn't be heard, 'count of I played into a mute and was frightened." He's recorded a number of sides with Parker, including a couple of albums, and some things including "Milestones" and "Half Nelson" under his own name on Savoy.

On the Parker tune "Ko-Ko," Dizzy Gillespie was playing piano and had to double on trumpet for Miles because Miles said he was too nervous to play. The label has Miles' name on it as trumpet, and has caused some confusion.

The Eckstine band, he believes, was the best of all modern units, with the possible close second of Claude Thornhill's band when Gil Evans was writing for it and Lee Konitz was in the reed section.

"Thornhill had the greatest band of these modern times," Miles says, "except for Eckstine, and he destroyed it when he took out the tuba and the two French horns. It was commercially good and musically good. For the Capitol records I made last year, I wanted to get a band as close to the sound Evans writes for as I could.

"I'm going to try to get Evans to do four more arrangements for our next record date with Capitol, and have John Lewis and Gerry Mulligan do some writing, too. I'll use the same instrumentation, and the same men."

Miles' favorite musicians, who form a huge, formidably heterogeneous group, including Lewis, whose composing and arranging skills he greatly admires; Evans; Will Bradley, "who writes like Stravinsky"; Parker; Konitz; Freddie Webster; Vic Coleson (who worked with Hawkins before Joe Guy, and is now out of the business); Fats Navarro, whose ability to play high and fast and still sound pretty he finds amazing; Bechet; Billie Holiday; Louis Armstrong; Gillespie, who Miles says is still progressing; and on and on.

In fact, it would be difficult to find a musician for whom the easygoing Miles wouldn't have a good word.

He has nothing good to say, however, about band promoters ("Look what they've done to Dizzy") and club operators. The night club operators especially. "They don't treat musicians with enough respect," Miles complains. "They think all jazz musicians are irresponsible drunkards."

Sept. 21, 1955
Blindfold Test: Miles and Miles of Trumpet Players
by Leonard Feather

> The "Blindfold Test" is a listening test that challenges the featured artist to discuss and identify the music and musicians who performed on selected recordings. The artist is then asked to rate each tune using a five-star system. No information about the recordings is given to the artist prior to the test.

For a long time, Miles Davis and I had been trying to get together for a "Blindfold" session. I was determined that when the interview did take place, it would be something out of the ordinary run of Blindfold Tests; and that's just the way it turned out.

Every record selected was one that featured at least two trumpet players. As you will see, this selection of material did not faze Miles.

Miles was given no information whatever, either before or during the test, about the records played for him.

CLIFFORD BROWN
"Falling in Love With Love" (Prestige)—Brown, Art Farmer, trumpets; Bengt Hallberg, piano.

That was Art Farmer and Brownie blowing trumpet. The arrangement was pretty good; I think they played it too fast, though. They missed the content of the tune.

The piano player gasses me—I don't know his name, I've been trying to find out his name. He's from Sweden. . . . I think he made those records with Stan, like "Dear Old Stockholm." I never heard anybody play in a high register like that. So clean, and he swings and plays his own things; but, they had the piano up too loud in the ensembles. If there's anything that drags me, it's when they put the piano up too loud in the control room.

Aside from the trumpets, I didn't care for the other soloists at all. . . . Also, I think that Arthur should improve his tone and that Clifford should swing more. Four stars, though.

ROY ELDRIDGE AND DIZZY GILLESPIE
"Algo Bueno" (Clef)—Eldridge, Gillespie, trumpets; Oscar Peterson, piano; Herb Ellis, guitar; Louie Bellson, drums.

That was Diz and Roy. Sounded like Oscar Peterson on piano. Guitar messed it all up—and the brushes. And, one of the four-bars that Dizzy played wasn't too good. One of the fours that Roy played wasn't too good. They're two of my favorite trumpet players; I love Roy, and you know I love Diz.

I don't know why they recorded together . . . sounded like something of Norman Granz's . . . one of his get-togethers. It's nice to listen to for a while, but Oscar messes it up with that Nat Cole style; and that kind of rhythm section, with brushes.

It's not that kind of song. You can't play that kind of song like that, with those chords. There's another way to swing on that. It could have been much better. I'd give it three stars on account of Diz's and Roy's horns.

BUCK CLAYTON AND RUBY BRAFF
"Love Is Just Around the Corner" (Vanguard)—Clayton, Braff, trumpets; Benny Morton, trombone; Steve Jordan, guitar; Aaron Bell, bass.

Sounds like Buck Clayton; the other sounded like Charlie Shavers. I don't know who was on trombone; sounded like Jack Teagarden. I don't know about that rhythm section.

Maybe they want to play like that, huh? But the bass and guitar—they always seem to clash when they play 1–3–5 chords that don't vary. You know—C, C, G, G, 4, 4, 5, 5, like that—seems to be some clash in there. When they play straight four-four I like it. I did think the guitar was too loud. Two stars.

DON ELLIOTT AND RUSTY DEDRICK
"Gargantuan Chant" (Riverside)—Dick Hyman, comp., arr., piano; Dedrick, first trumpet solo; Elliott, second trumpet solo; Mundell Lowe, guitar.

Sounds kind of fine. Sounds like Howard McGhee and Ray Nance, but I don't know who it is. The arrangement was pretty nice, but not the interpretation. Piano, whoever he is, is crazy. That's about all I can say about it. Two stars.

Guitar was nice. I preferred the last trumpet solo to the earlier one for that kind of thing.

Metronome All-Stars
"Look Out" (Victor)—Sy Oliver, comp., arr.; Tiny Grimes, guitar; Flip Phillips, Georgie Auld, tenors; Buddy DeFranco, clarinet; Harry Edison, Cootie Williams, Rex Stewart, trumpets; Teddy Wilson, piano.

Gee, that sure sounded like an All-Star record! Sounded like Teddy Wilson. I think I heard Harry Edison, Georgie Auld, Cootie Williams, Al Killian. Guitar player was nice. I don't know who that was. Sure was a funny arrangement.

I don't know who could have done that arrangement. . . . Pretty nice record, though. It kinda swings. I couldn't tell the clarinet player; I can't tell anybody but Benny Goodman and Artie Shaw and Buddy DeFranco. It was sort of a short solo. . . . Give it four stars. I liked that.

Charlie Barnet
"Terry Tune" (Columbia)—Clark Terry, Jimmy Nottingham, trumpets.

That was Clark Terry and somebody; I don't know who the other trumpet was. Sounded a little like Willie Cook. I don't recognize that band. I know Duke didn't write these arrangements. . . . For a moment it sounded like Maynard; but I guess Maynard would be doing more acrobatics. He always does.

I like Terry. . . . I met him in St. Louis when I was about 13 and playing in a school band. He was playing like Buck Clayton then—but fast, just the way he is now. So I started trying to play like Terry; I idolized him. He's a very original trumpet player; but I don't like to hear him strong-arming the horn just to try to be exciting.

He's much better when he plays soft, when he sounds like Buck. I like him when he plays down, instead of up, always upward phrases . . . I don't like that arrangement, though. I know it must be Terry's tune, 'cause it sounds like him. I'd rate it three stars on account of Terry. I don't know who that other trumpet player would be.

Bobby Byrne and Kai Winding
"Dixieland vs. Birdland" (from Hot and Cool Blues, *MGM)—Byrne, Winding, trombones; Eddie Shu, Mike Baker, clarinets; Howard McGhee, Yank Lawson, trumpets; John Lewis, Kenny Clarke, Percy Heath, rhythm.*

Jeez! . . . That was Howard McGhee and Percy, wasn't it? Kai Winding. Howard played nice. I liked the contrast idea . . . but I just don't know what to say about that record; there's too big a switch when they go from that riff

into the sudden Dixieland. . . . I like good Dixieland, you know . . . I like
Sidney Bechet . . . Kai and Howard swing. I'd give the record a couple stars
on account of Kai and Howard.

LOUIS ARMSTRONG
"Ain't Misbehavin'" *(Victor)—Bobby Hackett, Armstrong, trumpets; Jack*
Teagarden, trombone.

I like Louis! Anything he does is all right. I don't know about his statements,
though . . . I could do without them. That's Bobby Hackett, too; I always did
like Bobby Hackett—anything by him. Jack Teagarden's on trombone. I'd
give it five stars.

DUKE ELLINGTON
"Stormy Weather" (Columbia)—Harry Carney, baritone; Willie Cook, Ray Nance,
Cat Anderson, trumpets; Billy Strayhorn, arr.

Oh, God! You can give that 25 stars! I love Duke. That sounded like Billy
Strayhorn's arrangement; it's warmer than Duke usually writes. Must be
Billy Strayhorn.

   That band kills me. I think all the musicians should get together one
certain day and get down on their knees and thank Duke. Especially Mingus,
who always idolized Duke and wanted to play with him; and why he didn't
mention it in his "Blindfold Test," I don't know. Yes, everybody should bow
to Duke and Strayhorn—and Charlie Parker and Diz. . . . Cat Anderson
sounds good on that; Ray always sounds good.

   The beginning soloist sounded real good, too. That's Harry Carney, too,
in there; if he wasn't in Duke's band, the band wouldn't be Duke. . . . They
take in all schools of jazz. . . . Give this all the stars you can.

━━━━━━

Nov. 2, 1955

Miles: A Trumpeter in the Midst of a Big Comeback Makes a Very Frank Appraisal of Today's Jazz Scene
by Nat Hentoff

After a time of confusion and what appeared to be a whirlpool of troubles,
Miles Davis is moving rapidly again toward the forefront of the modern
jazz scene. He has just signed a contract guaranteeing him 20 weeks a year
in Birdland (the first three dates—two weeks each—Oct. 13, Nov. 24 and
Jan. 19). He has been added to the three-and-a-half-week, all-star Birdland
tour that begins Feb. 5, and there are reports—at present unconfirmed and

denied by Prestige—that Miles may leave Prestige for one of the major record companies.

Miles already had shown clearly this year how important a jazz voice he still is by his July performance at the Newport Festival, a performance that caused Jack Tracy to write: "Miles played thrillingly and indicated that his comeback is in full stride." A few weeks later, Miles surprised the international jazz audience by tying Dizzy for first place in the *DownBeat* Critics Poll.

But those listeners who had heard several of his Prestige records over the past year (particularly the "Walkin'"–"Blue 'n' Boogie" date with Lucky Thompson, J.J. Johnson, Kenny Clarke, Horace Silver and Percy Heath) decided on second thought that there really should have been no cause for them to have been surprised.

So Miles is now in the most advantageous position of his career thus far. He has the bookings, the record outlet, and he has the group that he's been eager to assemble for some months. As of this writing, on drums there's Philly Joe Jones, described by Miles as "the best drummer around today." On bass is the young Detroit musician Paul Chambers, who's recently been working with George Wallington at the Bohemia and of whose ability Miles says only, "Whew! He really drives a band. He never stops." On piano is Red Garland from Philadelphia. The tenor is Sonny Rollins, for whom Miles has deep respect. Miles has been trying to convince Sonny to leave Chicago and go on the road with him and finally, to Miles' great delight, he has succeeded.

"I want this group," says Miles, "to sound the way Sonny plays, the way all of the men in it play individually—different from anyone else in jazz today. We've got that quality individually; now we have to work on getting the group to sound that way collectively. As we get to work regularly, something will form up and we'll get a style."

As for records, Miles is dissatisfied with most of his recent output, since his standards call for constant growth and change, and his criteria for judging his own works are harsh. "The only date of mine I liked in the last couple of years was the "Walkin'" session (Prestige 182). And the one with Sonny Rollins (Prestige 187). The rest sounded too much alike."

Of the records he made in the years before, Miles looks back with most satisfaction to the set with J.J. Johnson that included "Kelo" and "Tempus Fugit" (Blue Note 5022), the earlier albums with Rollins (Prestige 124, 140) and the 1949–'50 Capitol sides with Gerry Mulligan, Lee Konitz, Al Haig, Max Roach, J.J. Johnson, John Lewis and Kenny Clarke (Capitol 459). He remembers, however, how tense those Capitol sessions were, and wishes he had a chance to do a similar date, only with a full brass section and with writing that would be comfortable for all.

Miles, as his sharply perceptive "Blindfold Test" (*DownBeat,* Sept. 21, 1955) indicated, is an unusually knowledgeable observer of the jazz scene. In a recent, characteristically frank conversation, he presented his views about several key figures and trends in contemporary jazz. This is a record of his conversation:

The West Coast: "They do have some nice arrangements. Jimmy Giuffre plays real good and Shelly [Manne] is good, but I don't care too much for the other soloists. Carl Perkins, though, is an exception—he plays very good piano, but he doesn't record enough. I wish I could get him to work with me. You know, that man can play bass notes with his elbows!

"My general feeling about what's happening on the coast is like what Max Roach was saying the other night. He said he'd rather hear a guy miss a couple of notes than hear the same old clichés all the time. Often when a man misses, it at least shows he's trying to think of something new to play. But the music on the coast gets pretty monotonous even if it's skillfully done. The musicians out there don't give me a thrill the way Sonny Rollins, Dizzy and Philly Joe Jones do. I like musicians like Dizzy because I can always learn something from him; he's always playing new progressions, etc. Kenny Clarke, too, is always experimenting."

Brubeck: "Well, Dave made one record I liked—*Don't Worry About Me.* Do I think he swings? He doesn't know how. Desmond doesn't swing, either, though I think he'd play different with another rhythm section. Frankly, I'd rather hear Lennie Tristano. Or, for that matter, I'd rather hear Dizzy play the piano than Brubeck, because Dizzy knows how to touch the piano, and he doesn't play too much. A lot of guys are so conscious of the fact that the piano has 88 keys that they try to do too much. Tatum is the only man who plays with a whole lot of technique, and the feeling too. Along with Bud Powell, he's my favorite pianist.

"Getting back to Brubeck, I'd say first he ought to change his drums. Another thing is that if Brubeck could play the piano like that pianist in Sweden—Bengt Hallberg—in combination with the way he himself already thinks, he would please a lot of musicians. Brubeck has wonderful harmonic ideas, but I sure don't like the way he touches, the way he plays the piano."

Tristano and Konitz: "Lennie has a different problem. He's wonderful by himself. He invents all the time, and as a result, when he works with a group, the bass player generally doesn't know what Lennie's going to do. I don't think, therefore, that Lennie can be tied down to writing one bass line. He should write three or four bass lines so that the bassist can choose.

"As for Lee Konitz, I like the way he plays. With a different rhythm section, he swings—in his way. Sure, there are different ways of swinging. You can break phrases and you can play seven- or 11-note phrases like Lee does, and they swing, but you can't do it all the time."

Bird: "Bird used to play 40 different styles. He was never content to remain the same. I remember how at times he used to turn the rhythm section around when he and I, Max and Duke Jordan were playing together. Like we'd be playing the blues, and Bird would start on the 11th bar, and as the rhythm sections stayed where they were and Bird played where he was, it sounded as if the rhythm section was on one and three instead of two and four. Every time that would happen, Max used to scream at Duke not to follow Bird but to stay where he was. Then eventually, it came around as Bird had planned and we were together again. Bird used to make me play, try to play. He used to lead me on the bandstand. I used to quit every night. The tempo was so up, the challenge was so great.

"Of the new altoists, Cannonball plays real good. He swings and has real drive, but he doesn't know the chord progressions Bird knew. Bird used to play things like Tatum. But if Cannonball gets with the right musicians—men like Sonny Rollins—he'll learn."

MJQ: "I was talking about small groups before. I can't omit the Modern Jazz Quartet—that's the best group out. That piece 'Django' is one of the greatest things written in a long time. You know, John Lewis teaches everyone all the music in that group."

Max Roach and Clifford Brown: "I don't like their current group too much because there's too much going on. I mean, for example, that Richie Powell plays too much comp. Max needs a piano player that doesn't play much in the background. Actually, Brownie and Max are the whole group. You don't need anybody but those two. They can go out onstage by themselves. What happens is that the band gets in Brownie's way the way it is now."

Writing: "With regard to big bands, I liked some of the arrangements this last Stan Kenton band had at Birdland, and, of course, Count Basie sounds good, but that's just swinging. I also admire the big band writing Billy Strayhorn does. Do you know the best thing I've heard in a long time? Alex North's music for *Streetcar Named Desire* (Capitol 387). That's a wild record—especially the part Benny Carter plays. If anybody is going to be able to write for strings in the jazz idiom or something near to it, it'll be North. I'd recommend everyone hearing that music.

"Now as for Kenton, I can't think of anything he did original. Everything he did, everybody else did before. Kenton is nowhere in the class with some-body like Duke. Duke has done more for jazz than anyone I could name. He takes in almost everything when he writes, he and Billy.

"You can really tell how a man writes when he writes for a large band. But funny things happen, too. Like if it weren't for Neal Hefti, the Basie band wouldn't sound as good as it does. But Neal's band can't play those same arrangements nearly as well. Ernie Wilkins, on the other hand, writes good, but the Basie band plays Neal's arrangements better.

"About the kind of things Charlie Mingus and Teo Macero are writing for small groups, well, some of them are like tired modern pictures. Some of them are depressing. And Mingus can write better than that. The 'Mingus Fingers' he did for Lionel Hampton is one of the best big-band records I ever heard, but he won't write like he did on that number any more. For one thing, in his present writing, he's using the wrong instrumentation to get it over. If he had a section of low horns, for example, that would cut down on some of the dissonance, he could get it over better. I heard one of Teo's works at Newport, but I don't remember it. And if I didn't remember it, I didn't like it.

"My favorite writer has been Gil Evans. He's doing commercial things now, but if you remember, he did the ensemble on 'Boplicity' and several other fine things around that time. In answer to that critic who recently asked why a song like 'Boplicity' isn't played by modern groups, it isn't played because the top line isn't interesting. The harmonization is, but not the tune itself.

"Other writers I like are Gigi Gryce—there were several nice things in the last date he did with Art Farmer—and Gerry Mulligan is a great writer, one of my favorites. Bill Russo is interesting, too—like the way he closes the harmony up. He sure loves trombones. He uses the brass section well.

"A lot of musicians and writers don't get the full value out of a tune. Tatum does and Frank Sinatra always does. Listen to the way Nelson Riddle writes for Sinatra, the way he gives him enough room, and doesn't clutter it up. Can you imagine how it would sound if Mingus were writing for Sinatra? But I think Mingus will settle down; he can write good music. But about Riddle, his backgrounds are so right that sometimes you can't tell if they're conducted. Billy Eckstine needs somebody like Sinatra, by the way, to tell him what kind of tunes to sing and what kind of background to use."

Instrumentalists: "There are other musicians I like. Stan Getz is a wonderful musician, and Bobby Brookmeyer is real good. The man I like very much is J.J. Johnson, because he doesn't play the same way all the time. And he's a fine writer. If J.J. would only write for a big band, then you'd hear something. The best small band arrangements I've heard in a long time are the ones J.J. writes for the Jay and Kai group, and that's only two horns. I liked, too, what he wrote for me on the Blue Note session. J.J. doesn't clutter it up. He tries to set the mood. He has the quality Gil Evans has, the quality I hope Gerry Mulligan doesn't lose.

"As for trumpets, Brownie plays real good. Yes, he plays fast, but when you're playing with Max, you play real fast almost all the time, like the time I was with Bird. Art Farmer is real good, but he has to get his tone together. Thad Jones, if he ever gets out of the Basie band, then you'll really hear him. Playing in a big band makes you stiff. It doesn't do a horn man good to stay in a band too long. Conte Candoli, for example, told me he hasn't been the same since Kenton. He can't keep a flowing line going. His lips tighten up and he has to play something high even though he doesn't like to play like that. I told him to lay off three weeks and start over again. Dizzy had to do the same thing after he had the big band. Part of that stiffness comes from playing the same arrangement again and again. The only horn players a big band didn't tie down were Bird and Lester.

"Now about drummers, my five favorites are Max, Kenny Clarke, Philly Joe Jones, Art Blakey and Roy Haynes. Roy, though, has almost destroyed himself working with Sarah [Vaughan] so long. He's lost some of his touch, but he could pick up again if he had a chance to play more freely. Elvin Jones, the brother of Thad and Hank, is another drummer who plays real good. Elvin comes from the Detroit area, which is producing some very good musicians."

Tradition and swinging: "Bird and [Coleman] Hawkins made horn players realize they could play fuller progressions, play more of the chord and still swing. I saw Stan Getz making fun of Hawkins one night and I said to Getz, 'If it weren't for Hawkins, you probably wouldn't be playing as you are!' Coleman plays just as well as anybody you can name. Why, I learned how to play ballads by listening to Coleman. I don't go for putting down a man just because he's older. Like some guys were once looking at a modern car, and they said, 'A young guy must have designed that car!' Why does he have to have been a young guy?

"On clarinet, I only like Benny Goodman very much. I don't like Buddy DeFranco at all, because he plays a lot of clichés and is very cold. Tony Scott plays good, but not like Benny, because Benny used to swing so much. No matter what form jazz takes—Lennie or Stan or Bird or Duke—jazz has to swing.

"What's swinging in words? If a guy makes you pat your foot and if you feel it down your back, you don't have to ask anybody if that's good music or not. You can always feel it."

Nov. 30, 1955

An Open Letter From Charles Mingus

Four editions of *DownBeat* come to my mind's eye—Bird's "Blindfold Test," mine, Miles' and Miles' recent "comeback story" as I sit down and attempt to honestly write my thoughts in an open letter to Miles Davis. (I discarded numerous "mental" letters before this writing, but one final letter formed last night as I looked through some pictures of Bird that Bob Parent had taken at a Village session.) If a picture needs to go with this story, it should be this picture of Bird, standing and looking down at Monk with more love than I think we'll ever find in this jazz business!

Jazz wasn't a business with Bird. That's probably why his scope could be so broad as to dig Monk, as I do, and even to dig the way Mingus writes presently. Perhaps even Teo. Some cats seem so hungry to make money with what they call jazz that they're scratching at those few eyes that focus on the least likely subjects—and this doesn't exclude some of our jazz critics. But back to the subject.

Bird's love, so warmly obvious in this picture, was again demonstrated in his "Blindfold Test." But dig Miles' "Test"! As a matter of fact, dig my own "Blindfold Test!" See what I mean? And more recently, dig Miles' comeback story. How is Miles going to act when he gets back and gets going again? Will it be like a gig in Brooklyn not too long ago with Max, Monk and me when he kept telling Monk to "lay out" because his chords were all wrong? Or even at a more recent record date when he cursed, laid out, argued, and threatened Monk and asked Bob Weinstock why he hired such a nonmusician and would Monk lay out on his trumpet solos? What's happening to us disciples of Bird? Or would Miles think I'm presuming too much to include myself as one?

It seems so hard for some of us to grow up mentally just enough to realize that there are other persons of flesh and bone, just like us, on this great, big earth. And if they don't ever stand still, move or "swing," they are as right as we are, even if they are as wrong as hell by our standards. Yes, Miles, I am apologizing for my stupid "Blindfold Test." I can do it gladly because I'm learning a little something. No matter how much they try to say that Brubeck doesn't swing—or whatever else they're stewing or whoever else they're brewing—it's factually unimportant.

Not because Dave made *Time* magazine—and a dollar—but mainly because Dave honestly thinks he's swinging. He feels a certain pulse and plays a certain pulse which gives him pleasure and a sense of exaltation because he's sincerely doing something the way he, Dave Brubeck, feels like doing it. And as you said in your story, Miles, "if a guy makes you pat your foot, and if you feel it down your back, etc.," then Dave is the swingingest by your own definition, Miles, because at Newport and elsewhere Dave had the whole house patting its feet and even clapping its hands.

Incidentally, since Duke Ellington has conducted several compositions without tempo, music to which it is not possible to pat your foot except by following his baton out of tempo, would you say, Miles, that Duke was not playing jazz on these compositions? Or is it safe for me to wager that foot-patting Miles digs Duke's invisible foot-patting music in a nonjazzical ad lib sense? The lack of foot-patting should make Duke kick less for us, according to your definition of swing. But I believe that foot-patable or footless, Duke's music, with or without tempo, manages to get down Miles' back and ring jazz bells for him. Just like Duke, Bartók, Schoenberg or Bird ring other bells for me.

I know Miles and his cult of self-esteemed creators, who are convinced of their clan's mystical powers of secret formula swinging, and they're cool as long as they are together to pat each other on the back. These self-appointed prophets should get together and lead the way as they miss those couple notes Miles speaks of while trying not to play the same old clichés, a fault that all but Bird is guilty of in the past era. Let them pave the way for whoever will follow.

Dave is content. So are Tristano, Duke, Max, etc.—and me, too. Miles' explorers would be very important to new development in counterpoint when and if they missed in different places and remembered to do it the same place on the same tune. And especially if it all happened on a Thursday night at 1:15 a.m. at Minton's and for no reason at all.

Miles, don't you remember that "Mingus Fingers" was written in 1945 when I was a youngster, 22 years of age, who was studying and doing his damnedest to write in the Ellington tradition? Miles, that was 10 years ago when I weighed 185. Those clothes are worn and don't fit me any more. I'm a man; I weigh 215; I think my own way. I don't think like you, and my music isn't meant just for the patting of feet and going down backs. When and if I feel gay and carefree, I write or play that way. When I feel angry I write or play that way—or when I'm happy, or depressed, even.

Just because I'm playing jazz I don't forget about me. I play or write me, the way I feel, through jazz, or whatever. Music is, or was, a language.

March 6, 1958

Self-Portrait: Miles Davis

A brilliant trumpeter tells in his own words how his career started.

You want me to tell you where I was born—that old story? It was in good old Alton, Ill. In 1926. And I had to call my mother a week before my last birthday and ask her how old I would be.

I started playing trumpet in grade school. Once a week we would hold notes. Wednesdays at 2:30. Everybody would fight to play best. Lucky for me, I learned to play the chromatic scale right away. A friend of my father's brought me a book one night and showed me how to do it so I wouldn't have to sit there and hold that note all the time.

My mother wanted to give me a violin for my birthday, but my father gave me a trumpet—because he loved my mother so much!

There was a very good instructor in town. He was having some dental work done by my father. He was the one that made my father get me the trumpet. He used to tell us all about jam sessions on the Showboat, about trumpet players like Bobby Hackett and Hal Baker. "Play without any vibrato," he used to tell us. "You're gonna get old anyway and start shaking," he used to say, "no vibrato!" That's how I tried to play. Fast and light—and no vibrato.

By the time I was 16, I was playing in a band—the Blue Devils—in East St. Louis, Ill. Sonny Stitt came to town with a band and heard us play one night. He told me, "You look like a man named Charlie Parker and you play like him, too. C'mon with us."

The fellows in his band had their hair slicked down, they wore tuxedos and they offered me 60 whole dollars a week to play with them. I went home and asked my mother if I could go with them. She said no, I had to finish my last year of high school. I didn't talk to her for two weeks. And I didn't go with the band, either.

I knew about Charlie Parker in St. Louis. I even played with him there, while I was still in high school. We always used to try to play like Diz and Charlie Parker. When we heard that they were coming to town, my friend and I were the first people in the hall, me with a trumpet under my arm. Diz walked up to me and said, "Kid, do you have a union card?" I said, "Sure." So I sat in with the band that night. I couldn't read a thing from listening to Diz and Bird. The third trumpet man got sick. I knew the book because I loved the music so much I knew the third part by heart. So I played with the band for a couple of weeks. I had to go to New York then.

My mother wanted me to go to Fisk University. I looked in the *Esquire* book and I asked her, "Where's all of this?" Then I asked my father. He said

I didn't have to go to Fisk, I could go to big New York City. In September I was in New York City. A friend of mine was studying at Juilliard, so I decided to go there too. I spent my first week in New York and my first month's allowance looking for Charlie Parker.

I roomed with Charlie Parker for a year. I used to follow him around, down to 52nd Street, where he used to play. Then he used to get me to play. "Don't be afraid," he used to tell me. "Go ahead and play." Every night I'd write down chords I heard on matchbook covers. Everybody helped me. Next day, I'd play those chords all day in the practice room at Juilliard, instead of going to classes.

I didn't start writing music until I met Gil Evans. He told me to write something and send it to him. I did. It was what I played on the piano. Later I found out I could do better without the piano. (I took some piano lessons at Juilliard, but not enough.) If you don't play it good enough, you'll be there for hours and hours.

If you can hear a note, you can play it. The note I hit that sounds high, that's the only one I can play right then, the only note I can think of to play that would fit. You don't learn to play the blues. You just play. I don't even think about harmony. It just comes. You learn where to put notes so they'll sound right. You just don't do it because it's a funny chord. I used to change things because I wanted to hear them—substitute progressions and things. Now I have better taste.

Do I like composing better than playing? I can't answer that. There's a certain feeling you get from playing that you can't get from composing. And when you play, it's like a composition anyway. You make the outline. What do I like to play? I like "'Round About Midnight." In fact, I like most any ballad, if I feel like playing it.

What do I think of my own playing? I don't keep any of my records. I can't stand to hear them after I've made them. The only ones I really like is the one I just made with Gil Evans [*Miles Ahead*], the one I made with J.J. [Johnson] on my Blue Note date about four years ago and a date I did with Charlie Parker.

People ask me if I respond to the audience. I wouldn't like to sit up there and play without anybody liking it. If it's a large audience, I'm very pleased because they are there anyway. If it's a small audience, sometimes it doesn't matter. I enjoy playing with my own rhythm section and listening to them. I'm studying and experimenting all the time.

I know people have some rhythm and they feel things when they're good. A person has to be an invalid not to show some sign—a tap of the finger even. You don't have to applaud. I never look for applause. In Europe, they like everything you do. The mistakes and everything. That's a little bit too much.

If you play good for eight bars, it's enough. For yourself. And I don't tell anybody.

━━━━━━

Aug. 7, 1958
Blindfold Test: More Miles
by Leonard Feather

> The "Blindfold Test" is a listening test that challenges the featured artist to discuss and identify the music and musicians who performed on selected recordings. The artist is then asked to rate each tune using a five-star system. No information about the recordings is given to the artist prior to the test.

The last time Miles Davis took the "Blindfold Test," in the issue dated Sept. 21, 1955, the feature bore the headline "Miles and Miles of Trumpet Players." Each of the nine records played for Davis featured at least two trumpet soloists.

This time, by way of contrast, I avoided this emphasis; in fact, a couple of the records played had no trumpet at all, and others used the horn only as a secondary instrument.

However, just for laughs, I retained one record out of the previous test, the Elliott–Dedrick Gargantuan Chant. In 1955, Davis thought it sounded like Howard McGhee and Ray Nance, said the arrangement was nice but not the interpretation, considered the piano great and liked the guitar, and rated the record two stars.

Davis won't know until he reads this that he was played the same record twice, three years apart. Now, as then, he was given no information about the records played.

JOHN LEWIS
"Warmeland" (from Dear Old Stockholm, *Atlantic)—Lewis, piano.*

I'll give it 10 stars. . . . On top of that, John loves Sweden, you know. I like John . . . his interpretation of a song is too much. Last night, Lennie Hayton played something for me from this same album, and like Lena Horne says, "All I do is sing the song like the man wrote it." That's how John plays the piano. I don't go for guitar at all, and John complemented him there. . . . All the stars are for John.

TINY GRIMES AND COLEMAN HAWKINS
"A Smooth One" (Prestige)—Musa Kaleem, flute; Grimes, guitar; Hawkins, tenor saxophone.

"A Smooth One." We used to play that in St. Louis. I don't know who that flute player was, but if he was up to the Apollo Theater when Puerto Rico was living, he would have blown the horn on that whole record. The guitar player was terrible. . . . I really can't say anything about it. Give it half a star just because Coleman Hawkins is on it.

BUDDY COLLETTE
"Cycle" (Contemporary)—Collette, arr., tenor; Gerald Wilson, trumpet; Red Callender, bass.

You know what that sounds like to me? It sounds like Gigi Gryce arrangements with Oscar Pettiford, but I don't know—all those white tenor players sound alike to me. . . . Unless it's Zoot Sims or Stan Getz. It must have been Ray Copeland on trumpet. . . . I don't know for sure, but I don't like that type of stiff trumpet playing.

That's a very old kind of arrangement—like an old modern picture with skeletons.

I'd rate it two stars.

SONNY ROLLINS WITH THELONIOUS MONK
"The Way You Look Tonight" (Prestige)—Tommy Potter, bass; Arthur Taylor, drums; Rollins, tenor saxophone; Monk, piano.

I know that's Sonny Rollins, but I don't see how a record company can record something like that. You know the way Monk plays—he never gives any support to a rhythm section. When I had him on my date, I had him lay out until the ensemble. I like to hear him play, but I can't stand him in a rhythm section unless it's one of his own songs.

I can't understand a record like this. I don't know who the drummer and bass player are. Is that "The Way You Look Tonight"? That's what I used to play behind Bird, only we used to play it twice as fast. I'll give this two and a half on account of Sonny.

EDDIE CONDON
"Eddie and the Milkman" (MGM)—Rex Stewart, cornet.

It's Don Elliott. . . . No, I don't know who that was on trumpet. In fact, Leonard, I don't know anything about that at all. It has a nice beat, but it sounded like Don Elliott to me, imitating somebody, but I know it wasn't him.

I like the piece, but you know Don is always "da, da, da, da, da." I know it isn't him because he doesn't have that much feeling. I'll give this four.

DON ELLIOTT AND RUSTY DEDRICK
"Gargantuan Chant" (Riverside)—Dick Hyman, comp., arr., piano; Dedrick, first
trumpet solo; Don Elliott, second trumpet solo; Mundell Lowe, guitar.

I don't know who that was, Leonard. Sounds good in spots, but I don't like
that kind of trumpet playing. The guitar sounds good in spots and the piano
player sounds good. It's a good little number except for that interlude and
that tired way of playing trumpet. I'll give that three stars. Who were those
two trumpet players?

JOHN LEWIS AND SACHA DISTEL
"Dear Old Stockholm" (Atlantic)—Lewis, piano; Distel, guitar; Barney Wilen,
tenor; Percy Heath, bass; Kenny Clarke, drums.

I like the tune. I'll give it four stars, especially for the rhythm section. I think
it was John Lewis and Kenny Clarke, but I'm not sure. Whoever they were,
they were very sympathetic and very swinging.

    I know the two other fellows—I like them very much. I think I can speak
better about the guitar than the saxophonist—Sacha Distel is the guitarist, and
I believe if he continues to develop, he will be very good. . . . I don't think he
has too individual a voice yet. I'll give this four stars for the swinging rhythm
section.

BOBBY HACKETT
"Albatross" (Capitol)—Dick Cary, E-flat horn; Ernie Caceres, baritone; Hackett,
trumpet.

I'll give it five stars. . . . I like that. The trombone player knocked me out.
Who was that playing baritone? . . . That trombone player gassed me. The
trumpet? It sounded better than Ruby Braff. I don't understand Ruby at all.
In that style I like Red Allen, Louis and Bobby Hackett plays nice, but I can't
tell anybody else.

SHORTY ROGERS
"I'm Glad I'm Not Young Anymore" (Victor)—Bill Holman, tenor; Rogers,
trumpet.

I know it's a West Coast record. Right? Shorty playing trumpet, and I've
never heard James Clay, but I guess it must be him. I don't know anything
about that.

    I'll give it two stars.

Jan. 7, 1960
The Enigma of Miles Davis
by Barbara J. Gardner

There is no room for the middle stance. You choose up sides, and you play on your team. He is either the greatest living musician or he is just a cool bopper. He is handsome and a wonderful individual or he is ugly and a drag. His trumpet prowess is getting greater every day or his scope is becoming more and more limited.

Any current jazz discussion can be enlivened simply by dropping in the magic name—Miles Davis.

Yet these arguments can be mystifying in the frequency with which the opponents switch positions. A musician in a conversation with fellow workers is likely to blast Davis. The same musician discussing Miles with his dinner host and hostess may change tunes in the middle of the chorus and sing nothing but the highest praise for the trumpeter.

Unaware of the chain of events they were beginning, Dr. and Mrs. Miles Davis, on May 25, 1926, named their first son Miles Dewey. Miles, his parents and an older sister, Dorothy, moved from Alton, Ill., to East St. Louis, Ill., in 1927. There, Miles' brother Vernon was born. The first 12 years included all the usual brother–sister squabbles. Yet, though there were normal childhood frictions, Miles was gregarious, amiable and had many friends.

Musically, his career began uneventfully on his 13th birthday when his father gave him a trumpet. Only his immediate attraction and dedication to the horn gave an indication of the mastery of the instrument he would later achieve. Even his family admits that in the beginning, the growing pains were considerable and Miles was no instant threat to any trumpet player.

"We still have a record packed away someplace that he cut with some rhythm and blues outfit," his sister recalled. "He was pretty awful. They don't even mention his name." But the woodshed was nearby, and Miles used it.

By the time Billy Eckstine brought his big band through East St. Louis in the early 1940s, the worst was over. Dizzy Gillespie and Eckstine convinced both Miles and his father that the quiet, reserved youngster should continue to study music. While the band was in town, Miles had the exciting experience of sitting in. He was so awe-stricken by Charlie Parker and Gillespie that he could hardly play.

Miles pulled up stakes in 1945 and at 19 made the trek to New York City, where he enrolled in the Juilliard School of Music to concentrate on theory and harmony. At this time, the idol of the jazz world was Charlie Parker.

Miles, too, was under his spell. He spent his entire bankroll searching the clubs and hangouts, trying to find Bird.

While his relationship with Parker, Eckstine and Gillespie had been discomforting for him in East St. Louis, it was not nearly so overwhelming as being surrounded by the giants who inhabited 52nd Street in the mid-'40s.

The same Dizzy who had invited him to sit in with the band in East St. Louis, who had encouraged him to come to New York and study trumpet, now sternly advised the newcomer to study piano so that he might learn how to build an effective solo.

The helpful and understanding Bird, who advised him to leave the woodshed and break into his own with the public, was making such departures in improvisation, rhythm and harmony that Miles was bewildered. It was no wonder that the frustrated neophyte, just in his 20s, would quit every night. Fortunately, he returned every day.

He underwent the usual influences. His first idol had been Roy Eldridge, a musician whose influence spreads throughout the contemporary trumpet tradition. Once having heard Gillespie, however, Miles decided to draw from this man his major inspiration. For a while there was a period of complete absorption, and Miles Davis seemed destined to become a second Dizzy Gillespie.

But by 1947, Davis had filtered from the Gillespie-ish playing all that was not natural to himself.

During that two-year period, he had worked with Parker, Eckstine, Benny Carter and Coleman Hawkins. He had so impressed the listening jazz public that he was voted *Esquire* new trumpet star of 1947.

Davis made his debut as leader in 1948. The first small group was replaced within months by a nine-piece unit whose exceptionally high musical caliber was captured on records. These celebrated 1949 recordings featured Lee Konitz, Gerry Mulligan, J.J. Johnson, Max Roach, Kai Winding and Kenny Clarke. Musical pre-eminence, however, was not enough to salvage this experimental group. The gig folded after two historic weeks, and the group disbanded, its members spreading their messages on separate paths.

Davis went to Europe. In 1949, France got its first glimpse of 52nd Street's new trumpet star. He played the Paris Jazz Festival.

But when he returned to New York, Miles passed into comparative musical obscurity. For a while illness plagued him, financial difficulties mounted, and musical appreciation and satisfaction made a sharp and rapid decline. This bleak pattern was brightened only by his three noteworthy events: he won the *Metronome* Readers Poll each year from 1951 to '53; he made the Jazz Inc. tour in 1952; and, above all, the musicians were still listening, learning, even copying.

It is this last fact that perhaps is most significant. It is the thing that, more than any other, explains the sudden reappearance and pervading eminence of the forgotten patriarch.

In 1957, there had come to be established a new sound in jazz, a new school of trumpeters, a new concept in communication in music. People began listening for the familiar characteristics and searching for their source. Re-enter Miles Davis, rediscovered, new star.

After throat surgery in 1957, Davis captured every coveted trumpet award in the United States and Europe. Readers of Holland's *Muziek Espress,* Hamburg's *Jazz Echo,* Paris' *Jazz Hot* and London's *Melody Maker* all awarded Miles first or second place on trumpet in 1958 or 1959. In the United States, he has been voted outstanding trumpet start by *Metronome* readers and has won the *DownBeat* Readers Poll award every year since 1954, except 1956, when he placed a close second behind his former mentor, Dizzy Gillespie.

As Davis now stands at the pinnacle of his musical career, he stands simultaneously at the nadir of sociability.

Ask any jazz fan who Miles Davis is. Most will say, "He's a fink, but he sure can play." Ask any club owner where he has worked. Most will say, "He's a headache, but the customers flock to hear him." Ask any musician. He probably will say, "He's an evil little bastard, but he certainly can play." In other words, two points seem glaringly in evidence—Miles is a difficult person to deal with, and Miles can play his instrument. Among his closest friends, and he has many, it is the consensus that Miles carefully cultivates both contentions.

The major accusation levied at him is indifference toward and lack of consideration for the audience.

Wearing what the well-dressed man will wear next year, Miles saunters diffidently onstage. Usually squinting through smoke from his cigarette, he briefly surveys his audience, chats momentarily with his sidemen and idly fingers his horn. Snapping off the beat, he assumes his characteristic stance, drawing the muted trumpet inward. He shoves the mute tight against the microphone and breathes out the notes, placing each sound just where he wants it. He hovers there for several choruses, then drops his horn and casually ambles away, off the stage sometimes, out of the room . . .

"No stage presence!" the customer will exclaim.

The appearance is certainly that he disinvolves himself from activities on the stand. But musicians who work with him deny this emphatically. The wily trumpeter is able to dissect every tune played during the set. Each musician's work is analyzed at the next rehearsal.

Why Davis chooses to wander about while the rest of the group plays is still as much a mystery as it was when he began doing it 10 years ago. It is by no means a newly acquired habit. Miles has never attempted to be a crowd pleaser, although these very eccentricities serve almost to transform him into a showman whose behavior, though often resented, is nearly as much a part of his audience appeal as his musical performance.

The quality of music that is presented is the major concern with Davis, and neither money nor threats can force him to compromise on this point.

During the spring of 1959 the Miles Davis Sextet, featuring John Coltrane and Cannonball Adderley, was contracted to play a Milwaukee night club. Adderley was hospitalized a few days before the opening. Davis agreed to go with the rhythm section and Coltrane. On the morning the five men were to leave New York, Coltrane contracted a virus infection and could not leave. The club owner insisted that Davis keep the engagement. Davis said, "No." The owner threatened to sue. Miles used his favorite unprintable epithet. The club owner sued—but Miles did not play the date.

There are few persons more noted for the use of flat, bald definitives than Davis. Only an inconspicuous withdrawal or reversal of a celebrated position would belie the assertiveness of his original proclamation. "I shall never work here again" was hardly dry on the printed page before he was back at work in the same club.

Among his most flagrant asserted positions is dislike for the ofay. This generalized overt exhibition of racial prejudice, however, has been undermined in practice throughout the entire pattern of his adulthood.

Since 1948, when he formed his first group, Davis has hired competent musicians regardless of race. Among his closest associates are white politicians, actors, actresses, musicians and citizens of many countries and many walks of life. He is no embittered hothead on this issue. His attitude has been arrived at because he has endured a series of cold, degrading and demoralizing experiences.

An instance: Arriving in Chicago during the summer of 1959, Davis rolled his imported Ferrari into a motel on Lake Michigan's shore only to be told there was a mix-up in the reservations. Sorry. Jazz great or not, there was no room available.

His refusal to accept publicly a poll award from a national men's magazine was prompted by his dissatisfaction with the discriminatory policies of the publication. Davis talked, as well as corresponded, with the publisher, explaining why he could not, in good faith, accept any commendation from the publication. In spite of the best efforts of the publisher, he has been unable to sway Davis' attitude.

This adherence to principle runs through his relationships. Once he has made up his mind, and cast his lot, he is more than reluctant to change his position. This is especially true regarding sidemen working with him. Both his present pianist and his drummer went through periods during which Miles had to adjust to and acquaint himself with their styles of playing.

"Miles thinks there is only one drummer in the entire world," a musician said at the beginning of 1959, "and that one is Philly Joe Jones." Miles seemed to give credence to this idea long after Jones had been replaced by Jimmy Cobb. Several times, he recorded only when he was able to secure Jones as his drummer. Gradually, this attitude began to fade, and Cobb at last was free to function without the ghostly sizzle of his predecessor behind him. Several months ago, questioned about Miles' affinity to Philly Joe, the same musician expressed amazement. "Well, Miles has that clean-cut Jimmy Cobb sound in his ear now," he said.

The exact pattern was followed when pianist Wynton Kelly replaced Red Garland. For months Miles was attuned to the blockish Garland swing, and he couldn't hear it in the melodic, stylish Kelly. But, sticking by their personal styles, and drawing from Miles' subtle hints in technique and execution, Kelly and Cobb came to be highly regarded by their employer.

Davis' ability to pick top musicians as sidemen is unerring, and the influence he wields over their musical expression is almost phenomenal. Sometimes by subtle suggestion, at times by brutal frankness, Miles whips a musical unit into a cohesive, tight-knit, power-generating single voice.

Not only does he usually walk away with top trumpet honors in trade polls, but like a powerful politician, he carries the ticket, and individual members of his group wind up well inside the first 10 of their categories.

This has been referred to as the "Miles magic." What are some of the elements that form the man and the magician in this trumpeter?

There is an undercurrent of loyalty and dedication to conviction that runs well-hidden beneath a temperamental guise. Examples of his generosity and loyalty are described throughout the industry.

Earlier this year in Chicago, a man wielding a knife appeared backstage and began threatening the trumpeter. A prominent New York musician— unexpectedly out of work, down on his luck and hung up in Chicago—was nearby. Seeing the man with the knife move in on Miles, the New Yorker knocked him cold with an uppercut.

Miles walked calmly away without saying so much as "thank you." Some bystanders were annoyed. Wasn't this more than adequate proof of Miles' insolence and ingratitude? Few if any of them knew the reason the New Yorker was present: Miles, hearing the man was in financial trouble, had invited him to play the date with his group. He had no need of the man, but offering a handout would perhaps have hurt the New Yorker's pride.

The fee Miles paid him was big enough to get him out of town and on to the next gig.

A contributing factor to Miles' attraction is his show of freedom and individuality. This exhibition strikes a chord within many persons who, on the surface, are critical of his attitude. He seldom allows anyone to bore him with small talk. A chatterbox is likely to find himself talking to empty space as Miles walks quietly away.

Although there are several individual writers and disc jockeys among his personal friends, as a professional, Miles has little use for persons in communications. He seldom gives interviews to writers and almost never appears for radio or television interviews. One reason he will not do them is that he is, in his speech habits, impetuously profane.

But perhaps more important than that is his extreme sensitivity about the loss of his normal speaking voice.

After a throat operation a few years ago, Miles was told by the doctors not to speak at all for several days. Someone provoked him, and Miles blurted out a retort. The damage was done. Now he speaks in a soft, rasping, gravelly voice. It is curiously attractive, when you become accustomed to it, and strangest of all, it somehow resembles the tightly restrained sound of his muted trumpet.

The striking, delicate-featured man who stands in almost shy uneasiness, mute against the microphone, is the antithesis of the confident, self-contained offstage Miles. There are those who believe this restless musician is the real Miles. Certainly his exquisite—at times even fragile—playing would not seem to be the expression of a braggart or a bully.

Standing somewhere between the unapproachable loner and the onstage lonely trumpeter is Miles Dewey Davis. At present, Miles is unwilling to share that person with the public. He expresses his conviction that each person has a right and a duty to live an independent existence.

If this attitude rubs many persons the wrong way, his popularity evidently rises with each disparagement.

It was not surprising that Miles in the past few months has won both the *DownBeat* International Jazz Critics Poll and the magazine's Readers Poll. What is surprising, however, is that despite all the criticism of his stage manner, the readers also voted him Jazz Personality of the Year.

Apparently a club owner was right when, not too long ago, he threw up his hands in exasperation as Miles sauntered offstage after a solo. After reciting to Miles a list of his sins, he said: "The trouble with you is that everybody likes you, you little son of a bitch."

Feb. 16, 1961

Miles and Gil: Portrait of a Friendship

by Marc Crawford

In the South Side Chicago home of his in-laws slumped a bathrobed, slipper-shod Miles Dewey Davis III with a bottle of Dutch beer on the table and Ravel's "Piano Concerto in G Major" coming from the stereo.

The dishes from the breakfast Miles had prepared (eggs and hamburger and tomatoes, garnished with salts of garlic and celery) rode at anchor in the kitchen sink, and almost forgotten was Miles' earlier refusal on the telephone to talk about his relationship with "Gil." At that time he had growled: "I don't like discussing Gil. I got too much respect for him to do that. It's almost like asking a man to discuss his wife."

But now Miles was relaxed, and pianists Arturo Benedetti Michelangeli was sending him into several shades of ecstasy.

"Listen to those trills!" Miles ordered. The sound of them was sustained as though they had been made by an electrified instrument, and Miles sat there, his first and second finger aflutter, demonstrating how the effect was created. "You know," he volunteered, "Gil thinks like that."

The "Gil" of whom he spoke was, of course, Jeff-tall Gil Evans, who, with Mutt-short Miles, forms one of the most creative and productive friendships in jazz. Miles appeared lost in thought about the 48-year-old, Toronto-born Evans, who wrote the arrangements for the celebrated Davis albums *Miles Ahead, Porgy and Bess* and *Sketches of Spain.* Suddenly he picked up the telephone and long-distanced Evans in New York. Miles asked him to catch the next jet flight for Chicago so he could hear Miles and his group at the Cloister and "just hang out." Evans had said he would, and Miles settled back to await his arrival.

"Gil is my idea of a man," Miles said. "Say you had a friend who was half man and half donkey, and suppose he even wore a straw hat, and you said 'Gil, meet George.' Gil would get up and shake his hand and never care what George looked like.

"You ask Gil a question—you get a straight answer. Like in New York, somebody asked him what he thought of Ornette Coleman's tonal organization, and Gil told him: 'That's Ornette's business. If it isn't good, he'll take care of it.'"

Now Miles got up to flip the record to the Rachmaninoff "Concerto No. 4" side. He stabbed the air with a flurry of vicious right and left hooks aimed at a hapless imaginary opponent. He had not been able that day to work out at Coulon's Gym, as is his Chicago custom, and he digressed to say he wished he had. Then he returned to his main subject: "Rachmaninoff and Ravel were way out—like Gil is way out. You know, my ambition has always been to write like Gil. I'd give my right arm to do it—no, my left one, because I'd have to write the notes down."

Words spilled freely from Miles now, which is rare, but then he was talking about what, to him, is a rare human being. "I first met Gil when I was with Bird, and he was asking for a release on my tune 'Donna Lee.' He wanted to make an arrangement for a government electrical transcription of it. I told him he could have it and asked him to teach me some chords and let me study some of the scores he was doing for Claude Thornhill.

"He really flipped me on the arrangement of 'Robins Nest' he did for Claude. See," said Miles, placing his left hand on the table that suddenly in his mind's eye had become a piano, "Gil had this cluster of chords and superimposed another cluster over it." Miles demonstrated, covering the left hand with his right so that the fingers of the hand above fitted between those on the bottom. "Now the chord ends," Miles explained, suddenly taking his right hand off the piano, "and now these three notes of the remaining cluster are gone," he went on, removing the thumb, first and second fingers of the left hand. "The overtone of the remaining two produced a note way up there," Miles swore, pointing at the other end of the piano. "I was puzzled. I had studied the score for days trying to find the note I heard. But it didn't even exist—at least, on paper it didn't. That's Gil for you.

"We've been friends since that first meeting. I got stranded once in St. Louis, and he sent me $75. I bet he's forgotten it." The expression on Miles' face was fine—warm and rare. All the sneer was gone. Not once had he walked off the bandstand, this Miles Davis in bathrobe and house slippers, alone in the big house with his music. "He's my favorite arranger, yet he's never really made money out of the business."

Miles had finished his own bottle of beer and was taking back half of the bottle he had provided his visitor. "You know, in New York we go over to each other's house, but we don't drop our problems on each other. When Gil is writing, he might spend three days on 10 bars of music. He'll lock himself up in a room of his house, put a 'Do Not Disturb' sign on the door, and not even his wife, Lillian, can come in. It's torture for her when he's writing. It's like he's out to lunch. Sometimes he'll get in there and play the piano for 12 hours. He's not only a composer and a hell of an orchestrator, he just knows instruments and what you can get out of them. He and Duke Ellington are the same way. They can use four instruments when others need eight.

"Listen to what Rachmaninoff is saying," Miles commanded suddenly, turning his attention again to the stereo. "Gil once said he would like to go to Africa and teach music just so he could hear all those African rhythms."

Now Miles was addressing himself to what Gil calls "a merchandising problem," which he claims has "nothing to do with music at all." Said Miles: "People always want to categorize music—jazz, classical. Put labels on it. But Gil says all music comes from the people, and the people are folk. Therefore, all music is folk.

"I used to write and send Gil my scores for evaluation. Gil used to say they were good, but cluttered up with too many notes. I used to think you had to use a lot of notes and stuff to be writing. Now I've learned enough about writing not to write. I just let Gil write. I give him an outline of what I want and he finishes it. I can even call him on the phone and just tell him what I got in mind, and when I see the score, it is exactly what I wanted. Nobody but Gil could think for me that way. He just has a gift of being able to put instruments together. Some people have it, some don't. Gil has it.

"He is as well-versed on music in general as Leonard Bernstein. And what the classical guys don't know is what Gil knows. They don't know folks. Gil is always listening to Gypsy, South American and African things. Every time he comes to my house, he's got some new record for me.

"Hey!" Miles laughed, "you know what Gil will do sometimes? You'll be playing one of his arrangements in 4/4 time, and, all of a sudden, you'll come upon a bar of 3/2. That Gil is something."

Since early morning and continuing through a pot of neckbones and pinto beans he had cooked himself, Miles talked about Gil. The street lights along Michigan Avenue had been burning for hours when the phone rang. "That was Gil," Miles said, hanging up. Evans' jet flight had just arrived at Chicago's O'Hare field, and he was now en route through town.

Less than an hour later, the doorbell rang and silver-maned Gil Evans filled up the door with his six-feet-plus. "Hi, Miles," Gil said. "Hi," Miles said casually. It was as if Evans had been there all day—or at least, had gone out five minutes before to get a pack of cigarettes. Then they sat down and watched TV, with nothing more to say. "Look," Miles would mutter, pointing to the action on TV. "Uh-huh," Gil would answer. But that was all the conversation that passed between them.

The incomplete utterances explained something Miles had said earlier. "Sometimes when I'm playing, I start a phrase and never complete it because it isn't necessary. I have communicated the idea. Let's suppose somebody tells you something that bugs you and then asks your opinion about it. You might just say, 'Aw!' and from the way you have said it, they get the message that you don't dig it." And in quite another vein here was the scholarly, soft-spoken Evans and the sometimes volatile and always hard-spoken Miles Davis achieving absolute communication with the sparest of sounds.

Next day they watched football games on television, ate well, smoked, drank, talked, joked and listened to music from other lands, joined by their wives, as in a family visit.

The day before, Gil had told me that he felt Miles was a "first-rate musician." "But," Gil said now, "that is what I felt yesterday. Today I feel he is a genuine artist and there are very few of them in the world today. I also think he's a pretty fine specimen of the human animal in most things he does. Today I admire his approach to life."

On only one thing does Evans seem to have his mind thoroughly fixed: "I only work for Miles and myself." He said he could not do anything he did not want to do, yet insisted he was a "commercial arranger," but only in the sense "that what I write is popular." And while Evans admitted that each year, his income seems to wind up some $500 under what his needs require, he rejects Miles' contention that he is just now receiving the acclaim his talents have long deserved. "I haven't been around music for 20 years just waiting to be discovered," Evans said, "nor am I a recent discovery. I am just now able to do the things I couldn't do before. My product just wasn't ready."

And, of course, Gil—christened Ian Ernest Gilmore Green by his Australian parents—is no novice to the musical world. He led his own band in Stockton, Calif., from 1933 to 1938. Skinnay Ennis later took it over, but Gil stayed on as arranger until 1941. Then he became musical architect for the Claude Thornhill Band, remaining with it until 1948.

Evans is a symphony of contradictions. Despite his vast knowledge of instruments, he never played one professionally until he took up the piano seriously in 1952. In recent years, he has been writing big band arrangements—with no standing big band at his disposal.

In October, however, he resolved some of this contradiction with the formation of his own 12-piece orchestra. "I need a band as a workshop," he said. "In the past, I didn't get to be around a band but once a year, like when Miles and I are doing something. Before, I had to hear music in my imagination." Evans' band recently recorded its first LP, titled *Out of the Cool,* for the Impulse label. It was released late in January.

The gangling Evans, who strikes you as a cross between Gary Cooper and Henry Fonda, likes to talk philosophy, poetry, travel, politics—but rarely does so with Miles. Yet he insists: "We think alike." Their communication is on the music level. "We are complementary in that we are opposites," Evans said. "My inclination is just less extroverted than his. We both like the same kind of music."

Modern music's Mutt and Jeff, however, rarely sit down and say, "Let's do this type of LP," and then plan around their decision. For an example of how they work, take *Sketches of Spain,* of which Evans says: "We were just ready for flamenco music and fell into it. We don't have anything specifically planned at present, but we will be doing some more things."

The compatibility of these two diverse personalities was first evidenced in the late 1940s, when Evans helped Miles and Gerry Mulligan set up their historic nine-piece band. Ever since then, they have shared a common wish: to go on growing musically together.

All the evidence indicates that they will.

―――――

June 18, 1964
Blindfold Test: Miles Davis
by Leonard Feather

> The "Blindfold Test" is a listening test that challenges the featured artist to discuss and identify the music and musicians who performed on selected recordings. The artist is then asked to rate each tune using a five-star system. No information about the recordings is given to the artist prior to the test.

Miles Davis is unusually selective in his listening habits. This attitude should not be interpreted as reflecting any general misanthropy. He was in a perfectly good mood on the day of the interview reproduced below; it just happened that the records selected did not, for the most part, make much of an impression.

Clark Terry, for example, is an old friend and idol of Davis' from St. Louis, and the Duke Ellington Orchestra has always been on Davis' preferred list.

Davis does not have an automatic tendency to want to put everything down, as an inspection of his earlier "Blindfold Tests" will confirm (Sept. 21, 1955, and Aug. 7, 1958).

The Cecil Taylor item was played as an afterthought, because we were discussing artists who have impressed critics, and I said I'd like to play an example. Aside from this, Davis was given no information about the records played.

Les McCann and the Jazz Crusaders
"All Blues" (Pacific Jazz)—Wayne Henderson, trombone; Wilton Felder, tenor saxophone; Joe Sample, piano; McCann, electric piano; Miles Davis, composer.

What's that supposed to be? That ain't nothin'. They don't know what to do with it—you either play it bluesy or you play on the scale. You don't just play

flat notes. I didn't write it to play flat notes on—you know, like minor thirds.
Either you play a whole chord against it, or else . . . but don't try to play it like
you'd play, ah, "Walkin' the Dog." You know what I mean?

That trombone player—trombone ain't supposed to sound like that.
This is 1964, not 1924. Maybe if the piano player had played it by himself,
something would have happened.

Rate it? How can I rate it?

CLARK TERRY
"Cielito Lindo" (from 3 In Jazz, *RCA Victor)—Terry, trumpet; Hank Jones,*
piano; Kenny Burrell, guitar.

Clark Terry, right? You know, I've always liked Clark. But this is a sad
record. Why do they make records like that? With the guitar in the way,
and that sad ———— piano player. He didn't do nothing for the rhythm
section—didn't you hear it get jumbled up? All they needed was a bass and
Terry.

That's what ———— up music, you know. Record companies. They make
too many sad records, man.

ROD LEVITT
"Ahi Spain" (from Dynamic Sound Patterns, *Riverside)—Levitt, trombone,*
composer; John Beal, bass.

There was a nice idea, but they didn't do nothing with it. The bass player was
a ———— though.

What are they trying to do, copy Gil? It doesn't have the Spanish feeling—doesn't move. They move up in triads, but there's all those chords
missing—and I never heard any Spanish thing where they had a figure that
went.

That's some old ————, man. Sounds like Steve Allen's TV band. Give
it some stars just for the bass player.

DUKE ELLINGTON
"Caravan" (from Money Jungle, *United Artists)—Ellington, piano; Charlie*
Mingus, bass; Max Roach, drums.

What am I supposed to say to that? That's ridiculous. You see the way they
can ———— up music? It's a mismatch. They don't complement each other.
Max and Mingus can play together, by themselves. Mingus is a hell of a bass
player, and Max is a hell of a drummer. But Duke can't play with them, and
they can't play with Duke.

Now how are you going to give a thing like that some stars? Record companies should be kicked in the ————. Somebody should take a picket sign and picket the record company.

SONNY ROLLINS
"You Are My Lucky Star" (from 3 In Jazz, *RCA Victor)—Don Cherry, trumpet; Rollins, tenor saxophone; Henry Grimes, bass; Billy Higgins, drums.*

Now, why did they have to end it like that? Don Cherry I like, and Sonny I like, and the true idea is nice. The rhythm is nice. I didn't care too much for the bass player's solo. Five stars if real good? It's just good, no more. Give it three.

STAN GETZ AND JOÃO GILBERTO
"Desafinado" (from Getz-Gilberto, *Verve)—Getz, tenor saxophone; Gilberto, vocal.*

Gilberto and Stan Getz made an album together? Stan plays good on that. I like Gilberto.

I'm not particularly crazy about just anybody's bossa nova. I like the samba. And I like Stan, because he has so much patience, the way he plays those melodies—other people can't get nothing out of a song, but he can. Which takes a lot of imagination, that he has, that so many other people don't have.

As for Gilberto, he could read a newspaper and sound good! I'll give that one five stars.

ERIC DOLPHY
"Mary Ann" (from Far Cry, *New Jazz)—Booker Little, trumpet; Dolphy, composer, alto saxophone; Jaki Byard, piano.*

That's got to be Eric Dolphy—nobody else could sound that bad! The next time I see him I'm going to step on his foot. You print that. I think he's ridiculous. He's a sad ————.

L.F.: *DownBeat* won't print those words.

M.D.: Just put he's a sad shhhhhh, that's all! The composition is sad. The piano player ———— it up, getting in the way so that you can't hear how things are supposed to be accented.

It's a sad record, and it's the record company's fault again. I didn't like the trumpet player's tone, and he don't do nothing. The running is all right if you're going to play that way, like Freddie Hubbard or Lee Morgan; but you've got to inject something, and you've got to have the rhythm section along; you can't keep playing all eighth notes.

The piano player's sad. You have to think when you play; you have to help each other—you just can't play for yourself. You've got to play with whomever you're playing. If I'm playing with Basie, I'm going to try to help what he's doing—that particular feeling.

CECIL TAYLOR
"Lena" (from Live at the Café Montmartre, Fantasy)—Jimmy Lyons, alto saxophone; Taylor, piano.

Take it off! That's some sad ————, man. In the first place, I hear some Charlie Parker clichés. . . . They don't even fit. Is that what the critics are digging? Them critics got to stop having coffee. If there ain't nothing to listen to, they might as well admit it. Just to take something like that and say it's great because there ain't nothing to listen to is like going out and getting a prostitute.

L.F.: This man said he was influenced by Duke Ellington.

M.D.: I don't give a ————! It must be Taylor. Right? I don't care who he's influenced by. That ———— ain't nothing. In the first place, he don't have the—you know, the way you touch a piano. He doesn't have the touch that would make the sound of whatever he thinks of come off.

I can tell he's influenced by Duke, but to put the loud pedal on the piano and make a run is very old-fashioned to me. And when the alto player sits up there and plays with no tone. . . . That's the reasons I don't buy any records.

July 2, 1964
Miles and the Fifties
by Leonard Feather

A problem arises in the nomination of any individual as symbolic of jazz in the 1950s. This decade, because of greater public acceptance and greater opportunities for learning on the part of the musicians, produced a broader assortment of new talents than the three previous decades combined.

Miles Davis is a particularly suitable symbol because his contribution straddles three decades. He was a direct product of the bebop of the 1940s. He was a progenitor of several phases in the 1950s—cool jazz; the new modern orchestral style and the Spanish influence, both represented by his collaboration with Gil Evans; the trend toward modal concepts, in some of the later combo performances. Through the latter, and through his launching of a series of important sidemen, Davis was also a pacemaker for the 1960s. In other words, he provides an all-purpose link from Dizzy Gillespie and Charlie Parker to Bill Evans and John Coltrane.

His importance as a cynosure for musicians seeking new avenues can be gauged from a glance at the personnels of the groups with which he recorded for Capitol in 1949 and 1950. John Lewis, who was to become the most important new combo leader of the middle '50s, and later a leading standard bearer for symphonic concert jazz, was a pianist and arranger on two of the three dates. Gunther Schuller gained some of his first exposure to jazz as a French horn-playing sideman on the third session. Gerry Mulligan, a key figure of the 1950s as a composer and combo leader, played on all three sessions.

As an instrumentalist, Davis was a pace-setter in leading the way to the increased use of fluegelhorn in place of trumpet in recent years. Davis adopted fluegelhorn in 1957, and it was soon taken up on a part- or full-time basis by Art Farmer, Shorty Rogers, Clark Terry and others. His improvisational style and sound seem to have had a direct influence on Farmer, Kenny Dorham, Donald Byrd and possibly even on Terry, who was Davis' own original influence.

Davis was even important as a launcher or reviver of themes. Though his career as a composer has been limited to simple instrumental lines, several of them, notably "So What" and "Milestones," achieved some general currency and were recorded by Gerald Wilson and others. Even his use of a standard tune often led to its general use among jazzmen. "Bye, Bye, Blackbird," "Someday My Prince Will Come," "On Green Dolphin Street" and "Stella by Starlight" were in little or no jazz use until he recorded them. Their subsequent adoption by other musicians was of a piece with the imitation of Miles' style of clothes; it had more to do with fad and fashion than with the superiority of these tunes over any other equally available popular songs.

There is also some connection between Davis' esthetic and social attitudes. Though this may not mean that any direct relationship exists between his birth and upbringing as an American Negro and his reputation as an iconoclast, or his decision to walk off the bandstand during a saxophone solo, nevertheless certain unusual aspects of his background are relevant to any discussion of his music.

Davis' identity as a Negro places him in the majority among important jazz figures; but as a very dark Negro he belongs to a minority. As a product of a well-to-do family he is again a minority member among jazz musicians; but his experience as a wealthy Negro's son is even less common.

"I got to thinking about my father last night," Miles said one day recently. "He died just two years ago, you know. I thought about how he spent his whole life trying to be better than the 'niggers'—and I started crying. . . . He could have been a musician, too, you know—I have slave ancestors that played string music on the plantations—but that wasn't what my grandfather wanted for him. He thought there were more important things to do than entertain white folks. So my father became a high-priced dental surgeon. And he owned a lot of land and raised pedigreed hogs. So I was never poor. Not as far as money goes. My father gave me an allowance, and I had a paper route and made money at that, too, and I saved money and used some of it to buy records."

Davis' grandfather had owned a thousand acres of land in Arkansas; Davis' father's land consisted of 200 acres in Millstadt, Ill., near East St. Louis, where the family lived from 1928, when he was two years old. His mother was, and is, prominent in Negro society.

Despite his lineage and respectable bourgeois background, Miles was no more immune than any other American Negro to the traumatic blow of a Jim Crow childhood.

"About the first thing I can remember," he once told a reporter, "was a white man running me down a street hollering, 'Nigger! Nigger!' My father went hunting him with a shotgun. Being sensitive and having race pride has been in my family since slave days."

Though there was little musical interest shown in Miles' generation of the Davis family, his personal enthusiasm was tolerated by his mother and encouraged by his father, who gave him a trumpet for his 13th birthday. Miles played in the high school band and was working professionally with a local group, Eddie Randolph's Blue Devils, by the time he was 16. He had an offer to go on the road with the Tiny Bradshaw Orchestra, but his mother insisted he stay home and complete his senior year of high school.

The next step for a youngster with financially comfortable parents was a college education. His mother wanted him to attend Fisk University, but Miles opposed the plan. His determination to stay with music was strengthened by an experience with the Billy Eckstine Band when it played in the area. A member of the trumpet section was sick, and Miles was drafted into the band for a couple of weeks.

Since the personnel then included both Dizzy Gillespie and Charlie Parker, the experience afforded him a foretaste of a top-grade professional life in jazz. He persuaded his father to let him continue his studies not at Fisk but at Juilliard, where he could take harmony and theory. He arrived in New York in 1945, immediately sought out Parker and became his good friend and protégé, as well as a disciple of Gillespie.

The prevailing new-music trend was bebop, with Gillespie and Parker as equal bellwethers. Because their partnership developed in Manhattan, and because of a somewhat distorted legend that has grown around Minton's, it has often been assumed that the new music of the 1940s evolved exclusively in New York City. The fact is that Davis' musical thinking had begun to take substantial shape long before he hit New York. A few details were brought out in the following exchange:

LEONARD FEATHER: Surely you must have heard some important people before 1945 and developed your style before you came to New York? I don't think everything happened in New York. A lot of accounts place everything at Minton's, but it wasn't that specific, do you think?

MILES DAVIS: No, because I heard Clark Terry in St. Louis. He used to play like that. Real fast, like Buck Clayton sounds.

L.F.: Did he play the new kind of changes and ideas?

M.D.: I think so. We were going around with a piano player in St. Louis who played like Bud Powell. Name was Duke Brooks. He made a record with Red Callender, and then he died. Duke couldn't read or write any music. We used to have a trio together in St. Louis. We played like the Benny Goodman Sextet. He was always showing me things Charlie Christian played.

L.F.: Maybe Charlie Christian was an influence around there.

M.D.: I think bop branched off from Charlie Christian. There was a trumpet player named Buddy Anderson from Kansas City. He was with Billy Eckstine, and he used to play like Charlie. He got TB, and later I heard he was in Oklahoma, playing guitar. He used to be real fast and light. And there was a boy from Oklahoma used to play with Buddy and with us. His name was Miles Pruitt. He used to play like Monk. There was another boy who played with us who played Kansas City blues and that kind of thing, but he had worked with Pruitt and he sounded like Charlie Parker. His name was Charlie Young. We all used to work together.

L.F.: There are a lot of people who were probably playing flatted fifths, and other things Diz and Bird were identified with, even before Diz and Bird became famous.

M.D.: Certain clichés and half-steps they used to play—from the sixth to the flatted fifth.

L.F.: I don't think any one person was responsible, but I think Charlie Christian helped spread it around the Middle West.

M.D.: He used to play fast like that, and from what I hear, he was the one. I never heard him in person. Duke Brooks used to play with Jimmy Blanton across the street from my father's office in a place called The Red Inn. They used to have fights and somebody would get cut every Saturday night. We used to go in there and hear them.

L.F.: You probably didn't play any style but your own, did you? You didn't start out playing like Roy, did you?

M.D.: I started out playing like anybody I could play like, but Clark Terry was my main influence. I used to follow him around.

L.F.: Terry was modern all along, wasn't he?

M.D.: Yes, he always played like that ever since I heard him. He used to hang out with Duke Brooks and Blanton; bands that used to come to town wanted them to leave, but they never would leave.

L.F.: Was Blanton that modern harmonically, do you think?

M.D.: I don't know. During that time in St. Louis, they used to say I sounded like Shorty Baker and Bobby Hackett. I couldn't ever play high. Anything I liked, I was trying to play.

L.F.: Then when you arrived on 52nd Street, you probably didn't hear anything completely different from what you'd heard before.

M.D.: I couldn't find anything I liked but Vic Coulson and Diz. I tried to play like Vic because I couldn't play like Diz; he was too high for me. I would get the chords from Monk—written in a hurry on matchbook covers, you know. And from Benny Harris. But those guys in K.C. and St. Louis and Texas . . . I knew a guy named Clyde Hicks, I think he was. He was a hell of an alto player, and he used to show me how to write. He used to play in Bird's style—that running style with changes. I also knew a guy named Ray something—played trumpet. He came to St. Louis and he'd play with us, and he was playing . . . We were playing with Eddie Randall and a boy named William Goodson. Everybody wanted Ray—Billy Eckstine wanted him.

L.F.: I guess these modern ideas were developing all over the place then. How did it reach the point where the whole bop thing became a fad? How and where did you decide to go from there?

M.D.: It's just like clothes. All of a sudden you decide you don't have to wear spats and a flower up here, you know? You wear the flower and leave off the spats, and then pretty soon you leave off both of them. After a while, what was happening around New York became sickening, because everybody was playing the clichés that people had played five years before, and they thought that made them "modern" musicians. I really couldn't stand to hear most of those guys.

In other words, by the late 1940s, bop, represented by the sartorial elaborations in Davis' figure of speech, had begun to grow stale. In order to revive it and recapture it from the cliché merchants who were all wearing the spats and the boutonnieres, all destroying it through indiscriminate, uninspired usage, it was necessary to step a few paces back and get a better perspective.

Some of the beboppers gradually learned that the revolution had been won and some of the conquered territory needed recultivation. It was this kind of thinking that led Davis, Gil Evans and a coterie of others in New York to resolve that new approaches must be fashioned out of the clichés of bop. Following are some of Davis' recollections of this phase, in which the "hot" jazz of bop evolved into the "cool" of 1949–'50 and the Capitol nine-piece band.

L.F.: How did the cool era begin?

M.D.: Well, for one thing I always wanted to play with a light sound, because I could think better when I played that way.

L.F.: Why were so many of Claude Thornhill's players involved in that at first—was it because of Gil Evans?

M.D.: I wanted Sonny Stitt with those nine pieces, but Sonny was working someplace, and Gerry [Mulligan] said get Lee [Konitz] because he has a light sound, too. And Gerry was playing his baritone—in fact, I didn't expect him to play. I didn't know Gerry until I went down to Gil's house and he was there.

We wanted John Simmons because we wanted everything to be light, but Gil said Joe Shulman could play real light. I liked Al McKibbon at that time, too, but he was busy. But that whole thing started out as an experiment. And Monte Kay got us a job at the Royal Roost. He's another guy who'd done a lot for modern music, but he never gets any credit.

L.F.: Did Tristano have any effect on you then?

M.D.: Well, I loved to hear him play by himself, because the others didn't know what to do. They would clash. Like Art Tatum—I didn't know anybody that could work with him.

L.F.: I think Lee had a pretty good understanding.

M.D.: Yes, he did. But I'd rather hear them just play together, the two of them by themselves.

L.F.: They had something in common with your approach in terms of the lightness and general feeling, more than most of the musicians at that time.

M.D.: They probably did.

Asked if he could distinguish between his style in the bop years and his later approach, Davis said, "A lot of things that I didn't do, or just didn't know about, I do now. Harmonically and technically. I wasn't phrasing as definite and pronounced as I do now. If you don't add something to a note, it dies, you know. Certain notes and melodies and the rhythm. If you don't cut into a rhythm section, it dies, too. You play behind the beat, the rhythm drops. But never play ahead of a beat unless you're superimposing some phrase against the beat."

"Do you think that what people meant by cool jazz involved mainly a solo style or an ensemble?" I asked. "Were they thinking of the Capitol record dates, or of you as an individual or leader?"

"I think what they really meant was a soft sound," Davis replied. "Not penetrating too much. To play soft you have to relax . . . you don't delay the beat, but you might play a quarter triplet against four beats, and that sounds delayed. If you do it right, it won't bother the rhythm section."

Gerry Mulligan's recollection of these events, as reported a few years ago, differs slightly from the Davis version:

L.F.: Was the fact that so many men on the Miles Davis dates came from the Thornhill band coincidental?

GERRY MULLIGAN: No, the Thornhill orchestra was a tremendous influence on that small band, because the instrumentation, when you get down to it, was a reduced version of what Claude was using at the time.

L.F.: Who had the idea of using French horn, tuba, etc.—you and Gil Evans, or Miles?

G.M.: It was pretty much of a group undertaking, the putting together of the band. There were two separate stages, the discussion and theoretical stage, and then when we got into rehearsal Miles was more of a prime mover, as far as organizing, rehearsing and all that. Gil and I spent the better part of one winter hashing out instrumentations. We used to spend a lot of time talking about it with everybody that was coming down there at that time, like John Lewis and John Carisi. It was at Gil's place; he had a basement room over on 55th Street in back of a Chinese laundry.

L.F.: Was this an attempt to get away from the conventional bop format?

G.M.: No, the idea was just to try to get a good little rehearsal band together. Something to write for.

L.F.: Then it was more or less regarded as a workshop experiment?

G.M.: Yes. As far as the "cool jazz" part of it, all of that comes after the fact of what it was designed to be. They used that title on the Capitol album, Birth of the Cool—maybe that was a good idea, but I don't know that it was particularly responsible for the birth of the cool. It certainly was an influence, though, in the use of small bands, for four-, five- and six-horn writing.

L.F.: Do you think cool means the ensemble sound or the style of the soloist?

G.M.: Well, Mel Powell said it in an interesting way. He said that the first impact of Benny Goodman's band in the 1930s was people saying how could all these guys play ahead of the beat, on top and ahead of it as an ensemble and do it together, and make it swing? It didn't sound like they were playing out of rhythm or anything. And when our date came along, he said, it was the complete opposite—how could we lay so far back, play so far behind the beat together, and sound like we were swinging and not slow down? So it was just as much a rhythmic as a tonal matter.

You hear a lot of four-horn writing today that sounds very much like the Miles band. In fact, there's a lesson that we learned, the hard way, out of that band; that we really didn't need the French horn or the—well, the tuba was needed from an orchestration standpoint, not so much for the sound; the sound was in the conception of the lead players mostly.

Miles dominated that band completely; the whole nature of the interpretation was his. That was why we were always afraid to get another trumpet player; it would have been ideal, actually, to have a second trumpet. We thought about it but never did it. We only worked two weeks at the Royal Roost in September 1948, then one more date about a year later, I think at the Clique Club; those were the only personal appearances the band ever made.

Despite the seven-year gap between the last Capitol session and the first Davis–Gil Evans Columbia LP (*Miles Ahead,* 1957), the expansion of Miles' setting from a nine- to a 19-piece orchestra seemed a logical though long-delayed outgrowth of the original concept. The trumpeter through the years had developed a style based largely on some aspects of his 1949–'50 work. It involved a more frequent employment of mutes, substitution of the fuller-sounding fluegelhorn for trumpet, a wispy and ethereal tone, sensitive use of pauses and a generally lyric sound and underplayed approach. The characteristic phrases of bebop, though never totally rejected, were dispensed with in many of the solos.

His discarding of much of the technical ability he has achieved seems like a deliberate attempt to demonstrate the expendability of such values.

"Years ago," Miles has said, "Gunther Schuller brought some guys from the Metropolitan Opera to hear me—in Canada, I think it was. They wanted to hear some jazz. One guy came over and said, 'Play "Body and Soul,"' so I played 'Body and Soul' for him. Then he said, 'What do you do when you play that?' He was trying to pick on me, make my playing seem like it was nothing, in front of some friends of his. But those same guys don't think like that anymore, because they are now trying to play things like I was trying to play. And they can't do it. So they must know there's something to it. And they know I can do what they're doing, because I went to school and learned that. 'You know,' I told this guy, 'when I was 10 years old, I started out where you are now. I used to play "Flight of the Bumblebee." The only reason I stopped playing it was, I found out I didn't like it. Can you play it?' And I said, 'I make as much money as you do, too, and more.' And he couldn't say nothing. He just said, 'I'm sorry.'

"But that was years ago. Nowadays, some of the teachers don't teach the way they used to, with that same old dry legit tone, because in the first place you can't get a job with it.

"The old symphonic repertorial music is going to go out. They're going to concentrate on the guys that write more or less modern music. Pretty soon all the schools of music will be together and understand one another and learn from each other's approaches, and you won't hear Beethoven's Fifth any more as a standard on a concert."

What was implied (and later stated outright by Davis) was that something on the order of *Sketches of Spain* might find its place in the concert repertoire.

The relationship between Davis and Evans began around 1947, when Miles was a member of the Charlie Parker Quintet. Intrigued by the work Evans was doing for Thornhill, he spent several days studying the score Evans had done for the orchestra on "Robbins' Nest."

"We've been friends ever since our first meeting," he told Marc Crawford (*DownBeat,* Feb. 16, 1961). "He's not only a composer but a hell of an orchestrator; he just knows instruments and what you can get out of them. He and Duke Ellington are the same way. They can use four instruments when others need eight.

"People always want to categorize music—jazz, classical. Put labels on it. But Gil says all music comes from the people, and the people are folk. Therefore, all music is folk."

The Davis–Evans collaboration technique is as subtly worked as Duke Ellington's with Billy Strayhorn. Davis used to send his own scores to Evans for evaluation. He found he was cluttering them up with too many notes and had to learn what not to write. A simpler solution arose; he began to give Evans a brief outline of his ideas, and when he saw Evans' score later it would represent exactly what he wanted.

"Nobody but Gil could think for me that way," Davis said. "He just has a gift of being able to put instruments together. Some people have it, some don't. Gil does. He is as well versed on classical music in general as Leonard Bernstein. And what the classical guys don't know is what Gil knows."

Davis recently elaborated on this theme. Through the years he has grown away from John Lewis and Gunther Schuller, both of whom took part in the Capitol record dates. He did not dig the Lewis–Schuller Third Stream approach of the late 1950s. He said he feels that Schuller particularly lacks the empirical jazz experience that has made Evans' co-operation so valuable to Davis.

"Somebody came to me a while back," he said, "and asked me to play with that orchestra that Gunther and John have been working with. What do they call it? Orchestra U.S.A.? Anyway, I just told him, 'Get outta here!' You know, when John Lewis writes for a big string section, it sounds like two strings."

Davis' musical thinking might be summed up succinctly as follows: The amalgamation of musical cultures reached its peak with Evans' work, which combined classical, jazz and ethnic elements. As for jazz, he observed, "There is no next trend. If there's another trend, then we're going backwards; because, look, you had Duke, and you had Charlie Parker and Dizzy, and you had Lennie Tristano, right? And they're all just leveling off. There's not going to be another trend unless it's the walking-off-the-stage trend."

A review of the 1950s fails to reveal any major inaccuracies in Davis' assessment. Despite the huge number of first-rate new talents, few if any were apocalyptically different. After Tristano, there was the Dave Brubeck–Paul Desmond surge, which, though musically successful and attractive, remained sui generis and did not prove vital in terms of general influence. There was the Modern Jazz Quartet, a delightful chamber-music group that nevertheless seemed to have reached a dead end not long after the decade ended, because of its self-imposed formal limitations.

Most other trends of the 1950s were mere echoes of earlier phases. Gerry Mulligan, in his work as a combo leader, symbolized a scooping up of a handful of schools, from Dixieland on through swing to bop. West Coast jazz in the mid-'50s was a thin dilution of cool jazz. Hard-bop, or neo-bop, was represented by Art Blakey's Messengers. Horace Silver's Quintet (with its overtones of the even earlier Gospel-ful harmony), and the Adderley brothers. It was not until just after the turn of the decade that the impact of John

Coltrane and modal jazz, Ornette Coleman and atonality, Herbie Mann and the polyethnic bag could be felt to any substantial degree.

Davis rounded out the decade with two more superb Evans collaborations. *Porgy and Bess* was released in 1959 and *Sketches of Spain* in the summer of 1960. For the most part, he spent the second half of the 1950s leading a series of quintets or sextets that served as a very loose, even sloppy backdrop, though they offered a procession of prodigious solo talents.

There will be no analysis here of the Miles Davis temperament. Too much has already been written, at the expense of discussions of musical facts and factors. When *Time* threw a few gratuitous barbs at him during its examination of Thelonious Monk (implying that Davis is raging at the white world and teaching his children boxing so they they can protect themselves from whites), Miles did not even bother to become incensed.

"They came to me three times to do a cover story on me," he said, "and I wouldn't have anything to do with them; so where do they get their information?"

Such matters are mild irritants but do not seem to bother him deeply; after 38 years of discrimination, coupled in recent years with success, financial security and patronization by white liberals, he has developed a protective armor heavy enough to inure him against solecisms.

Miles Davis, in short, represents restlessness and querulous doubt rather than riot and open rebellion, just as the lyricism of his solos, whether against a multitextured Gil Evans carpet of sounds or a quietly responsive rhythm section, is transmitted through a muted ball of fire more often than by an open horn.

Both as a human being and as a musician, Miles in many ways was the symbol of the '50s, the decade of our discontent.

―――――――――

Oct. 7, 1965
The Birth of the Cool
by George Hoefer

This is the story of a jazz album, *Birth of the Cool* (Capitol 1974), recorded more than 15 years ago. The music on it, although neglected by most listeners at the time, eventually became the inspiration for a new trend in jazz—the so-called cool school.

No one individual was responsible for the innovation, though the record is under Miles Davis' name; it was the culmination of a group effort involving such prominent modern-jazz figures as Davis, Gil Evans, Gerry Mulligan and John Lewis.

In actuality, the seeds of the cool style had been planted a decade earlier by the late pianist-arranger-bandleader Claude Thornhill when he started his own band in 1940.

After having made a name for himself as arranger for Hal Kemp, Ray Noble, Bing Crosby, Benny Goodman and the Bob Hope radio show (one of his most famous early accomplishments was the arranging and conducting of Maxine Sullivan's *Loch Lomond* recording), Thornhill established a band that has gone down in history as one of the most outstanding "musician's bands" of the swing era.

Thornhill had a definite conception of a band sound, and at first he did most of the arrangements himself. As Gil Evans told Nat Hentoff in a 1957 *DownBeat* interview, Thornhill's basic premise was "a sound based on the horns playing without vibrato, except for specific places where Thornhill would indicate vibrato for expressive purposes."

One of the great soloists with the early Thornhill band was Irving Fazola, the blues-oriented New Orleans jazz clarinetist with the liquid tone. Thornhill wrote an obbligato for French horns to accompany a Fazola solo, and the first time the band ran through the number Fazola was unaware of the addition until the pianist signaled the two French horn men to mount the stand—the leader wasn't sure what his clarinetist's reaction would be and decided to spring the innovation as a surprise. Fazola was so intrigued with the new sound that he went out and bought himself a bassoon. The French horns became an integral part of the Thornhill bands until 1948.

These two major concepts—the vibratoless horns and the addition of French horns—were well-established before Evans joined the band in late 1941 as arranger. The two men had worked together on the arranging staff of the Hope radio program, and Evans had been quite taken with Thornhill's ideas.

He told Hentoff, "Even then, Claude had a unique way with a dance band. He'd use the trombones with the woodwinds in a way that gave them a horn sound."

Within a year, Thornhill and Evans went into service, but the band had reorganized in late 1946, and Evans, as well as many of the original sidemen including the French hornists, returned. Evans now was the chief arranger, and many of the band's outstanding scores were his (*The Thornhill Sound,* Harmony 7088); he later was responsible for adding baritone saxophonist Mulligan to play and arrange.

A tuba (Bill Barber's) was added to the sound in mid-1947. Evans also gives credit for this innovation to Thornhill, though, in fact, the use of the instrument was a bone of contention between Evans and his boss. The leader liked the static sound of the tuba on sustained chords, while Evans wanted to use it for flexible, moving jazz passages.

Evans was responsible for getting arrangements of "Anthropology," "Yardbird Suite" and "Donna Lee" into the Thornhill book, and this resulted in the significant meeting of Miles Davis and Evans; the arranger went to the trumpeter to get clearance for the use of "Donna Lee."

Davis at this time was a great fan of the Thornhill band. He told a *DownBeat* reporter in 1950, "Thornhill had the greatest band, the one with Lee Konitz, during these modern times. The one exception was the Billy Eckstine band with Bird."

When Evans approached Davis on "Donna Lee," the trumpeter agreed to the clearance if Evans would give him some instructions on chord structure and let him study some of the Thornhill scores. Davis was fascinated by Evans' arrangement of "Robbins' Nest" with its unusual superimposition of chord clusters. He once commented, "Gil can use four instruments where other arrangers need eight."

By mid-1948, the jazz business was at low ebb, partly because of the second record ban. Thornhill's band was doing badly on a financial basis, and the pianist disbanded it for a while. Evans' one-room apartment on West 55th Street in New York City became an informal salon and workshop with the participants including Davis, Parker, Mulligan, Lewis (then pianist and arranger with Dizzy Gillespie's big band) and composers George Russell, John Benson, Brooks and Johnny Carisi.

Mulligan said in later years, "We all gravitated around Evans." Davis pushed the idea of getting a nonet organized, as suggested by Evans and Mulligan, whose basic idea was an experimental band with the smallest ensemble that would still give the writers the maximum possibilities. They decided on six horns plus rhythm.

Davis, who had enjoyed a comparatively long stay at the Royal Roost during the summer of 1948, was able to get a two-week date for the nonet at the Roost in September as a relief unit during Count Basie's engagement. He broke precedent by insisting the sign in front of the club should read, "Miles Davis Band, Arrangements by Gerry Mulligan, Gil Evans and John Lewis."

The personnel for the date was Davis, trumpet; Ted Kelly, trombone; Konitz, alto saxophone; Mulligan, baritone saxophone; Junior Collins, French horn; Barber, tuba; Lewis, piano; Al McKibbon, bass; and Max Roach, drums. Kenny "Pancho" Hagood, a former Gillespie vocalist, sang with the band.

This two-week engagement was the only time the band performed outside the recording studio or Nola's rehearsal hall. Basie was tremendously impressed and told a music journal writer, "Those slow things sounded strange and good. I didn't always know what they were doing, but I listened, and I liked it."

When the record ban ended in December 1948, two major labels, RCA Victor and Capitol, decided to go all out with bebop recording programs. Capitol had the more definitive and less commercial approach; it signed Davis pianist Tadd Dameron, singer Babs Gonzales, pianist Lennie Tristano, singer Dave Lambert and clarinetist Buddy DeFranco.

Trumpeter Davis had a contract calling for 12 sides, which were recorded in New York City at three separate sessions—January 1949, April 1949 and March 1950—with Pete Rugolo as A&R man.

On the first session, there were three changes in personnel from that heard at the Roost; Kai Winding, with whom Davis had been playing in Oscar Pettiford's group at the Three Deuces on 52nd Street, replaced trombonist Kelly; pianist Al Haig replaced Lewis; and bassist Joe Shulman replaced McKibbon. Five of the participants—Mulligan, Konitz, Collins, Barber and Shulman—were Thornhill alumni.

They cut two arrangements by Mulligan and two by Lewis. The opener was "Jeru," composed and arranged by Mulligan (the title derived from Davis' pet name for Gerry). This was followed by a Lewis scoring of a 1947 tune, "Move," written by George Shearing's drummer, Denzil Best, who originally titled it "Geneva's Move," in honor of his daughter; a Mulligan treatment of George Wallington's "Godchild"; and the closing number, Lewis' arrangement of Bud Powell's "Budo."

The Capitol brass must have been pleased with the results because they put out the pairing of "Move" and "Budo" on the label's popular 78-rpm series (Capitol 15404) within several weeks. The other two sides were held for their first bop releases in April.

On April 21, 1949, the second session was held with revised personnel: J.J. Johnson, who had just left the Illinois Jacquet Band, was the trombonist; Sanford Siegelstein (ex-Thornhill) played French horn; Lewis was the pianist; Nelson Boyd, who had replaced McKibbon with Gillespie's band, was on bass; and Kenny Clarke, then using his Muslim name of L.A. Salaam, was the drummer.

This date brought forth the Gil Evans arrangement of "Boplicity," a number composed by Davis under the pseudonym Cleo Henry. When asked in 1950 for his favorite example of his own work on record, Davis answered, "'Boplicity,' because of Gil's arrangement," and in the same interview he cited the bridge he played on "Godchild." His reaction regarding the composition is interesting. Once asked why all the boppers hadn't recorded "Boplicity," he replied that "the top line isn't very interesting, but the harmonization is," thereby giving all the compositional credit to Evans' scored ensembles.

The second number recorded on that April day was "Israel," a blues in a minor key, written and arranged by Carisi. This number, along with "Godchild," evoked the most praise at the time of release.

Two other originals, one by Mulligan and the other by Lewis, completed this session, made while Capitol was still happy with the bebop idea. These were "Venus de Milo" by Mulligan and "Rouge" by Lewis.

"Israel" was paired with "Boplicity" and was released with the second and last batch of the bebop series of 78s in October. Mulligan's "Venus" was held and released in late 1950, backed by "Darn That Dream," recorded during the third session. "Rouge" did not see the light of day until 1954.

That the third date, to permit Davis to complete the remaining four sides called for by his contract, did not take place until March 9, 1950, indicating there may have been some arm-twisting necessary. The personnel changes for this last date included Gunther Schuller on French horn in place of Siegelstein, McKibbon back on bass and Roach again as the drummer. Hagood was added to do the vocal on "Darn That Dream."

This time the scores used included two Evans arrangements of popular tunes, Johnny Mercer's "Moon Dreams" and the Van Heusen–Delange "Darn That Dream" (the only side not included in *Birth of the Cool*); a Miles Davis original, "Deception"; and the now well-known Mulligan score of "Rocker" (first titled "The Coop").

The first of these sides released (in November 1950) was "Darn That Dream," backed by "Venus" from the previous session. Mike Levin, *DownBeat*'s reviewer of the time, thought Hagood's vocal was "too tense," but he praised Evans' background scoring. "Here is an arranger who has learned the individual instruments and their sound possibilities," was Levin's comment. It never has been issued on LP.

The other Evans score, "Moon Dreams," along with "Rocker" (this Mulligan original was later recorded by the baritonist's tentet and released a year before this initial recording of the tune), and "Deception" were put on a Miles Davis 10-inch LP in May 1954 (Capitol 459).

Prior to the *Birth of the Cool* LP, several of these classics had been issued singly in jazz LP collections. Davis was represented in *The Modern Idiom* (Capitol 325) by "Budo" and in *Trumpet Stylists* (Capitol 326) by "Move," both released in mid-1952. A year later "Boplicity" appeared on *Cool and Quiet* (Capitol 371).

The 1954 Davis LP included re-releases of "Jeru," "Godchild," "Israel" and "Venus de Milo" in addition to the initial offerings of "Rouge" from the second date and the three tunes already mentioned from the third session. In

1957 this set was expanded to include "Budo," "Move" and "Boplicity" for the 12-inch LP *Birth of the Cool* (Capitol 762, recently re-released).

It is not true that these historic recordings went unnoticed at the time of their original release. *DownBeat*'s Levin said "Jeru"'s sounds "are extremely earable, far mellower than many bopped sounds" and that "Godchild"'s sounds "blend, and somebody actually worried about dynamics." He wrote equally favorably about the other tunes released in 1949–'50. *Metronome*, too, gave the releases high ratings, but their comments were tempered by their reviewer's high enthusiasm for Tristano's group. "Jeru," the review read, "sounds, with tricky accents, a little like a tune of the '30s in its use of instrumental ensemble. And why didn't Lee Konitz get a solo?"

During 1950–'51 Bill Russo and Lloyd Lifton used four columns in their "Jazz on Record" feature for *DownBeat* in analyzing the Davis solos on "Godchild," "Israel," "Move" and Konitz's alto solo on "Move."

Many musicians expressed praise at the time. The late pianist Herbie Nichols wrote a letter to *DownBeat* saying, "Miles proves melody and harmony in sufficient amounts will win out in the end." Bandleader Elliott Lawrence, who employed Mulligan as an arranger in 1950, said, "There is so much bad music that it is a relief when you come across something like those great Miles Davis sides on Capitol. Mulligan made up some of the numbers for us." Even antibopper Eddie Condon was impressed in a "Blindfold Test" when he heard "Move": "There's a lot of stuff going on; the arranger exercised his imagination. I like the whole sound—can't make much of the solos. It's the ensembles that hold this bebop performance together."

Andre Hodeir, the French critic and musician, devoted part of a chapter of his 1956 book, *Jazz: Its Evolution and Essence,* to this Davis band. He was greatly impressed by the arrangements, and in his summation of the band's importance he wrote, "Men like Evans and Mulligan seem to have understood that the principal objective of the arranger should be to respect the personality of each performer while at the same time giving the group a feeling of unity."

A lot has happened in the last decade that can be traced back to the experiences derived from the collaborative effort of the nonet: the Miles Davis–Gil Evans musical partnership, John Lewis and his Modern Jazz Quartet and Gerry Mulligan Concert Band, to name only a few.

Jazz record buyers may have missed the boat back in 1949, but today there are many who listen to the *Birth of the Cool* with the same affection the old-timers have for the Louis Armstrong–King Oliver duets on Gennett.

March 10, 1966

Miles Davis: A Most Curious Friendship

by Mike Zwerin

I have had a longstanding marginal acquaintance with Miles Davis. Our lives have touched in a number of minor episodes, which, I suppose, would be unimportant to me were it not for the fact that I like his playing so much. Anybody who plays that sweetly and intelligently has got to be beautiful inside—I keep thinking.

The first time I met Miles he gave me a job. It was 1948, and I was in New York on summer vacation from college. I was sitting in at Minton's Playhouse one night when I saw Miles standing, listening, in the back. When I was packing up my trombone, he asked me if I could make a rehearsal the next day at Nola's Studios. I said OK and drove home to Queens feeling pretty fine.

That was a fine summer for me, anyway. That summer I realized I had learned how to play jazz, learned in the sense that I knew I could do it— poorly, it was true, but at least the academic schooling was over. The rest I had to learn by experience. Doing it began that summer.

For the years before that, there often were weird people—sometimes junkies, and always funky—trooping through my parents' living room on their way upstairs to my little attic room where I had regular jam sessions. My father used to look up over his evening newspaper in disbelief as my raggedy bunch of jazz heroes passed by.

When I wasn't playing, I was listening in my attic room overlooking the Forest Hills Tennis Club. There was a picture of Charlie Parker on the wall over the upright piano. His records were always playing if I wasn't practicing my trombone. I would play along with them often, learning the tunes.

Another kind of learning started for me that summer. It was my summer with Charlie Parker, although I never did meet him. Bird made it hip to be an intellectual. His interest in reading, classical music and other similar things changed the style of hipsterism. If he knew about certain writers, or listened to Beethoven, that was enough to start many hipsters of the day doing those things. I can't say he started me reading, but he certainly accelerated my interest in literature. The wildness in his playing helped give me a lust for the wildness in novels, particularly Conrad and Hemingway. That part of my education started then.

Bird was the closest thing I've ever had to a hero. I was 18—a good age for having heroes—impressionable and absurdly romantic. Miles played with Charlie Parker at that time. I suppose some of my worshipping Bird was transferred to Miles because the night Miles asked me to a rehearsal

I remember feeling like a major-league ball boy who has just been told he will be given a tryout as a player.

Miles' band consisted of a lot of big names—Gerry Mulligan, John Lewis, Max Roach, Lee Konitz—plus Bill Barber on tuba, Junior Collins on French horn and myself. We played arrangements of tunes that were later recorded, such as "Jeru," "Boplicity," "Move" and "Israel." That the overall sound was right out of Claude Thornhill wasn't surprising since Gil Evans wrote many of the arrangements.

Miles was pleasant and relaxed but seemed unsure of how to be a boss. It was his first time as a leader. He relied quite a bit on Evans to give musical instruction to the players. Miles must have picked up his famed salty act sometime after that, because I don't remember his being excessively sarcastic that summer.

After we had worked at the Royal Roost on Broadway for two weeks, I went back to school and didn't see him for a long time. When I did, he was leading a quintet with Sonny Rollins, Red Garland, Philly Joe Jones and Paul Chambers at the Cafe Bohemia.

I was there with a French girl named Annette. Miles came over to our table and said, "Mike, you're getting fat." He smiled sweetly at Annette and started talking about pretty little nothings with her, turning on a full dose of his charm. He ignored me completely. She was impressed, but the start of his next set prevented him from continuing his attention. Annette and I left after a couple of drinks.

A year or so after that, I was leaving the Russian Tea Room with my mother and daughter when we ran into Miles and Gil Evans, who were going in. It was a bright fall afternoon, and Miles looked like he knew he looked like he had just stepped out of the pages of *Esquire*. He had on a well-cut jacket and beautiful gloves with belts. Smiling, he play-punched me in the stomach and said in that sandpaper voice of his, "You're getting fat, Mike."

The next time was in Paris. I was doing that thing Paris is so perfect for—"finding myself." This consisted mostly of walking all over the city, playing or sitting in the Old Navy Café on the Boulevard St. Germain. Because of complicated personal problems, I hadn't touched my trombone in five years. Each day in Paris, I would practice for about a half an hour, working to revive my long-neglected chops.

The Paris jazz scene was really quite provincial. There were few good players, most of whom were Americans—Kenny Clarke, Don Byas, Jimmy Gourley, Al Levitt, Allen Eager, maybe one or two others. The best French players were on the level of good people in provincial cities in the States— Pittsburgh or Dallas, for instance. I'm talking about my contemporaries, not the guys like Stephane Grappelli, Mezz Mezzrow or Bill Coleman, who were much older. (Both Mezz and Bill were more French than American by that time.) We liked their playing but considered them museum pieces and ignored them. Actually, I couldn't ignore Grappelli entirely, since he lived in the next room to me at the Crystal Hotel, playing Bach chaconnes on his violin in the afternoons. But it was definitely French provincial there, and an American jazz star was treated with respect when he worked in Paris.

It was 1957, and Miles was the big man: his clothes, his girls, his new loose rhythm section, his fresh open playing. So, all of us who hung out at the Old Navy were excited about Miles' arrival in Paris for a concert at the Olympia Theater and three weeks at the Club St. Germain, which was, conveniently, directly across from the Crystal Hotel.

However, the day of the Olympia concert, Jeannette Urtreger informed us at the Old Navy that, as far as she knew, Miles had not even arrived in Paris. Talk started: Where was he? The Olympia Theater was sold out that night, but by curtain time Miles' whereabouts were still a mystery. Finally the curtain went up, revealing Barney Wilen, René Urtreger, Pierre Michelot and Kenny Clarke all set up. They started in playing "Walkin'" and sounded fine.

But no Miles Davis. Barney took a tenor solo, and as he was finishing, backing away from the microphone, Miles appeared from the wings and arrived at the mike without breaking stride, just in time to start playing— strong. It was an entrance worthy of Nijinsky. If this choreography was good, his playing was perfect that night. He had recently made his "comeback" and was really putting the pots on. He was serious, and he was trying hard instead of just catting, as he does so often nowadays.

For the first week of his stay at the Club, as we called the St. Germain, I was down there almost every night. Once Wilen came over to where I was sitting at the bar and said, "You wouldn't believe what Miles said to me in the middle of my solo on the last tune. He said, 'Man, why don't you stop playing those awful notes.'" Barney was a hot, confident young player at that time and, fortunately for him, was not inclined to paranoia. He thought it very funny and had just gone on playing. Anyway, during that week, Miles greeted me only once. He said, "Mike, you're putting on weight."

At that time I was going out with a Mexican girl, Eva, who was studying at the Sorbonne. Eva had freckles, a lively spirit, and a body worthy of Maillol. I had promised several times to take her to the Club to hear Miles, but for one reason or another it had been delayed until his last day there. That afternoon I had an unexpected caller at the Crystal. It was Ursula, a skinny girl I had known vaguely back in the States and to whom something had happened in the six years since I'd last seen her: She was now spectacularly beautiful, with olive skin, dark long hair—and she had gained weight in the right places.

January 7, 1960   35¢

down
beat ®

AUGUST 30, 1962   **35c**

down beat

THE BI-WEEKLY MUSIC MAGAZINE

Condition Red — Allen, That
Trumpet On The Way Up · Ted Curs
Revolt In The Goodman Ba
— What Really Happene

MILES DAVIS X 3 = EVOLUTION OF AN ARTIST

ICD   **AUGUST 13, 1964**   **35c**

down beat

THE BI-WEEKLY MUSIC MAGAZINE

INTERNATIONAL JAZZ CRITICS POLL RESULTS

Final Results Begin On Page 14

NEWPORT REPORT

Complete Festival Coverage Begins On Page 10

Miles Upsets Dizzy

ICD MARCH 10, 1966   35c

down beat®

THE BI-WEEKLY MUSIC MAGAZINE

MILES DAVIS

APRIL 6, 1967   35c

down beat®

THE BI-WEEKLY MUSIC MAGAZINE

The Early Days
Of Miles Davis

By George Hoefer

Jazz Fans—1967

A Survey By Leonard Feather

Blowing Out
In Chicago—
Roscoe
Mitchell

MILES DAVIS

DECEMBER 11, 1969   50c

down beat®

EVERY OTHER THURSDAY SINCE 1934

Special:
Your Holiday Record
Shopping Guide to the
Best in Jazz, Blues&Rock

Miles Davis, Boxer:
An Offbeat Interview

Are Drummers Paranoid?

Gaspin' At Aspen:
The World's Highest
Jazz Party

John Mayall Blindfold Test

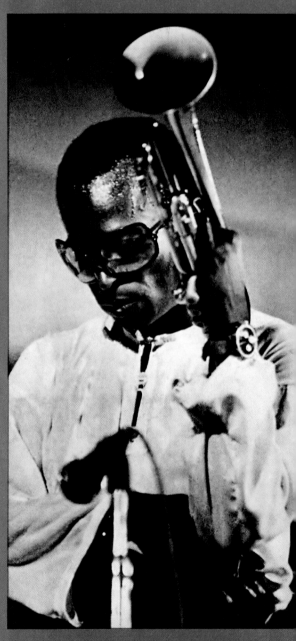

db music workshop

Paul Horn's "Paramahansa":
An Original Arrangement
For Flute Ensemble

Rock Group Audio, Part II

Jazz On Campus

MILES MOVES ON: AN EXCLUSIVE INTERVIEW

SEPTEMBER 3, 1970

down beat®

THE BIWEEKLY MUSIC MAGAZINE

Jazz Lives At Newport:
In-Depth Festival Report

New Music Products:
A Special Survey

Freddie Hubbard
Blindfold Test

music
workshop

Guitar Scale Tones

JULY 18, 1974   50c

the contemporary
music magazine

down
beat
®

Since she was leaving Paris the next day for the Middle East, I did the gentle-manly thing and invited her to join Eva and myself for the evening.

About 10 p.m. I made a splashy entrance into the Club, Ursula on one arm, Eva on the other. It was an entrance worthy of Allen Eager.

Miles was at the bar. As we sat down, he came over and put his arm around my shoulder—all of a sudden my good friend. He asked me how I had been and made it generally clear that he was concerned with my welfare. I asked him to have a drink with us, which he did, coming back to our table after each set.

Eva lived in a dormitory at the Cité Universitaire. There was a 1 a.m. curfew, so about 12:30 I left to drive her home. When I returned to the Club, an hour later, Miles and Ursula were deep in conversation. When I sat down, Miles looked bugged. He asked her what she saw in a dumb cat like me. I could never take Miles' saltiness seriously. It always seemed more funny than anything else.

As Miles was playing his last set, Ursula said to me, "Well, I guess I have a decision to make." I gave her my well-considered advice and paid the check. We walked out together. Miles was playing "When I Fall in Love," his look following us soulfully as we went up the stairs.

By the time I returned to New York City the following spring, I was practicing my horn two to three hours a day and had reached the point where I was good enough to play with some "weekend bands," like Billy May, Sonny Dunham and the Commanders. They worked mostly at Kiwanis clubs in towns like Harrisburg, Pa., or Binghamton, N.Y.

Traveling with these bands was raunch, a second-rate circus performing for people not interested in circuses any more. The big-band era was over. The worshipping girls who formerly clustered around bandstands were now worshipping somewhere else, as were most of the paying customers. The music didn't deserve better, anyway. It was tired, bad and unimaginative.

The life was unbelievably dreary—long drives, bad food, no sleep, plenty of booze just to stay sane. No life!

In 1959 I started about a year's stint with Maynard Ferguson. The money was still bad—less than $2 an hour if one included traveling time, which was most of it—but Maynard had a musical and personal excitement about him that was contagious. The band was boisterous and unsubtle. Most sophisti-cated people put it down. But he had that personal electricity so lacking in those other bands I'd been with, and that made it much more bearable.

Above all, though, it was a jazz band. Almost everybody in the band was a frustrated soloist, and Maynard constantly had to deal with requests for more solos by players who were sure their talents were not being fully used.

To most of us "stars" in Maynard's band, Miles was still the man. He was the jazz soloist, with the rhythm section, and he hadn't lost his originality—a musician whose style had remained modern and who had not been left behind by the new developments in music.

We worked at Birdland, opposite Miles, for a couple of weeks. One night, Miles was sitting at the table in the corner, which was reserved for musicians, listening to Wynton Kelly and the rest of his rhythm section playing the blues. Miles seemed annoyed. He said, "What the hell is Paul doing with the time?" The time seemed pretty good to me, but I didn't comment. When he got up—I assumed to do something about the situation—he turned to me and said, "You're getting fat, Mike."

A few months later, I moved into an apartment on 10th Avenue and 57th Street. Miles and John Lewis both lived one flight up from me. One day I went upstairs to ask John, whose apartment was right above mine, if he couldn't stop playing his harpsichord at three o'clock in the morning. I talked to him at his door. At one point, to be polite, I asked if my trombone practicing was too loud. A grumpy voice from behind me said, "Yeah, it's too loud." I turned around to see a funky Miles, in a ragged sweatshirt, dumping a bag of garbage in the incinerator.

Last Thanksgiving weekend, Miles was working at the Village Vanguard. He had been sick and hadn't played much in about six months, so he sounded a little weak. All the same, I would rather listen to a weak Miles than a strong almost anybody else—especially the way he plays a ballad. I love sparseness in music. Satie. Webern. Make one note do the job of many—imply, don't state. Miles can play jazz like that. He blew "Old Folks," and a young girl sitting near me said softly, "He opens up melodies like a flower."

The incinerator scene had been the last time I saw Miles, and since then I had lost 20 pounds. At the end of the evening I was standing in my thin glory outside the Vanguard when he came out of the club. He walked toward me, looked at me and passed right by without saying a word.

April 6, 1967
Early Miles
by George Hoefer

In a roundabout way, Miles Dewey Davis has elevated and dignified the status of jazz as an art form.

The well-known Davis image has been inflated, overstressed, misunderstood and as constantly criticized as if he were a part of show biz. The Davis rejection of nonessentials, not only in his music but also in his presentation of that music, can permit a listener the contemplation of a well-developed work of art. The molded sound lingers in one's being long after it has been heard; exposure to Davis' music is not a matter of an evening's entertainment easily forgotten.

It is this characteristic of purity that helps to give jazz status as a serious music.

It is significant that for the last decade Davis has received an acclaim and financial reward beyond that of many contemporaries, especially when one considers that his success has been acquired without opening a handbook on how to win friends and influence people.

It's been said that because of his nonconformist conduct, Davis is a master showman. This is not entirely valid. It is certainly not the way Davis means to be taken. He wouldn't go to all that trouble to win popularity.

Miles Davis is Miles Davis because he is Miles Davis, and the trumpeter's early years may give some clues to how he has become the artist he is.

The biographical facts have often been published—much to Davis' disgust. He once started a taped interview: "You want me to tell you where I was born—that old story? It was in good old Alton, Ill., on May 25, 1926. And I had to call my mother a week before my last birthday and ask her how old I would be." This introduction to a so-called self-portrait being taped for publicity purposes illustrates the Davis disdain for nonmusical facts and his self-conscious sense of humor.

Although born about 25 miles upstream from St. Louis, he became aware of the world in East St. Louis, Ill., where his parents had moved a year or so after Miles' birth.

When Miles was 13, Mrs. Davis wanted to give her son a violin for his birthday. Miles, with sardonic humor, later reported, "My father gave me a trumpet—because he loved my mother so much!" A few years later, when Mrs. Davis wanted to send Miles to Fisk University, Dr. Davis, a dentist, gave him the money to go to the Juilliard School of Music.

The main reason Davis got his son the horn was that one of his patients was Elwood Buchanan, a music teacher who visited the East St. Louis grade schools once a week. Buchanan recommended that Dr. Davis get Miles a trumpet.

In those days, St. Louis was considered a trumpet man's town. Many jazz trumpeters have come from the area; bandleaders Dewey Jackson and Charlie Creath, and Ed Allen, Joe Thomas, Harold (Shorty) Baker, Mouse Randolph, George Hudson and Clark Terry were among them. Buchanan would entertain his young pupils with stories about the exploits of these men at the jam sessions held at the Showboat on the west side of St. Louis.

Of his first lessons under Buchanan, Davis said, "Once a week we would hold notes. Everybody would fight to play best. Lucky for me, I learned to play the chromatic scale right away. A friend of my father's brought me a book one night and showed me how to do it so I wouldn't have to sit there and hold that note all the time."

Young Davis was still under the tutelage of Buchanan when he went into high school. There the instructor was on hand for daily lessons, and Davis made the high school band. It was about then that Buchanan told the young musician, "Play without any vibrato. You're gonna get old and start shaking anyway."

The pupil started, as he put it, "to play, fast and light, and no vibrato."

Clark Terry recalled his first meeting with Davis in an interview some years ago:

"I was with a band led by a one-legged piano player named Benny Reed. We were playing at a Carbondale, Ill., night club known as the Spinning Wheel. One afternoon we were engaged to play at a picnic grounds where there was an athletic competition between various southern Illinois high schools. There were several school bands in attendance with their teams. One of the bandleaders, who had the East St. Louis outfit, was an old friend of mine. He wanted me to meet a little trumpet player he admired very much and eventually brought the kid over to introduce us. The kid started right in asking questions—how did I do this, or that? We talked, but my mind was really on some girls dancing around a Maypole, and I kind of fluffed the kid off."

While still in high school, at age 15, Davis joined the musicians union and soon obtained a job with a St. Louis band, Eddie Randall's Blue Devils.

They were playing at the Elks Club in St. Louis when Terry again ran into the young trumpeter (Terry is six years older than Davis). "I was used to going up to the Elks Club in St. Louis to jam," Terry recalled. "One night, as I was climbing the long flight of stairs, I heard a trumpet player flying about on his horn in a way I couldn't recognize. Eddie Randall had the band, and I knew everyone in it but this little trumpet player. After I got over by the stand it dawned on me I'd seen the fellow before. As I said, 'Aren't you . . . ,' he broke in with, 'Yeah, I'm the kid you fluffed off in Carbondale.' We've often laughed about that since."

Another now well-known jazzman, saxophonist Sonny Stitt, also noticed Davis back in those days. It was 1942, when Stitt came through St. Louis on tour with Tiny Bradshaw's band. He dropped by the Rhumboogie, where the Randall group was playing for the floor shows. After listening for a while, Stitt told the young trumpeter, "You look like a man named Charlie Parker, and you play like him too. C'mon with us."

Stitt was serious and apparently able to get Bradshaw to offer Davis a job. "The fellows in the band had their hair slicked down," Davis remembered. "They wore tuxedos, and they offered me $60 a week to play with them. I went home and asked my mother if I could go, but she said no, I had to finish high school. I didn't talk to her for two weeks."

During the last two years in high school, Davis turned down several other offers to leave home for the road. Illinois Jacquet, who had taken over his brother Russell's band from Houston, offered Davis a job. Idrees Sulieman, the trumpet-playing manager of the last edition of McKinney's Cotton Pickers, also tried to get Davis to leave East St. Louis.

Right after graduation from high school in June 1944, Davis took a job with a small band from New Orleans. The group, known as Adam Lambert's Six Brown Cats, had finished a long run at Chicago's Club Silhouette, where singer Joe Williams worked with them. When the band was booked for a date at the Club Belvedere in Springfield, Ill., its trumpet player, Tom Jefferson, returned to New Orleans. The band included guitarist Adam Lambert, bassist Duke Saunders and drummer Stanley Williams. Davis played the only horn, and he received $100 a week. It was a good job for a start. The group was a modern swing outfit—but the gig only lasted two weeks. At the time, Davis was still trying to play in a Roy Eldridge–Harry James style.

A short time after he returned to East St. Louis, Davis heard that the Billy Eckstine Band was scheduled to play at the Club Riviera in St. Louis. In July 1944, young Davis showed up at the Riviera with his trumpet and was immediately recruited by Eckstine's music director, Dizzy Gillespie, to sit in for the band's ailing third trumpeter, Buddy Anderson. Miles later recalled, "So I sat in with the band. I couldn't read a thing from listening to Diz and Bird Parker."

The sitting-in stretched out for a couple of weeks, and the experience removed any doubt from Davis' mind about becoming a musician.

When September came along—and the Eckstine band had gone to Chicago for a date at the Regal Theater, with Marion Hazel slated to join in Anderson's place—Mrs. Davis was insisting that Miles go to Fisk.

But the young trumpeter took home the newly published *Esquire Jazz Book,* which was full of information and pictures about the jazz scene in New York City, and as he put it, "I looked in the book, and I asked my mother, 'Where's all this?'"

Mrs. Davis wasn't impressed, but Dr. Davis was and told his son he didn't have to go to Fisk. Since Miles had a friend studying at Juilliard in New York, it was decided that he could go there.

Shortly after the Chicago date, Charlie Parker left the Eckstine band. He may have informed Davis of his intention. At any rate, Davis was to say later,

"I spent my first week in New York and my first month's allowance looking for Charlie Parker."

It was some time later that he read that Parker would be at a jam session at the Heatwave in Harlem. Davis put in an appearance at the session and renewed the friendship. Meanwhile, he had been attending Juilliard days and hanging around Minton's and 52nd Street at night.

In addition to other studies, Davis studied piano at Juilliard. This was done at the suggestion of Gillespie, who had told him it would teach him how to build an effective solo. A few years later, after he had met Gil Evans and started to write music, Davis was to feel he had not taken enough piano lessons.

The schooling that had the most impact on the trumpeter, however, was out in the field where he met the modern-jazz men. He has acknowledged that he received considerable help from Thelonious Monk, Tadd Dameron and Gillespie, but his chief mentor was Parker.

"I roomed with Parker for a year," he has related, "and followed him around down to 52nd Street. Every night I'd write down chords I heard, on matchbook covers. Next day I'd play those chords all day in the practice rooms at Juilliard, instead of going to classes."

During 1945, trumpeter Freddie Webster was around New York and frequently played at Minton's. Webster had a singing tone with a beauty that especially appealed to Davis. Musicians still talk about the shows at the Apollo when Webster was playing with the Jimmie Lunceford Band. When the band performed "Stardust," Webster would be featured in a solo played from the balcony.

When Webster was playing with John Kirby at the Café Society Downtown, he would get Davis to teach him chords Davis had learned at Juilliard. In return, he helped Davis try to assimilate some of his (Webster's) tonal qualities.

At first Davis was hesitant in getting up to play with the jazz giants then inhabiting 52nd Street. Parker would try to get him to play, saying, "Go ahead. Don't be afraid."

But in early 1945, the street's spots were featuring saxophones more than trumpets. Some of the ice for Davis was broken in early May, though, when Herbie Fields, then featured with Lionel Hampton's band, used Davis on a Savoy record date. They cut four sides, but Davis later said, "I was too nervous to play, and I only performed in the ensembles, no solos."

That same month, Coleman Hawkins opened at the Downbeat Club with Joe Guy on trumpet. The featured attraction was Billie Holiday. Guy and Miss Holiday had just been married, and Guy didn't show up for work half the time. Davis would sit in when Guy didn't show, and he got into the habit of checking the Downbeat nightly to see if he was needed. If Guy appeared, Davis would go over to the Spotlite and sit in with Eddie "Lockjaw" Davis and alto saxophonist Rudy Williams. Eventually, Miles was hired by Eddie and spent a month at the Spotlite.

By fall, armed with this bit of experience and courage, Miles joined Parker at the Three Deuces. The altoist was then using pianist Al Haig, bassist Curley Russell and drummer Stan Levey. Davis has said, "I used to play under Bird all the time. When Bird would play a melody, I'd play just under him and let him lead the note, swing the note. The only thing that I'd add would be a larger sound. I used to quit every night. I'd say, 'What do you need me for?'"

After the Deuces, Parker went to the Spotlite, taking Miles along. The group then had Levey, Sir Charles Thompson, piano, and Leonard Gaskin, bass. Tenor saxophonist Dexter Gordon soon joined them. The gig ended after the Spotlite was temporarily closed in early November, along with seven other spots in a periodic clean-up on 52nd Street. Miles then went into Minton's with pianist Thompson and a drummer for a short while. Then came another stint with Hawkins, this time for pay.

Later in November, Parker's famous "Ko-Ko" recording session for Savoy took place with Davis playing "Billie's Bounce," "Now's the Time," and "Thriving From a Riff" (the trumpeter heard on the introduction and coda of "Ko-Ko" was Gillespie).

The sides were much better than the jazz critics of that time thought. The *DownBeat* reviewer of "Billie's Bounce" and "Now's the Time" hit hard at Davis. "The trumpet player, whoever the misled kid is, plays Gillespie in the same manner as a majority of the kids who copy their idols do—with most of the faults, lack of order and meaning. They can be as harmful to jazz as Sammy Kaye!" The reviewer ignored everybody else on the record, indicating he was, at least, musically short-sighted, for these sides were eventually to be considered classics.

Shortly after Parker went to the West Coast with Gillespie in late 1945, Davis quit Juilliard and returned to East St. Louis, where he found Benny Carter's band playing at the Riviera. They were headed for the Coast, and Davis joined the trumpet section. It was a big band with a book of ancient vintages except for a couple of arrangements by Bob Graettinger and Neal Hefti. Davis was not happy with the job, and while they were playing the Orpheum Theater in Los Angeles, he doubled by playing at the Finale Club with Parker, pianist Joe Albany, bassist Addison Farmer and drummer Chuck Thompson.

The musicians union frowned on the practice of doubling jobs, and Davis was fined when union authorities found out about it.

Davis left the Carter band and appeared with Parker until the Finale closed because of poor business. It was during this time that the first Pacific records for Dial were made. This time the reviews were kinder. Although most of the reviewers thought that Davis still sounded like Gillespie, they were beginning to refer to him as a brilliant young trumpeter. He was credited with playing one of the best solos on the Bird Lore take of "Ornithology."

After the Finale folded, work was hard to come by for the modern jazz men in California. Parker got together Davis, pianist Dodo Marmarosa, tenorist Lucky Thompson, trombonist Britt Woodman and guitarist Arv Garrison to play at a concert given in April at the Carver Club at UCLA.

Little else turned up. Parker's breakdown came in late July, and he went away to Camarillo State Hospital.

In August, Lucky Thompson leased the Elk's Ballroom on Central Avenue in Los Angeles for three nights a week. An announcement in the music press said the key member of Thompson's small band at the ballroom would be "the brilliant young trumpet player, Miles Davis, last heard here with Benny Carter." Young bassist Charlie Mingus was also listed as a member of the Thompson group.

The group soon broke up because Thompson joined Boyd Raeburn.

The Eckstine band reached Los Angeles during September 1946, and Davis was hired to take over Gillespie's chair. He spent five months with the Eckstine outfit and went east with it during late fall. After the band was dissolved in the spring of '47, Davis played around Chicago. He appeared on the South Side at Jumptown with Sonny Stitt and Gene Ammons for the jam session nights.

When Charlie Parker returned to New York City in April, he formed the group that was to stay together until mid-1948: Charlie Parker's All-Stars, with Parker, Davis, pianist Duke Jordan, bassist Tommy Potter and drummer Max Roach.

The band went into the Three Deuces and, in June, recorded for Savoy ("Donna Lee," "Chasin' the Bird," "Cheryl," "Buzzy") with Bud Powell on piano. Parker supposedly had an exclusive contract with Ross Russell of Dial at the time. Russell was unhappy with Parker, but went east in October and began a series of recording dates with Parker's All-Stars. Davis received some good notices for his work on "Embraceable You, Quasimodo" (one reviewer said this was as close to "Embraceable" as one could get), "Drifting on a Reed," "Don't Blame Me" and "My Old Flame."

When these Dials were reviewed, the writers were judging Davis on his own merits. It was noted that on these ballads the trumpeter had evolved a sound of his own. He was playing more in the middle register at medium tempos and using more sustained notes. As writer Barbara Gardner once noted, "By 1947 Davis had filtered from his heretofore Gillespieish playing all that was not natural to himself."

Davis had his first recording date under his own name in January 1948, for Savoy. With Parker playing both alto and tenor; John Lewis, piano; Nelson Boyd, bass; and Max Roach, drums, the trumpeter waxed four originals: "Milestones," "Little Willie Leaps," "Half Nelson" and "Sippin' at Bells."

When Ross Russell wrote his series of articles on bebop for *The Record Changer* in 1948, he said, "Miles Davis may be said to belong to the new generation of the musicians. There is now a mounting body of evidence that Davis is leading the way to, or even founding, the next school of trumpet playing."

By the end of 1948, Davis had organized his nonet, which subsequently made the famed Capitol recordings. A year or so later, the top bebop arranger of the 1940s, the late Tadd Dameron, was to say, "Davis is the farthest advanced musician of his day, and 'Boplicity' is one of the best small-group sounds I've heard."

Since then, Davis has sought new ideas for expressing himself musically. In an interview in 1958, he saw a new course for jazz, saying, "I think a movement in jazz is beginning away from the conventional string of chords and a return to emphasis on melodic rather than on harmonic variation. There will be fewer chords but infinite possibilities as to what to do with them. It becomes a challenge to see how melodically inventive you are."

Davis' playing influence has enhanced the stature of jazz, though, typically, he himself says, "I don't go with this bringing 'dignity' to jazz. The way they bring 'dignity' to jazz, by wearing their formal clothes and bowing and smiling, is like Sugar Ray Robinson bringing dignity to boxing by fighting in a tuxedo."

––––––

Dec. 11, 1969
"And in This Corner, the Sidewalk Kid . . ."
by Don DeMicheal

A little man scurries down the dark staircase of the dingy old building on Chicago's 63rd Street.

"Is this Johnny Coulon's Physical Training Club upstairs?" I ask him.

"Third floor," he pipes.

"Miles Davis up there?"

"Oh yes. You just missed seeing him box. Knocked a fellow down twice."

On the third floor, Miles Davis the boxer is busy skipping rope before a full-length mirror . . . Dittle-e-dop, dittle-e-dop, dittle-e-dop. His feet dance lightly over the rope and across the floor. There isn't an ounce of fat on him.

"Hey, Don," he says, not missing a skip. "You should have seen me box."

Dittle-e-dop . . .

"A man just told me you knocked a guy down twice."

Dittle-e-dop . . .

"Naw, man" . . . dittle-e . . . "We" . . . dop . . . "just sparred a little."

He drops the rope and goes over to a punching bag suspended at head height by ropes connected to the ceiling and floor.

He tries some combinations and jabs on the bag, dodging it as it bounces toward him. A heavy-set man comes up to him and starts sparring lightly, giving advice as Miles tries unsuccessfully to land a light blow. Miles stops and listens to the man, who is Kid Carson, a trainer. He tries what Carson tells him, finds it works and smiles.

Miles introduces me to Carson; Johnny Coulon (the little man on the stairs); and his eldest son, Gregory, up from East St. Louis, Ill., Davis' home town, for a visit.

"Greg won three titles while he was in the Army," says the young man's obviously proud father. "Plays drums, too."

"Can you beat your old man?" I ask, but the son is noncommittal, and the father chuckles.

"Hey, try to lift Johnny," Miles says with an impish glint in his eye.

This didn't seem to be a problem, since Johnny Coulon, who was bantamweight champion many, many years ago, weighs about 90 pounds. So I lifted him.

"Now try it again," Miles says, suppressing a laugh.

Coulon cannot be budged.

"Ain't nobody ever lifted him when he didn't want 'em to," Davis says. "Show him your pictures, Johnny."

Coulon conducts his standard visitor's tour among fading photos of such boxers as Braddock, Dempsey, Carnera, Tunney, Louis, Clay—all trying to lift the little man. In the middle of Coulon's reminiscences, Miles walks up in a white terry-cloth robe.

"Hey, man," he whispers gleefully, "keep your cool, but dig when I turn around." There in that cloth script one has seen on hundreds of boxers' robes is inscribed "Miles Davis." Miles looks over his shoulder and flashes that beautiful smile of his. Miles Davis, boxer, seems a happier man than Miles Davis, musician.

After Miles had dressed, we climbed into his Volkswagen bus (used to haul his quintet's electric piano) and headed for Floogie's Restaurant, one of his favorite eating places in Chicago.

"Turn on your recorder," he said. "We can talk while I drive." And we did, while Miles dodged the traffic.

The obvious question was first:

DON DeMICHEAL: Why do you box?

MILES DAVIS: It gives you a lot of strength. It's good for your wind. I mean, when I go to play something that I know is kind of impossible to play, I have that strength, that wind. And it blows the smoke out of your lungs from last night.

D.D.M.: Do you work out every day?

M.D.: Uh-huh. Like today I did about seven rounds, boxed four and worked out about three.

D.D.M.: Did you ever think about boxing a bout somewhere?

M.D.: It didn't go that way with me 'cause I always could box, you know? Anybody'd I'd box as a kid I could beat. It's just a natural thing. But I like to go up against trainers like Carson to find out what they know. Carson trains Eddie Perkins. Eddie's the welterweight champ. I boxed Eddie yesterday, four rounds. He's so slick, can't even touch him.

D.D.M.: How long have you been doing it?

M.D.: All my life.

D.D.M.: I mean working out in a gym.

M.D.: I started about 10 years ago.

D.D.M.: Anybody ever try to start some trouble with you? Say, in the club where you're playing?

M.D.: I'd kill a man in the club.

D.D.M.: I mean, does it ever happen?

M.D.: Uh-huh. If they start it, I just tell 'em, you know? I just say point blank, "Y'wanna fight?" or "What's happening?" A man in the street is no contest against what I can drop on him. Even if he hits me three or four times, he'll be tired. I don't get tired. I just tell him, "Go on down and enjoy yourself." A guy who doesn't know how to fight is the one who always wants to fight.

They think it's a big deal to fight, but it's the easiest thing in the world to whip somebody like that. Can scratch their eyes out, kick 'em in the groin, and then they say that's not fighting fair. But a fight is a fight. Ain't nobody gonna stand up to me and say watch the Marquis of Queensbury's rules. If I get in a fight, I'm choking the mother. I just box on account it makes you graceful, and it shapes the body nice.

D.D.M.: To play music you have to be in good physical shape.

M.D.: You can say that again. And the way I play . . . I play from my legs. You ever notice?

D.D.M.: Yeah, I've noticed how you bend your knees.

M.D.: That's to keep from breaking the embouchure.

D.D.M.: How does that keep you from breaking your embouchure?

M.D.: You see, when I play . . . You notice guys when they play—and this is some corny stuff—they play and they breathe in the regular spots; so, therefore, they play the regular thing.

D.D.M.: You're talking about two- and four-bar phrases, things like that?

M.D.: Yeah. But if you keep your embouchure up there and breathe out of your nose—or whatever comes natural—you can play different things. But don't drop your hands. (Sings broken-rhythm phrases to show what can be done by not dropping hands.) See, it'll fall in different spots. (Sings short, jerky phrases.)

D.D.M.: You break the flow.

M.D.: You break the flow, and it's the same thing. You're playing in a pattern. Especially if the time is getting mucked up, and you're playing in a pattern, it's going to get more mucked up 'cause you're going to start dropping the time when you drop your horn down, 'cause whoever is playing behind you will say, "Well, he's resting." You never let a guy know when you're gonna rest. Like in boxing, if I jab a guy, I won't relax, 'cause if I jab him, that's a point for me. If I jab him, then I'm gonna do something else. I mean, you've got to keep something going on all the time.

D.D.M.: If when you move, you break your embouchure, why move at all?

M.D.: You keep getting your balance. You keep getting your balance back. Certain things jerk you. Say, like last night I was playing triplets against a fast 4/4. Jack [DeJohnette, his drummer] was playing (Miles taps his fingers at a fast tempo against the dashboard), and I'm playing like (sings quarter-note triplets as he moves slowly up and down); it's got to break. . . .

D.D.M.: You mean different muscles, different pressures, to get the notes?

M.D.: Yeah. So you got to keep getting your balance and . . . I mean you just got to keep in time [with the body] so it'll swing, or so it'll sort of stay connected. It's according to how you think. When you box, you gotta watch a guy. You understand? You gotta watch him, anticipate him . . . you gotta say if he jabs, I'm gonna stop it with my left hand. All this stuff has to be like this (snaps fingers).

D.D.M.: Then you're saying the same thing's true in music.

M.D.: The things of music you just finish. When you play, you carry them through till you think they're finished or until the rhythm dictates that it's finished, and then you do something else. But you also connect what you finished with what you're going to do next. So it don't sound like a pattern. So when you learn that, you got a good band, and when your band learns that, it's a good band.

D.D.M.: A lot of times you'll let, say, eight bars go by during a solo without playing anything.

M.D.: Yeah.

D.D.M.: Doesn't that break the flow you talked about?

M.D.: It doesn't break the flow because the rhythm section is doing the same thing they were doing before.

D.D.M.: In other words, you're letting the tension grow in there.

M.D.: No, I'm letting it go off. Whatever's been happening has been happening too long; if it dies out, you can start a whole different thing.

D.D.M.: As a listener, though, I feel there is another kind of tension in those places, of anticipation of when you're going to come back in, of what's going to happen. So that in that space, I feel a tension growing . . .

M.D.: Yeah.

D.D.M.: . . . So when you come in, then the release comes.

M.D.: Sometimes if you do the same thing, it hits the spot.

D.D.M.: You mean: Do the same thing you ended with.

M.D.: Yeah. It'd be mellow, you know? (He turns to go into the parking lot.) You're not going to believe this . . . (drives up the sidewalk and turns into a parking place) . . . screw it.

D.D.M.: Say, you came driving out on the sidewalk the other day.

M.D.: Right . . . the Sidewalk Kid.

———————

Sept. 3, 1970
Miles in Motion
by Dan Morgenstern

I approach the prospect of interviewing Miles Davis with some trepidation. We've had a nodding acquaintance for years—since the time, way back in '48, when a little trumpet player named Nat Lorber (they call him "Face") introduced us on Broadway. I remember that Miles was wearing a beautiful dark blue double-breasted pinstripe suit. He's always been sharp.

Since then, in many brief encounters, in clubs, backstage at concerts, etc., Miles is sometimes friendly, sometimes not. And nine years ago, an evening at his house, I was with a whole bunch of writers and players in a "confrontation," as they call it now, between critics and musicians arranged by a press agent. Miles was a beautiful host. So why am I uptight?

I remember the house, in the West 70s, but as the cab pulls up and I spot Miles lounging near the entrance, it looks different. Above the front door, there is now a moorish turret. Miles greets me, and we enter. There are men at work inside. The place is being completely redecorated. An Egyptian mural graces the patio walls. A tempting honeydew melon rests on the kitchen table.

"Want a piece?" Miles asks. It's a hot day. He cuts two slices expertly. The melon is delicious, tasting just right at room temperature. "It's best when it's not too cold," Miles comments. "Come in here—I want to show you something," he adds, moving toward the front room.

There stands a new Innovex unit. "They sent me this," says Miles, turning on the power and picking up his trumpet. "Dig this."

A foot pedal has been connected to the unit, and Miles works it while he blows. The sound is not unlike that achieved by moving the hand in front of the bell, in this case Harmon-muted. Miles obviously likes the sound; he's never played wah-wah style, and this way, he can also bend the notes subtly. He turns up the volume to show the power of the speaker system. Then he puts the horn away.

Glancing at the multiple controls atop the unit, I ask if he uses any of the other devices. "Naaah," he shrugs disdainfully. Like any musician with his own good and distinctive sound, he has no desire to distort it. He likes the pedal effects and the amplification, but that's all.

"Let's go upstairs," he says. It's a duplex apartment, and the redecorating upstairs is finished. The living room is like a cool oasis. Everything is built-in—aside from a low, round table, there is no standing furniture. (A recent article about the house in *The New York Times* quotes Miles to the effect that he doesn't like corners. Everything is rounded off.) The soft, blue carpeting looks inviting, and when Miles answers the phone, he reclines on the floor. You can move freely in this place. The bedroom is so groovy that if it were mine, I might never leave it.

"You want to hear something?" Miles asks, approaching the wall that holds his music system—tape decks, amplifiers, turntable, some records, lots of tapes. He finds a reel he wants, unravels it and puts it on. The speakers, invisible, built into the ceiling somewhere, are a gas, and so is the music, by Miles' new band, obviously recorded live. It's quite a change from *Bitches Brew*—this man doesn't stay in one place too long. I listen, and let the music carry me away.

What I've heard, I learn, is from a forthcoming Columbia album, recorded live on three consecutive nights at the Fillmore East. It will be released in September, and is the first live Miles LP in many years. Keith Jarrett is on the band (as well as Chick Corea—Chick on electric piano, Keith on Fender Rhodes combo organ), and he is a significant addition. Miles is obviously pleased with him.

"Did you hear what Keith was playing behind me there?" he asks, rolling back the tape. "He's a bitch. Chick, too." After the passage has been replayed, he demonstrates at the piano, built into one side of the seating unit, and within easy reach from the hi-fi system.

"With a C going on in the bass, you can play anything against it," he explains. I ask if he does most of the writing for the group now, since Wayne Shorter's departure, and he says yes. When he has to write something for a record date, he adds later, he usually does it at the last moment, so it will be completely fresh.

"You write to establish the mood," he points out. "That's all you need. Then it can go on for hours. If you complete anything, you play it, and it's finished. Once you resolve it, there's nothing more to it. But when it's open, you can suspend it."

Suspension is a word Miles uses frequently when talking about his music—a music very much of today, in sound and in feeling. Once again, Miles is setting the pace, as he has been doing at frequent intervals since 1948 and the Capitol nonet. There was the pioneering quintet with John Coltrane, Red Garland, Paul Chambers and Philly Joe Jones; *Miles Ahead* and the other memorable collaborations with Gil Evans; the great sextet with Trane, Cannonball Adderley and Bill Evans, which in *Kind of Blue* established a whole new syntax for jazz improvisation, and then his series of surprises beginning with *E.S.P.* and running on through *Bitches Brew*.

When the Fillmore album comes out there'll be new surprises. In a sense, Miles is a perfectionist, but not the polishing kind. Once he has perfected a thing, he needs to move on to something new. His music today is in constant motion, ideas bouncing off each other, interacting; many things going on at once; cyclical, unresolved, suspended and full of suspense, electrified and electrifying.

Miles has some private business to attend to. He invites me to come back the following afternoon. "We'll go up to the gym. You can watch me work out."

Another sultry New York day. Inside it's cool and dark. We join our host in a cup of refreshing mint tea, then take a stroll to a nearby garage.

Again a surprise—no more red Ferrari, but a new battleship gray Lamborghini; a magnificent machine, low and trim, built like a racer. We shoot out onto the West Side Highway, heading north.

Miles drives with superlative reflexes like a pro, fast but not taking any dumb chances; not showing off, always in complete control. We learn that the Ferrari was "full of bullet holes," unwanted souvenirs of the stupid attempt on Miles' life by obviously amateur gangsters earlier this year.

What happened to them? "They're all dead," Miles answers matter-of-factly, not gloating. "I don't know how or where, but that's what I heard."

On our way to pick up Miles' trainer, we stop for a red light in Harlem. A young black man on a monumental yellow Honda rolls up next to us, eyeing the car with open admiration. "What kind is that?" he asks. "Tell him a Lamborghini," Miles instructs. The motorcyclist is on my side of the car, and Miles can't shout. I convey the information, repeating the unfamiliar name, and adding that it's an Italian make.

"Ask him how much is that Honda," Miles requests. "It's $1,600," the cyclist responds proudly, obviously pleased at the question. The car is more than 10 times the price of the Honda, but in asking, Miles has equalized them—two men admiring each other's strong machines.

At Bobby Gleason's Gym in the Bronx, a comfortable, old-fashioned place where some of the city's best fighters work out, Miles, in bright blue trunks, is shadow boxing under the watchful eye of his trainer, a slim, trim, soft-spoken man who looks and acts not at all like the stereotype of the ex-boxer. He's been with Miles for years.

Afterwards, while Miles does exercises in a corner, the trainer tells me: "He's really coming along. His reflexes are getting better all the time. And he's in top shape."

As I have noticed. Not an ounce of excess fat. All solid muscle, but not of the bulging kind displayed by some of the men in the gym. Sleek and compact like a panther. It's obvious that everyone around the gym and on the street outside knows and likes Miles Davis.

"Boxing is like music," Miles says later, as we drive downtown. "You keep adding to it." He works out four times a week, he says, and does 40 pushups and 40 situps each day.

He talks some more about music. "We're not a rock band. Some people get that idea because we're amplified, but with amplification, we can be heard, and we can hear each other. This is a new day, and we can do what we want. With a good system, you can play soft or loud, and people can hear."

"For years," he goes on, "I've been going to clubs to listen to something—like Ahmad Jamal playing piano—and once I'm there, I can't hear anything." And there are other things he dislikes about most clubs: "You have to give people something, not just take from them."

But he doesn't mind playing clubs, he says, provided things are right and the music can be heard. "For a while, I thought we had something good at the Village Gate (where, earlier this year, Miles had worked out an arrangement with owner Art D'Lugoff enabling him to book acts of his own choice to work opposite his band, getting the admission gate while the club took in the proceeds from drink and food sales), but Art didn't seem to want to keep it going."

We're nearing our destination, and Miles gives me fair warning to hold on before he negotiates a hairpin turn that takes us off the East River Drive.

"Our music changes every month," he says. "We extend each other's ideas. I may start a phrase and not complete it because I hear something else behind me that takes me to a different place. It keeps going further. Our Latin drummer [Airto Moreira] gives us something else to play off. Most of the guys in the band can play other instruments, and that expands their conception. Jack [DeJohnette] can really play the piano, and Chick plays the shit out of the drums. Keith plays clarinet. So when they ad lib, you know it's going to be something you like to hear."

In jazz today, there are many seekers of new ways. Often, the searching seems forced, and the results not natural. Miles Davis, however, has that rare gift of being able to give birth and life to new things that, no matter how startling, always seem natural and logical, and open up new roads for others to travel after he has moved on.

The sole photograph in Miles' living room, unobtrusively displayed, is a color shot of a pensive John Coltrane, dating from his days with the trumpeter. It's pure speculation, of course, but if he were still among us, I have a feeling that Coltrane, that restless seeker, might well once again feel very much at home with Miles.

———

July 18, 1974

Miles: Today's Most Influential Contemporary Musician
by Gregg Hall

In this interview with one of the most controversial figures on the American music scene, Miles Davis, I have attempted to bring before the reader facets contained within this remarkable man that have never surfaced in all his 48 years.

His general knowledge of music, humanity, politics, recording, sports and concern for the betterment of his race are all areas in which he excels.

As in his music, colors are used for effect. There is no in-between with him. Black equals good, and white equals bad, not to be confused with racism in any form, just a point of differentiation. His answers to some of my questions were brief, but this is Miles, and keep in mind that one sentence from him can be correlated to the average paragraph from most.

GREGG HALL: Miles, what's happening in contemporary music?

MILES DAVIS: Man, how do I know? I don't even know what that means.

G.H.: I mean you're the forerunner.

M.D.: I don't know, man, I can't give away all my secrets.

G.H.: No, man, I don't want you to give away all your secrets.

M.D.: Man, there ain't nothing happening with anybody else.

G.H.: I mean you're the leader.

M.D.: Yeah, well, there is something happening with us.

G.H.: You're calling all the shots. It's your band they're chasing!

M.D.: Yeah, do you really like my band? I don't think anybody likes it.

G.H.: You don't?

M.D.: You know, if I walk in a club, the guys hide the girls. If I don't have nobody with me when I go to clubs, I don't have nobody to talk to (*laughter*).

When I get through playing, I don't know if they liked me or not, you know, and I really don't care 'cause I'm giving them something they never heard before and will never hear again.

G.H.: Yeah, but isn't that part of that Miles Davis "mystique," you know what I mean?

M.D.: I don't know nothing about that shit. I'm a normal person, Gregg, and they just build me up to be something funny—you know, they say I just kick bitches in the ass, drive Ferraris, you know, man, and fuck four at a time.

G.H.: Oh! My man, using that horn (*more laughter*). You dig, but, there's this big mystique around you.

M.D.: I know it.

G.H.: It makes people terribly reserved when it comes to approaching you and things like that. I guess I can understand to a certain degree or maybe to a large degree how you feel and the resentment and animosity that you must have because of this. I guess that's because of your great abilities and the things you have done for music.

M.D.: Oh, you know, every time I change the stuff, you know, a new direction, they just copy me, man. Santana and them come around me and jive. Like with *Bitches Brew*—well, we don't play that shit no more. If I were white and had blonde hair, you know what I mean, then it would be a different thing—but I'm black, man, and they figure I'm supposed to be able to do what I do—Swing-Sweenge, man (*laughter*).

G.H.: Doesn't that make you stronger, though? Tell the truth.

M.D.: It always makes me strong, man.

G.H.: I mean, because you seem, at least to me, to be a person that's possessive of a lot of inner strength.

M.D.: Challenges always make me 10 times stronger. I love challenges.

G.H.: I dig.

M.D.: If somebody says step outside and let's fight—I'm ready.

G.H.: I know that.

M.D.: But really, man, I don't really fight. I've been listening to Puccini's "Tosca" for about 10 years, and I wanna play it, and I'm gonna play it one day. You know challenges like that really turn me on.

G.H.: Do you know who told me that?

M.D.: Who?

G.H.: Nesuhi Ertegun.

M.D.: What did he say?

G.H.: Nesuhi and I were talking last week, as a matter of fact. I talked to him, and I had him put some things on tape about you.

M.D.: Yeah, what did he say?

G.H.: He said some very beautiful things. He said that your intelligence was beyond reproach and that you were not only knowledgeable about jazz music per se, but you were knowledgeable about all types of music and all forms of music. He said your intelligence had never ceased to amaze him and that he had known you for 25 years and that he still remembers your phone call to him about Ray Charles.

M.D.: What did I tell him?

G.H.: When Ray first joined the label, you called Nesuhi and told him, "Hey, man, I know you got a guy on your label. It's a new guy and I hope you know what to do with him because he's very talented." And, Nesuhi said to you, "Who's that, Miles?" and you said, "It's Ray Charles, man, and I hope you know what to do with him." Nesuhi still remembered that, and he wrote it down.

M.D.: (*laughter*)

G.H.: Yeah, man, he put it down on the tape. So people don't really forget, man. A lot of people don't forget. By the way, Lonnie Smith was talking to me yesterday and we talked about you for about three hours on the phone last night. We were talking about his association with you and the growth that you gave him.

M.D.: Who said that?

G.H.: Lonnie Liston.

M.D.: Who?

G.H.: Liston Smith!

M.D.: Lonnie!!! Wow!

G.H.: Yeah, he loves you.

M.D.: Oh yeah, I taught him a lot of shit.

G.H.: He said you changed his whole lifestyle.

M.D.: Yeah.

G.H.: You dig, that you changed his whole style of living?

M.D.: Yeah.

G.H.: What is the mystical thing? You know you're a mystic or known to be a mystic and you affect people's lives in a different way.

M.D.: Well, you know, in the first place, I have always known what to wear for myself and then other people try to copy it.

G.H.: Well, you've always been a forerunner that way.

M.D.: Well, that's part of it, you know. Like when I go on the bandstand man, for 35 or 45 minutes, I'm playing by myself, and I'm sweating like a motherfucker and the bitches are just sittin' there looking to see what I got on and I'm playing my ass off, and they don't hear what I'm playin', you know, and then they get home and they say, "ooohhhh!" You know how people look up at you and size you up.

G.H.: Does it bother you?

M.D.: No, no, that shit don't bother me. Nothing bothers me but a bad trumpet.

G.H.: Well, you know that everybody that's somebody today came through that Miles Davis school.

M.D.: I wonder why they always call it the "Miles Davis school."

G.H.: Because you're the teacher, and that's where it's all coming from.

M.D.: I just bring out in people what's in them.

G.H.: Yeah, but how? Look what you did for Cicely Tyson.

M.D.: Yeah man, ain't that a bitch, so she could continue her career.

G.H.: Yeah, did Cicely ever know that your ulterior motive was in doing what you did?

M.D.: I told her, yeah, I taught her a lot of stuff. I taught her about eyes. You see, black people's eyes are so wide anyway, so I told her not to open her eyes too much. She had a habit of overacting. I taught her to be subtle, you know, and when it comes time to use some volume, she'd know it. Did you see what she did in *Sounder*—that was a motherfucker!! When she ran to Paul—uuhh!!!! Brings tears to your eyes.

G.H.: I dig. Miles, how did you like Pittman?

M.D.: Man, she used my voice. (*laughter*)

G.H.: Yeah, me and you were laughing about that before.

M.D.: You know, she'll call and say, "I'll be right over, I can feel something's wrong with you"—and I'll be sicker than a motherfucker. She does it all the time. Remarkable!! She's wonderful. She's a very talented woman!!! She plays piano and nobody knows. She won't play it for nobody.

G.H.: Did you teach her how to play?

M.D.: No, she's played piano all her life, and she can sing. She's very talented, you know.

G.H.: Well, who else do you like, Miles? What are some of your other likes and dislikes? What musicians do you like, and who do you listen to?

M.D.: Nobody—I listen to Stockhausen.

G.H.: Is that all? I talked to you before and you had a tremendous love for Al Green.

M.D.: Yeah, well, Al's OK. He's a good rhythm and blues man.

G.H.: Do you like Roberta?

M.D.: Yeah, I like Roberta. But, you know, if Al Green had one tit, I'd marry that motherfucker. You know who's a baddd motherfucker—Ann Peebles.

G.H.: Ann Peebles?

M.D.: Sssshhhhiiittt!!!

G.H.: You like her, huh, Miles?

M.D.: Helllll, yeah!!!

G.H.: Hmm, I'll have to check her out.

M.D.: Man, that bitch is a motherfucker, and Linda Hopkins, you know, and Aretha, man.

G.H.: You love Aretha.

M.D.: Man, there ain't nothin' happening that ain't happening with her.

G.H.: How do you feel about the success of John McLaughlin and people like Billy Cobham?

M.D.: I put that together, man.

G.H.: I know that. You were his Guru.

M.D.: (*laughter*) How did you know I was?

G.H.: Teo and I were talking about that in the interview we did. By the way, I would like to mention the fact that we did interview Teo for your issue, and man, he said some of the strongest, heaviest things I ever heard from anybody who works for the establishment.

M.D.: Oh, yeah?

G.H.: He said your relationship with him was just like a marriage. What was the reason why you didn't speak to Teo for two-and-a-half years one time?

M.D.: Cause he fucked up *Quiet Nights*.

G.H.: How did he fuck it up?

M.D.: In the studio he was busy looking at the score saying, "Jesus, you use these chords." I said, "Man, just record it and don't worry about no chords." You know what I mean, instead of looking at the score, he should have just brought out the sound. He fucked it up.

G.H.: And you didn't talk to him for over two years?

M.D.: I felt there was no reason to. You see, I could have had him fired. Goddard Lieberson was the president of Columbia then, and when I told Goddard about it, he said, "What do you want me to do—fire him?" But I said, "No."

G.H.: He's been with you for 17 years.

M.D.: He's a very talented musician.

G.H.: He said some very beautiful things. It wasn't hype, you know, and it wasn't bullshit. Miles, tell me, how do you really feel about Columbia?

M.D.: I think they're the saddest record company in the world—but, the greatest.

G.H.: But the greatest, too?

M.D.: Sure.

G.H.: Why do you think it's the saddest?

M.D.: They don't do nothing for niggers—nothing!

G.H.: You know, Freddie's over there.

M.D.: Freddie who?

G.H.: Hubbard.

M.D.: That don't mean shit. He don't have no ideas and no talent. All he does is run up and down the scales. I used to teach Freddie.

G.H.: You said he didn't have any talent?

M.D.: Man, he doesn't have any imagination. If you don't have no imagination, then you don't have no talent, right?

G.H.: If you get a pretty bitch with no personality, you might as well go out with a dog.

M.D.: Shit, at least the dog will bark. (*laughter*)

G.H.: Miles, you used to put women on all your album covers, and you stopped doing that. Why?

M.D.: Well, I put Cicely on one of my records.

G.H.: Yeah, Cicely was on *Sorcerer,* right?

M.D.: Yeah, I have a thing about helping black women, you know. Because when I was using dope, it was costing me a couple of grand a day, and I use to take bitches' money. So when I stopped to clean up, I got mad at *Playboy,* and I wouldn't accept their poll because they didn't have no black women in their magazine, you know. So I started putting them on my covers. So I put Cicely's picture on my record. It went all around the world!

G.H.: Why don't these things about you ever come out?

M.D.: I don't know, man.

G.H.: That's what this interview is about—trying to show a side of Miles that people don't ever see. Why don't they know what you did for Cicely Tyson, man?

M.D.: I also taught her the technique of filming. You see, black people aren't supposed to be filmed in technicolor. I gave her the key. You know that brown kind of hue—it brings out the red in your skin.

G.H.: You mean sepia-tone.

M.D.: Yeah, it brings out the red in your skin. You know, white people put all that makeup on themselves. I told Cicely to tell them to use that sepia-tone, you know. I also gave her some ideas about film. I wrote a little thing for her.

G.H.: For Cicely?

M.D.: Yeah, it was outtasight!!

G.H.: Well, what other little gems have you got that you've done for people that people don't know about, but they should know about, besides the Cicely Tyson story?

M.D.: Well, I got Roberta Flack $25,000 instead of $5,000 for Atlanta. She called me up, and she was so mad because her lawyer put her name down to appear for $5,000 on behalf of the mayor. So I straightened her out and she said she had already cancelled one date down there. I told her that when she refused a date she shouldn't say that she doesn't want to make it, but instead make her price so high that they either say yes or they say no. She finally got $25,000—and the place was sold out.

G.H.: There's another story floating around about you wanting to teach—to be a music educator because of your experience. Is there any truth in that?

M.D.: Shit no, man. They offered me a position at Howard University. I can't do that shit. I teach my musicians. I taught my drummer everything he knows about playing drums. I play drums myself. I'm teaching a young boy now that I have in the band. His name is Dominique. He's about 19, and he's from Bahia. He's a baddd motherfucker. He's like Hendrix. I have to show him the different chords. You know, Hendrix didn't ever learn any chords. You know, they came to me to get me to reorganize Hendrix's band.

G.H.: There's a story out there that you had no love for Hendrix.

M.D.: How did that story get out there? I went all the way to Seattle for his funeral.

G.H.: Then you did have a love for Jimi Hendrix.

M.D.: Of course.

G.H.: Miles, how do you interpret Herbie Hancock's success?

M.D.: Herbie tries to be too intellectual. He needs to be edited. But, he's the only one out there. Chick Corea's got a band, boy!!! Chick said that the greatest musical experience he ever had was working with me.

G.H.: You used some members of that band. I know that damn well. Lenny White was on *Bitches Brew*.

M.D.: Yeah, I had three drummers on that. I didn't give the critics the instrumentation. You know why? Because, when you give the critics the instrumentation, they know the musicians and they say that he plays this way or he plays like that. So, they didn't know who was in the band and they had to think for a change.

G.H.: You're full of little things like that.

M.D.: They make me sick. Critics don't do a motherfucking thing, and deejays don't do nothing, either.

G.H.: By the way, I saw you on the *Cavett Show*. He doesn't know what's happening.

M.D.: White folks do not understand black music, and I don't expect them to, you know. When I get through playing, I just walk off. I don't know whether they're applauding or booing. I really don't.

G.H.: Does it really matter to you?

M.D.: It wouldn't matter to me at all. Nothing matters except that the members of my band are satisfied with me and as long as I don't drag them—fuck all that other shit.

G.H.: Did you ever hook up with those black colleges you were telling me about?

M.D.: No, I'm trying to get that in line. I would like to do something, Gregg, you know, I always feel like I haven't done anything.

G.H.: That you haven't done anything?

M.D.: I always figure that, man.

G.H.: Well, maybe that's the creativity in you.

M.D.: I like when a black boy says, "Oohh! Man, there's Miles Davis." Like they did with Joe Louis. Some cats did me like that in Greensboro. They said, "Man, we sure glad you came down here." That thrilled me more than anything that happened to me that year.

G.H.: Then, does your original offer still hold that you'll play every black college for nothing?

M.D.: That's right. All they have to do is pay my transportation and pay the band. I really feel like I don't do anything. I would like for black people to look at me like Joe Louis. (*laughter*) Maybe it will never happen, maybe it's just wishful thinking. You know, Sugar Ray Robinson inspired me, and he made me kick a habit. I said, "If that mother can win all those fights, I sure can break this motherfuckin' habit." I went home, man, and sat up for two weeks, and I sweated it out.

G.H.: Sugar Ray did that for you?

M.D.: Man, he didn't know it!

G.H.: Oh, then he inspired you to do it.

M.D.: Yeah, when he started training—he wouldn't make it with chicks. He disciplined himself and all that! Man, now that's a motherfucker—and Jack Johnson, too!

G.H.: Miles, your idols have always been fighters.

M.D.: Yeah, because they don't miss—like Joe Louis didn't miss, and Jack Johnson was 20 years ahead of his time. Ray Robinson, too. You know my favorite fighter is Johnny Bratton. Fighters just turn me on and make me wanna do something.

G.H.: You said you feel that you don't do enough.

M.D.: I don't feel like I'm doing anything. I mean, so what, so I play music, but my race don't get it. You know what I mean, it's 'cause they can't afford it, man. I get tired of seeing black people walking in clubs with the girl in front of the guy and the guy with his hands in his pockets trying to be cool. (*laughter*) I mean, now, what is that shit? Gregg, do you know what I mean? You've seen what happens.

G.H.: Yeah, many times. Tell me, Miles, do you consider yourself successful?

M.D.: Sure!

G.H.: Financially, materially, or how?

M.D.: Well—I'm not a millionaire, but let's say I'm not successful the way I want to be successful.

G.H.: How does Miles Davis want to be successful?

M.D.: I just want to get to my race, man. I want them to quit "fibbin'" when they come in those clubs.

G.H.: Miles, what's going to happen musically? Where are you going to take the world next?

M.D.: I don't know, man. I got a lot of things in mind.

G.H.: I know you got about 80 LPs in the can.

M.D.: Right.

G.H.: How about *Big Fun*? Are you satisfied with that as a new direction?

M.D.: No.

G.H.: Columbia thinks it will be bigger than *Bitches Brew*.

M.D.: How???? I did *Big Fun* years ago. My next thing, *Calypso,* will set a new direction. The entire record will be one track.

G.H.: Miles, what are some of your political views?

M.D.: I love King Faisel!!! I love the way when they talk to white folks they got them "tommin'" like a motherfucker. Actually, black people should rule the world, 'cause without the oil we can't fly our planes and drive our cars, and we'd all freeze to death—man, 'cause we got all the oil! We got it fixed so when you go near it it will blow up, and if it blows up, it will take at least 20 years to fix it. So they ain't comin' near it. Ain't that some "slick" shit? (*laughter*)

G.H.: How do you feel about what's happening in Washington?

M.D.: That ain't nothin', it's just "tweedle dee and tweedle dum." That shit's been happening for years, man. They should leave the man alone, you know. He didn't do anything that ain't nobody else done before. You know that the Democrats used to give my mother $50 to vote. Ain't that shit.

G.H.: Where was this? In St. Louis?

M.D.: Yeah, and my father was running for state representative.

G.H.: Your father was a dentist, right?

M.D.: Yeah.

G.H.: Did he win?

M.D.: Hellll no!!

G.H.: When was this?

M.D.: Back in the '40s. Man, Nixon ain't no worse than no other president. John Kennedy was the worst president.

G.H.: Why do you feel that?

M.D.: He didn't do nothing but have a lot of hair. You know how white people like to have hair fall in front of their face and all that shit. Anyway, he started the whole thing—now he can't change that shit and the House of Representatives can't change it.

G.H.: Other than the physical arts, is there anything else you do well?

M.D.: I play the drums, you know.

G.H.: How are your legs, by the way?

M.D.: Terrible.

G.H.: Do your legs still hurt you?

M.D.: Whew, yeah. I wish I had some new ones.

G.H.: Do you exercise at all?

M.D.: I can't, man, 'cause it goes out of the sockets.

G.H.: Oh, I see. How bad is the pain when you play?

M.D.: It hurts like a motherfucker sometimes. I have to take about eight pain pills a day.

G.H.: Aren't they gettin' any better?

M.D.: No. I have that black disease. I don't have enough white corpuscles gettin' into my blood. I have very poor circulation. That shit hurts.

G.H.: Have you got a studio built in your house?

M.D.: Sorta.

G.H.: How much playing do you do each day?

M.D.: I never touch my horn unless I have a job. Then, it's fresh that way. In fact, I don't know how to play it. (*laughter*)

G.H.: Miles, you are responsible for putting a lot of cats out there. You know they all came through your school—like we said before. How many of those cats do you feel really know what you did for them?

M.D.: Herbie. Herbie wanted to quit when he first got with me. He said it didn't seem like there was enough music for him to play. I said, "Well, then lay back, motherfucker. You just told yourself what to do." He would play for a while and could not keep it up, and sometimes it just seemed like there wasn't anything for him to do.

G.H.: Who else do you hear from?

M.D.: Oh man, all of them come by—Tony Williams, all of them.

G.H.: Do you ever hear from Wayne Shorter?

M.D.: Yeah, he comes by too.

G.H.: Zawinul?

M.D.: Joe, yeah. All of them come by when they're making new records.

G.H.: Then, they all must know.

M.D.: They know, yeah, man, but when they get with their wives, then they're all my enemies. But, when they make a record, they come and ask me what I think.

G.H.: They've got to come back to the master.

M.D.: Like Jack DeJohnette. I fixed his stuff for him, and I usually fix all of Wayne's music up. Also, a lot of things that Gil Evans wrote, I really wrote.

G.H.: Anything come to mind in particular? Can you remember what you wrote that he put his name on? Does anything come to mind?

M.D.: Yeah, a couple of things, like *Sketches of Spain* and "The Buzzard Song" from *Porgy and Bess*, and I outlined all of his shit. They offered me $70,000 to get it on with Sly [Stone]. They wanted me to make Sly a hit record. It takes me three hours. When I got around Sly, I didn't say anything because we became fast friends. He's a crazy motherfucker, and I'm crazy, too. I took a gun over there one day and put it right to his head. I said, "Man, sit down, we will listen to this!" (*laughter*) Of course, there were no bullets in it. I want to write a musical. Could you imagine how that would be? Some hip shit.

G.H.: I'm hip. I sure would like to see you and Marvin Gaye get together. I would love to see the two of you get together, and I've already spoken to him about it.

M.D.: You spoke to him?

G.H.: Yeah.

M.D.: What did he say?

G.H.: He wanted to get together with you.

M.D.: No shit!!!

G.H.: Oh, yeah.

M.D.: He really likes me?

G.H.: He loves you, man. Marvin loves you.

M.D.: He really likes me—God damn! The next time you see Marvin, tell him that what he writes, if he wants me to play it, to just call me up and tell me where he is. He's a motherfucker! Man, I ain't never heard nothing like "You're the Man." And "What's Happening Brother"—God damn! That tune is so hip, boy, Marvin should do a show with it. I love him, man.

G.H.: Did you refuse to see Mick Jagger?

M.D.: Oh, fuck him. Who's Mick Jagger, anyway!

G.H.: I wanted to know why he wanted to see you.

M.D.: That's what I want to know.

G.H.: Did you ever find out?

M.D.: Yeah. One of his friends was trying to impress him by saying he knew me. Stevie Wonder, now there's a sad motherfucker. He thinks I stole Michael Henderson from him, but Michael came to me. I never did anybody like that in my life.

G.H.: Hey, man, don't you have a birthday coming up soon?

M.D.: Yeah, May 26. I'll be 48 years old.

Pull Quotes

"I've known him quite well for more than 25 years. He has always been extraordinarily kind, gracious and generous with me, and I count him among my real friends. As a musician, he is one of the five or six great people in the entire field of American music—of the entire century. He has always been in the forefront of new movements. He's had the biggest ears of anyone I know. He knows everything that's happening in every form of music. And, I think he is a genius."
                                                            —Nesuhi Ertegun

"More than a great trumpet player, Miles is a great artist. My debt to him is huge; if it wasn't for Miles Davis, I would play a little differently for sure, and I would write differently. His influence is very far-reaching among all contemporary music. His influence has even penetrated as far as Muzak—that's how heavy he is."
                                                            —John McLaughlin

"One of the best relationships in the world exists between Miles and me. He is my friend, and I understand and love his work."
                                                            —Bill Cosby

"As the forms of music continue to evolve through the years and decades, there are always certain musicians (composers or instrumentalists) who stand for their creative certainty and ability to constantly evolve their forms. These individuals seem to capture the true spirit of the contemporary world through their aesthetics, and also set the trends and standards for other artists who are their contemporaries. Miles is one of these beautiful people, and I totally love him. Thank you, Miles."   —Chick Corea

"Whatever Miles does, he tries to do for the music. If he feels he can't do justice to the music, those are usually the times he doesn't show up, or leaves early. But Miles can play more in a few notes than a lot of people play in a lifetime.

"The remarkable thing is that so many of the people who have sprung from his groups have been major influences themselves. Personally, I learned so much from Miles' conception of how to bring the most out of his sidemen . . . allowing them to shape the music. And as for his personality, it's unfortunate that people don't realize what a nice man Miles really is, how concerned he is for his audience and also for his friends. He'd give you the shirt off his back."   —Herbie Hancock

"Miles Davis is the only superstar that jazz has, not Mr. Basie, not Mr. Buddy Rich, not Mr. Kenton, none of these. Miles is the only superstar we've got. There are musicians who have made as much or more money, but they weren't superstars. Jazz people need superstars just like rock people."
                    —Chico Hamilton

"Miles is special and rare. He is an innovator and certainly ranks with Louis, Dizzy, Parker and Coltrane. He has influenced my appreciation and understanding of music."   —Bob Thiele

"Miles Davis' influence is all-pervasive in modern American music. Look at the *Billboard* chart, although Miles is not on it at the moment. In the last year, all sorts of groups who studied at the Davis Conservatory, from Chick Corea to Herbie Hancock, have been. Miles is like Picasso. He has made change into style, and wherever you go, you bump into little fragments of his music."   —Ralph Gleason

"Miles Davis, whether you like his music, love his music or hate his music, has a charismatic spirit that is the motivation of a whole area, a whole group of people; and he has the kind of magic that, even if you don't embrace him at that moment, you have to watch because he sort of has the ability to look into the future. Truly a giant. The moving force in contemporary music."
                    —Joe Fields

"Miles means the same thing as the name Rembrandt. The same thing the name Picasso means, Fellini, Bergman, Casals, Duke Ellington. We're just lucky to be alive when he's alive. He's a magical person."   —Joel Dorn

"Well, what do you say about him? Wherever he goes, it's a great trip. He's shown all of us the way for a long time now—and he's always been right . . . the lyricism, the cool: It's like he's a stepchild of Lester and Bird, that combination of hot and cool. Duke used to say that Miles is like—and I know you've heard this—Picasso."   —Quincy Jones

"On *Jack Johnson,* Miles instructed almost everybody individually about what he really wanted from them. He tried to show me, physically, what he wanted. It was nice to play with him without having him to speak to you verbally, because you could learn so much from what he said through his instrument. It's another way of communicating. And one of Miles' major attributes is that he knows how to do that first nature, rather than second nature."
          —Billy Cobham

"Consistently, beginning with his vital role in the creation of bop, at the outset of modern jazz, has Miles Davis signified trumpet progress. Small wonder he so strongly influences each successive crop of young players."
          —William L. Fowler

"His trumpet, theatrics, his escapades—lifestyle, the greatest conversation piece in 15 years. The loyalty to do things his way, his observation and uncanny talent to consistently pick the right musicians for his bands, he's like no one; no one is like him. A very special hero."   —Joe Zawinul

---

September 1980
Miles: Resting on Laurels? Changing His Silent Ways?
by Charles Mitchell

It's been five years or so since Miles Davis last performed in public or recorded any music that has been heard elsewhere than on studio or corporate tape machines. Since competition for listener attention in the overcrowded music arena remains as intense as ever, several great musicians in jazz and rock who've gone into seclusion, for even lesser periods of time, have slid into semi-obscurity. But Davis is not merely a great musician. He bears, however reluctantly, a symbolic stature as a focal point for directions in modern music. Most jazz enthusiasts under 35, regardless of the opinions they may hold of the individual phases of his development, await Miles Davis' return to the scene with the same intense expectations that rock people hold for a Beatles reunion.

We have to look outside of the music, to cinema and the visual arts, in order to find creator-personalities comparable to Davis in terms of impact; and these points of reference are no less than Marlon Brando and Pablo Picasso. The musician and the actor share an affinity for the controlled yet significant gesture, the performed essence, a result of concentrated internal selection from a vast repertoire of expressive options. This stripped-down approach to craft often obscures a wider technical command than is immediately apparent. But early on, both men must have realized that eschewing obvious displays of virtuosity would gain them the advantage of mystery, further cultivated out of the limelight by their fierce insistence on privacy illustrated by a close-mouthed hostility toward intruders.

Though even Davis can't match the depth and breadth of total oeuvre and influence in his field that Picasso achieved in painting and sculpture, both artists play a similar, Janus-like role in the modern eras of their respective art forms. They're synthesists, observing and interpreting past and current events from deeply personal perspective, while pointing out new paths for art to follow. Both failed to rest content with one of a variety of single styles, however revolutionary, they helped innovate, establish and then push further.

Davis, Brando and Picasso share yet another similarity. All three concerned themselves enough with personal image to practice their arts on a precarious interface with show business. In lesser men, this tightrope walking often results in rather nasty falls into self-parody; and Brando, indeed, has suffered some embarrassing moments with his willingness to risk everything artistically that has clashed with inferior material written solely to cater to his image. On the other hand is Picasso, with his voracious desire to remake everything, including all aspects of himself, from his own point of view. He turned the buffoonish dissonances of self-parody into art, amplifying his humanity while remaining larger than life.

Self-parody is lacking to the greatest extent in Davis' work, though much of its attendant visual packaging—from certain album graphics to onstage behavior—has ranged from off-putting to absolutely silly. Still, as soon as Davis starts making music, the only image that concerns him is the one he projects aurally. One can acknowledge this while still recognizing the essential value of Davis' extra-musical image in the formation of his charismatic position as contemporary music's reigning sage. Since his disappearance from the scene, in a haze of controversy surrounding his most recent playing, no one else has arrived to assume his place.

The last musician before Davis to mean as much to the music in this larger sense was Charlie Parker. Partisans of the jazz avant-garde may hold John

Coltrane and Ornette Coleman up for scrutiny, but the seminal achievements of these saxophonists lacked Davis' colossal stride over past, present and future—even though in purely musical terms they may be equally influential. In any event, it's highly symbolic that Davis received his professional baptism of fire in Parker's employ.

The true test of any embryonic talent is how strong an independent identity one can forge in the direct shadow of a giant such as Parker. Davis, a youngster who should have been uncontrollably swayed, realized from the beginning that he would not make a name for himself by trying to match the virtuosity of his boss or Parker's soulmate on Davis' instrument, Dizzy Gillespie. Davis' first recordings as a leader show that he was trying to fashion a more concisely edited, relaxed and simplified lyrical line that bop had previously heard. At the same time, the dense harmonic underpinnings of the new music were to be retained and even further crowded.

The trumpeter resisted temptations to play high and fast—perhaps because, as Gillespie once remarked to him, he didn't hear that way, or perhaps because Davis figured to set himself off from these musical terrors by playing it cool. Some of his early "mistakes" on Parker sides can be heard as tense attempts to reconcile his simpler desires with bop's will to unbridled virtuosity. Thus began a history of creative reaction, rather than personally embellished imitation, in pursuit of a unique voice.

The first Davis-led pieces featured Parker on tenor sax, a move that softened ensemble tone and frankly recalled the progenitor of easy lyricism, Lester Young. When the time came for Davis to step out from under Bird's wing, he continued to move in this more tonally subdued direction. The innately contrary nature that had him making his own way in the area of personal instrumental style also manifested itself in a search for ensemble inspiration where no one else was looking. He found it in some almost somber arrangements Gil Evans had done for the Claude Thornhill dance band. Davis, always the editor, opted for a nonet combination, the fewest number of instruments he needed to express harmonies and colors similar to Thornhill's. The result of Davis' application of bebop melody and harmony to this quieter instrumental blend (trumpet, trombone, baritone and alto saxes, French horn (!), tuba (!!), and rhythm section) was *Birth of the Cool,* Davis' first important contribution to jazz literature.

Whatever sins were later committed in this recording's name are not the leader's fault. Rhythm was not utterly neglected, as some contend: Kenny Clarke and Max Roach were the drummers, and provided strong momentum. But the possibilities expressed elsewhere in the music overshadowed its solid and conventional rhythmic content. Davis may have set a trap for less imaginative, more cerebral players, but he didn't step into it himself. True to form, he was expressing one or two colors of many possible to him. As if to confirm this, at a Paris concert, co-led by Tadd Dameron, two weeks after the second of three nonet dates, the trumpeter was found playing unexpectedly flamboyant, fiery horn in a pure bebop context.

Davis turned completely away from the cool in the early '50s, typically just as the impact of the session was beginning to register. Engaged in a personal war with drug addiction, he set about a decade-long musical project of opening up bebop—assessing what in the music was of lasting significance, what its limits were and how to move past them. Some warm and expansive Blue Note sessions with J.J. Johnson, Jackie McLean, the Heath brothers and others took a frank look at late bop jazz repertoire: "Woody 'n' You," "Tempis Fugit," "Ray's Idea." But the culmination of this look back in order to look ahead came, meaningfully enough, after Davis won his non-musical fight with heroin. It was the "Walkin'"/ "Blue 'n' Boogie" session of April 1954.

Once again, Davis the reactor and commentator made a statement of thoroughgoing significance. These sides averred the primacy of some old values that had been lost in the convolutions of bebop, especially its cool extensions. Strongest among these qualities was the blues form as a classic jazz essence capable of not only withstanding the most modern melodic development, but also framing and contextualizing it. Forsaken here were the complex harmonies and busy but quiet line movement of cool jazz; in their places appeared intensely distilled melodic forthrightness, crisp instrumental tones and unabashed rough energy.

Reflection on the exceptional playing here by a comparatively fresh pair of hands belonging to Horace Silver gives rise to further recollection of Davis' unequaled abilities as an employer of the best young talent. One is familiar with the litany of names from the '60s and '70s; but this gift stretches back to his first days as a leader, with the recruiting of Gil Evans, Gerry Mulligan and Lee Konitz for *Birth of the Cool,* continuing from a completely different tangent into the post-bop era with the hiring of Silver and a rough-hewn Sonny Rollins. Those two subsequently became paragons of the hard-bop style triggered by "Walkin'" and "Blue 'n' Boogie."

This shrewd location of voices from largely unexpected places bore fullest fruit with the assembly of Davis' first quintet, about a year and a half after "Walkin'." Such a delicately balanced group could only have been held together by a leader skilled in exacting interactive creativity from disparate elements first from within himself. By late 1955, Davis had reconciled and fused relaxation and intensity; reflective lyricism and the blues; sophisticated harmonics, compact melodic material, and unafraid rhythmic attack all into a cohesive instrumental style. No small achievement, and no wonder that he would seek to combine many of the same qualities in a small group.

Enter John Coltrane, a "hard" tenor player from Philadelphia who, as Martin Williams has pointed out, was a foil for Davis' lyricism as the trumpeter had conversely been to Parker. In the rhythm section, Red Garland, a light, almost casual stylist, was set against the flaming, barely controllable polyrhythmist Philly Joe Jones. Young bassist Paul Chambers rounded out the first quintet; unobtrusive on the first hearing, he subsequently revealed himself to be an ensemble welder of subtlety and strength.

As he had with Thornhill, Davis drew a certain amount of inspiration for this group from a strange source, this time Ahmad Jamal. This Chicago pianist affected various facets of the Quintet music, from repertoire (an affinity for clever melodic and harmonic reworking of hoary show tunes and standards) to rhythm (a jaunty two-beat that lent a calculatedly offhand quality). There's a more direct echo of Jamal in the easy openness of Garland's playing; but to his credit, the latter lined his approach with Texas blue steel, a strength sorely missing from the former. Especially when Garland accompanied Coltrane, the intense resolve of the first quintet prevented a wandering into merely pleasant trivia.

Davis had carried on all of his work within the jazz tradition up to this point, but four recorded orchestral reunions with Gil Evans moved him slightly outside of it. Contemporaneous with his combo playing in the late '50s and early '60s, they are essentially detours from this primary course, bearing virtually no resemblance to contemporary big band jazz either. Rhythm was largely de-emphasized on the Evans collaborations, while Evans painted a richly toned backdrop of dense harmonic colors from his orchestral palette. As one might guess, it was Davis' responsibility as soloist to provide forward movement and whatever "pure" jazz content there is to be found. But if one comes to these performances with high expectations in the jazz area, one will come away disappointed. They are more valuable on their own terms, exemplary of Davis' ongoing fascination with new sounds and new directions, jazz relatable to, but outside of, the mainstream.

Coltrane's rising star precipitated an amicable breakup of the first quintet, leaving Davis with a broad but stable repertoire of standards, blues and hard bop to constantly reconsider with fluctuating personnel. Despite the comings and goings, Davis was enjoying peak popularity. And he found the opportunity, in 1959, to explore more new possibilities, again just off the beaten path. It seemed like an isolated incident in Davis' career at the time, but *Kind of Blue* turned out to be an early tremor in the final earthquake of bebop. It was the harbinger of other developments, being worked out without Davis' direct knowledge, by an alto saxophonist in Los Angeles named Ornette Coleman.

Post-Parker jazz, which Davis had done so much to air out and simplify without rendering it trivial, was ready to break open completely. *Kind of*

Blue, recorded in one take with no prior rehearsal, cracked the music from the inside through the introduction of scalar patterns as the basis for modal improvisation, rather than the customary invention over chord systems of varying elaborateness. It was an undeniably rarefied climate, and Davis couldn't have attempted it without pianist Bill Evans present on four of the five selections. Evans' reflective concept of harmonics brought modern jazz into direct contact with the French Impressionist composers. Though the pianist is not a bluesman, the blues structures and their congruent modalities are broad enough in this music so that Evans could complement the hornmen rather than clash with them. They, in turn, could roam a free area of melodic activity while maintaining a blues feeling throughout.

Kind of Blue is a thoroughly haunting magic experience in music, over and above its considerable significance to the history of jazz. It exists on a level apart from Davis' other work carrying a melancholy freedom, without going "outside." Its melodies are simple, spare, memorable and uncondescending. Unlike *Birth of the Cool* and the Gil Evans collaborations, this session was not an isolated cul-de-sac for its leader. It opened up fresh territory, albeit unexplored by Davis for a few years to come.

It's difficult in retrospect to understand why Davis, the music's Janus, was so slow in confronting the challenge of the jazz avant-garde, especially in light of Coltrane's interest in Ornette Coleman and *Kind of Blue*'s own moves in an expanded direction. But the trumpeter expressed nothing but hostility for Coleman. One finds it hard to believe that he felt upstaged by the altoist, as he quite possibly did by Jimi Hendrix and Sly Stone 10 years later. A better explanation would be that Davis the sophisticate was put off by Coleman the primitive, who sometimes reached rather progressive conclusions by methods that seemed crude at face value. Still more plausible is the theory that Davis, unwilling to reject formal harmonic options out of hand, was working out his own answers, involving a further stretch of post-Parker limits to their most taut.

Four years after *Kind of Blue,* Davis consolidated a new, young rhythm section. Herbie Hancock seemed to be steering a middle course between two dominant courses of new piano: the impressionistic lyricism of Bill Evans and the percussive dissonance of Cecil Taylor. Ron Carter, an elusive counter-melodist with a penchant for unusual accents, was counted on to subtly guide the group, but loosely and broadly. And in Tony Williams, Davis discovered the Philly Joe Jones of the avant-garde—an irrepressible percussionist who listened to the soloist, unflaggingly maintained a swinging pulse and simultaneously orchestrated his own universe of splashing, rolling, independent polyrhythms.

The addition of saxophonist Wayne Shorter, following stints by George Coleman and Sam Rivers, brought the second quintet into full relief in 1964. Its early days were spent in further interpretations of Davis standards like "All of You," "Autumn Leaves," "My Funny Valentine" and various modal pieces. The group virtually threw themselves into these performances, as themes were treated tersely, brusquely, epigrammatically. Tight paraphrase was the general rule, followed by explosive improvisation at breakneck tempos. The music was wide open, yet severely controlled by strong implications from the accompanists—chords, riffs, linear fragments—which the soloists could choose from and work upon at will.

The second quintet soon evolved a fresh book of compositions unique to it. The ever present need, especially in Shorter and Davis, to prune their solos to bare essences, spilled over into the written music. The restraint with which it was constructed went against the grain of the times; but the intensity and freedom with which the players moved was of a piece with the emotional commitment of the more structurally loose and/or radical avant-gardists. As a result, the second quintet's albums are more listenable, a decade or more later, than most other music of the period. They consistently deliver fully realized musical insights. At a time when looking had become just as important as finding, Davis felt it unnecessary to externalize his search. He just presented the results, and they were classic.

Despite the high level of these performances, Davis' fascination with new textures and instrumental colors prevailed. The new rock had thunderstruck popular music with overwhelming force, undercutting jazz among young musicians of all kinds. Davis began flirting directly with electronics as early as 1967; but one also recalls that a much earlier innovation of his had been the muted horn, closely miked. It was a typically simple yet acute understanding of how electronics could modify a personal voice in a singular way.

Of course there were deeper reasons for Davis' increasing interest in electronics, rock and R&B in the late '60s. He and others had been engaged in opening up modern jazz since the early '50s. That task has been accomplished; but the popular thread in jazz had been lost in the process, as further and more extreme abstractions prevailed. It's possible that Davis, faced with a dwindling audience of elitists, was seeking to widen his own musical horizons while getting in touch with a new group of more liberal listeners, unafraid of electronics, rock or anything at all. Integrity was not at issue; Davis' identity was so strong by now that his musical standards couldn't be compromised, no matter what the newly evolving context.

In 1968, the trumpeter must have found that his carefully cultivated image as the impeccable, enigmatic hipster had become passé. He had become, in spite of himself, a respected musical elder. Assuming his mantle as the baddest of the bad went to more outrageous, uninhibited outlaws, Jimi Hendrix and Sly Stone. Despite their external flash, these performer-musicians were seriously involved in much of the same project for rock, blues and soul music that Davis had repeatedly undertaken in jazz—no less than the reinterpretation of basic musical language in a progressive atmosphere. But Davis clearly wasn't ready to go quietly to the old folks home. His famous remark in *Rolling Stone* that he could put together a better rock band than Jimi Hendrix was as much macho challenge as statement of musical fact.

While non-musical stimuli such as these can help spur a proud man to new achievements, music must be sustained by a more profound artistic will. In 1968–'75, Davis escalated his perpetual pursuit of ever-shifting instrumental texture and color. Underpinning these were a series of increasingly harsh riffs and ostinatos, loosely pasted together with broken pieces of thematic material. Everything was set in an expanded percussive field in which the thicker, but no less explosive, rhythmic attacks of Williams' successors Jack DeJohnette and Al Foster were amplified and embroidered by the "little instruments" of Airto Moreira and Mtume.

Davis' movement through electronic fusion swept across the muted, eerie ethereality of *In a Silent Way* (the electric *Kind of Blue*) and *Bitches Brew* to the more volatile, jagged and high-flying Fillmore band, the Davis ensemble most concerned with "free" collective improvisation. Changes in personnel led to *On the Corner*'s shift to a more repetitive, honed down, abstract funk, shaded with peculiar Indian colors of sitar and tabla drums. From this lean mixture, Davis again built up the density and heat. Three chattering, chanting, bickering guitars were added, and Davis himself played organ. Remaining were the welter of percussion and the omnipresent deep patterns of ex-Motown bass guitarist Michael Henderson.

Limits were again being pushed, tested and strained by Davis, this time ruthlessly, with less attention to editing. There's less open space in the post-*On the Corner* music than at any other time since *Birth of the Cool*. Except for random, unexpected, harrowing stop times, every moment is filled. There's so much sound in this boiling, teeming mass of pure rhythms, timbre and texture that conventional means of getting it out to the listener—concert sound systems, multitrack stereo recording—seem inadequate. Most of Davis' later recordings are technically muddy and obscure, compounding the difficulty of finding the handle on this alternately over-stimulating and forbidding, exhilarating and unfulfilling phase.

A certain amount of positive critical revisionism has lately occurred where *On the Corner*, *Get Up With It* and *Agharta* are concerned, but it has cleared little of the cloud of uncomprehending negativism that surrounded Davis when he left the active scene five years ago. Nonetheless, his return is anxiously awaited. Though it's more likely to happen than a Beatles reunion, Davis will undoubtedly face the exalted, probably unfulfillable, expectations attendant upon a near legend. He'll be a critical sitting duck.

If Davis does decide to come back, it will be in his utter disregard for anyone's artistic ideals but his own that will see him through. Long ago, he realized that a complete, contrary independence would serve his music and his image equally well. Commercial popularity has followed a separate axis, depending on each phase's congruence with public taste. It's significant that record sales, or lack thereof, have never compromised Davis' overall position of dominance when he has been active.

And if, after repeatedly unsatisfactory rehearsals and recording sessions, Davis finds all the possibilities exhausted and decides not to return, would it really be so hard to comprehend after the scope of his 30 years at the forefront? When one has redrawn the boundaries of contemporary music as often as this man has, rewriting the rules of the language time and time again, he has earned the right to silence. Still, one suspects that the ever-present need to react, comment and point the way ahead will soon bring about Miles Davis' waiver of his prerogative. When that happens, we can expect new directions to again be heard in the land.

December 1984
Miles Davis: "I Don't Mind Talkin' If People Are Listenin' "
by Howard Mandel

"I don't mind talkin' if people are listenin'," says Miles Dewey Davis, at 58 a pace-setter of what he described last summer as "social music." By every indication, people are indeed listening—and watching—as *Decoy,* Davis' fourth album recorded since his return to activity in 1979, tops sales charts, comes in No. 1 with *DownBeat* readers and shows up as a four-minute music video on discerning television networks.

"Just don't ask me no bullshit," his husky voice, unmistakable as his trumpet sound, warns over the telephone from his place in L.A. "I don't want to be compared to any white musician."

Comparisons are odious—and anyway, the only standard to hold Miles Davis to is the one he himself created in the past. Is he playing ballads as tenderly as he did in the '50s? Hear his version of Cyndi Lauper's "Time After Time." Does he still strip songs to their essence, then fill them with emotional nuance? You can tell by turning an ear to Miles playing a slow blues. Can he yet recognize young talents, and organize them for groundbreaking forays?

I'd say so; he's recruited guitarist John Scofield, saxists Bill Evans, Branford Marsalis and Bob Berg, senstitive percussionists, funky bassmen and especially, synthesizer player Robert Irving III—improvisers as estimable as any emerging in the '80s—to join him in daring studio sessions and onstage stomps.

Was there a time when people stopped listening, like before he quit appearing in public in the mid-'70s? "I don't know," mutters The Voice, "but I was bored with it myself. I was bored with the business end of it; that's always been terrible. You know, if you don't watch your money and have somebody who knows about how to invest it, somebody will steal you blind. Now, Columbia pays me very well; Columbia's doin' a good job on all its artists, especially me comin' back. But we still have to ask 'em for money time and time again—you know what I mean?"

Uh, probably not. In a series of brief news bites CBS has prepared for any television producer who'll air them, Miles paints with oils, reclines in his white-upholstered living room amid dramatic sculpture and otherwise seems quite comfortable addressing some off-camera presence in what appears to be his Manhattan penthouse. Sure he wants more—just as he might like the kids on the corner break-dancing to a Miles single, as they did to Herbie Hancock's monster "Rockit" last year. So he keeps working on it . . .

"The more we play, the more I play, the more I can perceive what we can do in concert—what we should do. Then by playing a lot of concerts, you can change the music. You get tired of hearin' it yourself. So the more we work, the more things change—the tempos change, we don't play songs in the same order, and little things that happen that are great, we keep 'em in. 'Cause I tape all the concerts, so I can hear what we can use and what we can't, what we both like—the people and the band, the players."

Live Miles tapes—could they be released? "Yeah, they can be released, a lot of 'em. And the good stuff, I take it off if it's good, and use it. We used a lot of in-person stuff on *Decoy*." Two cuts on side two, in fact, were recorded on 32-track live at Montreal's Festival International in '83, then spliced up in a mix by editing and adding another track of Miles' trumpet—not to replace, but as a counterpoint to his original line.

"I've found, like a lot of other guys, I guess, that studio music sucks," Miles confides. "There ain't nothin' happenin' in the studio; you don't get no feelin'. I just got through recording 'Time After Time,' and I don't ever play it but once a night, but we had to sit there and do it over and over. I had to do that on *Porgy and Bess*, and I swore I'd never do it again. It's not the retakes; it's the feelin' you put in it . . . I mean, you can't say 'I love you' twice. You have to say it when you feel it. And when I play a ballad, more than anything else, it's all me." Reports are that Miles has almost an album's worth of ballads in the can—though release is not in immediate sight. The same source indicated Davis wants to record only new material.

Whatever Miles is playing, he's putting himself all into it, as those raging uptempo live numbers prove. "When I get through with a concert, I've lost about three pounds," he mentions. And does Miles, whose former boxing workouts are well known, do anything special now to keep fit?

"I swim about an hour a day, in the pool," he says. Ah, L.A. "And what else? I practice every day. Got to do that—you don't practice, you can't play nothin'. Scales, mostly—trumpet stuff. Long tones are the best. If I can play a low F sharp, loud and clear, then I know my tone is there. I had to work real hard to get that tone back when I came back; it took me two years to get it right. Now that it's back, I'm gonna keep it." How important is tone to Miles? "If you don't have a pleasant sound, you can't play any melody. And my head is full of melodies," he answers.

Yet, "I play what we can play, not me," says Miles. "I never play what I can play; I'm always playin' over what I can play. I'm always tempted to play somethin' difficult, and usually it's a ballad, you know—the rest of the stuff is easy—but my love for ballads gets me in trouble. Well, not trouble—it's just that you have to have good tone, a workin' tone, or else you're gonna think the ballad sounds bad. My love for singers makes me play like that on trumpet. On 'Time After Time,' it's the song I like. There are some songs that belong to certain people—they're just made for you. I've met guys who've had pieces for me, too."

Like Bob Irving, credited with the title track of *Decoy* and the spooky made-for-radio processional, "Code M.D."—also co-writer with Miles of the brief trio "Robot 415," a tasteful embellisher of "That's Right," and a traveler with Miles' band? "Well, Bobby's learnin' real quick. I just add a little somethin', and I tell him different things, and when we talk, he has his tape recorder workin', so he doesn't forget what I tell him. So we add to that, and it comes out great. Really good. He's very thorough, and when I tell him, 'Bobby, this just don't work, you have to take this out,' he says, 'OK.' He does what I tell him. Took me six months for me to get him to be more selective."

And Scofield? "John is overplaying—he always overplays. I tell him about it; he goes, 'I know, I know, I know—I overplay.' I told him, 'When you get through playin' what you know, then play somethin'. Nobody wants to hear you practice onstage. Practice at home.' You can't tell that to everybody. I don't tell that to John every time he does it—just when he gets on my nerves."

What do you tell your bass player? "I give him a line to play, but I don't ask him for anything. If he plays too much of somethin' I don't like, I tell him.

I stop him. What I'm tryin' to get him to do now is not resolve anything. I told him, 'After you play the tonic, there's nothin' else to play. So don't play it.'

"Endings just drag me," Miles remarks when I mention his ploy at the New York Kool fest. Toward the end of a tune, ringing feedback seemed to seep from some amplifier. Irving, Scofield and bassist Darryl Jones all appeared mystified, and the drone kept on until they had all dropped to silence. Then Miles cooly dialed out the sound he'd summoned from his own keyboard bank. "I'm not playin' with them when I do that. I just like to continue on to the next number. When we stop abruptly sometimes? After you've heard it all, if you play things long as we play 'em, they don't mind stoppin' like that." They being the band—or the numbers themselves?

"We're gettin' away from the chords," the trumpeter explains. "Chords, they just get in the way. If I give Bobby a chord, it's the sound I want—and I tell him that the sound can go anywhere. When you take a sound, it only sounds wrong if you don't resolve it to somethin' else. I mean, the next chord makes the first one; it tells on the first chord, the first sound. If you hit somethin' that sounds like a dischord to everybody in the world, you can straighten it out with the next chord. So, we don't play chords. That is, we play 'em, but they're not . . . chord-chords."

"Hold the phone. Somebody's at the door," he directs. I think Miles' notion of sounds for chords and his revolution against resolution are similar to ideas both Ornette Coleman and Cecil Taylor have employed. When he returns, I ask if by leaving the strict chord structure, one can get a lot further. Is that where he's going?

"Yeah, there's nothin' happenin'. Like, where's Wynton Marsalis? Wynton's a brilliant musician, but that whole school—they don't know anything about theory, 'cause if they did, they wouldn't be sayin' what they say, and doin' what they do.

"The only thing that makes Art Blakey's band sound good is Art. They're energetic musicians, yeah, but it's the same structure that we used to play years ago, and it's too demanding on you. You have to play the same thing . . . if you play a pattern of fourths, or parallel fifths, or half-step chords and all that stuff, nobody's gonna sound different on that—everyone sounds the same. Why do you think Herbie don't want to play that anymore? He'd rather hear scratch music. I'd rather hear somebody fall on the piano than to play that. That newness will give you something—more so than all the clichés you've heard from this record, that tape. The only way you can get away from that is by being very selfish."

Selfish? "Selfish. I mean—don't listen. You don't listen to a trumpet player for what he's doin'; you listen for the sound, to his sound. You don't listen to Herbie for how he's playin' the piano; you listen for what the whole thing does. You know what I'm sayin'? You don't have to play 'The Flight of the Bumblebee' to prove to another trumpet player that you're a good trumpet player. Everybody can do that. The way you change and help music is by tryin' to invent new ways to play, if you're gonna ad lib and be what they call a jazz musician.

"I myself couldn't copy anybody. An approach I could copy, but I wouldn't want to copy the whole thing," Miles maintains with an emphasis that regrets those who would, so to speak, play-giarize. "Listen," he offers, "I would love to play like Dizzy or Buck Clayton or, you know, all those trumpeters who I heard who I liked. But I couldn't do it. Roy Eldridge—I couldn't play like that. I tried. I tried to play like Harry James—I couldn't do that."

When did he realize this inability? "When I played 'Flight of the Bumblebee' and thought, 'What the fuck am I playin' this for?' I was about 14. 'Carnival of Venice'—I said, 'Damn, what is all this?'"

But most young musicians coming up look for guidance and want to . . . "Have an idol? Yeah. You can see how difficult it is because you have so many records. When I was comin' up, I had three records. I had Pres' *Sometimes I'm Happy,* Art Tatum's *Get Happy,* Duke's *J.B. Blues.* And my mother loved Louis Jordan. Billy Eckstine and Dizzy. Coleman Hawkins playin' 'Woody 'n' You.' And that was about it. I thought everybody in the world, all the good trumpet players, played like Dizzy; when I got to New York, I found out things are different—you have to go your own way; you can't copy anybody. You know, just because you play a flatted fifth doesn't mean somebody's gonna hire you," he snorts derisively.

What would Miles tell a youngster seeking advice? "They have to get their own sound. Then, notes go with your sound. It's like a color. My color—I'm black, brown, with a little red-orange in my skin. Red looks good on me. You have to do the same with music. If you have a tone, you play notes to match your sound, your tone, if you're gonna make it pleasin' to yourself—and then you can please somebody else with it."

And composing for your band, or working things out with them live, you keep in mind their notes, as Duke Ellington did? "Right, that's right. Yeah. You know what they can do. John, the rest—these are some very talented musicians. If you play every night, and somebody does somethin', you remember that. If it's not somethin' we did 10 minutes ago, I say, 'Well, here it is, down on this tape—you can hear it again. You know what to do.' But your sound has to match what you think—not what somebody else thinks. Nobody can make like me, know what I mean? Louis [Armstrong] was the one you could copy; he was the easiest. You can't play like Dizzy."

What could you copy from Louis? "The sound, the tone. I liked the tone of Pres, of Louis and Buck Clayton and Ray Nance. That low register sound. I hear that."

Many older listeners don't hear the connection between your electric style and earlier improvised music. "Who cares? I mean, you go from 1984 on up, not from 1903."

But you wouldn't rule out doing an acoustic project again, would you? "No, I wouldn't mind. If the place was all right. You know, people have said I turn my back—but it's not like that. Onstage there's always a spot that will register more for the horn player; when I was playin' with J.J. Johnson, he used to say, 'I'll give you $10 if you let me sit in your spot tonight,' 'cause if it's a good spot for brass, that's what happens. But I would play acoustic with a nice guitar player, or a nice pianist like Keith [Jarrett] or Herbie or Chick [Corea] or George Duke, and record like that—it would be great. Not in Carnegie Hall—because the symphony, they got 70 guys playin' one note. They need some speakers in there.

"You can use acoustic; I've always thought so. I used to have big arguments with Dave Holland and Chick about electric pianos and stuff, but how many years ago was that? And you can see what happened."

What happened was electricity became the norm. Does Miles dig further adventures into hi-tech—Herbie's scratch music and such? "Yeah, that knocks me out. Because I know Herbie so well—he's like what people call a genius; he's something else. But Keith, Chick, they're all crazy like that in the genius way—they play so much there ain't nothin' left for them to do but funk with somethin' else. Herbie has to play with different things, because he's done everything else."

But that's OK? "Yeah. Give somebody some kind of goose, give 'em just a little kick. You owe that to music. A lot of guys are wearin' clean shirts, and drivin' new cars, from copyin' me. They have jobs. But they owe Dizzy somethin', and Louis, and people like that, for what they did that was great. Why not try to do somethin' yourself? Even if nothin' else but for the fans' sake, 'cause they done heard all this stuff. You don't play anything they haven't heard—it just comes out different. Well, everybody wants a new sandwich. Whatcha gonna put on a hamburger next? You know?

"Now, if we don't play some blues, in front of a black audience, ain't nothin' gonna happen, and I'm black, so that's what we're gonna play; if I was Chinese, we'd be playin' somethin' else. I still play the Harmon mute; I take the middle out of it. I'm not usin' wah-wahs or any of that, not this season. You know what I do, though? I play chords on the piano and play on top of the synthesizer. Hey, talk about prejudice, dig this: The synthesizer sound for trumpet is a white trumpet player's sound—a white trumpet sound. It is!

And the only way I can play it is to play over it with my trumpet. To me, they should get Snooky Young or one of the good first trumpet players and have him record to put his sound on the synthesizer. I'd love that—or my sound. I have an Emulator that Willie Nelson gave me, and I could put my sound on that—I might just do it. Or get Snooky to let me record him."

Can Miles always tell the difference between a black and white player through their sound? "I don't know, man—there are a lot of good white players out there now. Used to be a white trumpet player couldn't play over a high C—now they can do everything. But when I was at Juilliard, that white trumpet sound—that's what you used when you played concerts. You don't put that stuff on synthesizers for social music. They have to get that sound together; you should have a choice on a synthesizer between a black and white sound.

"See, it's a problem because they can't lose that schoolin'. Wynton has told me sometimes he thinks things he plays sound too white. I told him, 'Don't worry about it,' because he's a good player, and it ain't gonna be that white. He's sayin' that in order to play those strict phrases with the symphony orchestra, you have to play like them, 'cause they can't play with us."

When you played with Gil Evans' orchestra in the late '50s and early '60s, didn't Gil's orchestra match your sound? "Gil loves my sound, and my sound fits because I love his arrangements, like those for Claude Thornhill—I loved that pure sound. But when you mix, you integrate a band, it sounds different. You can tell when a rock band has a black rhythm section—it can hold a groove a little longer. And groups like Earth, Wind & Fire—they could mix a couple white trumpeters in there, use 'em right."

What else has Miles been digging? Prince? "Yeah, I heard Prince. You know, it's easy to write in between a crack; like in a song, if you sing, it's easy to fill a phrase. But to fill up 32 bars, for 15 minutes—then you got to admire a person for doing that. For what Prince's doing, filling his own backgrounds in, it's great, but only for a few minutes. I like to listen to groups like Earth, Wind & Fire, Prince, Michael Jackson, Ashford & Simpson. They only have a couple bars in which to do it, and they make the best of it. But if they had to do it in 32 bars, for half an hour, they couldn't do it because they're not groomed that way.

"Me, I'm basically a quarter horse. You know how a thoroughbred runs a mile? A quarter horse runs a quarter-mile. I think it's easier to do what Prince and them, and Quincy [Jones], too, do—fill in those cracks, if you can write like that. Playin'—if you let it flow, if you can stand it, long tunes are all right. But if you feel irritable when it takes going on, that means somethin's wrong. So you have to stop it. *Bitches Brew* and all that turned out great because I let it flow for a while, but there were also cues, and the musicians knew what to do."

I have one more question. Miles, since you came back, which of your songs or albums do you think is best?

"Best? That's a big word."

━━━━━

October 1988
Miles to Go
by John Ephland

"And Terence [Trent] D'Arby came up to my room in Milan, callin' me Mr. Davis. He said, 'I carry around *Kind of Blue*. I play it for inspiration . . . before I play.'"

Perhaps not every one knows who the young Mr. D'Arby is, or the kind of musical success he currently enjoys. He is a musician. "Mr. Davis" is a musician. There is a bridging across generations with Miles Davis. To anyone who has followed his career, if only by glances, his music is synonymous with change and an openness to new styles, new ideas. So it's no wonder that a young musician might find favor in the presence of the Prince of Darkness.

It's been a while since Miles has graced the pages of *DownBeat* (December 1984). *Decoy* was then the current rage, topping sales charts in addition to being voted best jazz album by *DownBeat* readers. (His electric jazz groups won top honors in '85 and '86 with both the readers and critics.) Another album for Columbia, *You're Under Arrest,* stretched his bandmates even further and included a few guest appearances (ex-sideman John McLaughlin for one). And then, next thing you know, Miles is recording a "concept" album with a new label, Warner Bros. When was the last time that happened? *Tutu,* complete with full-cover front and back photos of Miles, brought him together with bassist/composer/producer/arranger Marcus Miller in an album that streamlined the musical force on hand even as that inimitable trumpet voice continued to shine.

"Synthesizer programming" allowed for more guest artists. And yet, the sound was lean, simply providing—as always—"a program, a menu, a guide." If you have seen and heard Miles perform over the past two years (since *Tutu* was released), you know *Tutu* has served its purpose well, in the tradition of other great Miles Davis records: "It goes like this, but it goes farther when we play it, you know?"

Miles' most recent recording, *Siesta,* harkens back to a period when his love of Spanish music surfaced in a big way—with *Sketches of Spain*. Rightly dedicated to "The Master," Gil Evans, it continued the pace set by *Tutu,* using a spare lineup of artists alongside synthesizers and trumpet. Once again, Marcus Miller had a major role, playing along and composing the music as a film score. Although Miles plays on only about half of *Siesta,* when he does, "he doesn't just play solos; he creates moods (*DownBeat* review, April 1988)."

His current band includes Robert Irving III and Adam Holzman on keyboards, Kenny Garrett on saxophones and flute, Joseph Foley McCreary on guitar, Benny Rietveld on bass, Marilyn Mazur on percussion and Ricky Wellman on drums. And it is with this band that Miles continues to tour worldwide even as he receives more awards, shows up on TV, paints/sketches professionally, etc. And, as if all this wasn't enough, his vast catalog continues to be reissued in record and CD formats.

Miles has a lot to say, with subjects as diverse as Beethoven, performance styles and the impact of Charlie Parker.

Read on, and see if you don't agree that the Sorcerer has a few more tricks up his sleeve, and quite a few miles to go.

JOHN EPHLAND: Let's talk about your style of performance. You like to move around a lot.

MILES DAVIS: I walk around all the time because there's different sounds on stage. Nobody wants to stands still and play, you know what I mean? It's old-time, man; it's Jim Crow. Not Jim Crow, Uncle Tommish when you go to the microphone and you play and you step back and bow to the audience, like the audience is doing something for them when they are really teachin' the audience.

J.E.: I think of my wife, who is a dancer, and how she is always drawing comparisons between dance and jazz improvisational music. Music is movement, particularly improvisational music. So, creatively, your juices are flowing when you're moving.

M.D.: Yeah.

J.E.: Aren't your ideas coming a lot easier than if you're stationary?

M.D.: Sometimes, like when Trane heard the high sound of a soprano sax, you can pick up the higher sounds like that. It's not too hard, like not as high as a dog. When I first gave Herbie the electric piano, he really loved to play it 'cause Herbie would try anything. But Keith Jarrett, I got him an organ and an electric piano. He used to play them for me like this (*demonstrates moving around*). Same thing when I'm walkin' around that they do.

J.E.: Standing still?

M.D.: Yeah.

J.E.: And it's different for a drummer because a drummer, in a sense, is rotating on that stool; they've got all four limbs moving if they're really doing it.

M.D.: Marilyn, my drummer, she dances around when she plays. And Ricky, my drummer Ricky, he's just as steady as, he's a bull; he can play two hours, then take a solo. But I'm sayin', I know George Duke walks around and he plays his ass off.

J.E.: Speaking of Trane, there's a phrase I've read that you used in connection with him: "that thing." It was something subjective that you used when you heard something and it was the kind of sound that you wanted in your musicians.

M.D.: It's the thing that connects the melody with another melody, that shows a musician, that shows himself, you know; and it also shows me what he knows and what he doesn't know. For instance, Coleman Hawkins, the way he plays "Body and Soul," that's an old record and when Frank Sinatra used to phrase, he taught me how to phrase.

J.E.: He taught you how to phrase?

M.D.: Yeah, when Frank Sinatra sings, when I was at an early age, "Night and Day," the way he phrases; the way Orson Welles used to phrase, the way Orson Welles used to speak, the heavy accent that would stop short. Orson Welles had a way of speaking, it was like care. Most didn't know I have that. That's what I liked about him.

J.E.: All the people that you have mentioned were before this kind of mobile stage presence-type thing. For example, Coleman Hawkins or John Coltrane, when they would play, they would do that old thing where you go to the mic and solo, right?

M.D.: Well, you know the way John played, it was, all the stuff he played was throwin' him off-balance anyway. So it didn't matter whether he was standin' in front of the mic or what. And sometimes I can't remember him even goin' to the microphone or him bein' in the vicinity of the microphone. But not like old musicians with the bebop clichés and stuff. Dizzy just asked me, called me up the other day and said, "I gotta get me one of those microphones you got on your horn."

J.E.: He doesn't have one yet?

M.D.: No, he's been askin' me that for six months. I thought he had it. Well, I hooked it up for him, you know.

J.E.: One last question about Coltrane. How did you follow his later music on Impulse? Say, from *A Love Supreme* on?

M.D.: I never did hear his records after, you know, after he left the band.

J.E.: Did you follow his career much and the kind of music he was into?

M.D.: It was the same thing. It was the same thing playin' with me. I don't like, I didn't like the piano player.

J.E.: McCoy Tyner?

M.D.: I don't like all that bangin', you know? I like a piano player that gets a lot of sound out of the piano. Like a baby grand; gettin' a sound out of a baby grand like Bill Evans and people like that, and Herbie and Chick and George Duke. They know how to play the piano by itself and make it sound like a piano. I don't like the guys who make a livin' playin' in the mode.

J.E.: Playing in the mode?

M.D.: Yeah. We just did it because it's one style. You know, you can play the whole set like that . . . who could play after Coltrane? He played everything in the mode, you know, and McCoy just used to bang around, and I couldn't stand that.

J.E.: What were you looking for that wasn't there, that wasn't happening with McCoy's playing?

M.D.: He just didn't have any touch, you know? There's nothin' there. . . . The way he played with John, he kept the vamp goin', then he got monotonous. I know how Trane played, it would get monotonous if you'd sit there a long time. Even though it's a style; only he could do that and make it work. You know, when they played (*sings/hums a little of "My Favorite Things"*), what is that?

J.E.: "My Favorite Things"?

M.D.: Yeah. Only he could play that. There's some of those that I did just because of the way he plays. I used to give him sets of chords to play—three, and five, six chords in one bar, two bars, 'cause he always could do 'em. And to hear McCoy bang around like that and . . . this is only my opinion, what I like to hear. I couldn't see nothin' there. I could see Elvin Jones. Also, they didn't have a good bass player. Nobody else but him.

J.E.: So you'd say their best stuff was the duets? When John and Elvin would get off on just the two of them playing?

M.D.: Yeah, that's what I would want to hear.

J.E.: You've made a lot of records. What is the value of the recordings, beyond the immediate use of live material for possible new ideas? I've read that you're not that interested in your older records.

M.D.: It's like a program. It's like a menu, when you go out—say, "Here's *Tutu,* here's what they're gonna play. But, it ain't gonna sound like that. See, here's what they're gonna play, this is a guide, this is *Tutu.*" It goes like this but it goes farther when we play it, you know? That's all it is. Is that what you're talking about?

J.E.: Let me say it a different way. Say, for example, you talk about *Miles Smiles.*

M.D.: Which one is that?

J.E.: The album, *Miles Smiles*?

M.D.: I can't remember it.

J.E.: OK. What value is there in having records around except for people who want to listen to the kind of stuff you were listening to back then? In 10 years, is *Tutu* something you'll be glad was recorded?

M.D.: Yeah.

J.E.: You'd go back and listen to it?

M.D.: Yeah. You can always listen to it, is what I'm sayin'. When you play in person, *Tutu* is only a guide for what we might do. It's different on every take. A record, you can't do anything, man. . . . They should look at it like a program for a concert, like what we might play. All the rest is a composition.

J.E.: What about the whole "neo-classic" jazz scene?

M.D.: What is "neo-classic"?

J.E.: I guess that's a critics term. Take what someone like Miles Davis did in the mid- to late '60s, an all-acoustic jazz format, and 20 years later with a new group of players. You've dropped the all-acoustic format and have some very strong artistic reasons for doing so.

M.D.: Like I said, one thing is because I don't like to walk up and take a bow.

J.E.: Right. The electronics free you up.

M.D.: Well, you can hear better with electronics, the audience can hear better. They can hear every little thing that we have set up. They can hear everything.

Listen to this (*takes out a portable tape player, offers headset to me to hear a tape of their recent live music*). Can you hear that?

J.E.: I can hear what they're playing.

M.D.: You can hear it's separated. This was last night. You can hear everything, everybody's portion.

J.E.: Yeah, it's not muddy.

M.D.: Yeah. You know acoustic players, if you're not in the same room with 'em, you can't hear 'em. You can't hear the bass, you can't hear the piano, you can hear the drums; sometimes they're off-balance. If it was acoustic, there'd be no microphone, not at all. But if you're gonna put a mic by the drums, one by the piano, one in front and maybe another one for the saxophone player, one in front the the bass—it might as well be electric. That's what it is, anyway.

J.E.: You're not playing in somebody's room. You're playing for an audience.

M.D.: Yeah, for 4,000 people, 3,000 people. . . . And people on television, people have seen faces, half-smiles, cheap smiles, half-applause (*claps faintly*), you know? Expressions and movements that mean "I'm sorry," or "Yes." . . . They know when they look at you what is real or whether you're just bein' pretentious, or doin' this because you're really in the music. They can hear the note, they can hear everything. They can look at you, and when you play acoustic, I mean, they could tell you how awkward you must feel. They could see that, see your carriage. Don't you know when a guy wants to fight you? And don't you know when he's afraid or he's not afraid? You've seen cheap smiles on faces on TV. You know when you do this (*makes gesture of a phony facial expression*).

J.E.: Yeah. There's another job goin' on just to be on stage.

M.D.: Yeah. Well, you know, if you could hear it, you know you're givin' it to 'em, you don't have to do that. The applause, if they don't like it, they don't like it. And they usually do like it if you spend some time doin' it. You can tell the hard ones, why it's takin' some time. Most white people used to think, and the critics used to think, that black people just picked up this instrument and they did it because they all have rhythm. It's not so. A lot of people do a lot of workin' in music. You can tell Herbie put a lot of work into the piano. Ahmad Jamal—I can't see that in some piano players. If [Herbie] can prepare, then he can make you like what he wrote in 1988, or the way he plays in 1988. In 1944, he couldn't play like that—'cause, in the first place, the police didn't like black musicians; 'cause they thought they stole all the white women. Like what Orson Welles did at the Mercury Theater and scared everybody. Now you can't scare people, no matter what you do, you know? People are too hip now. Everybody's got as much music as I know. Even if they're not playin' it.

J.E.: What if they are playin' it?

M.D.: Well, you know that—OK, we played last night, Adam got up to play. I had to tell Adam, "In the first place, you're white. And white guys take long phrases. So you gotta be aware of what you can do. Don't start somethin' black and can't finish it, you know? Play what you can play. Don't try to do it like you see somebody else do. So, you know, set up the background so we can play comfortably." You gotta get rid of your ego. Nobody's gonna look at you and say, "That was a nice sound." You see the piano players in my band, and synthesizers, them motherfuckers have a habit of just turnin' it up real loud so that people can know what they're playin'. But in order to do that, you have to learn how to play like that. You know, you just can't say, "Let me play."

J.E.: Yeah. It's not just going to come out.

M.D.: Well, it's accordin' to what you learned. Adam used to tell me, "Guess what I'm learnin' in my class." And it's still the same old stuff they're teachin'. The bopper stuff. I told Adam, "Even if you have to get somebody else's personality, borrow it from him." You know what I mean? Like, if I'm gonna play basketball, I'm gonna do it like Magic [Johnson]. You know? It's not yours but at least you're doin' like he is. And pretty soon it might get to be yours.

J.E.: Is that something you followed when you were first coming up?

M.D.: Yeah . . . I've always wanted to play like Dizzy or . . . shit, there's so many guys . . . there's 10 fuckin' trumpet players; you gotta follow what you like about 'em. . . . If you gonna be a player and you wanna solo, you gotta get great soloists and see why they did certain things, you know? See where they come from. If they're comin' from Texas, or did they have a Baptist upbring-ing. Most soul singers sung in church. That's why they sound like that. They ad lib off the notes, which is flamenco music, the scale, like Arabic music, like Jewish folk songs, and stuff. Gypsies. That's like Baptists. Most white singers sing straight. They're just gettin' to play like soul music, you know. They copy, they borrowed sounds.

J.E.: So when you talk about soloing, do you just mean improvising?

M.D.: Yeah.

J.E.: How does that fit in with the players in your band that may not have the links to the history of jazz, that would give them that kind of tradition or basis?

M.D.: They have to find out what they like. Say I'm a piano player—so if I had any sense at all, I would have to go with Herbie, Chick Corea, Keith Jarrett. Herbie can't play like Keith, and Chick can't play like Keith. Nobody plays like Keith. Chick can't play like Herbie, but Herbie might be able to play like Chick; I doubt it because Chick plays like he would play drums. He uses his hands and he can only play one tempo, you know. Like the way I like to hear him. And that's a medium tempo like this (*gestures*). And the reason he can play like that, at that tempo, is 'cause he makes up his mind. With that tempo you have to make up your mind right away. You know, you can't be thinkin' of bein' cute.

J.E.: It was a different thing back then, when you first started with more than one keyboard player and it was Herbie or Chick or Keith or Joe Zawinul. And that was a different scene than it is now with more than one keyboard player. Or is it the same? Are we talking about the same kind of thing?

M.D.: No, you're talkin' about two different things. You're talkin' about orchestration and composition. I'm talkin' about what would a guy do to be a soloist. He has to copy one of those three.

J.E.: But were those guys doing that when they hit your band or did they come into it like you were working with Herbie?

M.D.: I remember he was playin' like Bud Powell. Tryin' to play like Bud, but to his technique he started adding doing like Bud and somethin' else, he played a style. He also, we introduced him to playin' like Ahmad Jamal, fakin' like that on a ballad, it's a medium tempo ballad. All three of them play the shit out of ballads. And that's where you can tell they do their own sound. And it's also like Art Tatum. You have to go past all those great soloists like Art Tatum. And you got that honky tonk music, boogie woogie, Lux Lewis, things like that. They're doin' it now. Like Huey Lewis and the News, that's all that is (*hums a few bars of one of their recent songs*). That sound is honky tonk music. I heard a lot of it lately. "The thing of rock & roll" . . . "The Heart of Rock & Roll"! (*continues to hum a few bars of the same song*) Honky tonk players play it. But you gotta realize it's 1988 and the shit rubs off on you whether you like it or not. All the television shows, all the MTV and all the black soul sound. And when you write music, it's gotta seep in. It's gotta be like that. You know? That's what the Top 10 says—that everybody's alike. Those that aren't in the Top 10, you probably get some good music. Beethoven was in the Top 10. Not the best, but one of the favorites. In Beethoven's era, it was like the Top 10. You know, five composers that played what the queen would like, what the king would like. But the ones that they didn't like had a new sound, you know? They probably sounded like John Cage (*laughs*). They say, "We can't use that, we can't do no waltzes." . . . It's just havin' an open mind. You can't just say, "I'm gonna be like him." "I'm gonna be better than him." You can't get in that kind of thing. The reason you say you can do it is because whoever does it does it so good that it fits. You know? But when you leave them and you don't hear it, you can't do it. Like if you look at a painting, like cubism, man, you know, and you say, "Oh yeah!" But if you hadn't seen a cube, it wouldn't have been there. Bob Berg, I used to tell, "Bob, why do you play in this spot? You not supposed to play in this spot." He said, "It sounded so good, Chief, I had to play it." I said, "The reason it sounded so good is because you wasn't playin'." As soon as he jumps in, he fucks it up. It's a hard thing playin' with a group.

J.E.: Is that related to your counsel on "Play what's not there"? That's the flip side?

M.D.: I was only sayin' that sometimes when you look at another form of art that you can see, maybe a guy wants to play out of key for about four or five bars . . . sometimes you see something so bold with your eyes that you say, "Why can't I play what I hear?" You know? "Why should I be afraid to play that?"

J.E.: Well, was it? Why is that? Because of the ego?

M.D.: That's the critics. Critics do that to a musician. [The musicians] want to impress the critics. Herbie, we used to go to Germany. I hate to go to Germany with Herbie.

J.E.: 'Cause Germany means something to Herbie?

M.D.: Well, his wife is from Germany, and there are a lot of good musicians in Germany. Piano players have discipline. They say, "You must practice eight hours." Herbie pulls back his sleeves and shit, and he plays a whole fuckin' concert, a concerto off of "My Funny Valentine." . . . But the drive that he [the white critic] gives a black man is to try to strive to be good. But it's also an Uncle Tom way of thinkin'. It's like a white collar Uncle Tom. You know, "I wear a shirt and tie 'cause I'm comin' downtown to shop and I don't want anybody to think I'm stealin'." So they dress up. It's also a bad way to go into music. Some people who go in like that are very good musicians, but that's it. They have no ideas.

J.E.: No heart?

M.D.: Yeah. They just play music for . . .

J.E.: They're playing for other people instead of themselves?

M.D.: Well, they're playin' so a white critic will like 'em, you know?

J.E.: Black critics aren't like that?

M.D.: I don't know any black critics.

J.E.: Critics are making musicians always look over their shoulders?

M.D.: They usually do, you know. I know a couple of guys that really . . . one time I had Jimmy Cobb, and a critic said he sounded like he had an axe in his hand. Which sometimes he did. But what he really didn't notice was that Jimmy used to drop tempo a lot of times, you know. Maybe he didn't know what to say. Constructive criticism. He should've said, "I didn't mean nothin'." But a day later, the critic came down to see us and Jimmy said, "There's that motherfucker. I ought to go punch him in the mouth." A critic'll do that. A second thought goin' in your head.

J.E.: Do critics have a place?

M.D.: They have a place, yeah. But, it's just that the musician shouldn't cater to 'em. If your own peers don't tell you how sad you are, the critic can't tell you, you know? A lot of times a critic says, "That sounds good," and you think it sounds like shit. But it's individual taste. And it does destroy a lot of careers.

J.E.: And that's why it's important to have a musical community? Where people talk to each other?

M.D.: Yeah.

J.E.: Nobody's out there in a race with each other. Other artists are not competition. They are fellow artists. I mean, that mentality wasn't back there in the '40s and '30s when Lester Young would come to Kansas City and try to blow out Coleman Hawkins. Is that a game the critics made up?

M.D.: No. But that's the trouble about it. He told me about Coleman Hawkins and his old lady.

J.E.: Who did?

M.D.: Lester Young. We went on a tour together. He said he had been waitin' on Coleman to come through Kansas City a long time. But his old lady was, "Where are you goin'?" Can you imagine that? Coleman's in town and he's got his horn. Ready to go out. So he knocked her down and went out. And when he came back he [made love to her].

J.E.: So where's that at in the context of musical community?

M.D.: Because they want to play together. Usually guys who want to play together get ideas from each other.

J.E.: They were playing together. They weren't seeing each other as competition in a bad sense.

M.D.: Yeah, it was competition.

J.E.: But in a good sense.

M.D.: Yeah. They both played two different styles. Bean [Hawkins] could never play like that. I used to rehearse the band. In those days, guys jammed together, you got ideas. Lionel Hampton wasn't the only guy throwing sticks on the floor. That came from St. Louis. When I was there, guys used to play like that. If a band wanted a show drummer, they'd come through St. Louis. Fats Navarro and I used to play together. He'd come get me and we'd go downtown and jam. You know, we'd go to Minton's and jam and we'd start soundin' alike when we were jammin'. And away from each other we'd play our own thing.

J.E.: Bird picked up a lot of his ideas from other people that came through K.C. before he split for New York.

M.D.: He had to. If you listen to Ben Webster, you can hear Bird. You can hear the same breaks, like in "Cottontail" and "C Jam Blues." It sounds just like Bird. And Ben was a supporter of Bird when people and critics didn't know what to write. You know, didn't know if he was a fluke. I was a young man then, and I know that movement was goin' on.

J.E.: The critics were confused?

M.D.: They were confused between Earl Bostic's speed and Jimmy Dorsey's, the way he played alto. . . . But Bird wasn't in any competition at all. He was just one of those things that happen every 100 years. I mean, he could do anything. He was a complete musician. He was just like Art Tatum. Art Tatum heard one of those player pianos with two people playin'. He thought it was one.

J.E.: And so, that's what he went with.

M.D.: Right. But Bird was just one of those people. And Duke Ellington. During Coleman Hawkins' time they had, just before with Fletcher

Henderson, Horace Henderson, Duke Ellington, they used to write an encore for the saxophone. . . . When bands used to play together they'd try—well, this isn't subtle at all, but they would have a battle of the bands; used to see the most difficult saxophone section solos. Not solos, but sections. Playin' an out chorus. Which is like what Ralph Burns wrote for Woody—"Four Brothers"; they used to do that all the time.

J.E.: And that was a capella?

M.D.: No. With the rhythm section. Horace Henderson's band. Fletcher Henderson and his brother and the arrangements they used to have. You can look back at Duke's old arrangements—they always had saxophone out choruses, you know? (*does some riffing*) "Cottontail." Doin' this they were soundin' like Bird (*more riffing*). And Bird's followers were dancers. That's the reason they played in two-part phrases. The time step was like (*demonstrates*). You know it was like two-bar phrases. That's the way you get that style. But he had about four or five styles. He had a style like that (*gets up and does a tap step*). You've seen it (*a "Tea for Two" step*), but fast. He wrote like that. (*He sings along with the step, to "Moose the Mooche."*) "Moose the Mooche" is like that. Free phrases. The way he writes it, it was different. When he first played it, Lucky Thompson put his saxophone down and started laughin'. He said, "Look at this." The notation was so different. When he first played it, Lucky Thompson had read, it wasn't like that (*more "Moose"*). You know, the accents comin' more differently. And now you have Prince, the way Prince writes. First beat and the third. Things that happen here that really hold it together. Like last night, I told our drummer, I said, "Marilyn," I told both of them, "I want something that hangs together." (*He counts off a four-beat measure, accenting the first and third beats.*)

J.E.: Kind of like a variation on a reggae beat?

M.D.: No, it's just somethin' that would hang a rhythm section together. You know, say like it's tiltin' a little bit and the rhythm section has a little wrinkle in it; you can do that, you can always pull it together (*counts off, again accenting the first and third beats*). It's not reggae. It comes from that, it comes from 4/4. Reggae's like a half (*counts off half-step beats*).

J.E.: It's a shuffle, almost like a tap dance?

M.D.: Like a half-shuffle.

J.E.: Getting back to playing, do you like the festival scene, the big crowds vs. the club days?

M.D.: There's nothing wrong with big audiences, you know? The only thing wrong is some halls, like Avery Fisher, the sound floats. And some of 'em, like—where did we play?—we played somewhere, and there was an echo, there was like a big (*makes echo sound*). That's all we'd use. It'd be funny, and we'd play around with it, play with it. But there's nothin' wrong with a good audience.

J.E.: So, is there anything to be gained from playing a small club anymore? Is there anything you miss about playing a small club?

M.D.: Yeah, the closeness, you know? You can hear each other and you get a better feelin'. When you're like tight, you know.

J.E.: What do you have planned ahead?

M.D.: I want to play music, try and get it on record. But in a live format—'cause live records are so great. You can feel the enthusism in everything, you know? And like I said, a record is only like a program. "This is what they might play, and it might sound like this. If it's worse, it would sound like this." But, there are so many pluses when you play in-person. You'd be surprised how different the band sounds with Marilyn and Benny. It's like a perfect marriage, you know. Marilyn is like a whole drummer. I have yet to tell her what to do. A drummer like her, she's a woman and she moves around when she plays; she knows when the shit don't fit 'cause she can feel it, you know? She's a helluva drummer, man. And Benny plays on top of the beat.

J.E.: You never went back to an orchestral setting. Have you thought about that much?

M.D.: I did one in Copenhagen. Yeah, this year. *Aura*. It was the last one I did for Columbia. I got this Sonning Award. It's like $10,000. It's an award that a guy set up. A rich guy in Copenhagen, I guess, Sweden. Leonard Bernstein, Isaac Stern and myself [have] gotten it. So I went over there. And of course they wanted me to play. So, I played and accepted the award. The radio band played it.

J.E.: Conceptually, what's happening?

M.D.: Well, Palle Mikkelborg wrote this composition that shows what I've done from . . . the styles I've played up 'til now. And he made a scale out of my name. And that's where I met Marilyn. We had about four drummers up there, 10 trumpets, we had a full brass section, saxophone stuff. About 20 pieces. So Palle, he wrote this composition, a helluva composition. I left Columbia. It was my last album.

J.E.: When was it recorded?

M.D.: About three years ago.

J.E.: And it's been in the can ever since?

M.D.: When I left Columbia, I went to the National Endowment for the Arts, 'cause they would pay for the last, to make an additional recording, which was $1,400 . . . And they [Columbia] wasn't interested, so I did it with some of my own money. And that's one of the reasons I left them.

J.E.: They were holding back?

M.D.: Well, one reason, they didn't put out "Time After Time," which I told 'em I'd done two years before they put it out. . . . Anyway, I left. Gotta good deal with Warner Bros. . . . One of the greatest rock 'n' roll records they [Columbia] ever heard was *Jack Johnson;* which it is. It's a motherfucker, you know? It just happened. I wrote it for Buddy Miles. But they buried it. Like, under "Film Music." Instead of puttin' it out and puttin' some thought into it, you know? You can give 10 minutes to anything and, think about it, it'd be better than what it is.

October 1988
Miles Davis: The Enabler, Part I
by Gene Santoro

There's an archetypal story told by nearly every musician I've ever talked to who's worked with Miles Davis. Melted down, its various versions run together something like this: "We were sitting in the studio jamming, and the tapes were rolling like they always were," says MilesMan. "Miles was just standing with his back to us, and all of a sudden he spun around and said, '(Fill in the blank with some very specific directive like, "Don't let me hear you playin' none of that bebop shit," or, "Why don't you learn how to leave some space in there?").' It was about the only straight direction I ever got from him."

There are other, more revealing angles to it, as Herbie Hancock has related different times to different folks, including on the excellent PBS-aired documentary *Miles Ahead*. "He told us to not practice," marvels the keyboard great. "He said that he was paying us to practice on the bandstand, at the gig; he wanted the freshness of conception that would come about that way. It's an amazing idea, being paid to practice in front of an audience."

He amplified that basic idea earlier this year in *DownBeat* (June 1988). As he told Josef Woodard, echoing his former boss, "Many times, I'll start with an idea and something else will come out of it. Rather than me try to follow the idea I originally had, I just go with what I have." When Woodard asked him if he'd learned some of his lessons about leading groups from Miles, Hancock replied, "Absolutely. About teamwork, listening and not being afraid to lean on the band for ideas and direction—allowing space for the band to be part of the direction. Miles never told us what to play, never told us what notes to play."

Welcome to the through-the-looking-glass world of Miles Davis, bandleader. If there are as many styles of leading a group as there are leader, Miles' approach has still got to rank among the most unusual—and, when the band lineup is equal to it, one of the most challenging and stimulating. Basically, it combines leadership with democracy.

Imagine this godfather standing in the studio, off to one side, silent, listening, only very occasionally even nodding his head to indicate some form of disapproval for their initiative. The posture allows him to feign omniscience and maintain his necessary critical distance from whatever is evolving; it also allows him to get people to do things he wants them to do, but without having to spell out just what that is, what the implications of any particular move will be. It frees up the horizon, and lets—in fact, makes—all that work itself out, in its own time, along its own dynamic, for each of the individuals involved. The sleight of hand involved is that, unlike a true padrino, it seems Miles rarely has a hidden agenda: He's there to hear what happens, and then deduce where it can go. Thus, his attitude forces players to be participants in the democratic model that we call a jazz combo even as it helps to clarify his next direction in the leader's restlessly searching mind.

But leading a band is more than a matter of personal style; to a large and very real extent, it helps determine the shape of music history. A couple of key examples should make how that comes down obvious.

Everybody knows (despite James Lincoln Collier's racist denigrations in his feeble attempt at a "revisionist" biography) how Duke Ellington set up what was essentially a closed feedback loop between himself and his band members. He kept his players on salary and used the studio and bandstand as compositional sketch pads. If during the course of a workout or jam a Johnny Hodges or a Tricky Sam Nanton or a Juan Tizol hooked a melodic idea that grabbed the Maestro, he'd seize it (sometimes with credit, sometimes not) and weave his rich orchestral tapestry around it. In the process, it would become a total composition, something living in a fully ramified way, quite apart from the scrawl or flash that had given it birth.

There's an odd way in which the nature of the relationship—which has functioned as a model for so many outstanding jazz leaders—helps explain why so few of Duke's sidemen ever went on to become imposing bandleaders in their own right, even aside from the very real socio-economic considerations involved. Everything that came out of Ellington's band flowed through his hands and was therefore shaped in his image, regardless of its genesis. Sure, he appropriated the players' input, and custom-wrote parts and solos with their personal attacks very much in mind, but in the end the overall sound, the nature of the material, became embedded in the ongoing body of work that was the Duke Ellington Band—despite changes of personnel, even despite their staggeringly individual voices.

Partly, of course, this resulted from the nature of a big band and the simple fact that its material had to be written in order to keep it coherent onstage; but that's not the only reason. Whenever Ellington shifted directions, the move tended to come in formal shifts, a change of compositional formats—from tunes to suites, for instance. Once he'd evolved it during his early days, the characteristic imprint of his sound remained, overall, fairly consistent.

Except for his own sound on trumpet—and even that has veered in different directions over the course of 40 years—there is no such sonic continuity in the equally long, equally fruitful, equally seminal career of Miles Dewey Davis III. Deliberately. Where Ellington's various lineups purposely maintained a strong link with their predecessors via compositions and arrangements, however elastic, Miles' groups are about change, often to the point of radical discontinuity. Each of them projects a divergent but characteristic feel that very much reflects not only the time and place surrounding that band whenever it flourished but its own internal makeup as well. It looks real simple, on paper, in hindsight.

Gather boppers who are big-band alumni, get big-band arrangers to radically revamp voicings and section work, and you've got the basic recipe—genius is always the unpredictable ingredient—for something like *Birth of the Cool*. Lose Cannonball Adderley, and the Coltrane-fired quintet that results speeds into regions Adderley would never have disturbed. Replace Red Garland with Bill Evans, and suddenly *Kind of Blue* creates a kind of revolutionary focus for the various paths that explorers as temperamentally and sonically unlike as Ornette and Mingus and George Russell and Sun Ra were following out. Use Tony Williams' fractured time signatures and frenetic pulses as the foundations to build a lineup upon, and the centripetal forces thrust outward to power Hancock, Shorter, Carter and the Boss himself while they undermine the notions of the hard-bop idiom, and thus allow the music to expand and be reformulated. Become intrigued by Jimi Hendrix and Sly Stone so that you delve into electronics and the favorite ax of the postwar baby boom, the electric guitar, and jazz-rock fusion spirals out. Obliterate the individual identities of your band, even to the point of refusing to list credits on your albums, because you become obsessed with textures rather than solos, and you wind up with the studio-intensive, rock-funk experiments on *On the Corner,* where the endless ribbons of tape can be edited and mixed in ultramodern fashion into nothing like what the individual band members may have had in mind when they were jamming in the studio. And so on, and so on.

From one perspective, then, Miles Davis as a leader is the epitome of Zen, the blank shrug that answers the clichéd question of which, creatively speaking, came first, the chicken or the egg, the band or the concept. From another, he's haunted—so fixed and focused on the never-ending flux of whipping up the currents of human life that he is driven by mortality and by mortality's flip side, the urge to write your name somewhere so others coming later will see you've passed this way. His method is to gather change's inevitable winds around him, to become the eye of the hurricane time after time—puns intended. And so he deliberately places his own creativity on the line, surrenders it to be at the mercy of the band he heads; his course is set to a large degree by the sounds raging from his personnel. Of course he picks them, but less to align with too many preconceived notions of where he's headed than because he's reacting to how they might get him someplace—and this is the key operable word in Miles' vocabulary—new.

What new is or will be, exactly, arises from the friction, the tension, the dialectic between Miles' studied technique of near non-direction and the band members' evolving sense of community and purpose, their gleaning from his oblique hints what salient points he's hearing about what they're doing. It completes an ironic circle, to say the least, one Duke's men would never have had to deal with. Miles' players are effectively always trying to guess what he's making of their attempts to guess what's on his mind, when in the end, of course, what he wants—and when it works, what he gets—is what's on their minds: He wants them to plot out their own methods for having the musical conversations we call improvisation. If it seems convoluted on paper, and if it's shredded more than one sideman's nerves, it just happens to be a remarkably flexible and democratic way to cohere a group. With the wrong individuals, if they lack either discipline or initiative to the large extent Miles demands, or even with the right individuals on the wrong night, it can make for more of a muddle than a statement. But then, that too is precisely Miles' point.

Miles himself spoke to me about it this way: "I don't lead musicians, man. They lead me. I listen to them and learn what they can do best. Like Darryl Jones play a bass line, and he forgets it. I won't. I'll say, 'Darryl, you did this last night, do it again.' He'll go, 'What?' I'll say, 'It's right there on the tape [of the show].' That's what gives playing that feeling, like when you see a pretty woman and say, 'Shit, wait a minute.' Listening to what they do and feeding it back to them is how any good bandleader should lead his musicians.

"I go nuts with the first interpretation of a piece. The musicians can fuck me around; if they do it wrong the first time, I'll go off. I'll say, 'Think about the note, think about what you gonna do.' Then again you have to think, they're trying to do what you want 'em to do. So sometimes I'll say, 'OK, show me what you want to do'—which is worse, nine times out of 10 (*laughs*). But you have to have that give and take. That's why athletes have coaches, know what I mean?"

November 1988
Miles Davis: The Enabler, Part II
by Gene Santoro

When a musician has gone through the rigorous training offered by the College of Hard-Bop Knowledge that's otherwise known as Art Blakey's Jazz Messengers, you can tell it almost immediately. There's a certain minimal level of polished sophistication, a guaranteed technical and emotional adeptness with the musical syntax of the stylistic language they've worked through while the dean egged them on to their limits with his chomping hi-hat and press rolls. This is one way the music can be taught: as an oral tradition that deals with each player one-on-one, taking off from basic musical skills and working out an individual voice that extends from those skills in front of peers and audiences on the spot, under pressure, in the glare.

It's a pedagogy that reaches back to the historical method of apprentice-ship, of teaching by a master. Schools, on the other hand, are based on the supermarket premise that you can buy training in a prepackaged format of courses and workshops and catalogs. As a result, they generally manage to produce competent players who can make fine studio musicians precisely because, in the end, they haven't undergone the two-step process of the oral tradition: first comes being weeded out, then follows the searching individu-ation that almost inevitably results from repeated scorchings on jam sessions and bandstands. Look at it this way: You can continue in most any music school as long as you come up with the tuition and pass the tests; you can continue playing gigs with Blakey only if you start from basic competence and grow—and when you've grown to the point when he deems you're ready, he throws you out of the next and into the real, live musical world to scramble for yourself. At that point, your chops become your weapons, your tools for survival.

But one reason for the apparent consistency among Blakey's graduates also points up a key weakness amid so much strength. From Bobby Watson to

Wynton Marsalis, their achievements tend to result from their focused—some would say narrowed—vision of the possibilities for the music, a concentration on a small musical segment sliced from the heterogeneous collection of genres bundled uncomfortably together under the much-hated and misleading rubric called jazz. Marsalis' constant preaching about the notion of jazz purity, so inherently misguided and weird about sounds that have been mongrelized from birth, derives as directly from his time with Blakey as does predilection for suits and ties on stage; if he sounds like a modern day fig, it's because he is.

And to a great extent, what he is is what Blakey helped make him. Where the master drummer's deep and fierce commitment to the sounds of his youth is not only understandable but typical—folks tend to cling to what they came up with—that same commitment sits oddly indeed on players often nearly a half-century his junior. And yet that commitment, in his case, seems to produce players in the mold.

In a way, it's an educational conundrum that turns on an unresolvable problem—the definition of jazz. On the one hand, the schools paint a false picture of musical ability and training with their freeze-dried concepts offered as a smorgasbord that—so the theory goes—anybody can sample from and then develop something to say; on the other hand, Blakey's educational method, though it more realistically weeds out wanna-bes from the real players and grounds the survivors in battle-tested techniques, seems from its results to be necessarily circumscribed by the syntactical and structural limits set down by his style. You learn them rigorously and well, but rarely do they get pushed passed the generic scope of hard bop into something truly different. So the point becomes nuance, finessing the accomplishments of the past, dotting Bird's i's and crossing Dizzy's t's.

Or, most ironically in Marsalis' case, endlessly reworking Miles Davis. Ironically because, in order to remake the chameleonic Miles into the figurehead image required by his neocon ideology, Marsalis and his cohorts have had to fit the ceaselessly changing contours of Miles' musical output onto their own hard-bopper's procrustean bed and lop most of the limbs off with wanton abandon. What makes the undertaking especially odd is, of course, the neocons' crude but insistent homiletic pieties about the Value of History and such.

For Miles Davis, history and musical education form a double-edged sword. His own background stressed bandstand learning over school training: remember that he came to the Big Apple ostensibly to study at Juilliard, but actually to enroll in beboppers' classes with Bird and Diz, and that even in St. Louis formal learning always attracted him less than jamming with players like Clark Terry. But remember, too, that even at his greenest he never mimed Dizzy's trumpet; instead, he deliberately sought a voice as utterly unlike his elder's as he could while still remaining musical. That drive alone distinguishes him from Blakey grads like Marsalis, who are more than content to bask in the sounds that made their septuagenarian Blakey a rebel when he was younger.

Miles himself nailed the problem, in these excepts from an interview with Howard Mandel in the December 1984 *DownBeat:*

"Wynton's a brilliant musician, but that whole school—they don't know anything about theory, 'cause if they did, they wouldn't be sayin' what they say, and doin' what they do.

"The only thing that makes Art Blakey's band sound good is Art. They're energetic musicians, yeah, but it's the same structure that we used to play years ago, and it's too demanding on you. You have to play the same thing . . . if you play a pattern of fourths, or parallel fifths, or half-step chords and all that stuff, nobody's gonna sound different on that—everyone sounds the same. Why do you think Herbie don't want to play that anymore? He'd rather hear scratch music. I'd rather hear somebody fall on the piano than to play that. That newness will give you something—more so than all the clichés you've heard from this record, that tape.

"The way you change and help music is by tryin' to invent new ways to play, if you're gonna ad lib and be what they call a jazz musician. . . . I thought everybody in the world, all the good trumpet players, played like Dizzy; when I got to New York, I found out things are different—you have to go your own way; you can't copy anybody. You know, just because you play a flatted fifth doesn't mean somebody's gonna hire you."

The fierce—and for him, unresolvable—dialect between past and present is at the heart of Miles' music; in fact, it pushes it relentlessly into the new. For Miles, anything new is what's important. Which isn't to say the new is always and automatically more valid than what came before—any notion of progress in art is problematic, and any notion of progress in art as an automatic evolution unfolding through this time is simply ludicrous. Was Miles "better" than Dizzy? Was Mozart "better" than Bach? Was Jimi Hendrix "better" than Robert Johnson? And how many angels can dance on the head of a pin? These are questions not worth asking, at least not in that form.

For Miles they're questions that are simply irrelevant. Some Hegelian notion of progress has nothing to to do with it; the iron law of change that runs through life itself is all that counts. Motion is life, stasis is death—it's as simple and as basic and as relentless as that. But change is not merely caprice or whim for Miles any more than it was for Darwin. Rather, it's a strategic interplay of forces—in Miles' case, the literal interplay on stage, and conceptually between himself and the musicians he picks for his band—that allows the chance of adaptation, and hence survival.

That's not just a conceit. The assumptions underlying all his musical moves are that nothing worth making comes without risk, and that you can't risk something you don't believe in or truly need. For Miles that something is his music. His vehemence toward critics comes at least partly from his constant awareness that what for him is life at its most fundamental is for them just another texture in a universe of sound.

Or actually, another set of textures—Miles in motion. And here is where we come back to Bu and the schools. Miles doesn't teach; he functions more like an agent provocateur within the context of what his musicians already know. Armed with the dynamite of his own history, knowledge and personality, he blasts them loose from what they've done before and perhaps try to repeat in his band. When the treatment takes—and, as with any pedagogy that's based around oral training an an apprenticeship system, it can't and isn't meant to take every time, just with the folks who can catch on to the particular master's technique and concepts—it opens up each musician's past for future explorations by forcing it to be reconsidered in a completely different light. In other words, it empowers them to discover their own voices.

It's a methodology that, like life, produces both successes and failures. But unlike the "success" imposed by the school-style training, its range is expansive: It sets no upper or lower limits by virtue of its alienated, fragmentary nature. And unlike the Jazz Messengers, it hoists no overarching musical credo as a banner to live for. How could it, since Miles' music at any given point is the product of a particular set of musicians and viewpoints colliding, firing, coalescing?

In that sense, it's Herbie Hancock who represents Miles' triumph as a teacher. Herbie can—and does—do it all, from his gently swinging acoustic piano music to movie soundtracks to the techno-funk hits that have drawn Marsalis' misdirected wrath. And yet, before he started with Miles, he was a Blue Note bopper dyed-in-the-keys. But he also embodies the outreach so valued by Miles that it's one of his few recurrent ground rules: "When you get through playin' what you know, then play somethin'."

Miles sees it this way: "You know, when I had Herbie, I'd say to him, 'Herbie, sometimes don't use your left hand.' If he'd do that he'd be much freer, like Ornette Coleman used to do; it's much freer to not have anyone shovin' you, you know? Those chords can be a cage. So when Herbie played without his left hand, goddamn, it was somethin' else.

"Now, I try to make my musicians avoid clichés by the way I write and arrange. I write all the clichés to this already, so once they've played all those things, the musicians got to find somethin' else to play (*laughs*). Gil did me like that. I'd say, 'Gil, man, you got every chord, every note that I was gonna play, you got it. Now what the fuck am I gonna play?' (*laughs*) So I played the melody."

Another triumph of Miles' pedagogy found ways to play every melody but the one that was written, proving again that one mark of a truly successful teacher is how well his best pupils can discard him. When John Coltrane signed on to Miles' outfit, he was an interesting post-bopper with a debt to Dexter Gordon. His rapid progression with Miles' fabled mid-'50s groups needs no rehash here. But, as he told Ralph Gleason at one of his own turning points in 1961, "I've been going to the piano and working things out, but now I think I'm going to move away from that. When I was working on those sequences that I ran across on the piano, I was trying to give all the instruments the sequences to play and I was playing them too. I was advised to try to keep the rhythm section as free and uncluttered as possible and if I wanted to play the sequences or run the whole string of chords, do it myself but leave them free. So I thought about that and I've tried that some, and I think that's about the way we're going to have to do it. I won't go to the piano anymore. I think I'm going to try to write for the horn from now on, just play around the horn and see what I can hear. All the time I was with Miles I didn't have anything to think about but myself, so I stayed at the piano and chords, chords, chords! I ended up playing them on my horn."

While Miles usually has kind words for graduates like Herbie and Chick Corea and Keith Jarrett, his highest accolade so far has been bestowed on Marcus Miller—he not only plays Miller's tunes, but has let Miller produce him and play nearly all the accompanying instruments. For a kid from south Jamaica who started playing bass because he dug the funk of Mandrill and Graham Central Station, it's a long way to come.

The way Miller tells it, "At that time I still didn't feel like I had an identity. Miles was the one who made me nail something down as far as style. See, the music he was playing didn't really have any predetermined bass style to it—I had to come up with something, and that forced me to come up with something of my own. The tape would just be rolling all the time, so sometimes it wouldn't be so hip, but sometimes it would be serious."

As serious as the next lesson in the book of Miles: "I learned to feel good about what I do, because it's a basic representation of myself; your playing is gonna get criticized or praised, so you better make sure it's you. If you start playing stuff you think people will like and then nobody likes it, you'll really feel like a jerk (*laughs*)."

And yet that "you" is not an exclusionary concept, but one that allows you to choose which other voices you'll accept as mentors based on your own needs. Sometimes it creates an awareness that extends past the musician's own literal knowledge simply because he's become a thread running through the vast and tangled history that is Miles Davis' music.

Listen, for instance, to the way Miller talks of how *Tutu* and *Siesta* were generated. "I saw it developing as a conversation between me and Miles. You know how jazz musicians used to do albums with the big bands: They'd play the melody, then solo for 16 bars, then play the melody again. That's how I envisioned these albums. Gil Evans was a big influence; I knew him, and I've really been influenced by him as a person. But I never really checked out *Sketches* [*of Spain*] until a couple of years ago.

"What I did check out, though, was one of my main influences—Herbie Hancock's writing, especially around his *Speak Like a Child* period. He was writing really interesting stuff, using chords he didn't even have names for—they just worked. Then one day I pulled out *Speak Like a Child* and I read on the back that Herbie during that period was inspired by Gil Evans (*laughs*). So now I understand why people tell me that *Tutu* sounds like *Sketches* for the '80s."

October 1991
Miles Plays Gil at Montreux
by Bill Milkowski

He has said "Time After Time" that he would never again tread on old musical ground, that it was against his "Human Nature" to go backward and play music from the past.

Well, miracles do happen.

It started with a fax from Montreux Jazz Festival founder Claude Nobs to the late Gil Evans' widow, Anita, saying that Quincy Jones had this marvelous idea. He wanted to re-create live *Sketches of Spain,* the classic Miles Davis album arranged and orchestrated by Evans. The catch? Quincy wanted Miles, in person, to play it as part of the festival's 25th anniversary.

"When Quincy first called me, I said, 'Of course we'd like to do it, but I can't imagine Miles doing it,'" said Anita, who provided some of Gil's original charts for the project. "'You don't have a problem here, you just gotta talk Miles Davis into it.' And Quincy said, 'I already have. I used love. I've been on him. I told him it would be my dream come true to do it.'"

With that, a miracle was conceived, nurtured and born. Miles, for the first time, accepted the challenge to go back more than 30 years and perform the arrangements of Gil Evans from not only *Sketches of Spain,* but also from *Birth of the Cool, Miles Ahead* and *Porgy and Bess.*

Billed as "L'Evenement" (the Event), the festival ground buzzed with anticipation. Could Miles, the renegade of the cutting edge, turn back time? Could he leave his funk and fusion trappings backstage and, for one fine evening, embrace these classic scores? After all these years, did he still have the chops to put his muted touch on complicated Gil Evans arrangements?

"I called up Quincy after the first rehearsal and said, 'You know, we really gotta get Miles,'" said arranger Gil Goldstein, who transcribed a great deal of the material. "Then I started to get nervous about Miles being able to play all of this stuff without coming to a rehearsal, because it's a hell of a lot of music. It's like classical music. You have to play it with the orchestra."

Miles didn't attend rehearsals in New York, where a combination of the Gil Evans Orchestra and the George Gruntz Concert Jazz Band met to prepare for the gig. He opted to catch up with the band at Montreux.

"But, I did bring the music to his house before he left, just so he could start looking at it," Goldstein said. "The first rehearsal in Montreux was full of confusion. A million things were still up in the air as far as details of what was really gonna happen. People were uptight about various business issues. It was just a kind of nervous not-knowing-what-was-going-to-happen environment. Quincy showed up at 2 p.m. That was the first time we had actually met face to face.

"By 11 p.m., Miles showed up. It was unbelievable, just the perfect entry for Miles Davis. We were rehearsing 'Boplicity' [from *Birth of the Cool*] and he just kind of walked in right at the first phrase, sat down and started taking out his horn."

The next evening, Miles received a hero's welcome as he made his way to the Casino stage and took his place before the 45-piece ensemble. With Quincy conducting, they opened with the lush, lightly swinging "Boplicity." And, from the first notes, all doubts were erased. The crowd was transported to jazz heaven.

One of the most enraptured listeners in the house was Quincy himself, who conducted the piece with obvious glee, smiling like a child on Christmas morning. After the number, he remarked to the crowd, "This is a great way to feel 17 again."

The sight of Miles Davis performing this classic material from the 1950s was like watching Muhammad Ali climb back into the ring with his jab intact. For jazz purists, it was a monumental comeback, a welcome return to the fold after years of jiving and vamping. Miles showed up and delivered the goods, blowing with the kind of confidence, soulful phrasing and dramatic power that few critics thought he still had in him.

Sitting up front alongside Miles were soloists Wallace Roney on trumpet and Kenny Garrett on alto saxophone. Roney functioned as a kind of safety net, occasionally doubling Miles' parts. This not only relieved Miles of any pressure of having to cut the difficult passages single-handedly, it also freed him up to take greater liberties with the melodies through his own adventurous phrasing.

The Miles magic was very much intact throughout the *Miles Ahead* medley. His seductive, muted trumpet work on "Springsville" and "My Ship" caused audible sighs from the audience and had Roney shaking his head in disbelief. The tone was captivating, unmistakably Miles; the lines characterized by masterful restraint, uncanny use of space, and a kind of sly, behind-the-beat phrasing on ballads that once caused Gil Evans to call him "a sensational singer of songs."

Miles' skillful timing was especially apparent on the title cut from *Miles Ahead,* which also featured a flowing, boppish alto solo from Garrett. On "Blues for Pablo," Miles engaged in spirited open-horn exchanges with Roney, who, throughout the program, would glance over at his hero with the eyes of a rookie watching Babe Ruth.

The idea of having Roney shadow Miles came up spontaneously during the first day of rehearsals at Montreux. "Miles didn't show up and we needed somebody to play his part," said Goldstein. "At first, we were going to have [trombonist] Benny Bailey do it, but at the last minute we gave it to Wallace Roney, who was one of the trumpets in George Gruntz's band. So, Wallace was up there playing Miles' part when Miles finally walked in during 'Boplicity.' Wallace just kind of stayed up there and started playing unison lines and trading solos with Miles.

"It was a great experience for him, and I think Miles really dug playing with him. And, I don't think that anybody could've done it as good as Wallace did in terms of just having real courtesy and respect and still play his ass off. He had to walk a kind of fine line between being a brat and being totally respectful. And, I think he was both."

But onstage, others were playing their asses off, too. Mike Richmond supplied a formidable bass presence, anchoring the pieces along with Grady Tate, whose brushwork on "My Ship" was sublime. Kenwood Dennard took over the drum chair on "Gone" from *Porgy and Bess* and kicked the band into high gear, inspiring some fiery eights between Miles, Roney and Garrett.

Miles dug deep on "Summertime," another muted-trumpet vehicle for the maestro, buoyed by a cushion of oboes and alto flutes. Delmar Brown added an earthy edge here with some lively, syncopated keyboard comping. Garrett responded with his finest solo of the evening, blowing more horn than he's ever had a chance to play in the context of Miles' electric band. Garrett also contributed some strong alto work on "Here Come de Honey Man," though

Miles seemed indifferent to this serenely melodic piece, virtually laying out and relying on Roney to cover his parts.

The evening closed dramatically with two pieces from *Sketches of Spain*. With glasses in place, Miles diligently read the charts down, navigating his way through "Pan Piper" (which, unfortunately, was marred by a sharp E string on Carlos Benavent's electric bass) and culminating beautifully with the flamenco-flavored "Solea."

The next day, a group gathered to watch the videotape of "L'Evenement" at Claude Nobs' chalet in the mountains. Members of the orchestra stood in awe of the aching tone, the vocal expression, the sheer power and unpredictable choices that Miles made throughout the evening. If a videotape of this performance is ever made available, a lot of skeptics are going to have to eat their words. (Memo to Messrs. Wynton Marsalis and Stanley Crouch: Dinner is served.)

"It was really a struggle sometimes getting all of the diverse realities together for this," said Anita Evans. "It just seemed unbelievable that it could happen. Every year for the past 25 years somebody would call up and ask Gil if they would get together and do it again. Depending on what year, either Gil would refuse or Miles would refuse. So, I had long ago gotten over the thought that I could possibly ever hear that happen. Gil was always thinking about the future or what he was doing next. He didn't want to look back. Miles had the same attitude. And, after all, some of this paper hadn't been unfolded in 34 years.

"So, you can imagine, it must have been scary for [Miles], not that he would ever admit it. But he braved it out, he showed up, and the music was beautiful. All the elements were set into place, then Miles came in and did what he does . . . those magical tones and colors, his masterful sense of time and space. He just breathed his Miles Davisness at the right moment while the orchestra played the stuff. I'm still floating over how beautiful it sounded."

Perhaps trumpet veteran Lew Soloff put it more succinctly: "That's one soulful motherf**ker."

In character, Miles didn't speak after the show, but his feelings about the music were captured in more ways than through his playing. "To me, one of the nicest things of the whole experience happened on the last rehearsal," Goldstein said. "I kind of walked over to Miles to give him some changes I had written out, and he was just standing there listening to the band rehearse *Sketches,* and he said, 'Nobody will ever write like that again.' It was obvious that he loves Gil's writing, but it was just nice to hear him say it again."

December 1991
Miles—A Life
by Howard Mandel

Miles Davis, the trumpeter and composer whose restless musical innovations and provocative image affected world culture with the values of jazz, died Sept. 28, 1991, at St. John's Hospital and Health Center in Santa Monica, Calif., where he'd been hospitalized for weeks following a stroke.

Davis, born May 25, 1926, in Alton, Ill., and raised in East St. Louis, Ill., was given a trumpet for his 13th birthday. Two years later he had a union card so he could perform with Eddie Randall's Blue Devils. Clark Terry was his mentor, and Davis filled in for an ailing trumpeter with Billy Ecsktine's band in 1944. That September he enrolled at Juilliard School of Music in New York and was befriended by Charlie Parker and Dizzy Gillespie, who brought him into bebop circles. The next year, Davis recorded with singer "Rubberlegs" Williams and quit his formal training. In November 1945, he recorded "Now's the Time" and "Ko-Ko" in Parker's quintet. Davis' August 1947 debut as a recorded leader featured Parker on tenor saxophone.

In 1948, with a coterie of composers, arrangers and players who gathered at Gil Evans' 52nd Street apartment, Davis formed a nine-piece band that originally recorded *Birth of the Cool.* In 1954, he overcame the effects of heroin addiction to affirm his singular style and talents as a soloist, songwriter and combo leader. Recordings with Sonny Rollins, Horace Silver and Thelonious Monk preceded Davis' establishment of a memorable, popular and influential quintet with John Coltrane, Red Garland, Paul Chambers and Philly Joe Jones, documented on Prestige and Columbia Records.

Davis' speaking voice, permanently scarred from shouting soon after throat surgery, reflected the intimate import of his trumpet sound. His elegance and extravagance, dramatic outbursts and lyrical moodiness were mirrored in his lifestyle, which fascinated fans who might otherwise know little of jazz.

Davis, however, never rested on his achievements or celebrity. He progressed from a classic modal album, *Kind of Blue,* to interpretations of Gershwin's *Porgy and Bess* and Joaquin Rodrigo's "Concierto de Aranjuez," both orchestrated for large ensembles by Gil Evans. His great acoustic '60s quintet gave way to breakthroughs in electrically amplified and studio manipulated albums, including the jazz-rock foundation *Bitches Brew.* Davis experimented with extended free improvisations, funk and new pop formulations, also creating jazz soundtracks.

In 1975, afflicted with health problems and drug habits, Davis retired, returning with the 1980–'81 album *The Man With the Horn.* Throughout his last decade he toured and recorded prodigiously, co-wrote with Quincy Troupe *Miles: The Autobiography* and accepted a Grammy Award for lifetime achievement. His final performances were re-creations of his Gil Evans collaborations conducted by Quincy Jones and a reunion concert in Paris with protégés and friends from diverse phases of his career. Davis' three marriages ended in divorce: He had three sons, a daughter and four grandchildren. A memorial service Oct. 5 at St. Peter's Lutheran Church was attended by several hundred admirers. The Rev. Jesse Jackson, Bill Cosby, Quincy Jones, Herbie Hancock, Max Roach and George Wein were among the speakers, and the rock star Prince's letter was read.

December 1991
I Don't Wanna Be Kissed
by John Ephland

The Prince is dead. I first heard about it in a local bookstore, when the owner recognized me and asked if I knew that Miles Davis just died. He happened to be listening to National Public Radio when the first few strains of "Blue in Green" wafted through the store, followed by a voice reporting the details of Miles' passing.

Miles is no more. Even if a certain record company chooses to bless us with any of its vast quantity of unreleased material, there will be no more new Miles, not to mention live performances, controversial brushes with the media or interviews.

The void created that fall afternoon found me tumbling back through the years, remembering the riches bestowed upon a young, awestruck music lover by a jazz trumpeter in the throes of one marvelous muse after another. *Kind of Blue* was a revelation. *Porgy and Bess* was a love song shared with a junior high sweetheart. *"Four" & More, My Funny Valentine,* back to *Milestones* and the Prestige sides and forward again to the '60s quintet albums. Coltrane, Bird, Gil, Bill, Monk, Newk, J.J., Tony, Jack, Wayne, Philly Joe . . . the list seems endless. Yeah, a new album from Miles was just that, new! "Directions in Music by Miles Davis": *Filles de Kilimanjaro, In a Silent Way, Bitches Brew.*

Miles was inconsistent, contradictory, his autobiography a maze of occasionally interesting but generally unsettling revelations, his fits of violence and abrasiveness saddening, and his penchant for celebrity status and anything new—all these realities could be distractions to the music. As with many great artists, however, Miles was a man largely misunderstood. Having met and interviewed him for *DownBeat,* it was obvious to me that, like Mingus, Miles' rough, volcanic exterior protected a shy, warm and lyrical underbelly.

Musically speaking, to say that Miles eventually "turned butt to the beautiful in order to genuflect before the commercial," as writer Stanley Crouch recently put it, is to miss the point. A conservative position on jazz, which allows little or no room for musical dialog (with rock 'n' roll, "European devices," whatever), is a prescription for folk music only, insulated and codified and one diametrically opposed to Miles' artistic thirst for imagination, possibility and open sky. Not just a trumpet stylist, Miles the conceptualist and bandleader has changed forever the way we hear music. As J.J. Johnson stated after learning of Miles' death: "There's no question that Miles was one of the key figures in the evolution of jazz since the 1940s—maybe *the* key figure."

Several months ago, we at *DownBeat* began planning a special issue to celebrate Miles' career. Sadly, it's become his memorial. Things around the office are different these days. There's an unsettling buzz, phone conversations with relevant parties, requests to send flowers to family, even a cartoon and poems for Miles faxed and mailed to us.

The balance has shifted. And people feel it down deep. In this special issue on Miles Davis, we hope you find solace, not to mention a little big fun.

December 1991
Sketches of Miles
by Howard Mandel

For those who've come to jazz during any of the 45 years since America got hip in the aftermath of World War II, it's hard to accept that Miles Dewey Davis III—Junior, the Cool One, the Black Prince, the Man with the Horn—is dead. All his life he was a survivor. The precocious and relatively privileged son of a rural Illinois oral surgeon, Miles dropped out of conservatory training to study the hard blues of New York City nights in the fast company of Bird, Diz, Monk, Newk, Blakey—and he never looked back. Brilliantly original and rangy, he forged an international career of mass popularity, artistic credibility and influence, winning a total of 29 *DownBeat* polls for best trumpeter in the process. He was a public contradiction, apparently arrogant but at some musical core tender and shy, he was always in touch with his tradition but always ahead—*way* ahead—of the pack.

"Miles' sound entered into whatever he played," says Jackie McLean, who essayed Davis' originals "Bluing," "Dig," "Out of the Blue" and "Denial," plus the standards "My Old Flame" and "It's Only a Paper Moon" in October 1951 as a 16-year-old alto saxist in the 25-year-old trumpeter's band. "I didn't love all the things he did in the later years with his fusion bands, but as long as *he* was playing he captured that tone, and the music was his."

What a tone it was, and what it sang of Miles' soul! Crisp and/or cooing, crooning, muted or mewling, fierce as though shredding complacency or tender as a man treading on eggshells, Miles' playing the trumpet is at once and forever identifiable and inimitable.

"I admired that," McLean admits, "and wanted it—a real personal sound, a sound people could recognize in just a couple of notes as *mine*." What Miles' sound said created controversy throughout a musical community, reacting in thrall or dismay to his dry but overtone-rich, middle-register "voice," the poised charts of *Birth of the Cool,* the dramatic economy of his '50s combos, the moody modal lyricism of *Kind of Blue,* the orchestral manifestations conducted by Gil Evans, the fluid freedoms of Miles' '60s quintet, his psychedelic adventures in the later '60s, excesses of the '70s, reemergence in the '80s, and completely uncharacteristic recapitulation of old times in Montreux and Paris just last summer. Ironically, touchingly, the pioneer of future jazz—personal expression over basic blues structures and vamps (not to exclude composed passages and processes), taking advantage of popular rhythms, tunes and state-of-the-art studio techniques—ended up reprising his roots and early successes, performing Gil Evans' scores and his own hits with famous sidemen of his past.

"To me, the fusion wasn't serious enough or deep enough," says McLean, citing an unorthodox position on Davis' exploration of music far from the bop with which he'd begun. "Miles played a very technical, traditional music before 1969, following Ellington and all the great masters. Then, for fame or money or something—I'm sure *not* because of his musical tastes—he decided to go this other way. I like some of the newer stuff. 'Mandela' and a few other tunes. And you've got to give him credit: he's the one who set up this whole marriage between rock 'n' roll, or rhythm 'n' blues, and traditional jazz. He opened up a whole market for people who play something heavier than 'Here come Charlie' four-chord rock."

This view prevails among many players of Miles' generation: Tommy Flanagan, Jimmy and Percy Heath, Milt Jackson, J.J. Johnson, John Lewis, Max Roach and Art Taylor from his Blue Note and Prestige albums come to mind. Since trumpeter Wynton Marsalis assumed a jazz leadership role, adapting some of the look and attitudes Miles posed in the '50s upon joining Columbia Records, the reboppers have embraced this opinion, too. But some musicians appraise Davis' post-acoustic jazz otherwise.

"Every style he played became a genre," keyboardist Gil Goldstein pro-claims, waiting at the bar at Sweet Basil before a set with the loud, young Miles Evans band. Goldstein prepared Gil Evan's fragmentary charts for Davis' Montreux fest concert at Quincy Jones' request, and is a font of back-stage stories regarding that videotaped event. "Even the things everybody hated, that the musicians said were bullshit, now they're all styles. To me, that makes the whole thing about Wynton and their debate so stupid. How are you going to compare these guys? *Everything* Miles did became a classic."

Chick Corea, among other collaborators from Miles' last 25 years, agrees. "He put the cap on a certain style of acoustic jazz music with Herbie and Ron and Tony and Wayne," Corea says of Davis' great combo with Hancock and Carter and Williams and Shorter. "And then he let the world of changing harmonies go, started going into vamps and jungle music, primitive rhythms and abstracted melodies. The years *we* were on tour"—Corea worked from '68 to '70, with Shorter, Dave Holland, Keith Jarrett, Joe Zawinul, David Liebman, Steve Grossman, Jack DeJohnette and various others—"the sets I played in would be one improvisation from beginning to end with a few little cues from Miles to change the tempo or the key. Every tune we played was in this incredible abstract form; the meat of the rendition was a free improvisation."

Though one of the most experimental, transitional and productive periods of Miles' prime, he was poorly documented from the late '60s to the mid-'70s. "They [Columbia] never released any live stuff from that band—it was too 'out,' I think. There's not much you could say about this music or do with it," Corea suggests. "There weren't any particularly memorable melodies or songs. But I remember a fun, searching energy and spirit of improvisation. There never was a studio version of the music we played, either."

Teo Macero, Davis' Columbia producer from *Kind of Blue* in '59 through *Star People* in '83, regrets dozens of lost opportunities and notions gone awry. "CBS didn't want live albums of Miles," he reports. "Some executive would always want him to go back to a quartet setting, or do another *Sketches of Spain*—not that they liked *that* when it was recorded. I used to tell them, 'He's a great artist. You can't screw around with a great artist, you've got to encourage him to move forward.' He should have done something with the London Philharmonic. He and Gil wanted to do something together again.

"Miles changed every five years, whenever he got a new girlfriend. I thought *Jack Johnson* was a step in the right direction. I wanted to put out a record every month by Miles. I wanted to take a sound truck on the road with the band and record everything they did. But I didn't control the purse strings. Even his covers were controversial, the cartoons, the big-bellied black lady on *Big Fun*—and I had to fight the stupidity every day.

"As documentation, there are cassettes that Miles gave me, recorded on the road, and takes that are still in the can at Columbia or here in my place, which are important parts of his legacy. He paid his dues, but his was a typical artist's life. The work is not recognized until they're gone. I can't believe that still goes on."

Miles was no Van Gogh—more like Picasso. Most, if not all, dimensions of his music, sound and attitude were hailed worldwide during his life. Still, his death sends us back to our memories and record collections, seeking out the overlooked pleasures. The music is put in fresh perspective by the passage of his time, and ours.

"I think there's more to be understood than what we've gotten so far," says Dan Morgenstern, director of the Institute for Jazz Studies at Rutgers University. "Especially that music of the '60s starting with *Miles Smiles* and going to *Filles de Kilimanjaro*, which is a step toward the fusion stage. *Bitches Brew* and all that has some fascinating stuff that the people who were involved, except perhaps Wayne Shorter, didn't pursue. And I'd like to point out that Miles was quite a trumpet player. Listen to the way he plays with Tadd Dameron on that Paris Jazz Festival date in '49. He's playing off Dizzy, he hits some high notes, he plays that bebop. There are people who say he created his own spare, lyrical style because he couldn't play the other stuff. I don't think that's true. He could have cut it, if he wanted to pursue that.

"Instead, he found his own voice, which is the point of the whole thing. And it wasn't by default. He could hit some pretty incredible notes even in his 60s."

What was incredible about those notes, and what remains so elusive of the analysis of Miles' art, is the power of personality behind them. "There's this one track on *Miles and Monk at Newport,* with Coltrane and the sextet, which is one of my favorite Miles performances," Chick Corea recalls. "They do a version of 'Straight No Chaser,' an F blues, and his solo on it, four choruses or so, is totally marvelous, simple masterpiece. I've listened to it over and over again, and once for a lark I transcribed it, wrote it down.

"Miles' solos are really interesting to look at on music paper, because there's nothing to them. On a Trane solo or Charlie Parker solo, you can string the notes out and see all the phrases and harmonic ideas, patterns, all kinds of things. Miles doesn't use patterns. He doesn't string notes out. It's weird. Without the expression, and without the feeling he put into it, there's nothing there."

"What I learned from Miles is that he goes with his feelings of the moment," says guitarist John Scofield, who toured with Davis from '82 to '85, recording *Star People, Decoy, You're Under Arrest* and bits of the soundtrack *Siesta*. "You have to learn to trust your own human instrument to read what's supposed to happen. That, for me, is the great message from Miles.

"We would play in huge venues to thousands of people, and he was able to reach those people and have them love the music. They loved it because of a feeling that came from his trumpet playing and the mood of the musicians around him. He was able to convey that to us in unspoken ways, and create a mood though music right there on the spot. Not the same mood as the night before . . . different, but picking up on certain things.

"It made me realize the power of his tradition, which I think *is* the jazz tradition," Scofield reasons. "I've never met anybody who is more of a bopper."

"*Siesta* and *Tutu* were projects," explains Marcus Miller, the multi-instrumentalist who produced Miles' three albums on Warner Bros., and continues working with people like Luther Vandross and Dave Sanborn. "They were not representative of how he usually made music. I envisioned *Amandla* as closer to the sound of his band, with Ricky Wellman on drums, Foley on guitar and Kenny Garrett playing alto. I would never contend that what he did could compete with what Miles did in the '50s, but it served a purpose in his career.

"What Miles told me was, 'Hey man—you brought me back!' People were talking about him again. I put rhythms that are going on now with elements that Miles had been into before. A lot of people could relate to that. I got him out from behind his mute, so you could hear that beautiful tone. Older people with open minds enjoyed it, and young people *loved* it.

"The first thing I learned from Miles was about being true to yourself," Miller explains. "Here was a guy who was acclaimed and criticized, and nothing that was ever said to him made him change what he felt he had to do. That's very important for a musician to learn, because you can be so easily swayed by people who have nothing to do with what you're about. They only know what you've already done; they have no idea of your goals.

"You've heard people say, when their parents have died, they finally feel like adults? Even if they're in their 50s? That now they're really on their own? Musically, I feel that way about Miles. I'm on my own now. This is it now. Figure out what to do, and do it. Right now, I'm working on an instrumental record of my own."

In that sense, Miles may yet serve as a father to us all.

May 1993
The Digs
by Bob Belden

Since the death of Miles Davis (Sept. 29, '91), much has been stated or rumored about his great legacy, both from a recording standpoint as well as personally. Where is he buried? Where are his horns? What music is in the can? How many more tributes can we expect?

Well, to begin, Miles Davis is buried at Woodlawn Cemetery in the Bronx. He lies near the Duke Ellington family site. One of his horns is buried with him and the rest are in his family's possession. All of his personal effects remain with the family, including music, scores, tapes and mementos. His family has sought protection from unauthorized uses of the Miles Davis name by incorporating and copyrighting (for trademark purposes) his name. All merchandise with his image must bear the © mark or you'll know that it's illegal.

As far as the music is concerned, let's start with the definitive discography on Miles compiled by Jan Lohman, *The Sound of Miles Davis* (Jazz Media), available through True Blue Music, Stamford, Conn. The book lists 925 recording sessions in chronological order. No doubt, this will serve as a guide for many a "Milesologist" as well as a pain for Columbia, Prestige and Warner Bros., the labels that hold the lion's share of his music. The PBS show that featured Miles, *Miles Ahead,* has been updated to include scenes from Montreux '91, the now-famous concert with Quincy Jones (see *DB* October '91).

Now for the CD news. The seven-CD *Complete Live at Plugged Nickel 1965* import from Sony Japan was a very limited item, and apparently will not be reissued again (see "Reviews" October 1992). Tower Records in New York City couldn't even get them on the floor, this set was so hot. Collectors are paying $250–$350 for it. The question arises as to what Columbia will do when there are so many rabid fans for the music.

Well, Columbia plans to release a series of CD boxed sets of unissued material with original albums, all in chronological order. In June, we'll see the rerelease of *The Sorcerer, On the Corner, Miles in the Sky* and *Miles and Monk at Newport.* As a bonus, Columbia says it will issue *Miles Ahead* in its original version, not the CD of second takes that's on the shelves now. (So, buy the available *Miles Ahead* now, because it's bound to be an instant collector's item.) According to Columbia's Gary Pacheco, the label intends to reissue all of Miles' Columbia albums. Longtime Miles producer Teo Macero has been busy assembling unreleased material that should start flowing soon. He has found the "lost" 1963 *The Time of the Barracudas* session with frequent collaborator Gil Evans and Miles that was a suite for a play that was never used. Herbie Hancock, Ron Carter and Tony Williams round out the 13-piece band.

Macero says there "is a lot more material than people" still in the can, and that Columbia is finding new stuff all the time. How many CDs will be issued is not known, but needless to say, there are still treasures in the vaults.

Miles Grammy-winning album *Doo-Bop* (Warner Bros.) has reached nearly 300,000 sales worldwide. According to Warners publicist Bill Bentley, the "Montreux '91" concert will be released May 25, with a video due out May 11. The fate of the "Paris '91" concert—with Hancock, Wayne Shorter, John McLaughlin and Joe Zawinul among the performers with Miles—has not been decided due to the immense undertaking of artist clearances. Warners, unlike other companies, actively pursues the issuing of bootleg CDs, and has stopped many from coming out. Warners only has rights to a few more Miles sessions, and those will be chosen carefully.

People in tribute to Miles? Many. Saxophonist and former Davis sideman Joe Henderson (*So Near, So Far,* for Verve—see "Reviews" March '93), Byron Olson (*Sketches of Miles,* Angel), *The Miles Davis Trumpet Tribute* (Columbia), Keith Jarrett (*Bye Bye Blackbird,* ECM) and Herbie Hancock all have lovely tributes. Hancock has been on tour with a tribute band, and Blue Note may issue a live album with the group (Hancock's recording is with Shorter, Ron Carter, Tony Williams and Wallace Roney—see *DB* Sept. '92). And Qwest Reprise has plans for a fall release of their own with this band. Trumpeter Sal Marquez waxed *One for Dewey* (GRP). Individual tracks dedicated to Miles: Jack DeJohnette ("Miles," on *Fifth World Anthem,* Manhattan), the Yellowjackets ("Dewey," GRP), Wolfgang Muthspiel ("Miles," Antilles). Concerts: Carnegie Hall with Zawinul, Dave Liebman and Wallace Roney at Manhattan School of Music and in Japan in August '92 at the Mt. Fuji Festival, and Freddie Hubbard and Terumasa Hino joining the Bob Belden Ensemble for a tribute to both Miles and Gil Evans.

So there is your news update. I'd like to be more specific about the dates of releases, but the major labels tend to shift their needs as circumstances change. Questions/predictions/wish list for the future: I'd like to see a movie made, one with the music in the foreground. As for reissues, how about "The Complete Miles Davis/Gil Evans Collaborations"? With the success of *Doo-Bop,* will Columbia issue more electric and crossover Miles?

All in all, the future looks bright for the legacy of Miles Davis. There are critics and historians who tend to dismiss or underplay the significance of Miles' contributions, but with the complete picture coming into sharper focus every day, his music is bound to be the final testament. That music will prove to be, as close collaborator Teo Macero believes, "one of the greatest musical legacies of the 20th century."

December 1995
Miles . . . "What Was That Note?"
For the record, former friends and collaborators celebrate the legend who played it one note at a time.
by Bob Belden and John Ephland

A voice shouts from the audience, "Ray Brown! Paul Chambers! Percy Heath!" as the bassist begins to solo. A heckler? Another bass player? No, it's just a cat from the neighborhood that really digs the band, especially Ron Carter. And he's not afraid to show it. Thirty years later that "heckling" actually "seems to indicate to me that the listening audience at that time had a great sense of jazz history. They weren't coming in for the first time. They were coming there because they knew of the history, not only of music vis-à-vis Paul Chambers *and* Ray Brown, but they were familiar with Miles Davis' personnel before I got there."

Thirty years ago this month, this little vignette was taped and is now generally available stateside for us to hear because Columbia Records, along with Mosaic Records, has begun an ambitious program to release every note that Miles recorded for the label from 1955 until 1976. Starting with *The Complete Live at the Plugged Nickel* and continuing with *Miles Davis and Gil Evans: The Complete Studio Recordings,* most of the Miles Davis legacy will be restored to the highest standards in the industry.

Ron Carter's poignant recollection of this unknown fan explains why playing in clubs was so special. "We got a lot more playing time [as a group] then," remembers Carter. "A lot more time to develop a band library, develop a band camaraderie, to develop a band personnel, a personality with the audience, a chance to work out details in the course of an entire night. It was a great environment to play in." But it took some time for Miles and the group to get to that magical, developmental place.

The first step in moving forward was to scout out new talent. In December of 1962, Davis and his former sideman Philly Joe Jones went to a club to hear a new drummer in town. Philly Joe raved about his playing, and that impressed Miles. It was Tony Williams. Miles also needed to find a new bass player, so again he checked out a new young bassist on the scene. "I was working with Art Farmer at the Half Note," says Carter. "[Miles] took me to a corner, and said that he was putting together a new band and wanted to know if I could leave for California next week." This band was Frank Strozier, George Coleman, Harold Mabern, Carter and Jimmy Cobb. When Davis returned to New York in May of 1963, he kept Coleman and Carter, and added Williams and Herbie Hancock to the quintet.

"We kind of sensed that this was going to be the band for a while," recalls Carter of his first rehearsal with Hancock and Williams. "And once we had the sense that this was the band for a while, rather than just another six-week tour, it became kind of more free. You could try things out, knowing that your job doesn't depend on the success or failure of what you do at that moment."

This sense of freedom would play a big part in the making of the quintet. By the time George Coleman had left and Sam Rivers joined the group in 1964, the direction was ". . . kind of stretching out," according to Sonny Fortune, who saw this quintet. But when Wayne Shorter joined in August of 1964, the dam finally burst wide open.

This quintet spent nine months getting familiar with each other, and the concept and attitude were dramatically affected. The direction of any given number would suddenly shift to another sphere, and that would lead to another, and so on. The quintet made one live album, *Miles in Berlin,* and one studio album, *E.S.P.* But by April of 1965, Miles stopped performing due to a hip ailment. The quintet became a quartet and continued to play whatever gigs they could. "When Miles didn't make a set, we became the 'Miles Davis Quartet,'" says Marshall Hawkins, the bassist who replaced Carter on live gigs in '68. (Hawkins had left Shirley Horn to go with Miles.) This quartet format is where Wayne and the rhythm section would experiment. (Williams' "Pee Wee," on Miles' *Sorcerer,* is an example of the quartet sound.)

After a long layoff, Miles began to play again. A gig in Philadelphia with Reggie Workman subbing for Carter and a week in Detroit with Gary Peacock set the stage for the quintet's December '65 engagement in Chicago. The Plugged Nickel was hardly the setting for a legendary recording. "The club was 20 feet wide and 100 feet long," says trumpeter Bill Byrne, who performed at the club often with Woody Herman from 1965 to '67. "It had a long bandstand like the Metropole in New York, but it barely held 100 people. It was in the nightclub district near Rush Street, and musicians liked the room."

On the first night, Reggie Workman was flown in to play. From the second night on (Dec. 22), Carter was back and the tapes rolled. Many herald this recording as Miles' first real venture into stream-of-conciousness playing, but as Dave Liebman points out, "It is really the end of an era, certainly regarding Miles' playing. But what's great about it is that he has these young cats, especially Herbie and Tony playing standards from such a different standpoint. That's why it's such a remarkable record. I mean, I couldn't see them going into the studio and doing another version of 'Green Dolphin Street.'"

The catalyst for many of the band's forays into the unknown was Carter. "My concern," Carter says, "was, could I make these guys play something different and/or develop what they had developed, or begun to develop, the night before or the set before?" The first impression for some people is that the band played free. "I think that the idea of being free, as is generally defined, is a great misnomer," observes Carter.

"This band has always been my favorite for really taking chances, but still keeping the form," admits John Scofield. "But I think that it was a time in jazz when freedom and free music had influenced the young guys who were playing form."

Or, as Shorter puts it, "When we played there was a lot of chance-taking. We had arrived at that point where Herbie fully fathomed what Miles was talking about, about when to play and when to not play as an accompanist. We were all taking liberties with expressing the sequence of the harmony, spinning single-line stories. And taking all kinds of harmonic liberties worked. Herbie had fast ears. And he was right there, comping, as if he were saying with a big smile, 'I'm right underneath you. Isn't this beautiful, don't we make a great couple?' With Tony, (*Shorter imitates the cymbal sound*) ding da ding, right there."

As for Shorter, his playing on these sets has become the stuff of legend. It's often considered to be his best playing with or without Miles. "It's wonderful to listen to Wayne," says Keith Jarrett. "Some of the best playing I've ever heard of Wayne—in fact, his best playing—is on there."

"We did three sets a night, every night, and in New York, we worked until 4 a.m. on Fridays and Saturdays," Carter recalls. These working conditions explain the pacing that Hancock and Williams employed throughout the Chicago gig. Concert sets would often compress a whole night's energy into 45 minutes; so when the band had a chance to lay back and develop, they took advantage of it. Miles also left the door open for the musicians to share something and to work together for a common cause and play to the best of their ability.

Says Jack DeJohnette, "He'd want you to play things that you didn't know: 'Don't play me what you know. I don't want to hear that shit.'"

Gary Peacock recalls, "When you were playing, you could hear him listening."

Running parallel to this universe of band music was Miles' association with Gil Evans. Aside from their masterpieces *Miles Ahead* ('57), *Porgy and Bess* ('58), *Sketches of Spain* ('60) and their triumph at Carnegie Hall ('61), the duo's recorded output dropped substantially after their bossa nova sessions, *Quiet Nights* ('62).

The two had worked together over the course of three decades. So why was their output so meager? Starting with the *Birth of the Cool* sessions in 1948 through *Quiet Nights,* there was a musical momentum that Miles and

Gil had achieved that was stunning and highly original. Beginning with *Quiet Nights* and ending with "Falling Water" in '68, the total recorded output was approximately 40 minutes' worth.

Was it because Miles was hearing differently, without an orchestra in mind? "That may have been it," says Miles' most important producer, Teo Macero. "Miles was starting to use different instruments that didn't require an orchestra. Miles and Gil didn't speak very much after the mid-'60s, but they remained good friends."

Hard to believe, Evans' tone poem "Falling Water" was the only complete performance that Miles and Gil recorded with the quintet, orchestrated also for Hawaiian guitar, mandolin, two French horns, harp, tuba, five woodwinds, tympani and marimba (with Hancock on Wurlitzer electric piano). According to Macero, who came up with the title, "Everything was falling apart. The music was very complicated, with odd time signatures. The orchestra wasn't getting it, so I went out there to conduct. Some of the best records I made were when I was standing right next to Miles!"

Time of the Barracudas, recorded in '63, consists of short musical cues that were intended to be used as incidental music in the stage play of the same name. Miles and Gil's last-known live collaboration was the Greek Theater concert in Berkeley, Calif., in April of '68. Unfortunately, no known recording of this concert exists, either in Columbia's vaults or from private sources.

The sound of the quintet's rhythm section did not easily translate to Evans' conceptions for Miles. However, you can hear the quintet appropriating (via Gil's uncredited assistance) the Evans approach to accompaniment throughout the quintet album *Filles de Kilimanjaro* ('68), where ensemble bass lines, pedal points and a unique sense of song form are utilized.

When all is said and done, however, what will remain of the orchestral music of Miles Davis and Gil Evans centers on the more famous collaborations, with the most significant perhaps being *Sketches of Spain*. As with all Miles Davis recordings, there is a story. Macero's recollection was that "it took 16, 17 sessions to complete. For the first six, Miles was sick. We didn't even have anything except rehearsals. That session ended at 2 in the morning with the album unfinished. I told Gil we had to wind things up. Gil asked for a half-hour to make the missing four bars [to Rodrigo's 'Concierto de Aranjuez']. He never finished the four bars, but we came up with material nonetheless. There may have been one overdub. With Miles, all you had to do was let him play."

But beyond Miles and Gil, and the Plugged Nickel, there have been other recordings, other memories. Some may remember the first time they listened to *Kind of Blue* or *Nefertiti,* and many can recall the first time they saw Miles live at a club or a concert. Most of our opinions about him are shaped by recordings, appearances or word of mouth. But the people who were around him often had different perceptions of the man.

"I see him as a wave that kind of stayed pretty even," Sonny Fortune observes.

"Being a Gemini," remarks Horace Silver, "he could be cool, and he could be a little touchy. But he was a genius."

"When we hear that sound," Keith Jarrett says, "that sound is the closest thing to music. It's like the sources without any ornaments on it. There's a bunch of notes you can choose, you can be a virtuoso of your instrument and beat everyone at the battle of the bands—that isn't what music's about. What he gave in that instance was letting go of so many things we think are so goddamn important, that protect us. It was vulnerable, it was powerful. You know, you're not supposed to be powerful and vulnerable at the same time. Jazz at its best is always that. Miles wasn't a drummer, but the way he played that note was more related to a deep sense of pulse than 95 percent of the drummers that've played at any one time."

"When I joined the band, I had been playing the bass for four and a half years," says Marshall Hawkins. "He had great patience and let me find myself."

"For me," says Gary Peacock, "there was an enormous silence that was made present. it was so complete, so full. I want to live there all the time. It's palpable, you can feel it, it's tactile. And he let it go; he never hung on to it. He could play the same. Why does it always sound like he played it for the first time, the same thing over? The answer is because every time he played it, it was the first time he ever played it. . . . There was something going through his playing that transcended him, and that was more significant than he was."

Don Alias recalls that when he got the call to join the band in '69, he thought Miles wanted him to play drums. "I showed up at my session with my drums, but Miles said he wanted me to play percussion, because, as he said, 'No one plays percussion the way you do.' But he let me play drums on the *Bitches Brew* date, on 'Miles Runs the Voodoo Down.' I put that second-line thing on that tune."

"Miles used to stay with my family when he came to the Bay Area," says Eddie Henderson. "I went up to him one day and said, 'My parents said that you played the trumpet, but that you played wrong.' He just looked at me funny and shrugged it off. Well, I proceeded, out of respect, to buy one of his albums. It was *Sketches of Spain*. After listening to it, I realized I had made a mistake in judgment about Miles' playing, and began to learn every note he played on that album. He came back to town and dropped by, and I rushed into the living room and confronted him. 'I just learned your solos of the *Sketches of Spain* album . . .' and played, note for note along with the recording, his solo. I finished, and proudly looked at him for positive reaction. He looked at me and said, 'That's OK, but that's me,' and walked into the kitchen. It hit me at that moment, but it took years to sink in."

Dave Liebman recollects an event during a tour of Brazil in 1974. "It was my last gig with him . . . São Paulo, Brazil. He had been sick, and we had to cancel gigs. Anyway, he got back on stage, and was pretty out of it for a day or two, I mean in-the-hospital-type [of out]. He looked over at me and said, 'That was a close one,' and then he played his *ass* off. I mean, maybe the longest solos of my whole time with him. He was hitting hard, man, you know, high notes and everything."

"Miles was also self-critical in a way most people don't realize," Jarrett recalls. "One time, we were getting on a bus to leave for somewhere—sometimes he took buses from his apartment in New York—and I was in his apartment with him for a while. And he was in his room with all his clothes, and he was looking at this wall-to-wall closet and wall-to-wall shoes, and clothes, and stuff. And he'd come out of his room with one thing on, and then he'd go back in, and then he'd come out of his room and he'd have something else on, and he'd be hanging around. And it was time to leave, and he was doing this thing, and finally, I guess he finally decided on what he was wearing and came out, and he and I were walking together to the bus, and he says, (*Jarrett guffaws*) 'Bitches and clothes, bitches and clothes!'"

"He gave me a set of hi-hats at a session in '69," Joe Chambers remembers. "I got 'em right now. He must have thought I needed them; I had a pretty ragged set at the time. Chick Corea, Joe Zawinul, John McLaughlin and Wayne Shorter were on the date.

"He was all music, a serious musician," Chambers continues. "He was a true artist. One time I went to his house in the mid-'70s, when he was 'retired.' The first thing he said to me was that he got into the music for the love of it—it was the first thing out of his mouth before we did anything else."

Gary Bartz remembers a time, in 1971, when the band was on a plane in Europe. "Whenever we traveled, people thought we were the [Harlem] Globetrotters or the Jackson 5. On this one flight, a man in the seat in front of me kept looking back and staring at me. I mean, he just kept looking at me with this funny expression on his face. Finally, I couldn't take it anymore, so I leaned over the aisle where Miles was sitting and said to him, 'Man, this motherfucker keeps looking at me, and I'm getting sick of this crap.' And Miles says to me, 'I'll make him stop,' and stares right at this guy 'til he gets his attention. Miles puckered his lips and blew the cat a kiss real feminine-like, and he never looked at us again."

"I'll tell you something funny," Jack DeJohnette laughs. "It's just one line, 'cause Miles never said much. He described my playing as a drunk falling up the stairs. It was a great compliment. Most of the time he was funny. And he could be serious; he could be a lot of things. He was many people. But I'll tell ya, man, I miss him; I wish he was around. There was so much meat in what he said."

Ron Carter recalls being impressed with how Miles was aware of everyone's part. "We were in the middle of this tune . . . and there was this piano solo. Miles would always get a spot on the stage somewhere between the second eight and the end of the last eight [bar phrases], so he could always get a view of what had developed in his absence. And we were playing this chord some kind of way, it was probably a . . . G-9, and I played B in the bass, and he asked me, 'What was that note?' It's hard for me to talk to him at the same time as I'm playing, because, remember, we're *on* stage. So I said, 'It's a B.' He said, 'What's it doing there?' And I said, 'Well, it's the third of the chord and it makes the ninth sound like a root.' He said, 'Oh!' And it struck me funny that he would pick out that note out of all of Herbie's playing to be important to him—to question, 'What is that note, and what is it doing there?'"

For Peacock, "There are two things that impressed me most about Miles: One was that he liked to be approached as though he were a human being; but if you approached him like he was a star, he could be really disagreeable in the extreme. And the other thing was that, whatever promo shit might be happening off the bandstand, when he came to the music, all that was going on was music. He didn't bring any other agenda into the music with him."

What, may you ask, would the Milester think of all this hubbub? Most of his former sidemen agree that he had a distain for the "show-biz" trappings that are a part of our culture. Are we hearing what he wanted us to hear? Maybe we should let someone who was as close to his music as anybody, producer Teo Macero, have the last words.

"Miles trusted me," Macero recalls. "He'd walk in, play and walk out. He even wanted to use four-letter words on his recordings! We were always experimenting from different sources. For example, I used to send his trumpet through an amplifier while he was playing into a mic and record the sound that would go through the amplifier—two or three tracks of Miles at one time. Examples include 'He Loved Him Madly' from *Get Up With It, Bitches Brew, Star People*. I might include a cassette of Miles from being on the road and add it; Miles would want it in there. There were a lot of loops for that first side of *Jack Johnson*. Special echo machines, what might be called a digital delay today, were invented for Miles. I used to use the wah-wah pedal in editing sessions. Miles never came to the editing room, maybe four or five times.

"With Miles, from the start of a session you were on. I wanted to catch everything, without inhibiting the musicians. I wanted to capture Miles in his totality, to make it a collection of things to come. I wanted to record the artist of the century—all of the recorded material as part of his legacy.

"If you look back, everything was a gem."

———

May 2001

Dark Prince in Twilight: Band Members and Close Associates Discuss the Last Years of Miles Davis' Life

by Dan Ouellette

A year before he died, Miles Davis headlined the opening night of the 1990 Chicago Jazz Festival. It was a transcendent set marred by brief stretches of less-than-sparkling play. Davis guided his electric septet through funkified and rock-inflected pieces, esoteric jazz meanderings and pop covers drenched in improvisational genius. Miles was in fine shape, playing at his minimalist best—selectively squeezing out fragments of themes on his horn, emotively suggesting melodies and occasionally unleashing a whirlwind of muted blasts. It was Davis' placard period, when he introduced and drew attention to his bandmates by holding up poster-sized white cards with the names of the supporting cast printed in black. Five-string lead bassist Foley and alto saxophonist Kenny Garrett got the biggest applause, even louder at times than Miles himself.

Taken on its own merits, the set was easily one of the highlights of the festival. But, for many in the last decade of his life, the Miles mystique had worn thin. He had been a revolutionary musical thinker from the '50s into the early '70s, but what in the world was he doing now? There were justifiable reasons for Davis' declining approval ratings, especially the continued fallout from his notorious silent years (1975–'80) when he was sick (a litany of maladies including a bleeding ulcer, walking pneumonia, insomnia, a hernia, bursitis and arthritis that required surgery to fit him with an artificial hip), chemically debilitated (from cognac to cocaine and oftentimes a cocktail mix of many painkilling, mind-numbing substances) and volatile (including well-documented violence toward the women in his life). His reemergence in the early '80s was hampered at first by his sub-par technique on the trumpet, which had gathered dust during his inactive years, but he made significant recordings later in the decade, including 1986's *Tutu* and 1989's *Amandla*.

However, many chastised Miles. Still sore at Davis for what they perceived was his jazz betrayals and backslide, they dismissed the final years of his career as stagnant and insignificant. Yet those close to Davis—particularly musicians he enlisted to perform in his last bands—offer quite a different viewpoint of his twilight years. In this rarely pried-open period of Miles' life, he is revealed as a drug-free, no-bullshit but caring man and peerless artist still striving for new sounds right up until his death on Sept. 28, 1991.

From 1985 to 1991, a total of 32 musicians performed with Davis, often in a septet configuration. While he wasn't quick to fire personnel, neither was he overly patient. Yet, by all accounts, those who were in his employ recount the experience as the most valuable in their careers. He was a no-nonsense taskmaster, but he also parceled out nuggets of wisdom to his bandmates, who, not surprisingly, called him "The Chief."

Electric bassist Foley, who came on board in 1987 and toured with Miles for his last concerts in 1991, is emphatic in stating that it was only through The Chief's generosity that he is who he is today as a musician. "Anyone who played with Miles after 1969 was lucky, lucky, lucky. As bad as Scofield is—I love him—he was lucky. Rick Margitza was no Coltrane. Rick was lucky. Miles had two jazz bands, period: the one with Trane and the one with Herbie, Wayne, Ron and Tony. Those guys in that period played with Miles. Miles didn't have to play with any of us. We should all be glad we talked more than five minutes with him, let alone appeared with him onstage."

"Job security didn't exist," says Kei Akagi, who signed on as a keyboardist with Davis in March 1989 and left the gig in January 1991. "You always had to be prepared to be fired, which forced you to put your all into the moment. It made us play better. Miles kept us on our toes because he expected something new every night. What I learned from Miles was that ultimately a musician's past has no meaning. It's only the present and the future. After playing with him I looked at music quite differently."

Akagi, who notes that he sometimes bore the brunt of Davis' cuss attacks for musical blunders as well as just because he was in a bad mood, says that he has never again experienced what the leader brought to the band. "It's hard to explain, but what he created among us went beyond mere empathy into an almost telepathic state. On nights when he was physically strong, it was almost as if he controlled us without telling us what to do."

The band's live performances mutated over the course of a tour, says keyboardist Adam Holzman, who was enlisted in 1985 and was in Davis' working band for four years until the end of 1989. Davis was a galvanizing influence who was constantly striking out into new territory, taking the band with him, but the pace of change was slow. "Miles was absolutely a trailblazer, but it wasn't as if lightning struck every minute. But you'd recognized at the end of a tour how much we developed."

Davis critiqued every night's performance after listening to its playback. That generally prompted one-on-one meetings with band members backstage the next night. "He'd make suggestions," Holzman says. "Even if you didn't nail things, he'd be encouraging."

As for Davis' recommendations for improvement, Holzman says they were often cryptic. "His suggestions weren't crystal clear, but they got you thinking. One time instead of referring to a riff or chord change, he said, 'You should subdivide what you're playing.' It was up to me to interpret that or run the risk of falling flat that night."

Tenor saxophonist Rick Margitza, who played in the band in 1989, recalls Miles calling him backstage before a performance one night and telling him simply that his fingers were coming up too high. "I was left to go back on my own to figure out what he meant. But he was right. I was expending too much energy, so I worked at keeping my fingers closer to the keys."

Miles was serious about music right to the end. Wallace Roney spent a lot of time with Davis in his later years. Although he performed on stage only once with Davis—at the historic 1991 Montreux Jazz Festival concert (the *Miles & Quincy Live at Montreux* retrospective was released shortly after his death)—he had been a close personal friend since 1983. One of seven trumpeters who performed at a Radio City tribute to Davis, Roney was taken under his idol's wing.

Upon learning that Roney was borrowing a trumpet for the Radio City gig, Davis invited Roney to his West 77th Street home and bestowed on him a Martin Committee horn. "After the Montreux show, Miles gave me a red one," says Roney, who still bristles at the criticism his mentor received for the concert that was a look back at the music he had played throughout his career. "That concert was so beyond criticism. Miles was making a statement. It was his last testament, the music that he wanted to leave us with. I didn't realize he was that sick, but he must have known."

Roney recalls his Montreux experience, particularly playing *Sketches of Spain,* where he was assigned Davis' solo part. It was a daunting challenge, but Roney says, "The only thing a creative artist can do is apply the lessons you've learned from the innovations and take the music somewhere else." However, in the middle of his improvisation, Davis walked off the stage. While initially unnerved, Roney overcame his apprehensions. "Miles wasn't standing near me, so I just let it all go and went for it. After the piece, Miles came back onstage, told me he walked off because he was tired, then whispered, 'You're good. No more humble stuff. You're great.'"

Roney also remembers conversing with Davis about the old days. "He liked talking about Charlie Parker, Monk, Trane, Coleman Hawkins, Philly Joe, and he was especially interested in what innovations old bandmates like

Herbie and Wayne were bringing to the music. He even talked about getting the '60s quintet back together. He liked having Ricky Wellman with his go-go drum beat, but he talked about wanting to play that cold-blooded groove. That's when he'd bring up Tony Williams and what a genius he was. Miles wanted Tony to play with him at the Paris concert after Montreux, but he had other commitments. I remember Miles telling me how sad he was. He asked me, 'How come Tony won't play with me any more?'"

Hanging with Miles on the road was an experience. Percussionist Mino Cinelu remembers going to Davis' hotel room one night and witnessing him in a playful mood doing a dance to the Michael Jackson song "Beat It." Margitza recalls Davis sitting in his hotel room with binoculars observing people. "It was fascinating sitting with him at the airport too," he says. "Miles watched people and then made comments about them, like this person used to be a junkie, that couple is really unhappy."

Twenty-three at the time of his enlistment into the Davis band, Foley was a pop music omnivore. "In my bag, I had everything from the B-52s and Zappa to the Jackson 5 and Funkadelic. Miles was ears to it all. He loved Teddy Riley's 'Groove Me' and I remember George Clinton's 'Knee Deep' split his head open." In fact, Foley was present when Davis and Clinton first met backstage at a show in Detroit. "They were both in awe of each other. They just gawked at each other, smiled and didn't have much to say. It was so deep."

Cinelu, who first played with Davis in 1981 and later returned for a two-year stint in 1987–'88 during what he calls Miles' "Prince period," recalls that they often talked about world music from India, the West Indies and Africa. "Miles knew all about Fela Kuti and was interested in the beat and strength of rap music. Of course, he also talked about Louis Armstrong, Bird and Gil Evans, whose death really affected him. It was the first time I ever saw him really sad. But he was always thinking about the future, asking me to show him traditional rhythms from places like Martinique and Haiti."

Change was a given for Davis, says bassist Marcus Miller, who first hooked up with him in 1981 during his comeback. (After retiring from his touring band in 1984 Miller went on to work with him producing *Tutu*, the *Siesta* soundtrack and *Amandla*.) "Miles heard Prince and he flipped," Miller recalls. "He said he had to get that sound into his music. It was the same with African rhythms. He had to figure out how to incorporate that into what he was doing." He pauses for a moment and then adds, "You know, I go into Sweet Basil and see cats who are 65 doing a perfected version of what they did at 25. That wasn't Miles. He was always pushing. That appeals to me."

When Davis was off the road and not in the studio for any number of extracurricular projects (such as contributing to the *Hot Spot* and *Dingo* soundtracks, guesting on the title track of Shirley Horn's *You Won't Forget Me* album and adding trumpet overdubs to Easy Mo Bee's rap tracks on *Doo-Bop*), he hung at home, either in New York or at his house in Malibu, Calif. Peter Shukat, Davis' attorney beginning in 1975 and his manager from 1987 to his death, notes that Miles didn't change much in the last four or five years of his life. As others attest, he says Davis was drug-free during this period, yet as unpredictable as always.

"In a word, I'd describe Miles as mercurial," says Shukat, who now represents the Davis Estate. "Some days he loved you, some days he hated you. Some days he would talk to you. Other days he wouldn't. But to the end, he was moving forward. My theory on him performing with his back to the audience was that he didn't want to look back."

Another person who spent a lot of time with Davis was his nephew, Vince Wilburn Jr., whom he fondly called "Nef." He played drums in the band from 1985 to '87. Wilburn admits that it hurt when his uncle fired him, but he insists they didn't have a falling out. Wilburn says that Miles loved football and watched games on TV. But his biggest love was boxing. The two would often attend fights at The Forum in Los Angeles or watch pay-per-view on TV. He also went shopping with his uncle, who favored hip designers like Versace. He notes that Miles owned horses, some of which were prize-winning show horses.

Even though Miller didn't work with Davis much after 1989, the bassist and his wife would drive up to visit him in Malibu. "When we went to his crib, there was always music in the background playing and his artwork was everywhere—on the floors, walls. In his last years, Miles painted and sketched nonstop. One day he was working on a piece and I asked him how much it would sell for. He said, $50,000, unless he got sick. Then the value would go up."

Miller also notes that shortly before Davis passed there was talk of a new project focusing on Brazilian music. "Quincy Jones wanted to work on it," he recalls. "I can't remember the exact details, but Johnny Mandel's name came up. I was going to work up some music, but Miles died before anything got off the ground."

Davis spent most of his time in his last few years painting and sketching (diagnosed as having suffered a stroke in 1982, Davis acted on a doctor's recommendation that he take up drawing to regain strength and dexterity in his partially paralyzed right hand). Little of his artwork has been seen. That changes this month when the book *Improvisations: The Drawings of Miles Davis* will be published on what would be his 75th birthday (May 25) by Publications International, Ltd. The book features 85 drawings, most of which come from Bag One Arts, the New York City gallery owned by Yoko Ono.

In his compelling book about the icon's last years, *Miles Beyond: The Electric Explorations of Miles Davis, 1967–1991* (Watson-Guptill Publications), Paul Tingen notes that Davis lived fast and hard right up until the time of his death. After the Montreux concert in the summer of 1991, Davis assembled much of the same personnel for an outdoor Paris concert at a venue called La Vilette. It was another look back at Miles' career with many of the musicians he performed with over the years. Many of the participants, including Chick Corea and Dave Holland, report that it was a wonderful experience, with the trumpeter and bandleader playing with renewed vigor.

However, after Davis played at the Hollywood Bowl on Aug. 25, 1991, (which turned out to be his final concert—the tune "Hannibal" from the show is documented on the posthumously released album *Live Around the World*), his health took a dramatic turn for the worse. Drummer Wellman noted that soon after the show Miles began vomiting blood and was quickly admitted to the hospital. Three days later he suffered a stroke that paralyzed the left side of his body. Davis suffered another stroke on Sept. 28 and died.

As Tingen points out in his book, "Almost all the musicians who had ever worked with him expressed deep shock and total surprise; like many, they had assumed that Miles would always be there. He had seemed to transcend the laws that apply to the rest of us."

Foley, who was with Davis on the bandstand to the end, waxes philosophical about The Chief's death. "As Miles got older, he often didn't feel really well. It's not easy for a horn player to perform because you've got to use a lot of energy to blow. It's not like playing the keyboards. But the only time he felt better was when he was playing. He had to do it. His life was like a comet. He swept down and then moved on."

October 2005

Behind the Cellar Door: The Making of the Explosive, Mostly Unheard Live Miles Davis Electric Sessions

by Dan Ouellette

Thirty-five years after it was recorded and five years after it was ready for release, the six-CD box set *Miles Davis—The Cellar Door Sessions 1970* has finally arrived. It opens yet another window into the life of the musician who, as Keith Jarrett says, was always "forging new ways of coming at things." In this case, the porthole on Davis' creativity is his plunge into the funk/rock jazz varietal that he was developing in rock venues like the Fillmore East and West.

During the week before Christmas 1970 (Wednesday, Dec. 16, through Saturday, Dec. 19), Davis called Columbia Records to record four nights of his electric quintet (and sextet) at the Washington, D.C., jazz club the Cellar Door. His band, still small compared to his larger outfits in subsequent years, featured Jarrett on electric keys, Gary Bartz on saxophones, John McLaughlin on electric guitar (only on the final night of the gig), drummer Jack DeJohnette, percussionist Airto Moreira and bassist Michael Henderson, the first pure electric bassist to play in Davis' bands. The group never recorded in a studio, as Davis chose then to free himself from a constrictive atmosphere that would impede what he was looking for improvisationally.

Playing only a few numbers from *Bitches Brew* ("Sanctuary" and "It's About That Time") and bulking up the proceedings with new compositions (such as "Inamorata" and "What I Say"), Davis and crew ripped into raucous and funky sets that surprised the audiences as well as the onstage musicians.

The final night was partially released by Columbia as *Live-Evil;* however, five-plus hours of inspired performances were stored away until co-producer Adam Holzman, a veteran of Davis' '80s bands, played the sleuth and unearthed them. The box set he produced with Bob Belden is a living document of the time period where Davis was flying high, but also, as Moreira says, tethered to the earth by deep-trenched funk.

DownBeat has dug a little deeper into the gig by asking key players, including musicians and producers, to offer their insights. (Henderson was unavailable for interview for this story, so his quotes are pulled from the liner notes to the Columbia/Legacy box set.)

Behind the Set

Adam Holzman: I was hired by Miles' estate in the late '90s to go through his personal tapes, including cassettes and seven-inch reels from the late '60s through the '80s. It was like the "Blindfold Test" of all time to figure out the context and who the sidemen were. When I came across the Cellar Door sessions, I got excited because this was the closest thing to what should have come out. Columbia had an involved system for labeling and storing masters, so each time I tried tracking down the tape numbers, I kept coming back to *Live-Evil*. So I called around to various Columbia storage facilities and finally found the masters stored in New Jersey.

Bob Belden: The reels were marked with numbers. [Adam] tracked down what they were and discovered virgin master reels that hadn't been listened to since 1971. Part of my job was to help shape the music, to get the mix right. On *Live-Evil,* everything was compressed into the center. But Miles had a stereo

iles at the Three Deuces, 1948, with Tommy Potter (bass), Charlie Parker (saxophone),
uke Jordan (piano) and Max Roach (drums, not pictured).
ownBeat Archives)

Miles receives
his 1958 Critics
Poll and Readers
Poll plaques
from *DownBeat*
Associate Editor
Dom Cerulli.
(*DownBeat* Archives)

Gil Evans, left, explains the problems experienced during the recording of *Sketches of Spain* during a press party at New York's Penthouse Club. Jazz promoter Pete Long and Miles look on.

(*DownBeat* Archives)

Miles and French bandleader Michel Legrand during a recording session in 1959 that produced *Legrand Jazz* on Columbia.
(*DownBeat* Archives)

Gil Evans conducts a 19-piece orchestra for Miles' television debut, "The Sound of Miles Davis," in 1960.
(*DownBeat* Archives)

Miles with saxophonist Wayne Shorter at a 1964 performance in Berlin wit his classic quintet.
(Jan Persson)

Miles at the same Berlin date with pianist Herbie Hancock, drummer Tony Williams and bassist Ron Carter.
(Jan Persson)

The classic quintet with Miles, Shorter Carter and Williams (Hancock not pictured) in Copenhagen in 1964.
(Jan Persson)

Miles and bassist Dave Holland at the 1968 Newport Jazz Festival in Rhode Island.
(Alain Bettex)

Left: Miles shows his styl
at the 1968 Newport Jazz
Festival.
(Alain Bettex)

Below: Jack DeJohnette
(drums, left), Airto More
(percussion), Gary Bartz
(soprano saxophone), Jan
Santos (congas), Miles an
Keith Jarrett (keyboards)
at Zellerbach Auditoriun
University of California,
Berkeley, on Oct. 14, 197
(Bassist Mike Henderson
also onstage, but not
pictured.)
(Veryl Oakland)

iles shows his moves onstage at Stanford University in October 1972.
eryl Oakland)

Miles works the wah-wah pedal at Northern Illinois University, 1971 (Floyd Webb)

Miles casts his spell on the crowd at the Park West in Chicago on Feb. 6, 1983. (Paul Natkin/ Photo Reserve)

image in mind. So, for these recordings, we stretched the sound out so that everyone has a pocket. We also mixed this in surround sound, but I doubt if that will ever come out.

Holzman: *The Cellar Door* is akin to *The Plugged Nickel* because it's the only other box to capture Miles live in a club over an extended period. During this time, the set list didn't significantly change for two years, so each night the songs were canvasses to express different ideas. That way it's easier to play and stretch, easier to improvise freely and have everyone else follow. It takes a long time to find the right canvas. This is a living example of the link between Miles' earlier and later material and bands.

The Players

Keith Jarrett: This band never recorded. I remember talking to Miles when we were at the Jazz Workshop in Boston to get CBS to record us there. The music was so good, the sound was so punchy. Everyone knew it: the band, the audience, Miles. But it was too short a notice.

John McLaughlin: Miles was, first and foremost, a sublime artist. He never had anything to prove to anyone. He was a consummate artist with impeccable intuition. With this band as with all his other bands, Miles was pushing the frontiers of music to the limit. It just so happened that I was there with a guitar, and having grown up with not only his music, but also rock and blues, I was in the process of bringing these diverse elements together. Miles knew that instinctively, which is why he hired me. Don't forget that as early as 1959, Miles was already in the process of bringing different musical cultures together. Check out the recording *Miles Ahead* with the Gil Evans Orchestra and how marvelously they brought flamenco and modern blues together.

At that time I was playing with Tony Williams, and Miles wanted me in his band whenever I wasn't busy with Lifetime. The Cellar Door gig coincided with some time off with Lifetime.

Airto Moreira: We knew we were doing something that had never been done before. The band made an effort to integrate all the members, with Miles taking charge. He made sure the music wasn't flying. It was settled, because that's what he wanted. We were looking to fly, to take off, but he wanted to keep the music on the ground.

Jack DeJohnette: Miles wanted to get that high-energy thing. He was looking to get to that younger audience without compromising his musical integrity. He wanted to capture the groove with a greater jazz sensibility. Having Keith and Gary in the band took it to another jazz level, and the band jelled with Michael, who put in a nice funk foundation.

Michael Henderson: Working with Miles was spectacular. . . . I was gaga over the fact that we were all in one building for four days because a lot of creative stuff happened. . . . Four days of hanging together, having dinner together. . . . I was a little separate because of my age, but it didn't matter because I was serious at an early age. We all treated each other with respect.

Gary Bartz: When you're in a band, it's like being on a basketball team. You have to find a way to play with the guys. I'd worked with Jack before, but not with Keith and Michael. So we had to learn to play together. Miles handpicked everybody, so it wasn't a frivolous thing. This band stuck. I was in it for two years. I joined when Dave Holland and Chick Corea were in it with Keith and Airto. Personnel changed, but once Michael came Miles had what he was looking for.

Jarrett: Michael was new. My memory of him was that he didn't know the jazz side. But now I listen and realize I wasn't paying attention then to how great he was. I appreciate that now listening to the tapes. Of course, Jack is Jack, playing like a machine gun. No one can play like him.

At the Gig

Bartz: I had been playing with Miles for a while, but this was like a home-coming for me because I'm from the Baltimore–Washington, D.C., area. My mother came because she always loved Miles and Lee Morgan. Miles never had to take a club gig, but every now and then when he felt like playing he'd book one. Normally we were playing concerts, where we had much longer to lay out. In a club we had to do a little more editing because we couldn't play as long in a set.

McLaughlin: The sessions are a window into the "live" Miles at that time. When you think of who was in the band, and how they were playing and reacting to Miles' discreet and ambiguous directions, it's amazing. Keith was playing like a man possessed on two keyboards, and we all had wah-wah pedals, except Jack. When you listen to these recordings, you can hear everybody playing their heart out.

Jarrett: I'm thankful the music didn't sound worse. Of course, I wouldn't have written any liner notes for the release if I didn't like it. But the pianos were in bad shape. I wouldn't have played those instruments except for Miles. The Fender Rhodes was off its game. I remember going up to the control room at the gig. I wanted to hear the recording. I didn't want the pianos to sound like pianos, not like an electric piano or organ. Basically, I wanted them to sound like John's instrument, which they couldn't do.

DeJohnette: Miles liked to capture the music. He was always experimenting, like with *Bitches Brew,* where the tape was always rolling. He played with an idea and cued people into it. But Teo [Macero] gets the credit for editing all those hours and putting them together. Miles didn't have the patience to sit in the studio, so that week at the Cellar Door was where he could organically capture the music. He was able to hear it develop night by night on a small stage.

Bartz: Every night was different. You never knew in what direction Miles would take the band. It was better for me because it usually takes me one night to get used to the sound of a room. It was good to be stable for a week.

Engaging the Audience

Moreira: The Cellar Door was one of the best places to perform in D.C. It was a small space, almost as if we were sitting with the crowd, right there in your face. You could see and feel everybody's reactions and hear people making comments. The vibe was intimate.

McLaughlin: There was a great reaction from some people, and a somewhat confused reaction from others. This band was pretty wild, and in 1970 Miles upset more than a few people with this new music, especially the jazz purists.

Bartz: Everywhere we played the crowds loved the music. They heard *Bitches Brew,* so they knew what Miles was doing. It was different in Europe, where people weren't happy. But in the U.S., the fans expected this new Miles. We were playing the Fillmores and places like that.

Henderson: We performed at the Cellar Door for only about 74 people on the first night, but they were all locked into what we were putting down. Their mouths were hung open and their jaws were locked. They were drawn into the intensity of our collective creative expression. The next night, there were more people, about 100 to 200 people throughout the first and second sets.

Belden: You wonder what people were thinking. You can hear that the crowd was not totally into what he was doing. But to Miles, there was no more joy than confounding people paying money to hear him.

Rewind and Listen

DeJohnette: I knew the record company was recording every night. But listening back to it now is quite a surprise because you can hear the process at work. The solos were different each night, as well as the tempos.

Jarrett: When I heard these tapes, I was relieved. There was actually a record of what that band was getting into without John. Everyone knows *Live-Evil,* but they didn't know the previous three nights.

DeJohnette (regarding "What I Say"): Miles had been listening to Jimi Hendrix and Buddy Miles, and he was looking for something like that. So he came up with a groove, a vamp and a shout chorus. He wanted to see how much he could get out of a little groove. He trusted me to develop it. I kept it locked in to propel the intensity. I like the way it eventually builds. It starts at high energy and goes up from there. I was fired up by that, so I'm glad it got captured.

McLaughlin: Miles was in a perpetual state of evolution and growth. *The Cellar Door* is just a glimpse of Miles, and where he was at that time. It's safe to say that Miles was the first true innovator of jazz and rock, no matter what people may say about me and the Mahavishnu Orchestra. Miles was there before everybody.

Belden: Some people thought that Miles had completely lost his mind. Others disagreed, saying that he was forging new paths. But Miles was just being a musician as well as a businessman. At this time, he was moving away from the club circuit, into concert settings where he could control the gate. Miles was into the idea of self-empowerment. *The Cellar Door* was his way of musically dealing with emancipation.

Jarrett: This was a strong period for Miles. That was true almost the entire time I was with him. I don't think people realize how strong he played. You can hear it on these tapes. There are times when he's playing the whole history of jazz.

Place in History

Belden: This is one of the best examples of jazz/rock. These guys got more of a focused sound out of their instruments than the rock guys. Miles was capturing Cream and ° and extending it into improvisation in a powerful live setting. After this came fusion, most of which sounds childish compared to this.

Holzman: This is truly the missing link of Miles' career, where his straight-ahead jazz was transformed into his wilder electric bands that came later. If these gigs had come out closer to the time they were recorded, the direction of electric jazz would have been different. People's understanding of groove and mood would have been enhanced. Jazz/rock got notey, fast and showy: pretty to look at, but no substance. But this is electric jazz with a lot of substance.

Moreira: These tapes are an important piece of information that was lost. It's a missing link on the period where Miles chose to go straighter to the beat and the groove. This was almost like the end of an era and the beginning of another.

McLaughlin: There's a great sense of vitality in the music, and freedom also. Don't forget that 1970 was a very volatile time in the United States with the Civil Rights Movement, the Black Panthers and the strong anti-war movement. Miles' music reflected the social upheaval.

Belden: What you hear in *The Cellar Door* is anti-establishment at its highest, but it's also entertaining to musicians. On *The Cellar Door,* there's no darkness, but beauty from everybody. Miles was not an abstractionist. He believed that in the midst of all the madness, if you played beautifully, it wasn't madness any more.

The *DownBeat* Reviews

All ratings are out of five stars unless otherwise noted.

July 15, 1946
Charlie Parker
"Ornithology" ★★
"A Night in Tunisia" ★★★
Dial 1002

Ross Russell's latest experiment arrived cracked, so there was a little difficulty reviewing it. "Ornithology," named for the Bird, is still the reigning fav. Drummer Roy Porter bothers me a bit; there are times when his counter beats interfere with the pattern being played. Trumpet man Miles Davis follows in the Dizzysteps admirably, and Lucky Thompson once again proves he has more than a big tone. Whole side is a little stiff for my dough, while I prefer "Tunisia" as made by Dizzy Gillespie with the Boyd Raeburn band. Rhythm is much looser on this side though, while Parker plays one fantastic four-bar section crammed with notes and an idea that persists all the way through his chorus. This is some excellent jazz here, re-bop or otherwise.

—Michael Levin

April 21, 1948
Charlie Parker
The Parkers
Savoy 509
★★★

"The Parkers" refers to brothers-under-the-bop, Charlie and Leo, on their respective altos and baritones, and if this was intended to be a carving contest, the Bird came away with the honors despite Leo's lively performances. This is good bebop, and the album with its varied personnel offers good examples of some of the best known modernists, as for example: the Parkers; trumpeters Miles Davis, Maggsi Evounce and Fats Navarro; and Albert Ammons' boy, Gene, on tenor. "Nelson" has good Davis and Parker solos. "Bird" is one of those flash tempo boppers. "Minton's" has some of the Fabulous Fats' fluent horn, and "Wild Leo" has enough Leo on it to last for some time. The Bird has good moments on all the sides, particularly on "Cheryl."

—Tom Herrick

"Half Nelson"; "Goin' to Minton's"; "Cheryl"; "Bird Gets the Worm"; "Wild Leo"; "El Sino."

Aug. 11, 1948
Charlie Parker Quartet
"This Is Always" ★★
"Dewey Square" ★★★
Dial 1019

Pianist Duke Jordan opens "Dewey" with quarter-note triplets, which make you think you're listening to a 6/4 time intro, with drummer Max Roach answering the question, "How obtuse can you get?" Miles Davis' trumpet is that of a quiet Dizzy. Charlie must have dropped into the Russell recording studio by accident. Different personnel on "Always," Erroll Garner's piano sounding like a "you'll astound your friends" teacher's example, behind Earl Coleman's vocal. Coleman, incidentally, sounds as though he was freshly cut with a slash knife. You can practically trace a melody throughout Parker's chorus! Garner off-beats eight and Coleman bleeds to death.

—Tom Herrick

Dec. 15, 1948
Charlie Parker
"Barbados" ★★
"Parker's Mood" ★★★
Savoy 936

The Bird's personnel on this date included Miles Davis, trumpet; Curley Russell, bass; Max Roach, drums, and an unnamed pianist. "Barbados" is Afro-Cuban in character with alto and trumpet solos plus the bop riff. The slow "Mood" belongs mostly to Parker, and he displays his usual great talent for making every chorus sound unlike any other he has played.

—Tom Herrick

Dec. 29, 1948
Miles Davis All-Stars
"Sipping at Bell's" ★★★
"Milestones" ★★★
Savoy 934

Trumpeter Davis is among those at Savoy who have taken turns as label-leader. In this instance he's supported by the Bird, drummer Max Roach, pianist John Lewis and bassman Nelson Boyd. "Sipping" is a moderately fast bopper with better than good solos by Davis and the sax—the "sax" being officially listed as Charlie Parker's alto on the label but is a tenor to us.

"Milestones" is a trifle slower but equally entertaining riffer, bop style with a very fine Davis trumpet solo. His playing on both of these sides is about the tastiest we've heard from him.

It's all middle- and low-register stuff with not a single reach into the higher stratas, and both solos have a richness of ideas and smooth flow that he must have felt very good about in listening to the playback. Good piano on both sides, too.

—Tom Herrick

Jan. 28, 1949
Charlie Parker
"Embraceable You" ★★★
"Bongo Bop" ★★
Dial 1024

"You" is a prime example of the heights of originality that the Bird can soar to when he's in the mood. He plays impeccably with a richness of ideas and change of pace that at once astounds you and then enables you to coast a bit while assimilating what went before. "Bop" is bop, but the "Bongo" part is a misnomer, for it is merely a riff tune with conventional rhythm. Miles Davis is on the No. 2 side on trumpet, and Max Roach is on both.

—Tom Herrick

April 22, 1949
Miles Davis
"Budo" ★★
"Move" ★★★
Capitol 15404

Capitol is in the bop market for sure, and with a rather imposing lineup of boppers under trumpeter Davis, plus French horn and tuba, yet. Both sides on this release are fast bop tunes markedly similar in construction, and the difference in ratings is due principally to the superior solos on "Move."

Miles' chorus on "Budo" is spotty, and Lee Konitz, alto, Gerry Mulligan, baritone, and Kai Winding, trombone, have only a single chorus to split among them. On the flipover, leader Davis plays exceptionally well and Konitz does likewise. But drum solos are nowhere—even by Max Roach.

—Tom Herrick

May 20, 1949
Miles Davis
"Godchild" ★★★★
"Jeru" ★★★★
Capitol 57-60005

Two more sides from that peculiar combination Cap supervisor Pete Rugolo recorded in New York including trumpet, trombone, alto, tenor, French horn, tuba and three rhythm. The sound, however, is extremely earable, far mellower than many bopped sounds, and with a wild opening unison of tuba and reed moving up through the other horns. The figure is credited to George ("Lemon Drop") Wallington, while leader Davis makes his trumpet solos hang together more than usual, and with pretty tone, too. The sounds blend and someone actually worried about the dynamics. My goodness, shortly there will be studio bop bands. Good Kai Winding trombone plus Gerry Mulligan baritone help the side along. "Jeru" is Mulligan's score, and again well done. Credit, too, to the fine relaxed rhythm work of Joe Schulman, bass, Max Roach, drums, and Al Haig, piano.

—Michael Levin

June 17, 1949
Charlie Parker
"Crazeology"
(Part I) ★
(Part II) ★★★
Dial 1034

This is a slightly insane record. The engineers, on side I, ran two tables playing the same master about two seconds behind on the same disc. This is what
came out. It sounds like the 1922 short-wave radio reception, but Symphony
Sid, N.Y. disc jockey, has been playing it to death, and so Dial issued it. It was
take No. 4 on the session, so Ross Russell made up for the garbage on side I by
issuing on side II one cut of the opening and Parker's chorus, a second take
of Parker's chorus, a third take of Parker's chorus and the finale, labeling it
"Three Ways to Play a Chorus." I found it fascinating to compare Parker's
three solos on the same tune, all made within 15 minues of each other. Miles
Davis' trumpet and J.J. Johnson's tram are well represented, and Max Roach
is substantially reared at the drums.

—Michael Levin

Oct. 21, 1949
Miles Davis
"Boplicity" ★★★★
"Israel" ★★★
Capitol 57-60011

The same wonderful sound as on Davis' previous side of "Jeru" and
"Godchild," this combines tuba, French horn and other blowing gentry for
very soft, melodious sounds as well as good solos. While the playing isn't quite
as clean on these sides as the ones before, it is still delightful, relaxed bop,
well conceived and integrated. Davis' playing, as well as Gerry Mulligan's
baritone, is worth hearing. "Israel," by brassman Johnny Carisi, utilizes some
fine moving passages in single instrumentation, which, unfortunately, the boys
don't render with quite the due justice necessary.

—Michael Levin

Dec. 1, 1950
Miles Davis
"Venus de Milo" ★★★★
"Darn That Dream" ★★★
Capitol 7-1221

Two more sides with that softly blended sound of French horn, tuba, trumpet, baritone sax and trombone, which Miles has used to great success before. I find this stuff extremely pretty, often movingly stated music. Kenny Hagood sings "Dream," takes it too impressively and misses the neatness of phrasing the song demands. The scoring behind him once again is well done. It would be a wonderful thing if every young arranger in the country were forced to write for units of this size so that he actually learned the individual instruments and sound possibilities instead of the mere massed blotches of color the Kenton tradition demands.

—Michael Levin

April 6, 1951
Miles Davis
"Morpheus" ★★★★★ (out of 10)
"Blue Room" ★★★★ (out of 10)
Prestige 734

Miles on "Morpheus" again attempts something different, this time using a sextet. Evidently he's trying for the same chamber music sound and feel he got on his Capitol sides, but here has only three horns to work with—trumpet, tenor (Sonny Rollins) and trombone (Bennie Green). It isn't very cleanly played, however, and the arrangement allows for few solo opportunities, although Miles sounds fine in his short burst.

"Blue Room" is another recording director's attempt to get sales by playing the melody straight. Davis is rather unfamiliar with the tune.

—Jack Tracy

Sept. 7, 1951
Lee Konitz Sextet
"Ezz-thetic" ★★★★★ (out of 10)
"Hi Beck" ★★★★ (out of 10)
Prestige 743

After giving Lee's "Rebecca" the highest rating yet this year (in a three-person review last winter) this may be unduly disappointing. It just isn't attractive listening, to these ears. "Ezz-thetic," dedicated to Ezzard Charles, is a flashy thing by George Russell in which the repeated figure has only a debilitating effect. Miles Davis plays sustained notes while Lee pushes a hurried counterpoint and Max Roach and Arnold Fishkin work out frantically on drums and bass. "Beck" is better in that Lee's solo is prettier and gayer, but Miles buzzes around to no effect, and the whole thing doesn't hang together.

—Pat Harris

Sept. 7, 1951
Miles Davis
"Down" ★★★ (out of 10)
"Whispering" ★★★★ (out of 10)
Prestige 742

Two very bad sides from Miles, cut at the same session last January that produced "Blue Room." Sonny Rollins, Bennie Green, John Lewis, Percy Heath and Roy Haynes give this aid. But no one seems at all interested in playing, and a completely lifeless and uninspired performance results. Release of items like this can do neither the artist or the label much good.

— Jack Tracy

May 7, 1952
Charlie Parker
"Star Eyes" ★★
"Au Privave" ★★★
Mercury 11087

Nothing much happens on "Star Eyes," but turn it over and catch some bop reminiscent of the halcyon days. Bird, Miles, young Walter Bishop (the songsmith's pianist son) and Max all blow their best on this fast blues. Teddy Kotick completes the quintet. The title, we understand on unimpeachable authority, means nothing.

(No byline)

<hr>

Dec. 3, 1952
Miles Davis
"Dig? (I & II)" ★★
Prestige 777

Here we have some six minutes of "Sweet Georgia Brown," extracted from Miles' LP. Miles, altoist Jack McLean and tenor Sonny Rollins are not helped a bit by the rude, unswinging drumming of Art Blakey.

(No byline)

<hr>

Feb. 11, 1953
Miles Davis
Young Man With a Horn
Blue Note 5013
★★★

Miles' environment here: J.J. Johnson, trombone; Jackie McLean, alto; Gil Coggins, piano; Kenny Clarke, drums; and Oscar Pettiford, bass. Swingingest sides are "Donna," a comely McLean variant on "Georgia Brown," and "Chance It," an old opus by Oscar also known as "Something for You" and "Max Is Making Wax." Though Miles' articulation and intonation are still sometimes bothersome, his two slow solo sides, "Yesterdays" and "Ocean," are long on ideas. J.J., McLean and especially Oscar have some good solos.

(No byline)

"Dear Old Stockholm"; "Would'n You"; "Yesterdays"; "Chance It"; "Donna"; "How Deep Is the Ocean."

<hr>

April 3, 1953
Miles Davis
"Bluing" ★★
"Blue Room" ★
"Out of the Blue" ★★★
Prestige 140

Blue Period is the title of this LP, and it was certainly that for us, as we thought back to Miles' great Capitol sides and reflected how sadly that great promise, that exceptional talent, has been betrayed.

The first 23 bars of "Blue Room" are simple and beautiful, and Miles gets through them without a fluff. By bar 32 you find yourself mustering, "Damn, if only he could have made it through the chorus." After an awkward pause as if the take has ended, Sonny Rollins' tenor takes over for 16 bars that sound as if they were patched on from another take. "Out of the Blue" is not blues, but a string of choruses on the changes of "Get Happy" with a long, long solo by Miles divided between moments of inspiration and others of vacuum. This is the most effective performance of the three.

The entire second side is occupied by nine minutes of desultory blues blowing by Miles, Rollins, Jackie McLean's alto and Walter Bishop's piano. Where it aims at relaxation it merely reaches lethargy, winding up with complete chaos when the front line goofs, Art Blakey is left playing by himself, and Miles is heard commenting, something to the effect that they'd better make another take. Alas, they didn't. Informality on records is one thing; sloppiness is another.

(No byline)

―――――――

June 17, 1953
Miles Davis
Miles Davis Plays the Compositions of Al Cohn
Prestige 154
★★

Miles Davis Plays the Compositions of Al Cohn, it says here, and sure enough he does. Surrounding Miles with Sonny Truitt's trombone, Al Cohn's and Zoot Sims' tenors, plus John Lewis, Kenny Clarke and Leonard Gaskin, Prestige has evidently endeavored here to recapture some of the glory that was Capitol's, and Miles', when he last recorded with his own organized band some four years ago.

Alas, Al and the guys aren't equal to the task. These are fair swing arrangements with nothing startling to offer in new sounds or new harmonic directions. There are some superior samples of what Barry Ulanov described so vividly as Miles' "eggshell trumpet"; there are good solos by others, too; but Klook's drums get in the way at times, and the ensembles just don't make it. As a theme, "Adults" is the only attractive item of the four, and it's still nothing to gas you.

As genuine admirers of Little Willie and of Cohn, we wish we could feel more than two stars for his set, but it just doesn't succeed in what it evidently set out to do.

(No byline)

"Tasty Pudding"; "Floppy"; "Willie the Wailer"; "For Adults Only."

Nov. 18, 1953
Miles Davis
Miles Davis, Vol. 2
Blue Note 5022
★★★

A largely inconclusive session—except for Art Blakey. Recorded in April, before Miles left for the coast, the sides contain some of his better recent solo moments, but he rarely seems to feel wholly free or relaxed.

Davis is at his best here on the two bittersweet ballads, Walter Fuller's "Waited" and J.J. Johnson's "Enigma." Being primarily a lyric trumpet player, Miles does generally express himself more memorably at slow and medium tempos. His intonation is not the steadiest nor is that of some of the ensemble choruses (e.g., "Tempus Fugit").

J.J. is almost always apt but is not given enough space to extend his ideas. Young tenor Jimmy Heath, Percy's brother, displays—as of this date—little tonal or imaginative distinction. Pianist Gil Coggins isn't heard fully enough to warrant expanded appraisal, but I'd certainly like to hear more.

Percy's bass work is first-rate, and his tone has become more full and sure over the last two years. It is Art Blakey, however, who rides through these sides like William the Conqueror. Not only does he lay down a remarkable, swinging beat, but his individual aid to each soloist is reminiscent of the imaginativeness of the late Sid Catlett (hear Art behind Johnson in "Tempus Fugit").

That third star is wholly due to Blakey.

—Nat Hentoff

"Tempus Fugit"; "Enigma"; "Ray's Idea"; "Kelo"; "I Waited for You"; "C.T.A."

Feb. 10, 1954
Charlie Parker
"She Rote" ★★★★★
"K.C. Blues" ★★
Clef 11101

"Rote," on the changes of "Beyond the Blue Horizon," flashes a fiery pair of opening choruses from Bird that should chase quite a few altoists back to the woodshed. He's superb, both here and later in the record. Between, there's a solo from Miles Davis in which he plays confidently and movingly, obviously inspired by Parker's opening lance, and a piano contribution from Walter Bishop. Max Roach and bassist Teddy Kotick give unwavering backing.

Flip side is a throw away, once-through blues of only mild interest.

—Jack Tracy

June 16, 1954
Miles Davis
Prestige 161
★★★

First four were made in May 1953, with John Lewis, Percy Heath and Max Roach, and were reviewed as an EP. Second side was recorded in January of this year with Horace Silver, Percy Heath and Art Blakey. Though there are small lapses in intonation and execution throughout, Miles blows interestingly for the most part, but he apparently needs the stimulus of at least one other horn to improvise at his best.

His most cohesive work here is on Charlie Mingus' "Smooch" and on the simple blues "Blue Haze," where he comes on in spots like Rex Stewart. Miles has rarely sounded as warmly relaxed as on "Haze." Rhythm sections on both dates acquitted themselves with distinction.

—Nat Hentoff

"When Lights Are Low"; "Tune Up"; "Miles Ahead"; "Smooch"; "Four";
"That Ole Devil Called Love"; "Blue Haze."

═══════

Aug. 11, 1954
Miles Davis
Prestige 182
★★★★

Prestige has recently been recording at Rudy Van Gelder's in New Jersey and
using better material in its pressing. Believe me, the difference is enjoyably
noticeable. Miles uses the unit he worked with at Birdland, and for a week at
Basin Street a couple of months ago: Lucky Thompson, J.J. Johnson, Horace
Silver, Percy Heath and Kenny Clarke. The first side goes a few seconds more
than eight minutes, after which the sextet walks for more than 13 minutes.
The Silver–Heath–Clarke rhythm section could even swing the Pittsburgh
Pirates. Lucky hasn't had this kind of recording opportunity for quite a while,
and it's good to hear his firm, drivingly intense tenor on both sides. J.J. also
sounds well, especially in his extended choruses on "Walkin'." Same is true of
Miles, who sounds more relaxed on "Walkin'" than "Blue 'n' Boogie." Closing
ensemble on the former is too drawn out while what little ensemble work
there is on "Blue" wasn't carefully enough planned. It's a good, vigorous date.
With a little more advance work, it could have been a five-star session.

—Nat Hentoff

"Blue 'n' Boogie"; "Walkin'."

═══════

Nov. 17, 1954
Miles Davis
Prestige 185
★★★★

With Miles are altoist Dave Schildkraudt and an excellent rhythm section of
Horace Silver, Percy Heath and Kenny Clarke. High point of the set is Miles'
lovely interpretation of "You Don't Know What Love Is." His reading is
real "soulful," as he might say. "Solar," which has a lunar quality, is warmly
relaxed, and there are good moments in the uptempo "I'll Remember April"
(7:50), which takes all of the second side.

Among the chief kicks there is Silver's humorous, loosely swinging piano. Schildkraudt, a Stan Kenton alumnus, is an altoist of power and passion, but his conception tends to fall choppily into fragmentary phrases. His solo lines are not yet integrated into flowing, cohesive entities. Good recording. No notes.

—Nat Hentoff

"Solar"; "You Don't Know What Love Is"; "I'll Remember April."

March 9, 1955
Miles Davis, Vol. 3
Blue Note 5040
★★★★

In this recital, Miles is excellently accompanied by Horace Silver, Percy Heath and Art Blakey. The first and last three originals are by Miles. One of the two best originals of the set, however, is Thelonious Monk's characteristically quizzical "Well, You Needn't." The Rodgers and Hart "It Never Entered My Mind" is taken slowly with a deliberate simplicity that is somewhat more stolid than lyrical. The other four line-patterns are good vehicles for extended variation by Miles, particularly the haunting, blues-filled "Weirdo."

It would have helped to further sustain the interest of the date if there had been at least one other horn, but the rating remains high for the strongly alive rhythm section and for Miles, who blows with imaginative and tonal style—a style unmistakably and influentially his own. A very attractive cover design.

—Nat Hentoff

"Take-Off"; "It Never Entered My Mind"; "Well, You Needn't"; "Lazy Susan"; "Weirdo"; "The Leap."

May 18, 1955
Miles Davis
Prestige 196
★★★

Volume 1 of the Miles Davis All-Stars has one tune to a side. Milt Jackson's "Bags' Groove" goes more than 11 minutes and Miles' new original, "Swing Spring," lasts nearly 11 minutes. The All-Stars are Milt Jackson, Percy

Heath, Kenny Clarke and Thelonious Monk. The outstanding soloist is Jackson, and the rhythm section moves well, with Heath and Clarke being an especial gas.

Miles has his moments (e.g., the final choruses on "Groove"), but I've heard him in more incandescent form. And Monk has known more fruitful hours (much of his lengthy exercise in understatement on "Groove" strikes me as valuable only if it's meant to be a parody). All in all, both tunes lasted too long and not enough care was given to organizing the session. Good recording quality.

—Nat Hentoff

"Bags' Groove"; "Swing Spring."

=====

June 2, 1955
Miles Davis
Birth of the Cool
Capitol 459
★★★★★

Not only has Capitol reissued four of the important Davis–Mulligan–Evans 1949 new directional experiments, but also included in this LP are four others that have never been released before. Three of them were cut in 1950—Gerry Mulligan's "Rocker," Miles Davis' "Deception" and an arrangement of Johnny Mercer's "Moon Dreams," the last half of which is of unusually rich textural interest. The personnel on those three had Miles, J.J. Johnson, Lee Konitz, Mulligan, John Lewis, Al McKibbon, Max Roach, John Barber (tuba) and Gunther Schuller (French horn).

The other new recording, Lewis' "Rouge," was recorded in 1949 on the same date as "Israel." On that session, Sandy Siegelstein was on French horn; Nelson Boyd, bass; and Kenny Clarke, drums; with the rest of the personnel the same. The band changes on the "Jeru/Godchild" date were Kai Winding, trombone; Junior Collins, French horn; Al Haig, piano; and Joe Schulman, bass.

The four heard here for the first time are just as absorbing as the other results of these collaborations (not all of which are included in this LP). The unusual instrumentation—for that time—was skillfully utilized by the arrangers to provide new ensemble colorations and a unity of complexly knit sound that has influenced modern jazz ever since. And with all the paper work, the sides swing with a lightness and crispness of attack that will keep them alive for many years. Not everything worked out perfectly at these sessions, but so large a percentage of the searching was successful that these are among the major historical guideposts in recorded jazz.

—Nat Hentoff

"Jeru"; "Moon Dreams"; "Venus de Milo"; "Deception"; "Godchild"; "Rocker"; "Israel"; "Rouge."

Nov. 2, 1955
Miles Davis
The Musings of Miles
Prestige 7007
★★★★★

Miles' first 12-inch LP enlists the aid of bassist Oscar Pettiford, Philadelphia pianist Red Garland and drummer Philly Joe Jones. The two originals, both sparely built but intriguing, are by Miles. Pettiford is solid; Jones has a lot of fire along with taste and works very well behind Miles; Garland is good but has a frequently idle left hand on middle and up tempos that thereby takes a dimension away from most of his choruses. Miles is fine, and plays with so much heart and intelligently original conception that he's consistently cooking. Dig, for example, his simple lyrically effective muted work on "I See Your Face Before Me," the way he renews "A Night in Tunisia" and the blues-deep warmth of his horn in "Green Haze." Good, informative notes by Ira Gitler.

—Nat Hentoff

"Will You Still Be Mine?"; "I See Your Face Before Me"; "I Didn't"; "A Gal in Calico"; "A Night in Tunisia"; "Green Haze."

Nov. 30, 1955
Caught in the Act: Jeri Southern, Miles Davis, Terry Gibbs
Birdland, New York

Jeri Southern's first Birdland appearance in six years was as welcome as a warm, sunny day in the dead of winter. It is the largely indescribable quality of personality that is Jeri's primary power. She comes through as a girl who feels music sensitively and who doesn't dig distorting it for quick commercial gain. Equally effective is her sound, and her attention to lyrics so that there is no mistaking the story contours of each song.

There are very few singers like Jeri who make it equally well at Birdland and the Blue Angel and still remain uniquely themselves. Her choice of numbers is uniformly intelligent and apt for her particular style with a song. On one set, she caressed "You'd Better Go Now," moved in to a darkly effective "Black Is the Color of My True Love's Hair," then jumped lightly through "This Can't Be Love," "Something I Dreamed Last Night" and "Something Wonderful," which created other moods, chiefly a marked reluctance on the part of the audience to hear the set end.

Miles Davis' band made for a generally effective complementary billing with Jeri. Miles himself had not played as consistently and strongly in a New York club in some time, but the band as a whole is not cohesive yet.

Terry Gibbs' quartet was the third unit on the bill, and swung all the way with bassist Herman Wright, drummer Jerry Segal and the attractive—and always moving—Terry Pollard. Gibbs himself so obviously enjoys playing that he communicates much of that enjoyment to the audience.

All in all, this was as good a bill as Birdland has had in some time—always excepting, of course, Count Basie.

—Nat Hentoff

Dec. 14, 1955
Miles Davis
Blue Moods
Debut 120
★★★★★

The album is called *Blue Moods,* and the title is exact. Miles is backed with taste and intelligence by Charlie Mingus, Teddy Charles, Britt Woodman and drummer Elvin Jones. Everyone falls sensitively into the reflective twilight scene, and everyone plays excellently. Miles has the major share of solo space and demonstrates again how lyrically he excels in this kind of context. Mingus is characteristically strong and penetratingly imaginative in both solo and section. Woodman has only one solo ("There's No You"). It's a good one, and he should have had more. All the spare, well-knit arrangements (except for Mingus' equally capable one of "Alone Together") are by Charles.

—Nat Hentoff

"Nature Boy"; "Alone Together"; "There's No You"; "Easy Living."

May 30, 1956
The New Miles Davis Quintet
Prestige 7014
★★★★

The New Miles Davis Quintet is the unit with which he's been traveling for several months—tenor John Coltrane, pianist Red Garland, bassist Paul Chambers and drummer Philly Joe Jones. Miles is in wonderfully cohesive form here, blowing with characteristically personal, eggshell tone, muted on the standards, open on the originals. And he continues to grow in his searching quality of being able to get so inside a song that he makes it fit him as if to order without injuring the essence of the work as first written. Coltrane, as Ira Gitler notes accurately, "is a mixture of Dexter Gordon, Sonny Rollins and Sonny Stitt." But so far there's very little Coltrane. His general lack of individuality lowers the rating.

Garland plays some of his best choruses on record here, combining imaginative sensitivity with relaxed light-fingered swing. Chambers lays down a support that could carry an army band. His tone is full and never flabby and his time is right. He has only one solo, a building one on "The Theme." His bass is somewhat over-recorded in places.

Philly Joe is pulsatingly crisp as usual, and he has apparently curbed a previous tendency to play too loudly too often. The last tune, a uniquely attractive original, is by Philadelphian Benny Golson. A very good set, particularly worth absorbing for Miles. He himself deserves a five.

—Nat Hentoff

"Squeeze Me"; "There Is No Greater Love"; "How Am I to Know?"; "S'posin'"; "The Theme"; "Stablemates."

Oct. 17, 1956
Miles Davis
Miles Davis and Milt Jackson, Quintet/Sextet
Prestige 7034
★★★★

A basic personnel of Miles, Milt Jackson, Percy Heath, Arthur Taylor and pianist Ray Bryant becomes a sextet on the first and third tracks with altoist Jackie McLean. Both are his tunes. "Bitty" is by Thad Jones, and Bryant contributed "Changes."

In contrast to many current sets that emphasize written frameworks and/or extended form, these conversations are in the tradition of improvised solo jazz with practically all the responsibility on the soloist, however fetching the starting lines and sequence of changes.

Bags' statements are as close to "pure" elemental jazz as the Hot Five of Louis Armstrong. Nothing he plays is extraneous or self-consciously rhetorical; it's all part of the swinging marrow of his jazz self-expression. Miles, more reflective, is less abandoned than Bags but no less hot-from-the-inside. McLean has the least solo space, and blows what he has with jagged warmth.

Bryant is impressive, playing with logic, imagination, heat and force. The rhythm section is steady. Bags is fine all the way through; Miles flows particularly in his muted solo in the oddly melancholy "Changes," but also has intense personal reflections of value elsewhere. As a no-frills, this-is-my-story collection, the LP is recommended.

—Nat Hentoff

"Dr. Jackie"; "Bitty Ditty"; "Minor March"; "Changes."

Dec. 26, 1956
Miles Davis
Collector's Items
Prestige 7044
★★★★½

Collector's Items is in two parts. The first side was cut in January 1953, and is released for the first time. It's the session with Charlie Parker on tenor that Sonny Rollins talked about in the Nov. 28, 1956, *DownBeat.* Sonny is also present on tenor with a cooking rhythm section of Philly Joe Jones, Walter Bishop and Percy Heath. The most arresting track is the mournful "'Round About Midnight," which has Bird's best tenor and Miles' best trumpet of the date.

For the rest, his tenor work is inevitably intriguing and forceful, and I wish there had been more recorded examples of his work on the horn after he had been playing it for some months (on this date, he has a new tenor that was christened on the date). Sonny also plays with heat. Miles is in good if not outstanding form, and Philly Joe is somewhat too loud in places. Bird is called Charlie Chan on the envelope.

The newer session (the last three tracks) has better Miles, considerably improved Rollins (with fuller, warmer tone and more cohesive idea structuring) and a superior rhythm section of Tommy Flanagan, Paul Chambers and

Art Taylor. Flanagan also solos with flowing distinction. Miles wrote the first two, and the third is Dave Brubeck's. The improvement in Prestige's recorded sound in three years, incidentally, is illuminating.

"Vierd Blues" is a fine demonstration of the continuing, freshening, earthy validity of the blues in modern jazz, with Sonny blowing one of his most eloquent choruses on record. This track has superb Miles and another excellent Flanagan solo. Miles treats the Brubeck ballad with sensitive intentness. Sonny is less lyrical, but his solo is built interestingly. And Flanagan, one of the few younger pianists with a quality of touch and lyricism akin to Hank Jones, speaks briefly. An important record.

—Nat Hentoff

"The Serpent's Tooth" (two takes); "'Round About Midnight"; "Compulsion"; "No Line"; "Vierd Blues"; "In Your Own Sweet Way."

May 16, 1957
Miles Davis
'Round About Midnight
Columbia 949
★★★★★

First, let me say that you should buy this LP immediately. Perhaps even two copies, since you may wear out one playing it and you will want another. This is the kind of album to which one returns time and time again because it is, in its way, a perfect thing, a slice of modern jazz conceived and executed in the very best style.

To those of you who may have heard this group (the album was made by the unit with which Miles has been touring for some time now) and have been disappointed, I want to point out that this album has captured all the best of the group and that Columbia and George Avakian have managed to make them sound on record as they have sounded only occasionally in person.

There is a mellowness, a lack of hostility and a ripe, romantic grooviness to the sound and spirit of this album that makes it an utter pleasure to hear.

The cover picture shows Miles with fingers in his ears, a position that some have emulated when Jones has been busy playing with less thought about dynamics than one might wish. On the album, however, he has been restrained either through electronics or by other devices, to use brushes at least part of the time behind Miles, and the result is an extraordinary example of the Milesian extension of single horn solos over rhythm. It is hard to see what can be done next.

Miles is in exquisite form. His inferential, tentative, haunting, low-pressure direction (reminiscent sometimes of Bunk Johnson—of all persons) is at its best in "'Round About Midnight," "All of You" and "Bye, Bye Blackbird," in which his essentially melodic conception seems particularly at home.

Miles plays with a dainty, almost delicate manner as he probes the melodic possibilities in these tunes, setting up a romantic, glowing mood in his first choruses that allows him to improvise endlessly in the second half of his solos. The break at the end of Davis' initial statement in "All of You" is as close to a wail as he produces on this album and yet it is a very moving thing. His solos build beautifully to logical climaxes, and Coltrane, who customarily enters after Miles, seems here to have more of the melding of Pres and Hawkins and less of the bad tone which has been his lot up to now.

In "All of You," Coltrane and Chambers set up what is almost a duet, and although Jones has switched to cymbals, it does not detract but rather adds. Garland, with his occasional excursions into the use of locked chords in his second choruses plays very effectively throughout the entire album. His chorus on "Blackbird" was particularly impressive for the manner in which he walked in, dancing along in a most attractive, elfin fashion.

Chambers has a long solo in the bop classic "Tadd's Delight," which, while it is impressive as all of his solos are, seems to indicate he has yet to master his tone problem.

Avakian's notes are informative despite an almost maidenly reluctance to mention Capitol when discussing Miles' previous important recordings.

—Ralph J. Gleason

"'Round About Midnight"; "A-Leu-Cha"; "All of You"; "Bye, Bye Blackbird"; "Tadd's Delight"; "Dear Old Stockholm."

Personnel: Davis, trumpet; John Coltrane, tenor saxophone; Red Garland, piano; Paul Chambers, bass; Philly Joe Jones, drums.

Aug. 8, 1957
Caught in the Act: Miles Davis Quintet
Personnel: Davis, trumpet; Sonny Rollins, tenor; Paul Chambers, bass; Red Garland, piano; Art Taylor, drums.
Reviewed: Cafe Bohemia, New York, two sets midway in the second week of a two-week stand.

I first heard Davis play in person at the Newport Jazz Festival two years ago. At that time, I was amazed that any human could achieve such a distillation of pure sound from an instrument so often thunderous. If anything, Miles has gone on making his tone purer and purer until it now is the gentlest of whispers when muted, and a subtle but somehow forceful and glowing sound on open horn.

He is ranging into exploration of dynamics as well as tone texture. On several of the originals, he built choruses expertly, one piece fitting neatly into the next, to a gleaming full shout, which, with Miles, is not loud but rather declarative. On other choruses, he would fall away to the subtlest of whispers, making his solo line a vehicle as fleet and delicate as a glance.

Perhaps it is the forceful presence of Rollins in this group that is bringing out this burst of artistry in Miles. Surely, Rollins is of some effect on his leader. Sonny's choruses, too, are constructed with craftsmanship—now rough-edged and brimming with virility, now soft and nearly timid but always sure of footing and aimed at a goal constantly achieved before he takes his horn from his lips.

The third melodic voice in the group is Chambers, who always has sounded like a section on record. In person, his full-bodied tone brings him out of the rhythm section, and his melodic voice is felt constantly in ensembles and behind the horns.

Garland is flexible and strongly rhythmic in the group, and supple in solos. On "Diane," for example, he varied the texture of his playing. From a longish line of dominantly right-hand phrases, he worked into a building series of powerful chords excitingly catapulting to a logical climax.

In addition to standing alone as a fine solo, it perfectly set off Miles, who followed with short bursts of melody blown in his liquid muted sound. Taylor's often bombastic drumming was edited to the dimensions of the pace set by Miles.

One final comment: "Bye, Bye Blackbird," long a sentimental favorite of mine, is as familiar a song as "Stardust." But never have I heard it blown with such feeling and depth as by Miles, who, though muted, achieved more genuine emotional impact than many could with the fuller range of sound available on open horn.

Audience Reaction: A full house, rather unusual for midweek, remained remarkably quiet, and even more remarkably attentive to the group. The response was warm and sustained after each number, particularly after the solos.

Attitude of Performers: The group is neat in appearance, and on the sets caught was quite businesslike, apparently absorbed in its work. Miles was in a buoyant mood, strolling down into the audience after his solos to chat with friends.

The lone failing of the group is in not announcing titles of tunes and thereby giving the audience a peg on which to focus its concentration. It might help album sales, too.

Commercial Potential: This group, now very good, could well become great. It has the talent necessary. It is booked to return to this location in July and to record for Columbia this summer.

Summary: Miles is increasing in stature as an artist. But while savoring his playing, don't neglect the rest of the group. There is that much going on.

—Dom Cerulli

Sept. 19, 1957
Miles Davis
Cookin' With the Miles Davis Quintet
Prestige 7094
★★★★★

All the tremendous cohesion, the wild, driving swing, and the all-out excitement and controlled emotion that was present at the best moments of the Davis quintet has been captured on this record. Jones has said these sessions, made in 1956 and the last of Miles' Prestige recordings, are the best Davis has made. I am inclined to agree.

Miles was in exquisite form; Coltrane sounds better here than on any except the group's Columbia LP; Chambers is well-recorded, and his solo on "Blues by Five" is particularly gratifying. Philly Joe Jones and Garland work together in their intricate system of rhythmic feeding in a fashion that has seldom been done, if ever, before by any rhythm section.

There are many moments of pure music and emotional joy on this album. Note the traces of Davis in Coltrane's solo on "Airegin"; note Miles and Philly Joe at the end of Davis' first solo on "Tune Up"; note Jones and Garland behind Coltrane on the same tune; note how Jones doubles up against the pulse behind Coltrane on "When Lights Are Low."

Garland contributes a golden solo on "Lights" and on "Five." In the same tune, note how the rhythm section continues the melodic outline behind the solos.

As to Miles, his peculiar blend of pure melody and acidulous accents never has sounded better. His "squees" and "whees" come at the moment you least expect them. On his own composition "Tune Up," he gets a remarkable show

tune type of sound in his statement of the melody and then prefaces his improvisation by a series of two-note phrases with the accent on the second one. This
is extremely effective. "My Funny Valentine" is a slow one, done thoughtfully
and almost sedately at times, with Jones on brushes behind Davis.

However, it is "When Lights Are Low," Benny Carter's great tune that
is mislabeled "Just Squeeze Me" on my copy, that is the classic number. This
is the second version of it Miles has recorded, and it is interesting to note
that the tempo is almost exactly the same this time. This is one of the best
arrangements this group had; an inventive melding of simplicity and thorough
exploration of the harmonic and rhythmic possibilities.

Miles' wispy statement of the melody is followed by Coltrane's ruminative
solo, Garland follows with his best work of the date, a long solo the second
half of which is locked chords, and there is a short bit of Davis presaging
the unison out chorus. This is one of the best LPs of the year and makes one
wonder why the group rated so few votes in the Jazz Critics Poll.

—Ralph J. Gleason

"Airegin"; "Tune Up"; "When Lights Are Low"; "My Funny Valentine";
"Blues by Five."

Personnel: Davis, trumpet; John Coltrane, tenor; Red Garland, piano; Paul
Chambers, bass; Philly Joe Jones, drums.

Dec. 12, 1957
Miles Davis
Miles Ahead
Columbia 1041
★★★★★

This is an extraordinarily well-done album with absolutely no point at which
you can wish for more if you, like John Lewis and so many others, have
wished for a big band with delicacy. If so, here it is, playing 10 beautifully
arranged (by Gil Evans) selections and sounding a good deal like the best of
Claude Thornhill with Miles.

Miles' use of the flugelhorn on this album does not in the slightest detract
from his communication. Rather, it lends a certain spice to it, as he extracts
from this sometimes blatant instrument all its mellowness and fullness. There
is no piano, but this is not noticeable at all, because what occurs here is a
remarkably flexible set of scores, written with a suppleness, fluidity and skill

that should immediately bring Gil Evans to the front rank of contemporary jazz writers. And long due.

With the exception of Miles and an occasional bit of Paul Chambers, there is no one else on this album who can be said to solo. It is interesting to consider this effort—for which all thanks, not only to Miles and Evans and the band, but to Columbia and George Avakian for making it possible—in comparison to other big band experimental albums in recent years.

Some of them, notably the recent Johnny Richards and now and then a flash from Shorty Rogers, have had a quality of excitement that this album does not have, deliberately I am sure. But aside from that, the tonal effects, the coloration, the subtlety, the lack of tension and the pure, lyrical quality is comparable only to Duke and Ralph Burns' *Summer Sequence*. This is not, by intention, an LP to raise you off your chair screaming. It is one to bring you close to almost unbearable delights in music in much of the same way the Modern Jazz Quartet does, and which only Duke has consistently been able to do with a big band. The handling of the brass, with its muttering, spouting, rolling figures is a thing of liveliness that grows with each listening.

Miles' solos throughout have an almost ascetic purity about them. They are deliberate, unhurried and almost inevitable in their time. On "Miles Ahead" he comes bouncing and skipping in almost as though he were the legendary Piper, dancing his way along leading everyone. The brass figures that follow Miles on this side are so Thornhill-ish it's startling.

One of the most exquisite numbers on this album—and that is a good word to apply to all of them, by the way—is Dave Brubeck's tribute to Ellington, "The Duke." It's a bit of pure description that immediately calls up Duke and remains in your mind after the LP is through.

Andre Hodeir, in his excellent notes, says, "I don't have room enough to point out all the beauties that I have discovered while listening over and over to the orchestration of these 10 little concertos assembled in a vast fresco." It cannot be expressed better than that as far as I am concerned.

The 10 selections are, by the way, arranged as a program of continuous music, each following without pause. This makes it doubly pleasurable to hear; but it is not alone the sort of jazz that demands full attention. This is some of the best mood music produced since Duke.

—Ralph J. Gleason

"Springsville"; "The Maids of Cadiz"; "The Duke"; "My Ship"; "Miles Ahead"; "Blues for Pablo"; "New Rhumba"; "The Meaning of the Blues"; "Lament"; "I Don't Wanna Be Kissed."

Personnel: Miles Davis, flugelhorn; Bernie Glow, Ernie Royal, Louis Mucci, Taft Jordan and John Carisi, trumpets; Frank Rehack, Jimmy Cleveland

and Joe Bennett, trombones; Tom Mitchell, bass trombone; Willie Ruff and Tony Miranda, horns (Jimmy Buffington replaced Miranda on one session); Bill Barber, tuba; Lee Konitz, alto; Danny Bank, bass clarinet (Edwin Caine replaced Cooper on one session); Paul Chambers, bass; Art Taylor, drums.

May 15, 1958
Miles Davis
Relaxin' With the Miles Davis Quintet
Prestige 7129
★★★★

After all that walkin' and cookin', it's time for Miles and men to relax. That's what they do here. This is an informal, one-take-a-tune session, complete with asides from Miles to Prestige's Bob Weinstock and a false start on "Everything."

Miles plays muted horn on all but "Woody 'n' You" here. He plays with his customary delicate, intricate impact. Chambers is superb. Garland plays effectively in support and solos authoritatively. Jones, less oppressive here than in past conquests, contributes inspirationally, too. The material is of interest, with the standards particularly well handled. It's pleasant to hear a coordinated jazz group approach such tunes.

There is a hesitancy and lack of melodic content in Coltrane's playing at times here that hampers his effectiveness for me and lowers the rating of the LP. This is particularly true on the first two tracks, on which his solos seem to me to be rather aimless and somewhat strident. However, he is quite fluent on "Oleo" and "I Could Write a Book." His efforts, throughout the LP, lack a consistent quality.

In general, however, this is an attractive set. And when all the members of the quintet are inspired, as on "Book" and "Oleo," it is a valuable demonstration of conceptual prowess.

Ira Gitler's notes are frank and informative.

—Don Gold

"If I Were a Bell"; "You're My Everything"; "I Could Write a Book"; "Oleo"; "It Could Happen to You"; "Woody 'n' You."

Personnel: Davis, trumpet; John Coltrane, tenor; Red Garland, piano; Paul Chambers, bass; Philly Joe Jones, drums.

July 23, 1959
Miles Davis/Gil Evans
Porgy and Bess
Columbia 1274
★★★★★

The inherent pensiveness of Gil Evans' writing and the introversion of Miles Davis' playing produces something akin to a gas flame turned as low as it can be without going out. Its heat is quiet, but very intense.

What is possible to say now about Gil Evans? This man has genius. He is one of the few living composers whose magic passes all the technical tests for stature without dying in the process. He has taken what he wanted and needed from the classical tradition, and yet remained a jazz writer, safely evading the lure of contemporary classical music, which has written itself up a blind alley. In his control and reserve (notice "Summertime") he can put you in the mind of Sibelius, who may have been the last classical composer to express himself naturally and without calculation of effects because he felt it that way. Yet Evans is unique, and his development has been quite personal. His debts are to himself: There are things in this album that hark back to his days of writing for Claude Thornhill.

The *Porgy* songs are quite submerged in this album, soaked up by the personalities—or rather, the joint personality—of Evans and Davis. You forget the underlying structures and, since the music used is not in the standard AABA pop song form to begin with, the album becomes a remarkable jazz experience, both for the musicians and the listener, who will be forcibly reminded of the great seriousness and the serious greatness in jazz, the universality in it that Andre Hodeir is always talking about.

Some of the best of Miles is to be heard in this album—along with some of the sloppiest. There are cracked and fuzzed notes and other things that just shouldn't have been let go ("Strawberry" may make all but the most uncritical Davis fans squirm). Why these things were let pass is anybody's guess. Maybe Miles didn't care. Maybe they were let pass in accordance with the dubious faith that even mistakes are part of the whole and therefore to be admired in jazz. Maybe it is because the executives-in-charge think that Miles' stature is such that these considerations are small in comparison—which, as a matter of fact, is true.

In any case, the Davis–Evans relationship has again produced superb music. In the jazz albums of *Porgy,* this one is in a class by itself. Which figures: It named its own terms.

—Don Gold

"The Buzzard Song"; "Bess, You Is My Woman Now"; "Gone, Gone, Gone, Gone"; "Summertime"; "Bess, Oh Where's My Bess?"; "Prayer (Oh Doctor Jesus)"; "Fisherman, Strawberry and Devil Crab"; "My Man's Gone Now"; "It Ain't Necessarily So"; "Here Come de Honey Man"; "I Loves You, Porgy"; "There's a Boat That's Leaving Soon for New York."

Personnel: Miles Davis, featured trumpet; arrangements by and orchestra under the direction of Gil Evans; Louis Mucci, Ernie Royal, John Coles, Bernie Glow, trumpets; Willie Ruff, Julius B. Watkins, Gunther Schuller, French horns; Jimmy Cleveland, Joseph Bennett, Dick Hixon, Frank Rehak, trombones; Phil Bodner or Jerome Richardson and Romeo Penque, flutes; John (Bill) Barber, tuba; Julian Adderley, Danny Banks, saxophones; Paul Chambers, bass; Philly Joe Jones or Jimmy Cobb, drums.

Aug. 6, 1959
Caught in the Act: Miles Davis Sextet
Jazz Seville, Hollywood
Personnel: Miles Davis, trumpet; Julian "Cannonball" Adderley, alto; John Coltrane, tenor; Wynton Kelly, piano; Paul Chambers, bass; Jimmy Cobb, drums.

In his first appearance on the West Coast in over two years, Miles Davis presented not a group as such but a very good rhythm section backing three star soloists. Not only were all six musicians not onstand together during any set on opening night, but there was no ensemble playing to speak of and, when the group was reviewed, Cannonball laid out completely during two consecutive sets.

The character of the sextet's engagement—for a reputed $2,500 a week—threw into razor-sharp focus the question of night club entertainment vs. untrammeled expression by jazz artists of varying maturity. While there can be no questioning the validity of the instrumentalists' right to express themselves in the jazz art, the debatable point remains of social responsibility to an audience paying through the nose to hear and see them.

Miles would informally open a number, blowing down into the mike, oblivious of the audience. Coltrane would follow, strolling out of backstage shadows, to blow long and searchingly on the changes of, say, "All of You," or the blues. Pianist Kelly, from his spot on floor level invisible to most of the audience, would solo for, perhaps, four easy and funky choruses. Then Miles would appear onstand again to take the tune out.

As to the individual solo work, Cannonball was forthright and original in expression; Miles raw and searing with open horn, insinuating and subtle with mute tight on the mike. Coltrane communicated a sense of inhibition (sometimes even frustration) with his calculated understatement and contrived dissonance. On the whole, the tenor man's contributions suggested superficially stimulating, lonely and rather pathetic self-seeking. Is this truly the dilemma of the contemporary American jazz artist? One hesitates to believe so.

For all the showcasing of the frequently brilliant soloists, one yearned to hear ensemble performance by these three horns of established merit. But apparently nobody had eyes—or the musicians were not prepared to offer such fare.

Some highlights of the solo work included Cannonball's compulsive strength and vigorous attack on a medium blues; Coltrane's multinoted minor exposition leading to an extended solo characterized by quick and frequent long flurries of notes that seemed vainly to seek the anchoring of a definitive feel for the solo mood; Chambers' infrequent arco solo excursions, brilliantly and facilely executed, and Miles' close-muted incisiveness.

Predictably, the audience—which packed the Seville opening night—expressed appreciation with much palm-beating. (Possibly the jam-session atmosphere engendered by the attitude of the musicians onstand got through to the customers.) In any event, this long overdue appearance by Miles and companions in Los Angeles set the locals straight on the current New York mode of jazz presentation.

—John Tynan

Oct. 1, 1959
Miles Davis
Kind of Blue
Columbia 1355
★★★★★

This is a remarkable album. Using very simple but effective devices, Miles has constructed an album of extreme beauty and sensitivity. This is not to say that this LP is a simple one—far from it. What is remarkable is that the men have done so much with the stark, skeletal material.

All the compositions bear the mark of the Impressionists and touches of Béla Bartók. For example, "So What" is built on two scales, which sound somewhat like the Hungarian minor, giving the performance a Middle

Eastern flavor; "Flamenco Sketches" and "All Blues" reflect a strong Ravel influence.

"Flamenco" and "Freddie Freeloader" are both blues, but each is of a different mood and conception; "Sketches" is in 6/8, which achieves a rolling, highly charged effect, while "Freeloader" is more in the conventional blues vein. The presence of Kelly on "Freeloader" may account partly for the difference between the two.

Miles' playing throughout the album is poignant, sensitive and, at times, almost morose; his linear concept never flatters. Coltrane has some interesting solos; his angry solo on "Freeloader" is in marked contrast to his lyrical romanticism on "All Blues." Cannonball seems to be under wraps on all the tracks except "Freeloader" when his irrepressible joie de vivre bubbles forth. Chambers, Evans and Cobb provide a solid, sympathetic backdrop for the horns.

This is the soul of Miles Davis, and it's a beautiful soul.

(No byline)

"So What"; "Freddie Freeloader"; "Blue in Green"; "Flamenco Sketches"; "All Blues."

Personnel: Davis, trumpet; Julian "Cannonball" Adderley, alto; John Coltrane, tenor; Bill Evans, piano (all tracks except "Freeloader"); Wynton Kelly, piano ("Freeloader"); Paul Chambers, bass; James Cobb, drums.

Oct. 1, 1959
Miles Davis
Miles Davis and the Modern Jazz Giants
Prestige 7150
★★★★½

There are few jazzmen whose creative resources are so great that any recorded example of their work is of interest. This reissue of 1954 and 1956 Davis sessions includes at least three such men: Milt Jackson, Thelonious Monk and Davis himself.

The earlier date (all titles but "'Round About Midnight"), which also produced "Bags' Groove," reveals a somewhat uncomfortable Miles, blowing with and against a free-wheeling, but only half-sympathetic group. Davis' approach to jazz, which leans heavily upon the sensitivity of his pianist, is left tattered by the jarring individualism of pianist Monk, whose playing is not designed to flatter or inspire Miles. In spite of all this, enough memorable moments came from the session to make this a very worthwhile LP.

"Swing Spring," in particular, demonstrates that Davis was ready to lead the way out of the cliché-ridden, I-can-blow-stronger-than-you arena into which many jazzmen had stampeded by the mid-'50s.

"Midnight," performed by the most esthetically satisfying of all Davis groups, is a musical essay on the virtues of lyricism and horizontal structure, combined with harmonic insight, a classic performance that should be in any thoughtful collector's library.

(No byline)

"The Man I Love (take 2)"; "Swing Spring"; "'Round About Midnight"; "Bemsha Swing"; "The Man I Love (take 1)."

Personnel: Tracks 1, 2, 4, 5: Davis, trumpet; Milt Jackson, vibes; Thelonious Monk, piano; Percy Heath, bass; Kenny Clarke, drums. Track 3: Davis, trumpet; John Coltrane, tenor; Red Garland, piano; Paul Chambers, bass; Philly Joe Jones, drums.

———

March 17, 1960
Miles Davis
Workin' With the Miles Davis Quintet
Prestige 7166
★★★★★

Even if it is quite possible that this is the least earth-shattering of the three Miles' LPs from this series of sessions, it still rates five stars because it is the sort of thing that is going to be owned and played and dug and redug for all time.

Few bands in the history of jazz have had the quality of this group. And not the least indication of its total importance is the individual importance of all its members then and now. Imagine if somebody had had the sense and initiative to take King Oliver and his Creole Jazz Band into the studio and leave them alone to cut their book, or that [Billy] Eckstine's great band had been let go at length. We can be everlastingly grateful to Bob Weinstock of Prestige for these recordings.

By now, everyone is familiar with the pattern and sound of this group. It does not seem sensible to essay any particular analysis here. Just let it go down like this: Red Garland plays particularly well on "Ahmad's Blues" (it's a trio) and Coltrane on "'Trane's Blues." But that's just the way it hits me. Actually, the whole LP is a gas. I don't see how anyone can do without it.

—Ralph J. Gleason

"It Never Entered My Mind"; "Four"; "In Your Own Sweet Way"; "The Theme (take 1)"; "Trane's Blues"; "Ahmad's Blues"; "Half Nelson"; "The Theme (take 2)."

Personnel: Davis, trumpet; John Coltrane, tenor saxophone; Red Garland, piano; Paul Chambers, bass; Philly Joe Jones, drums.

━━━━━━━

Sept. 29, 1960
Miles Davis/Gil Evans
Sketches of Spain
Columbia 1480
★★★★★

This record is one of the most important musical triumphs that this century has yet produced. It brings together under the same aegis two realms that in the past have often worked against one another—the world of the heart and the world of the mind.

So much of the jazz we hear today is one-sided. Either it is cold and calculated, with a minimum of feeling, like a lot of West Coast ensemble jazz, or it is a sloppy gush of terrifying emotion, like the music of some of the party-line hard schoolers.

But calculating brain and feeling heart need not cancel each other. Under the best conditions, one becomes the other—the mind feels; the heart thinks. This happy union has not often prevailed in jazz. Indeed, one camp abuses the other, and each threatens to suck dry its heritage. For this reason, we would all be well-advised to curl up in a quiet room and listen at length to this newest product of the Evans–Davis collaboration. Somewhere in the labyrinth, they have found the answer.

To give this "answer" in words is approachable but ultimately impossible. What is involved here is the union of idea with emotion, precomposition with improvisation, discipline with spontaneity. Every big band chart with built-in improvised solos is an attempt at this synthesis. But almost always there is simply compatible juxtaposition, not a true synthesis. (Let's except the music of Duke Ellington. He has succeeded more consistently than anyone else.)

The real value of *Sketches of Spain* lies in the fact that the intellectualism is so extreme, and, at the same time, the emotional content is so profound.

Evans' writing shows that he has been in good company. There are strong traces of serious contemporary European music, especially Bartók and Stravinsky. The mind reels at the intricacy of Evans' orchestral and developmental techniques. His scores are so careful, so formally well-constructed, so mindful of tradition, that you feel the originals should be preserved under glass in a Florentine museum. Yet the sheer emotional impact is overwhelming, almost embarrassing, in its power and honesty.

Similarly, Davis' playing is often so well thought out that you are overpowered by the cold logic of the man's brain. Yet there is nothing cold about the tears that Miles weeps for every man.

The experience you go through listening to this music is extraordinary. If you generally hear music as a series of moods, or emotional states, you will suddenly notice that you are hearing something else too: the connection of this part to that, the interplay of the large, formal sections, the careful building up of a certain harmonic progression, or of a certain melodic idea, the ingenious development of a thematic fragment.

On the other hand, if you tend to hear music analytically, as I do, this record will twist your ears too. Suddenly there will be no desire to figure out Miles' scale patterns, or to rush to the piano to check that ending chord. Instead, you will be willing—I mean compelled—to accept this music as an experience in virtue of itself, and not as a combination of so many analyzable details.

In short, this music is freedom incarnate. It transcends artistic prejudice—even, so help me, esthetic point of view.

Sketches of Spain is a suite of Spanish-influenced music. Both Davis and Evans delved into early Spanish folk material for much of their inspiration. The result is about as "Spanish" as Bartók's "Concerto for Orchestra" is "Hungarian" or Stravinsky's "Petrouchka" is "Russian." But it does make brilliant integral use of Spain's musical flavor.

The first side starts out with a 16-minute masterpiece, "Concierto de Aranjuez." This is the best track of the album. It is, to my knowledge, the first jazz work containing improvisation that stands complete in an extended form. It isn't a bunch of little pieces strung together, it is one long organic piece, like the first movement of a late Beethoven quartet. Joaquín Rodrigo composed the work.

"Will o' the Wisp" is taken from a 1915 ballet score of Manuel de Falla. It contains some high sustained French horn notes of insurpassable beauty.

"The Pan Piper," which begins the second side, is closest to the identifiable jazz style for which Miles is best known. He plays in a Harmon mute here, over delicate ostinato figures from the orchestra. It ends, however, with a whimper. I would rather hear the worst kind of goof than be subjected to the torture of a fade-out "ending."

"Saeta" is the most "Spanish" of the five works. It is the story of a religious procession, which approaches and recedes with very authentic-sounding trumpet fanfares. The bulk of the piece consists of wildly emotional playing by Davis. In the flamenco tradition, this part is sung by a woman, on a balcony, who is addressing an image of the crucified Christ. "It is the measure of Miles' stature as a musician and as a human being," Nat Hentoff says in the liner notes, "that he can absorb the language of another culture, that he can express through it a universal emotion with an authenticity that is neither strained nor condescending." I noticed in this passage an element of strain, of overreaching, but there is no dishonesty.

The final track, "Solea," is a little disappointing but only in that it doesn't match the inspired near-perfection of the others. Miles runs into difficulties.

Miles' style is so personal (though not especially intimate) that the listener feels he is actually experiencing the moment of creation. Also, at his best, Miles has the quality of inevitability, like Beethoven: One feels that every choice has been rightly made. These are the factors that have contributed to myth of the divinity and/or infallibility of Miles. Miles isn't divine and he's not infallible. He gets hung, and everybody knows it.

But the pain is only temporary. And hearing him get out of a jam is almost worth hearing him get into it. There is, for instance, one passage in "Solea" where, during a descending run of 16th-note-triplet–eighth-note figures, he gets so hung up that, toward the end, when the immediate future looks hopeless, you can almost hear him fling (musically) his patented two-word epithet right through his golden horn. Evidently disgusted, he stops playing for a long time. But when he comes back, it is with an ascent of such startling beauty that you know he did it all on purpose.

Miles Ahead (Columbia 1041), *Porgy and Bess* (Columbia 1274) and *Sketches of Spain* form a kind of terrifying triumvirate. If there is to be a new jazz, a shape of things to come, then this is the beginning.

To Davis and Evans goes not the distinction of five or 10 or a zillion stars in a review rating, but the burden of continuing to show us the way.

—Bill Mathieu

"Concierto de Aranjuez"; "Will o' the Wisp"; "The Pan Piper"; "Saeta"; "Solea."

Personnel: Davis, trumpet; Evans, conductor; large orchestra members unidentified.

July 6, 1961
Caught in the Act: Miles Davis
Carnegie Hall, New York
Personnel: Miles Davis, trumpet; Hank Mobley, tenor saxophone; Wynton Kelly, piano; Paul Chambers, bass; Jimmy Cobb, drums; 21-piece orchestra directed by Gil Evans.

Davis has never played more brilliantly than on this May night. Criticisms of his group can be made—Mobley was hardly more than a boppy intrusion; Kelly seemed overcome by Erroll Garner's success at Carnegie; Chambers and Cobb were only adequate—none of which is important in terms of what Miles played.

Even the names of the selections are unimportant. The trumpeter felt and paced his program differently from what had been announced. It caused some consternation, but his decisions were based on firm musical judgment regarding one composition, based on a judgment of his own emotional strength in terms of two other listed songs. (He left the stage at intermission with barely enough strength remaining to get to his dressing room.)

The concert was marked by excellent taste, an improved sound system (though it had its faults), gifts of red roses to the ladies, a cloth backdrop to enliven the bare stage and artful lighting.

Evans' rich, somber scores were, as usual, perfect complements to Davis' middle-register brooding. The combo's playing (the program was evenly divided between large- and small-group selections) was as usual, and as criticized; it was at its best on a fast blues highlighted by two-bar challenges between Davis and Cobb.

But all the impressive features of the concert were insignificant in the face of Miles' performance. He soared away from his usual restraint and limited register, playing high-note passages with tremendous fire, building magnificent solos that blazed with drama. The ballad "I Thought About You" was an open, emotional experience.

Few jazz performances have touched the heights of that evening. It was jazz at its finest.

—Bill Coss

Sept. 14, 1961
Miles Davis
Steamin' With the Miles Davis Quintet
Prestige 7200
★★★★½

This album is from the memorable 1956 recording dates by the Davis quintet. It is the last in the series that included *Cookin'*, *Relaxin'* and *Workin'*. This release takes its place with the other three as examples of free blowing at its most stimulating. Theme and variation, though it has been lamented and disparaged by critics and musicians, is still the heart of jazz, the proving ground.

The two horn men have, of course, become two of the strongest influences in contemporary jazz. At the time of these recording sessions, Davis had almost perfected his laconic, wistful manner of playing, but Coltrane had not yet found his direction. Though he plays well on this album, Coltrane tends to jump from idea to idea, seldom finishing what he has started. His solo on "Diane" is his most erratic in the album. On the other hand, when Coltrane follows through on ideas, his playing, as on "Well, You Needn't," is exceptional.

The aspect of Miles' playing that struck me the hardest was not his variations so much as his theme statements. There have been few jazzmen who played the melody as if it were anything but a chore to go through before getting to the blowing passages. Lester Young, Charlie Parker, young Louis Armstrong and Stan Getz are among these few who were and are able to express themselves through more-or-less straight melody passages. Davis must be included. His first chorus theme statements on "Surrey With the Fringe on Top" (he does the bridge, but it's an improvement on the original), "Something I Dreamed," "Diane" and "When I Fall in Love," if transcribed for another instrument would retain the Davis stamp. While it is easy to recognize any number of jazzmen as they state the melody, the recognition is more the result of the player's overall sound than his phrasing, his expansion and compressing of the original note values, or his editing of the melody. And these are the characteristics of Davis—and Bird, Pres, Louis and Getz. The only negative points of Miles' performance of melody is his dependence on the mute-in-mike device and his intonation—he's usually about that far flat.

His playing on the non-ballads, "Salt Peanuts" and "Needn't," should not be overlooked. Sometimes we get too taken with Miles' way with ballads and forget that he can be extremely fiery on up tempos. On these non-ballads in this album, his approach to each is different. His solo on "Peanuts" combines his earlier bop style with his latterday lyricism. On "Needn't" his solo is straightahead melodic improvisation.

The ensemble on these two tracks should be noted. Instead of stating the theme the same way [Charlie] Parker and Dizzy Gillespie did ("Peanuts") or as Thelonious Monk does ("Needn't"), Davis and Coltrane play abstractions of these two themes: Note values are extended in some cases, shortened in others, and on "Needn't" the two horns intertwine in a sort of round.

Garland's solos come as a letdown after Davis' or Coltrane's. Only on "Peanuts" and "Needn't," the album's best track, does he abandon his sometimes-nagging, splashing playing and dig in. The difference between romanticism and sentimentalism and the difference between tart and sugary playing is clearly defined when Davis' beautiful—the only word for it—solo on "Something I Dreamed Last Night" is compared with Garland's effort on the same track.

Jones is tasteful throughout and has a long solo on "Peanuts," in which he acquits himself admirably. Chambers is Chambers, strong in section, excellent in solo.

This album is a must for anyone seriously interested in jazz.

—Don DeMicheal

"Surrey With the Fringe on Top"; "Salt Peanuts"; "Something I Dreamed Last Night"; "Diane"; "Well, You Needn't"; "When I Fall in Love."

Personnel: Davis, trumpet; John Coltrane, tenor saxophone; Red Garland, piano; Paul Chambers, bass; Philly Joe Jones, drums.

Nov. 23, 1961
Miles Davis
In Person, Friday and Saturday Nights
Columbia 820
★★★★

These tracks were recorded at the Blackhawk in San Francisco. I am reviewing them as a two-record set, but each LP is available singly, as *Friday Night,* consisting of the first six titles below, and *Saturday Night,* the last six.

The recording is generally very good except that Davis' intimately close-miked sound is on the verge of distortion (without quite making it) on "Fran-Dance" and "Bell." One other flaw is also apparently technical, a decided drop in tempo between Davis' opening solo in "All of Me," and Kelly's portion—a tape splice, it would seem.

When Davis is good here, he is good indeed, and the only places where he is not really good are on "Fran-Dance," on which his lower register clouds up and he gets repeatedly hung on a single lick, a cliché in fact, which he somehow never executes cleanly. And more or less the same idea hangs him on "Blackbird," though only briefly. Those are the only places where fluffs bothered me as such. Also, I have never thought much of "Fran-Dance" ("Put Your Little Foot Right In") as material, and this seems to be a rather diffuse performance of it.

This visit to "All of You" also seems diffuse: Davis' first solo brings up some good ideas but never really finds its direction. His return at the end rebuilds things excellently, however.

On "All of Me," Kelly is good. He tries for less than Davis, of course, but his playing has direct organization. Next to Davis, Kelly is the soloist here. I particularly admire the way he has fallen into a somewhat preassigned, [Ahmad] Jamal-ish role in this group. Even when his ideas are not exceptional, they are usually good, and he always delivers them with personal force and conviction. He has an interesting solo on "Oleo," with a good variety of phrasing, fleetly delivered, and his solo on "Bell" is marred only by some rather predictable phrase lengths that he employs toward the end.

However, little can be made out of "I've Found You," which features Kelly alone. Granted, it is very well done, but such an out-of-tempo version of a pop tune, confined to a one-chorus statement with a few embellishments and some altered chords, seems to belong under the conversation in a chic cocktail lounge, no matter how well done.

Mobley is capable but the weakest soloist in this company. When Kelly lays out behind him on the very fast "Walkin'," for example, his time seems to falter. My first impression of "Walkin'" was that it was an impatient version, played fast through the boredom of having to answer the request for a hit record night after night. It is not; Davis is on top of the tempo, and he plays very good blues of his own special kind, with a wonderful climax to his solo. And if there is one lesson that his phrasing could teach, it is that one needn't clutter up a solo with notes at any tempo, that if one concentrates on melody and continuity, his lines can be simple, his pauses eloquent.

Mobley runs clichés on "Blackbird," including some out of Sonny Rollins, and on "So What," which is built on two scales rather than chords, one is soon conscious of the underlying mechanical framework during Mobley's episode.

On "Neo," Mobley is emotionally compelling from the first, but before he is through, he has played almost all those flamencan phrases that usually show up on the sound tracks of pictures about bullfighters.

On that same "Neo," which is more or less out of *Sketches of Spain,* Davis is eloquent, almost as movingly eloquent as he was on "Saeta"—and that means that he is almost as eloquent as any jazz musician is likely to get. The materials of "Neo" are very simple, and the temptations to run Spanish clichés or fall into a monotony of sound, melody or emotion are enormous. Davis gives in to them not at all.

I was fascinated by "Blackbird." Davis' theme statement has become a tantalizing, suggestive sketch of the original. There is an effective little modulation now, and the trumpeter's variations are better here than on any version of this piece I have ever heard him play. He also has new ideas on "Bell." I did feel, however, that "Oleo" has become a bit too fast for its own good.

"No Blues" has a medium funky line, taken at almost perfect tempo for the melody and the kind of variations that Davis comes up with. His emotional range in this performance is something to hear, all the way from his own version of simple earthiness through the kind of blues lyricism at which he is unique and including some humorous, "corny," on-the-beat licks en route.

Best of all is this fast version of "Well, You Needn't." I have not heard such sprightly, nearly breathless and original rhythmic interest from Davis since that superb solo on "Boplicity." I play his section of "Well, You Needn't" in delight and almost in disbelief. I shall remember his ideas there and on "Blackbird," and his eloquent speech on "Neo," for a long time.

I hear a lot of people in this man's work. Foremost I hear him, unmistakably. I also hear Lester Young, I hear Freddy Webster and I hear ideas of Dizzy Gillespie and Charlie Parker transmuted and put to such very different use that they are almost unrecognizable.

I hear a personal use of sound that also sometimes suggests that Davis is trying to reinterpret the whole range of sound of the Duke Ellington trumpets of 1939—Cootie Williams' plunger and Rex Stewart's half-valves—in a highly personal way, or a simply open or Harmon-muted horn. But more than anyone else, after Davis himself, I hear Louis Armstrong. There, I said it. I said it only for this reason:

Several people have tried to describe the emotion they hear in Miles Davis. It has been called effete lyricism, forceful lyricism, ecstasy. One man says that he hears in it nothing but defeat and despair. Another hears the whining and complaining of a disgruntled child. For me there is, beneath the sophistication and the thorough transmutation, the same kind of exuberant, humorous, committed, self-determined and forceful joy in Miles Davis that there is in Louis Armstrong.

—Martin Williams

"Walkin'"; "Bye, Bye Blackbird"; "All of You"; "No Blues"; "Bye, Bye"; "Love, I've Found You"; "Well, You Needn't"; "Fran-Dance"; "So What"; "Oleo"; "If I Were a Bell"; "Neo."

Personnel: Davis, trumpet; Hank Mobley, tenor saxophone; Wynton Kelly, piano; Paul Chambers, bass; Jimmy Cobb, drums.

April 26, 1962
Miles Davis
Someday My Prince Will Come
Columbia 1656
★★★★½

If anything, this set stresses Davis' highly introspective side. On four of the six selections he is muted, lonely and/or mournful. "Old Folks," "Drad-Dog" and "I Thought About You" are typically lovely statements. His moods are extremely lyrical and emotionally moving.

The other two selections find him playing open but relatively subdued. Their titles are a sore point, for Columbia has chosen to call them by names other than the ones they appeared under (in different versions) in Miles' *Friday and Saturday Nights at the Blackhawk* album. Are they trying to fool the public or has it got something to do with song royalties? Anyway "Teo" is really "Neo," and "Pfrancing" is "No Blues."

Another misleading fact is that the group is billed as a sextet, when in reality it is only a sextet on the title number. I can understand Davis' request for no liner notes (I assume that is why there are none), but that shouldn't have prevented Columbia from specifying the tunes on which Coltrane and Mobley play.

After Miles leads off "Someday My Prince Will Come" with a wonderful sweet-and-sour muted solo, Mobley comes in, mellow, simple and evenly flowing, as Cobb effectively switches to sticks. Kelly is both melodically and rhythmically stimulating. Then Coltrane caps everyone with an effort that reaches for and finds unexpected combinations of exquisitely held notes and rich, rapid runs. There is a haphazard pacing to "Prince," but it does not detract from it. Davis and Kelly each have sections that serve as interludes. After Davis has restated the theme, Kelly stretches out in a closing section that kind of evaporates rather than ends.

The only other number with Coltrane (and Mobley is not on this one) is the aforementioned "Teo," a minor tune cast in a modal vein. Davis' solo is an aftermath of *Sketches of Spain;* Coltrane's is the forerunner of "Olé" (originally "Spanish Tune"). Modal playing can be monotonous, and there are arid periods in each one's solo. Coltrane, however, builds to a pitch of excitement, and Davis, who has two solos, finishes strongly with the second.

Mobley is on all other selections. He is subdued and thoughtful on "Folks" and appropriately distant in an abbreviated bit on "Dog." His best is on "Thought," where he picks up Davis' second chorus, wherein Cobb has injected some insinuating stick pulse, and carries the mood perfectly until the tempo comes down again and Davis returns.

Mobley is not especially inventive on "Pfrancing," but he swings surely in the way he places his notes.

Davis, after a good opening, bogs down. The solos by Chambers and Kelly take the honors here. The latter has three separate good ones, and Chambers is fine, with some really exceptional moments. Kelly is excellent throughout the album, both in solo and accompaniment. Some of his two-handed sections in the upper part of the keyboard, put one in mind of Bill Evans, in mood if not in style. His single-lines are simultaneously hard and soft.

Cobb and Chambers groove perfectly together and with Kelly. The rhythm section, individually and as a whole, is very well-recorded.

Howard McGhee was quoted recently as saying that Davis used to play "more." In part, this is true. I find solos like "Bluing" (Prestige, 1951), although technically inferior to his trumpet playing today, touch me more than the kind of blues playing that is represented by "Pfrancing." And then, of course, there are "Bags' Groove" and "Walkin'" of 1954. But the Davis of the 1960s is another man and, as a result, has a different musical attitude. Just because he is playing less, in terms of notes, doesn't mean his powers have lessened.

Anything Davis does is important. This is one to get. And that Coltrane solo on "Prince!"

—Ira Gitler

"Someday My Prince Will Come"; "Old Folks"; "Pfrancing"; "Drad-Dog"; "Teo"; "I Thought About You."

Personnel: Davis, trumpet; Hank Mobley, John Coltrane, tenor saxophones; Wynton Kelly, piano; Paul Chambers, bass; Jimmy Cobb, drums.

July 5, 1962
Miles Davis
The Beginning
Prestige 7221

Prestige has instituted a reissue program including Miles Davis' *The Beginning*, originally titled *Musings of Miles*.

The Davis album was his first 12-inch LP, and, supported by pianist Red Garland, bassist Oscar Pettiford and drummer Philly Joe Jones, the trumpeter turns in an excellent performance, his playing ranging from a finely etched version of "I See Your Face Before Me" to an abstract but forceful "A Night in Tunisia" solo. He sounds like a pixie with guts on "I Didn't," his solo seemingly floating in space. On "A Gal in Calico" he plays a wonderfully dancing solo.

—Don DeMicheal

Aug. 2, 1962
Caught in the Act: Miles Davis/Oscar Brown Jr.
Music Box Theater, Los Angeles
Personnel: Miles Davis Sextet (Davis, trumpet; J.J. Johnson, trombone; Hank Mobley, tenor saxophone; Wynton Kelly, piano; Paul Chambers, bass; Jimmy Cobb, drums). Oscar Brown Jr.; Floyd Morris Trio (Morris, piano; Lyle Ritz, bass; Howie Oliver, drums).

While Davis got top billing during this nine-day concert series organized by Dandetta Productions, the star—from the standpoint of audience reaction—unquestionably was 35-year-old Brown.

Night after night, performance after performance, Brown's presence, repertoire and almost uncanny rapport with his audience added up to a unique entertainment experience and, in this reviewer's conviction, the certain knowledge that in Oscar Brown Jr. we have the most exciting entertainment figure in decades.

The overall concert presentation was in itself an unusual and highly effective wedding of the contemporary jazz of the Davis sextet and the broader appeal of Brown.

Davis was in consistently good form as, indeed, were the other members of the group. Trombonist Johnson's solo on the medium-up "On Green

Dolphin Street" was memorable, as was Davis' open-horn solo on a slow and evocative "Old Folks." There was marked consistency of stimulus from the rhythm team of Kelly, Chambers and Cobb to which tenor man Mobley and the other horns seldom failed to respond.

These Music Box concerts were intelligently programmed, with the Davis group playing one long set prior to an intermission after which Brown was introduced by an overture played by the Morris trio.

Brown's impact was instantly electric. He opened with his own "Humdrum Blues"; followed by Bobby Timmons' "Dat Dere"; the tender "Brown Baby" was its message of human dignity; the humorous "Signifyin' Monkey"; Nat Adderley's "Work Song," which was delivered with powerful impact; "Rags and Old Iron"; the hilarious "Hazel's Hips"; a profoundly moving memorial, "Hymn to Friday"; "Mister Kicks"; "A World Full of Grey"; and the satiric and extremely funny "Don't Blow Your Cool."

Brown is not merely a highly effective singer but also a consummate actor who coordinates body movement with facial expression and gesture in the manner of Yves Montand.

He draws his material—which is largely original—from urban Negro life with a perception and sensitivity enabling him to range from pointed social comment to satire and humor that is essentially Negro—rich, full and warmly rewarding. And because of the universality of his grasp of the material and the power of his own theatrical personality, he drives home these aspects of Negro culture with frequently stunning force.

Brown, therefore, is possibly the first Negro performing artist to project a wholly Negro concept to wide audiences outside that milieu and to make it stick on its own terms. This is his gift, and this is why he appears destined for a remarkable future in theater.

—John Tynan

Sept. 13, 1962
Miles Davis
Miles Ahead
Columbia 8633

If Davis was groping for his way with Parker in 1946–'47, and had it within his grasp in 1955, there was no doubt he'd found and mastered it in 1957, as can be heard on the first of the Davis–Gil Evans Columbia collaborations, *Miles Ahead,* recently released in simulated stereo or "electronically re-channeled," as Columbia says. Davis plays fluegelhorn throughout.

This piece of music—and you should listen to this album as if it were a sequential composition—is made even more brilliant by the "stereoing." Whether he sounds languid ("My Ship"), full of anguish and torment ("Blues for Pablo"), or elfish ("New Rhumba"), Davis proves his artistic excellence and his deserving to be called jazz's most dramatic player by his work on this album. Even on "Maids of Cadiz," which contains little improvisation, his tone and feeling are enough to transfix.

Much of the credit for the diamond's beauty must go to the setting, of course, and it is Evans' writing and conducting that perfectly sets off Davis' brilliance.

—Don DeMicheal

Oct. 11, 1962
Miles Davis
Miles Davis at Carnegie Hall
Columbia 1812
★★★★

Subtitled *The Legendary Performance of May 19, 1961,* this is a recording made at Carnegie Hall on the occasion that brought Miles Davis and Gil Evans together for their first public concert.

The occasion was an exciting one. Clearly it made a tremendous impression on several critics who heard it that night; the comments of three of them are used instead of liner notes. For those of us who were not lucky enough to be present, it comes as something of a surprise.

There are some 46 minutes of music on the album, but Evans' orchestra is heard on little more than a fourth of the footage—"Spring Is Here" on side 1 and the closing track, a three-tune segue, on side 2 (also the introduction only on "So What").

As you might expect, there are passages of rich beauty by Davis. Evans' writing needs no further endorsement here. The two reservations that must be made about the set are, foremost, the substandard recording and balance on the orchestra, and second, the availability of other versions of every tune heard on both sides, except "Spring." In spite of a number of exquisite solos, on the whole it would seem that the definite statements on most of these numbers were made earlier. "Someday My Prince Will Come" in particular is noticeably below the standard of the previously released version.

On the more informal tracks, namely "So What" and "No Blues," Davis plays with (and here I quote from John Wilson and Bill Coss, who happened on the identical phrase) "tremendous fire." Kelly, too, has some magnificent moments. Cobb and Chambers are in optimum form, though the balance tends to bring out the drummer a little too heavily at times when Kelly is soloing. (This review is of a monophonic copy; possibly the balance is better in the stereo version.)

Mobley, who has had to take the brunt of what little criticism has been leveled against the combo, plays with bristling confidence throughout and he is especially impressive on "So What" and "Oleo." The latter track has a curious editing aspect: the first eight bars and half of the second eight are missing from the opening chorus. But immediately afterward Davis tears into a wild, long solo during which the awkward start is soon forgotten.

If you don't own the earlier LPs in which these items were recorded initially, buy them first. Then, for comparison shopping as well as for additional subjective satisfaction, move to Carnegie.

—Leonard Feather

"So What"; "Spring Is Here"; "No Blues"; "Oleo"; "Someday My Prince Will Come"; "The Meaning of the Blues"; "Lament"; "New Rhumba."

Personnel: Davis, trumpet; Hank Mobley, tenor saxophone; Wynton Kelly, piano; Jimmy Cobb, drums; Paul Chambers, bass; unidentified 21-piece orchestra, Gil Evans, conductor.

———

April 25, 1963
Caught in the Act: The New Miles Davis Sextet
The Blackhawk, San Francisco
Personnel: Miles Davis, trumpet; Frank Strozier, alto saxophone; George Coleman, tenor saxophone; Harold Mabern, piano; Ron Carter, bass; Jimmy Cobb, drums.

The question of whether Miles Davis would organize a new group as a result of sideman trouble that befell him in Chicago some weeks ago was answered here in March. Only one familiar figure from his previous group—drummer Jimmy Cobb—was on stand with the trumpet star.

In the front line were altoist Strozier and tenorist Coleman, whose appearance bears a sketchy resemblance to a tall Cannonball Adderley. Pianist Harold Mabern, like Coleman and Strozier, is a native of Memphis, Tenn. Towering over them all was slender, six-foot four-inch bassist Carter.

Booked for a three-week engagement, Davis telephoned the club a few nights before his scheduled opening and obtained a week's delay. He said the left side of his face was still swollen from a root canal operation on a lower molar.

That the organization of the new group also was a factor seemed indicated by the fact Mabern did not arrive here until the third night of the gig. Pianist Vic Feldman, recruited from Los Angeles, filled in for him.

Once Davis and cohorts were ensconced on the Blackhawk stand, they began striking musical sparks that continued to fly for the remainder of the combo's two-week stay.

As was to be expected, their juxtaposition with the great trumpeter stimulated the new sidemen—Strozier and Coleman in particular. And the presence of unfamiliar associates turned up the burner under Davis. So pronounced were his fiery forays into the upper register, some listeners wondered if he was using a new, smaller mouthpiece. (He wasn't.)

Ensemble playing never has been an important factor in any Davis combo, so the fact that the new group had held but one rehearsal prior to its debut went largely unnoticed. Cobb, whose playing is not flashy but whose contribution to Davis' groups has been consistently low-rated, was as dependable as the Rock of Gibraltar. Carter, who has his bachelor's from Eastman School of Music (where he played in the Rochester Philharmonic under Howard Hanson) and his master's from Manhattan School of Music, played no bowed solos, but his pizzicato—while not up to predecessor Paul Chambers' best— was consistently firm, musical and interesting.

Strozier, an honor graduate of the Chicago Conservatory of Music and, like Mabern, a former member of the MJT+3, shows promise of becoming a major voice on his instrument. His excellent technique is coupled with good ideas, and his sound, which reflects traces of his two favorites—Johnny Hodges and Sonny Stitt—is his own.

Coleman, who formerly played with Max Roach and Slide Hampton, is still forging his own style. His exemplar is Charlie Parker and "many" tenor players, he said, and references to Parker, John Coltrane, Sonny Rollins and, occasionally, Lester Young—as well as a dash of the flavor Coleman distilled while working with B.B. King—was heard in his extended solos.

In his comping, Mabern was always alert to the soloist, and his own solos, which stress a two-handed chordal approach, were interesting and well done.

Of Davis it need only be said that he continues to prove himself one of the great improvisers, which is to say creators, in his music and the possessor of an unsurpassed ability to create and maintain a mood.

He consistently proved these points here with tender, heart-wrenching essays on "I Thought About You," "On Green Dolphin Street" and "All of

You." Such numbers as "Walkin'," "Flamenco Sketches" and an extended exploration of "The Theme" also were staples.

The change in personnel began when trombonist J.J. Johnson left the group a couple months ago in order to fulfill several writing commitments.

Chambers, who had been with Davis since 1955, and pianist Wynton Kelly, with the trumpeter since '59, split with Davis some weeks ago in Chicago, though they may not have intended to. Davis said his group was booked for a St. Louis engagement to begin four days after the Chicago job, but at the conclusion of the Windy City job, Chambers and Kelly went to New York City without a word of notice. Neither appeared for the St. Louis gig and as a result Davis had to cancel, a happening for which he is being sued by the club-owner.

Some time before this, Davis had canceled a Detroit engagement to protect Chambers from possible arrest in connection with a marital legal action. This cancellation resulted in another suit against Davis.

"They both wanted to come out to San Francisco with me," Davis said, "but even though they're both excellent musicians, I had to say, 'No.'"

—Russ Wilson

Sept. 12, 1963
Miles Davis
Seven Steps to Heaven
Columbia 2051 and 8851
★★★★★

This LP is the result of two sessions held this spring, the first in Los Angeles, the other in New York. The Los Angeles session, with Feldman, Carter and Butler, produced "Basin Street Blues," "I Fall in Love Too Easily" and "Baby, Won't You Please Come Home"; the other three titles stem from the second date, with the trumpeter's present group—Coleman, Hancock, Carter and Williams. Davis played exceptionally well on both dates, though each brought out a different facet of his artistry.

There is a spell of melancholy cast over the Los Angeles performances, partly because the three selections are slow tempoed and balladic in nature, partly because Davis plays only muted—and he tends to play "sadder" muted than he does open. But more than anything, it is what he plays and how he phrases it that casts the spell.

On each of the three tracks, there is a general downward curve to his solos; that is, the phrases may rise, but at the critical point they descend, either in a short run or a slur, and even as they rise there are innumerable points where Davis slurs individual notes downward. It's as if he were continually turning down the corners of his highly melodic improvisations.

Davis also often uses the low register of his horn, sometimes in breathy fashion on "Basin," "Love" and "Baby"—on the last named he ends his solo with what must be termed a sigh. And as always, his playing is very human, with voice-like inflections that give his work a "singing" quality, not unlike that of a Billie Holiday or an Edith Piaf.

On the other hand, his playing at the New York session is almost joyous. Certainly there are turned-down corners, but not as many as on the other three tracks.

It should be noted that "Seven Steps to Heaven," "So Near, So Far" and "Joshua" are not taken at slow tempos, but this is not necessarily the reason for the joy evident in Davis' playing—he's conjured up melancholy at fast tempos before. There is a shift in his playing here, a general upward curve to his solos—rising phrases and runs up scales to the high register. He also uses the upper register more on these tracks than the others—and he makes what he goes for, which is something one could not always say about some of his other recordings.

Both sessions resulted in classic Miles. All three tracks from the Los Angeles session are superb. And there is a remarkable "Joshua" solo that must stand as a model of how to construct a solo—there is one part, for example, where he uses a scale first in its entirety and then returns to it periodically but only uses part of it to make his point—which is a simple enough idea, but how many jazzmen think of something like that?

And so strong is Davis' playing on both sessions that one never bothers about how many choruses he plays, how long or short his phrases are, how he gets through a certain set of chords—just as long as he keeps playing. Which, I guess, is the mark of a true artist at work.

Of the others on the album, Feldman, who wrote "Joshua" and collaborated with Davis on "Seven," and Carter are the more sympathetic accompanists, though Hancock solos brilliantly, particularly on "Seven" and "Joshua."

Feldman combines parts of Bill Evans and Red Garland in his solos but plays harder than either of those two former Davis sidemen. In general, he does an excellent job of following Davis' unpredictable twists and turns.

Butler occasionally seems at a loss as to what to play behind Davis, sometimes double-timing for a few bars and then dropping back; he sounds more comfortable backing Feldman. Williams, however, goes straight ahead in his accompaniment, and the young Boston drummer displays mature taste in his "Seven" solo, which is a characteristic uncommon to most other 17-year-olds.

Coleman is unimpressive in his solos, though I've heard him play very well with the group in live performances since the record was made. The tenorist also falls victim to a recording imbalance in the stereo version that brings out Hancock's often busy accompaniment much too strongly, to the point of distraction, in fact.

But these are minor carps in light of the stunning performances by Davis on the record.

—Don DeMicheal

"Basin Street Blues"; "Seven Steps to Heaven"; "I Fall in Love Too Easily"; "So Near, So Far"; "Baby, Won't You Please Come Home?"; "Joshua."

Personnel: Davis, trumpet; George Coleman, tenor saxophone; Vic Feldman or Herbie Hancock, piano; Ron Carter, bass; Frank Butler or Anthony Williams, drums.

Sept. 12, 1963
Caught in the Act: Various Artists
Théâtre des Champs-Élysées, Paris
Personnel: Miles Davis Quintet, Sammy Price, Wilbert Harrison, the Harlem Beggars, Sunnyland Slim, Bill Doggett Band.

A very mixed bag: superb Davis, embarrassment for most of the rest with a catastrophic set for the Doggett band, and, finally, a near riot by the capacity house.

This was a festival in miniature made up of most of the visiting U.S. artists appearing at this year's Antibes festival.

Davis opened the show, and his group was about the only one that had an opportunity to perform adequately for reviewing purposes. The curtain went up one minute past 9 p.m., 31 minutes late, conforming satisfactorily to the noble Paris tradition of late starts. Davis had his new quintet with George Coleman, tenor saxophone; Herbie Hancock, piano; Ron Carter, bass; and Tony Williams, drums. As might be expected, emphasis in the quintet was on the solo capabilities of the musicians rather than on any kind of group sound.

Davis himself was in clean, decisive form and at his lyrical best, particularly on the opening "Autumn Leaves" and later on a long workout on "Stella by Starlight."

Williams, 17-year-old drum prodigy, created a mild sensation with his surging and propulsive drumming. Certainly this boy's name is destined to become a household word in the world of jazz.

Hancock's colorful chording and delicate ballad style proved that he is more than just a "Watermelon Man," and he was particularly effective on "Seven Steps to Heaven" and "Joshua."

Carter's dextrous bass was heard to good effect throughout, and especially on "Joshua." Coleman was adequate, but his somewhat anonymous style made one wish for a more individual instrumentalist to sustain interest.

The anticlimactic second half of the concert dissolved into bedlam—the worst display in years by the temperamental French jazz fraternity.

Paris audiences have long been noted for being ill-mannered and generally unpredictable, but in the last couple of years a certain maturity seemed to have settled in.

But at this concert Hugh Porter's Gospel quartet, the Harlem Beggars and singer-pianist Sunnyland Slim were barely tolerated, and despite pianist Sammy Price's valiant attempts to stem the gathering storm, singer Wilbert Harrison (attired, as a French newspaper put it, in a "jolie smoking jaune") got the bird 100 percent.

The unfortunate Bill Doggett with his down-home R&B band went through the motions on "High Heels" and "Ham Fat" before a rain of coins, peanuts and ice cream cartons obliged them to beat a hasty retreat. The boos rang out long and loud—evidently *le vrai* jazz in France does not have unlimited horizons.

—Alan Bates

———

March 12, 1964
Miles Davis/Gil Evans
Quiet Nights
Columbia 2106 and 8906
★★★★

This is a curious and not entirely satisfying album. The unsigned liner notes imply, while failing to make anything clear, that some or all the orchestral tracks could have been recorded two or three years ago—including, we are told, "most likely the first bossa nova music recorded in the country."

The Evans tone-color cornucopia, though inevitably less startlingly fresh in its impact today than in 1957, makes a superb backdrop for Davis; yet on the whole the matter of these performances falls far below the level of the manner. The first track, for instance, is a 95-second trifle that is finished before it has lasted long enough to set a mood, let alone sustain one. "Wait Till You See Her" is given a strange long-meter treatment.

Of the two bossa nova tracks, "Cruz" is by far the more effective, with Davis in an assertive mood that even includes touches of Harry Edison-like bent tones. The title number, perhaps because of the very inventiveness and harmonic audacity of Evans' orchestration, loses some of the simple charm that was its essence in several previous versions.

Perhaps the most successful track, measured by the yardstick of earlier Davis–Evans collaborations and the moods they created, is "Once Upon a Summertime," a somber minor performance in which Davis, the horns, harp and ensemble are ingeniously interwoven. The Evans flair is also in full bloom on "Song No. 1," though this is not the best track for Miles.

The final track is played by the Brooder with a rhythm section. George Coleman, listed in the personnel, is not heard. Both Miles, muted of course, and Feldman, accompanying and soloing with his customary sensitivity, achieve a consistent level of lyrical beauty throughout the six minutes. For no good reason the mood is abruptly broken at the end because Davis' comments were not edited out of the tape.

Caveat emptor department: The entire album offers less than 27 minutes of music. Evidently half an LP cut with Evans was spread thin enough, with the help of the quartet track, to stretch it over two sides.

—Leonard Feather

"Song No. 2"; "Once Upon a Summertime"; "Aos Pes da Cruz"; "Song No. 1"; "Wait Till You See Her"; "Corcovado (Quiet Nights)"; "Summer Night."

Personnel: Davis, trumpet; unidentified orchestra, Evans, conductor (1–6); Victor Feldman, piano; Ron Carter, bass; Frank Butler, drums (7).

April 9, 1964
Miles Davis
Diggin' With the Miles Davis Sextet
Prestige 7281
★★★★

Diggin' With the Miles Davis Sextet, recorded in 1951, offers further similarities and contrasts among its performers. All the men on the date—Davis, trumpet; Jackie McLean, alto saxophone; Sonny Rollins, tenor saxophone; Walter

Bishop, Jr., piano; Tommy Potter, bass; and Art Blakey, drums—are from Charlie Parker. By the time this album was cut, though, Davis, only 25, was well into the lyrical approach he has since perfected, but his sidemen were still very much in Parker's bag; it should be borne in mind, however, that in 1951 McLean was 19 and Rollins 22, ages at which musicians rarely have left fathers for selves.

And it is Davis who provides most of the album's interest. His solos are beautifully put together, statements that swing in a most delectable manner, gliding over the sometimes heavy-handed rhythm section.

Davis achieved an even more pervading air of melancholy in his playing in 1951 than he does today. Yet there is much heat in his solos on "Dig," "Paper Moon," "Denial," "Bluing" and "Out of the Blue"—a different heat, or swing, than was evident in the classic nonet sides he made in 1949 and '50.

There also is heat-swing in the saxophonists' work, but neither McLean nor Rollins comes through with anything as musically valuable as Davis does. Neither sounds as if he had mastered his horn or himself. In some instances Rollins falters clumsily or plays in a distressingly cautious manner. McLean, when not offering Bird calls, sounds extremely tense.

Yet, with its drawbacks, this record, these men, surely swing.

—Don DeMicheal

May 7, 1964
Miles Davis
Birth of the Cool
Capitol 1974

In the late '40s Miles Davis' bop-molded style moved more and more to the spareness and simplicity of understatement, becoming progressively more introspective in character. Surrounding himself with a number of growing jazz voices (among them arranger Gil Evans, pianist John Lewis, and baritone saxophonist Gerry Mulligan) who felt the need for a more reflective, challenging approach to jazz composition that would achieve a fuller unity between composer and improviser without sacrificing either's freedom, the trumpeter assembled a nonet in 1949 to play the works these young composers would create not only for its instrumentation but also for its specific solo voices.

The group played only one public engagement, but it participated in several recording sessions for Capitol Records. The recordings had a profound and far-reaching effect on jazz: The delicate, reflective sonorities of the instrumental blend; the unhurried, introspective mood of most of the compositions;

and the general tenor or unruffled calm that the numbers evidenced influenced a raft of jazzmen (most notably the denizens of the West Coast, who were to spawn a whole school based in the Davis experiments).

The Davis nonet, its size placing it on the borders of both combo and big band, was in effect an offshoot of the Claude Thornhill Orchestra; two of the Thornhill band's arrangers, Evans and Mulligan, were prime forces in Davis' band of arrangers.

For several years Evans, as Thornhill's chief arranger, had considerably widened the tonal range of the average jazz-dance orchestra by the artful employment of French horn and tuba in the band's orchestrations, its sound, as a result, taking on a rich, burnished and decidedly cooler—or less "hot"—coloration.

Evans, Mulligan, Lewis and trumpeter John Carisi (whose "Israel" was one of the nonet's finest achievements) carried these practices to their fullest use in their artful arrangements for the Davis unit. Chief among their accomplishments were the considerable expansion of tone colors open to the jazz group and the great variety of timbres that resulted; the production of a lighter, serene "floating" ensemble feeling; and the integration of the advances of bop into a fully ordered, homogenous approach of great attractiveness and charm. But perhaps even more notable was the freedom for exploration the recordings signaled.

—Don DeMicheal and Pete Welding

Aug. 13, 1964
Miles Davis/Thelonious Monk
Miles and Monk at Newport
Columbia 2178 and 8978
★★★½

This is a most curious collection, not the least curious aspect of it Columbia's decision to issue, along with the Monk–Pee Wee Russell performances recorded at Newport last year, four of the six numbers the Davis sextet performed at Freebody Park five years before that, at the 1958 Newport Jazz Festival. The notes have it, further, that Wynton Kelly is the pianist with the Davis unit, when it obviously is [Bill] Evans. And then there is Russell with Monk.

Davis plays excellently throughout. He gives more than passing allegiance to Charlie Parker and Dizzy Gillespie in the fiercely up-tempo version of

"Ah-Leu-Cha" that opens the album, playing with fire and power, spewing out a rapid scattershot of notes.

The more reflective, graceful and ardently lyrical approach that increasingly has become his particular province is displayed in the two performances that follow, Monk's "Straight, No Chaser" and "Fran-Dance" (Davis' appealing interpretation of the old "Put Your Little Foot Down"). On both of these, Evans' discreet, sensitive piano supports beautifully, complementing and gently reinforcing the trumpeter's luminous, limpid romanticism.

Coltrane was fast in the grip of his transitional sheets-of-sound approach and is not always effective in the context of Davis' playing. The tenorist here sounds as though the sheer momentum of his playing was carrying him forward, rather than any rush of ideas.

His most effective moments occur on "Two Bass Hit," which he has to himself, thus permitting him to shape the whole performance. The fact that his solo is not contrasted with those of the others is one reason that it comes off so well.

Adderley plays with assurance and bristling vigor, only occasionally reflecting Coltrane's turbulent manner. Evans, in both his accompaniment and in solo on "Fran-Dance" is delightful.

The meeting—one cannot say collaboration—of Monk and Russell is little more than interesting.

Theoretically, Russell's waspish, acerbic clarinet should have meshed with Monk's probing, angular piano. Theoretically, that is. In practice, however, communication breaks down somewhat; the conceptual and stylistic gap is too wide to bridge. Monk plays superbly, both in solo and in support, but the clarinetist merely sounds uncomfortable and out of his element. Russell never seems to get anything going; his solos never gather any momentum and fizzle out in a kind of doodling.

Tenor saxophonist Rouse, on the other hand, plays better here than I've yet heard him. His tone and the contours of his phrasing remind one very forcibly of Sonny Rollins' work with the pianist.

Monk's playing remains one of the marvels of jazz; the rhythm displacements with which he fills his solos are nothing short of amazing, and his playing is filled with wry, mordant harmonic delights. And his accompaniments are fully as creative as any of his solos.

The rating represents a compromise, of course. The work of Davis, Monk and Rouse is consistently high quality but is offset by the less impressive work, in comparison, of the others.

—Pete Welding

"Ah-Leu-Cha"; "Straight, No Chaser"; "Fran-Dance"; "Two Bass Hit"; "Nutty"; "Blue Monk."

Personnel: Davis, trumpet; Cannonball Adderley, alto saxophone; John Coltrane, tenor saxophone; Bill Evans, piano; Paul Chambers, bass; Jimmy Cobb, drums (1–4). Pee Wee Russell, clarinet; Charlie Rouse, tenor saxophone; Monk, piano; Butch Warren, bass; Frankie Dunlop, drums (5, 6).

Nov. 5, 1964
Miles Davis
Miles Davis in Europe
Columbia 2183
★★★★★

Cut at the 1963 Antibes Jazz Festival in France, this album finds Davis playing with great abandon. He takes a bushel basket full of chances: blowing flurries of notes, making unusual choices of notes, fragmenting his lines by laying out often or for so long that the continuity of his lines is threatened. He builds considerable tension with rests, but he usually releases it successfully.

One of the most exciting moments occurs on "Joshua." Davis stops playing, and Hancock—who seems somewhat confused—waits and then begins filling in the space. Before he's completed his figure, Davis jumps back in, taking the play from him and rocketing ahead.

Davis moves all over his horn, screaming in the upper register and also playing effectively in the lower. His muted work on "All of You" and "Autumn Leaves" is quite economical. It's amazing that he can play so few notes and still create those flowing, well-sustained solos. His phrases are of unpredictable length but fit together like the pieces of a jigsaw puzzle. He blows both long, suspended-in-space tones and perky, syncopated phrases.

Finally, Davis waxes extremely imaginative, even by his own high standards. After listening to the record a few times, one may find several dozen of his distinctive ideas lodged in memory.

Coleman swings compellingly, and he, too, is inventive. The catch is that he's often mouthing John Coltrane's vocabulary, and he even blows Coltrane-like harmonics. I was a little let down by his performance because I'd recently reviewed a 1961 Max Roach LP on which Coleman, in addition to the virtues he displays here, showed much more originality. He has the equipment to become a wonderful soloist. A striking effect is achieved during a section of his "Walkin'" solo when, at various points, the pianist and/or drummer lay out.

I've never before heard Hancock play as impressively. His style still contains elements of Bill Evans, Wynton Kelly and Red Garland; nevertheless, he has become his own man. On the fast selections (and they are taken way up), he makes the tempo with long, rich lines and, on "Milestones" and "Joshua," alternates these lines with impressionistic passages.

The rhythm section functions superbly. Williams plays a myriad of choice counter-rhythms and sensitively varies the timbre and volume of his accompaniments. Modern drummers have been criticized by older critics and listeners for dominating the soloists, but this charge is often groundless. In all probability, Williams inspires the soloists more by accenting and playing figures over the basic pulse than he would by confining himself mostly to keeping straight time.

Carter pours the coal on during the up-tempo pieces, but I get a bigger kick following his supple, secure section work on the bounce-tempoed standards. Here, his lively sound and melodic rhythmic ingenuity are heard to better advantage.

Davis has often recorded with musicians more famous than these sidemen (although they may become quite well-known in the next few years), but this LP is still one of the better ones he's made—and that's saying a lot.

—Harvey Pekar

"Autumn Leaves"; "Milestones"; "Joshua"; "All of You"; "Walkin'."

Personnel: Davis, trumpet; George Coleman, tenor saxophone; Herbie Hancock, piano; Ron Carter, bass; Tony Williams, drums.

Dec. 31, 1964
Miles Davis/Art Blakey
Jazz on the Screen
Fontana 67532
★★★★

There certainly is no diminution of the individual in the Miles Davis tracks on the *Jazz on the Screen* album. These are the performances Davis, tenorist Barney Wilen, pianist René Urtreger, bassist Pierre Michelot and drummer Kenny Clarke improvised in 1957 as background to the French film *Elevator to the Scaffold*.

(The music first was issued in the United States on Columbia as *Jazz Track*. But the material is owned by Phillips, of which Fontana is a subsidiary. Now that this company has issued the Davis tracks in this country, Columbia supposedly must withdraw the *Jazz Track* LP from the market, which is too bad, since the Columbia release, in addition to the movie music, has three long tracks by the Davis sextet that included pianist Bill Evans, tenor saxophonist John Coltrane and altoist Cannonball Adderley).

The movie music consists of 10 short tracks. The most moving performances are "Generique, L'Assassinat de Carala," "Julien Dans L'Ascenseur" and "Chez le Photographe du Motel," all fine examples of Davis in somber, melancholy mood. "Carala" and "Julien," in fact, are two versions of the same material, and "Chez" is cut from similar cloth.

Davis is less solemn, almost beboppish, on "Sur L'Autoroute," which is blowing on "Sweet Georgia Brown" chords, and "Diner au Motel." Something of the dark loneliness Davis conjures up on the more melancholy tracks is present on "Florence sur les Champs-Élysées," but here there is an impishness missing from the other tracks.

"Evasion de Julien" and "Visite de Vigile" are bass solos, which were effective in the film but on record are rather meaningless. And the remaining track, "Au Bar du Petit Bac," is of lesser stuff than the others with horns.

—Don DeMicheal

April 21, 1965
Miles Davis
"Four" and More
Columbia 2453
★★★½

The tempos are mostly the same—breakneck. Bad pacing.

Miles sounds raw, somehow unpolished. His best track is "Walkin'," on which he generates a good deal of heat, but they play it too fast. Miles cracks notes too often. It sounds as if he is overblowing the horn. I get chalk-on-the-blackboard squeak chills.

Coleman runs the changes, his surface facility leading me to expect more interesting music than he comes through with.

I don't like announcements on records. It's as if they have to prove that it really was recorded live. These announcements—there is one at the conclusion of each side—give the listener all the disadvantages of being at a concert, with none of the advantages.

Davis' rhythm section cooks—the time bubbles. Williams knows how to make clockwork interesting. His cymbal sound is crystal clear. Carter and Hancock are perfect. Davis' rhythm sections always have been distinctive, setting the style for others. Williams is part Philly Joe Jones and part Milford Graves—the best parts of each, I think.

Most of my three-and-a-half stars is for the rhythm section.

—Mike Zwerin

"So What"; "Walkin'"; "Joshua/Go-Go" (theme and announcement); "Four"; "Seven Steps to Heaven"; "There Is No Greater Love/Go-Go" (theme and announcement).

Personnel: Davis, trumpet; George Coleman, tenor saxophone; Herbie Hancock, piano; Ron Carter, bass; Tony Williams, drums.

June 3, 1965
Miles Davis
My Funny Valentine
Columbia 2306
★★★★ ½

No happier circumstances can exist in recording than to have an ensemble of instrumentalists who have something to say and an unhurried atmosphere in which to say it.

With no "single"-oriented producer to interfere with creativity here, Davis and colleagues take their sweet, eloquent time with five numbers recorded at a live concert in early '64. The shortest tune lasts nine minutes, which gives everyone ample opportunity to develop ideas, explore harmonic patterns and engage in conversation with like-minded swingers.

Davis' intense probing dominates. Each track bears the imprint of his swinging-steeped-in-pathos, his bent tones, and his linear excursions that alternately explode and subside.

Right behind him, or rather, right alongside, is the amazing Hancock, by far the most sensitive and imaginative young pianist on the scene today. While his solos forever swing (his stint on "All of You" is a model of inspiration), it's his comping here that reveals an extrasensory anticipation of Miles' wiles.

Another magnificent display of rapport can be heard in the walking, gap-filling, pedal-point prodding and even double-stopping of Carter.

Williams seems to be the victim of poor mike placement. On slow numbers he barely can be heard; on the up tunes, his contributions come through with less forcefulness than one is accustomed to hearing from this young phenom.

Of the five musicians, only Coleman leaves something to be desired. His Stan Getz-like tone is clean and crisp, but his ideas are too straightforward to match the harmonic and rhythmic daring of Davis, Hancock and Carter.

The title tune is given a wonderfully restrained treatment that captures the warmth of Lorenz Hart's lyrics. "Stella by Starlight"'s contours are etched impressionistically. In fact, this portrait of "Stella" is the most haunting account of a "woman" whose changes have always led musicians to put her on a harmonic pedestal. "All of You" shows Davis' penchant for tags, and they, in turn, elicit some muscular plucking from Carter. His glissandi behind Hancock's solo sound like a tailgating trombone.

"I Thought About You" does not adapt too well to the demands of jazzmen. Its changes are trite and the melody says less. What saves it from its own inherent mediocrity are Davis' introspective wailing, Carter's melodic solo and Hancock's double-time solo.

"All Blues" represents a much-needed brightness in tempo. Considering that the total playing time of the disc exceeds one hour, more uptempo tunes should have been included. As far as the instrumental quality of what is included, fast or slow, this album ranks with the best of Davis' recorded efforts.

—Harvey Siders

"My Funny Valentine"; "All of You"; "Stella by Starlight"; "All Blues"; "I Thought About You."

Personnel: Davis, trumpet; George Coleman, tenor saxophone; Herbie Hancock, piano; Ron Carter, bass; Tony Williams, drums.

Dec. 30, 1965
Miles Davis
E.S.P.
Columbia 2350
★★★★½

The theme of *E.S.P.* consists of 16 bars of a very mystic, haunting, thriller type of melody that repeats, with Davis and Shorter playing parallel, the tenor voiced a ninth above concert, which gets an alto–trumpet unison effect. It's a somewhat fresh approach to the usual unison trumpet and tenor playing.

Speaking of extrasensory perception, one has to be aware of what goes on during the creative act—the technical and psychological things, as well as the emotional, which will automatically be involved after one applies one's Fourth Wall (concentration) to the act/art of improvisation. (I don't want to clutter Miles' review with a lot of details and B.S.—I want to stick only to esthetics.)

In his solo, Shorter seems very familiar with the structure, as if he might have written "E.S.P." (Miles is listed as co-composer with Shorter), but as is usual with most excellent saxophonists, they can maneuver the vertical structure in such a detailed fashion that they oftentimes sound better than the composer's version—considering the saxophonist in question didn't write it. This is a natural technical asset of the reed family—25 to 30 keys compared with the brass family's customary three.

Miles, a vertical and horizontal improviser, solos next. Because of the technical deficiency of the trumpet, he is forced into a cat-and-mouse intrigue (arouse interest by baffling) with the horizontal and vertical layout of composition—unless he does it by choice, which I doubt. However, he plays mostly horizontally.

Miles is a master cobbler, softening his leather in the first chorus or so, pounding the leather where he will later stitch it—an astronaut taking his job out for a dry run in preparation for a trip to another planet. (I don't think all Miles' jets were working, but he made a soft landing.) *E.S.P.* can be—if not properly used—dangerous. If it's avant-garde like this, if it has higher aspirations with basic roots, then it must be built on something far-reaching. A lot of intuition—awareness—was necessary to bring this track off successfully, for it is quite easy to get lost from the form, making the title apropos.

"Eighty-one" has a cute intro within the 12-bar structure—the first four bars—then the next 12 bars carry a different melody, while retaining the 12-bar structure. This is a deviation from the blues, a modal type of blues. Hancock kind of saves this one from being monstrous, which seems to be one of the characteristics of most of the outgoing action.

Shorter plays daringly and well, rather deep-rooted in spots, folksy— which makes it. Miles also plays well on this track; he is set up by the vamp (which is used for all the soloists) in the first couple of choruses or so with the rhythm pivoted by Carter's big, precisioned beat and Williams' subtle drive.

"Little One" has a couple of modern, cathedral-type chords by Hancock— very reverent—but the third chord is lustier. Then there's a short mood thing by Shorter—a Gil Evans type of mood setting. Miles' entrance is beautiful and different, with a pianissimo unison by Shorter—very easy . . . easy now . . . easy. Cathedral chords come in again. Miles is heard in a sort of manufactured mood—vamp—then pulsating rhythm beneath Miles. Shorter follows up in much the same manner with some very personal moods and arpeggios. Hancock's solo also is in the same mood. The track closes in much the same fashion as it begins. It kind of fades into sleep—oblivion.

"R.J." has Miles hitting the track, swinging hard and soft, from the very beginning—no ensemble. Shorter follows with some different types of playing; he seems to have got sucked into the end of the "out" cat's exhaust pipe.

Different to be different? . . . But he plays well enough to overcome this and does. The idea here seems to be to try to pave the way for the avant-garde set—the jet set. Good collective playing, but I didn't dig the track too tough.

Williams is front and center at the beginning of "Agitation." This is nice to hear—a drum opener. Tony is still developing, but on the right beam. Not a [Max] Roach, [Buddy] Rich or a work of Art [Blakey] in the dramatic sense, but he has that youthful vigor that cannot be retained or regained. Something different.

Enter Miles and that famous Harmon mute, peeking and weaving his way—design—through the various vamps, tempos and moods. Shorter sounds best here in this Hank Mobley type of role. (He plays a lot of different roles while retaining his originality.) Of course, the Big John [Coltrane] influence goes without saying.

They go out with a canon, which is probably how—why—they selected the title.

Shorter sounds really wrapped up in "Iris"—beautiful. Then Miles wraps himself in the mood piece and plays some expressive high register up around D or E-flat. This tune seems kind of loose. It has a lot of that *Snow White and the Seven Dwarfs* action—sleep music, hypnotic. Well done.

"Mood"—Harmon again by Miles—after a few bars of Shorter merged beneath Miles, while the rhythm remains buoyant and full of life. Shorter plays under pretty much the same conditions; then Herbie kind of slumbers along . . . Wayne and Miles and out. Sleep . . .

I like to rate albums in the way that they move me emotionally as well as otherwise. Emotionally, as a whole, this one is lacking. It's mostly brain music. Miles is very crafty here and, because he is, so esthetic to the profession and perhaps enlightening to the avant-garde. I'm giving him a rating with reservations. This type of music has that drone thing that I don't like, but because of the almost flawless presentation, I give five stars—but only four stars for the writing and effort—and no stars for the overall sound. *E.S.P.* music in general is monotonous—one long drone. It's not for me.

—Kenny Dorham

"E.S.P."; "Eighty-one"; "Little One"; "R.J."; "Agitation"; "Iris"; "Mood."

Personnel: Davis, trumpet; Wayne Shorter, tenor saxophone; Herbie Hancock, piano; Ron Carter, bass; Tony Williams, drums.

June 29, 1967
Miles Davis
Miles Smiles
Columbia 2601 and 9401
★★★★½

This is Davis' most exciting album since *E.S.P.,* recorded by the same quintet and issued two years ago. Like the earlier record, this one is a confrontation with the avant-garde, and since the trumpeter is one of the spiritual fathers of the new jazz, what he and his sidemen do here is of considerable interest—aside from the intrinsic interest of the music itself.

Three of the pieces are by Shorter, a gifted composer/arranger as well as a fine player. They are "Orbits," "Footprints" and "Dolores." "Freedom," by saxophonist Eddie Harris, and "Gingerbread Boy," by Jimmy Heath, are given treatments quite different from their composers' recorded versions.

"Circle" is by Davis, and it is the album's best track. A lovely ballad, it focuses on the trumpeter's lyrical side, in contrast to the more aggressive playing in the other performances. Here is the essential Miles Davis, completely himself—and not a bit dated.

Elsewhere, he sometimes sounds a little like Don Cherry, but with more consistent command of both horn and structure. It is always commendable when an established player, especially a highly creative and original one, remains open to new ideas.

But no matter how experimental Davis gets, his improvisations remain melodic and logical. Even when they are not, strictly speaking, tonal in the Western European sense, they imply tonality and fall pleasantly on the tonally oriented ear. And he swings.

Though Davis remains the individualist, it is as a group that the quintet is at its most impressive, and, specifically, it is the extraordinary rhythm section that makes this one of the most cohesive and original groups in contemporary jazz.

There is almost uncanny communication among Hancock, Carter and Williams. At will, they can go from "inside" to "outside," never losing the thread of continuity so essential to jazz rhythms. And their collective sound (or rather, sounds) always enhances what goes on up front.

Each of the three is masterly, and there is, apparently, no disruptive rivalry among them. They are a unit—nobody ever seems to be saying "me, me," and even their solos are integrated.

As for the solos, which always benefit from the support that never flags, Hancock's are the most provocative of the sidemen's contributions. Hear him on "Circle," on which his imagination matches that of Davis, on "Dolores" and on "Freedom," and one will hear one of the outstanding pianists of the day.

Shorter, always a thoughtful, searching player, seems to be finding his true style, one that combines tradition with adventurousness in satisfying fashion. I liked him especially on his own "Dolores," with Carter working wonders behind him.

The bassist is splendid throughout—and so is Williams, whose crackling ensemble fills and momentous drive on "Gingerbread" are among many details that could be singled out for praise.

In their approach to musical "freedom," these five men never lose sight of the foundations of musical communication. They are always musical, and what they do makes sense. This is definitely a record to hear and hear again. And "Circle" is a masterpiece.

—Dan Morgenstern

"Orbits"; "Circle"; "Footprints"; "Dolores"; "Freedom Jazz Dance"; "Gingerbread Boy."

Personnel: Davis, trumpet; Wayne Shorter, tenor saxophone; Herbie Hancock, piano; Ron Carter, bass; Tony Williams, drums.

Jan. 25, 1968
Miles Davis
Sorcerer
Columbia 9532
★★★★★

No more big old fat old lazy melodies that cats can stand around riffing on corners, like "Bags' Groove" and "Walkin'" and . . . It's fine, though, nobody's standing around riffing on corners these days anyway—and Miles is, as he has been for 20 years, right on top of the times with superbly disciplined chaos.

Now, the substance of the sentences he plays seems as implicit in the punctuation marks as in the syntax. The structure of the phrase is secondary to the quality of the mood. Inflection and nuance seem to have become the vital guideposts of his statements (read: understatements), as befitting this extraordinarily sophisticated route to expression.

Instead of infallibly logical conclusions to neat little 32-bar choruses that must give rise to clichés somewhere along the line in horn solos that are unbreakably regulated by the changes dutifully registered by the slavishly comping piano and a bass that plays quarter-notes just because the time signature is in four and a drummer that keeps a steady beat, regard the infinite logic of the well-modulated scream, the piano that many times plays colors instead of chords, the bass that has learned to dance as well as walk and run, and the metamorphosis of the fourth dimension as revealed through the drummer that keeps the beat steadily changing.

Instead of the information usually found in the liner notes, the owner of this LP is treated to a bit of a phonetic Ferlinghetti by Ralph Gleason (who also did the cute thing with Davis' tune titles on *E.S.P.*). However, though we aren't told, in all but the last track, "Nothing Like You," the personnel is the trumpeter's current work force.

The leader, not boasting a single original on this album, unselfishly took advantage of the writing talent in his crew. Shorter owns "Prince of Darkness," "Masqualero," "Limbo" and "Vonetta"; Hancock wrote the title tune; and "Pee Wee" belongs to Williams.

"Nothing," written and sung by Dorough, in contrast to the more complex textures and color schemes of the rest of the material, is taken straightahead on devices reminiscent of King Pleasure and Babs Gonzales. It was cut more than five years ago by a different Davis group; almost certainly trombonist Frank Rehak, tenorist Shorter (then still with Art Blakey), bassist Paul Chambers, drummer Jimmy Cobb and Latin percussionist Willie Bobo. Its inclusion and tail-end positioning are startling, and though the musicianship is of a high order, one cannot escape wondering at its slightly atavistic presence.

On "Prince," Carter works in triple meter and Williams slashes in four with ricocheting rim shots, as Miles renders a treatise in late-'60s emotions. Everything moves separately toward the same end, the aggregate pulse seems derived from a pentagon of sources: six against two against four, and nobody bound to anything.

Williams' "Pee Wee" is a gentle ballad, without a drum solo or even percussive accents, and showcases Shorter's rippling fluidity and Hancock's quiet authority.

"Masqualero" finds Shorter a hair out of sync with Miles in stating the ominous, staccato theme, thus adding breadth and definition to the line. Hancock trails a string of brightly lit notes after the horns, and Williams' work acts like flying buttresses to the leader's expressive summits, before rumbling and stabbing through the tenorist's wisps of agonized lyricism and the pianist's gossamer tints.

"The Sorcerer" seems to work on ball bearings. Shorter calls laconically against the rhythm. The front line momentarily goes into ensemble, then swirls into symbiosis in an extended series of eights. After a beautifully haphazard ensemble, with Williams fracturing the pulse everywhere—shifting the aural focus as if it were something to view on a slide projector—Hancock's right hand splashes color around with the extravagance of latter-day Vincent van Gogh.

"Limbo" finds an eddying Hancock introducing the surging theme. Miles glides weightlessly across the rhythm, which has the activity of a freshly dynamited logjam. Shorter's movement is also friction-free and speedily functional on his featured spot, but Hancock reaffirms the restrained vector of the introduction on his solo. For the out chorus, the group returns to the rapids and a final cascade of sound from Williams.

For "Vonetta," Davis comes in with the long-noted poignancy of his Gil Evans days, and Shorter offers an unobtrusively guileful creation, while Hancock's harp-like musing underscores the top line. Interestingly, Williams maintains feathery stickwork on the snare head rather than resorting to the customary stick-on-cymbal or brush approach, and Carter's bass, like a Hollywood heiress, is found in all the right places.

Davis has always had an eye and ear for a great crew of musicians; this, as much as his own artistry, has kept most other jazzmen and listeners awaiting the trumpeter's next word. As usual, very few will be disappointed.

—Bill Quinn

"Prince of Darkness"; "Pee Wee"; "Masqualero"; "The Sorcerer"; "Limbo"; "Vonetta"; "Nothing Like You."

Personnel: Davis, trumpet; Wayne Shorter, tenor saxophone; Herbie Hancock, piano; Ron Carter, bass; Tony Williams, drums. Track 7: Davis, trumpet; Bob Dorough, vocal; others unidentified.

———

Oct. 3, 1968
Miles Davis
Miles in the Sky
Columbia 9628
★★★★½

Miles Davis has participated in one revolution in jazz and witnessed another, which, verbally at least, he refuses to accept. When that second revolution was taking effect, midway between Miles' 1956 quintet and his present group, it seemed that he might be trapped in a pattern of self-imitation. But, as this record and the recent *Miles Smiles* show, he has triumphantly renewed himself.

Miles has always been a lyrical player with an affection for the American popular song, and in many of his best solos (the second "When Lights Are Low," "All Blues") he created a wonderful tension by approaching and then withdrawing from the symmetry and sweetness of George Gershwin and Richard Rodgers. In one sense this way of playing can be called ironic. The player refers to a mood of simplicity and romantic sentiment and places himself at an emotional distance from it. If this describes the Miles of 1955–'60, it is clear why he has been unable to accept the essence of Ornette Coleman and John Coltrane, since Ornette has never found the popular song tradition to be relevant to his music, while Coltrane, for all the beauty of his middle-period ballads, finally abandoned it.

This record, one of the best that Miles has made with his present group, shows the effect of the Coleman–Coltrane revolution even as Miles denies it, for their assault on the popular song has pushed Miles along the only path that seems open to him, an increasingly ironic detachment from sentiment and prettiness.

Throughout this album, Miles takes material from his earlier days and darkens its emotional tone. His opening phrase on "Country Boy" recalls a fragment from his "Summertime" solo on the *Porgy and Bess* album, but here it is delivered with a vehemence that rejects the poignancy of the earlier performance. Even on "Black Comedy," his most straightahead solo here, the orderly pattern of the past is displaced and fragmented.

As Miles' playing becomes more oblique, he risks losing continuity altogether. That he doesn't is due, in large measure, to his wonderfully sympathetic group. Wayne Shorter's solos echo Miles' ironic temperament, and his tune "Paraphernalia" is a perfect example of the group's dead-pan comedy. It begins with a rhythm section vamp that in the past would have led directly into the theme. Here it is presented as an object in itself, over which the horns play a gentle, seemingly unrelated melody. During the solos the rhythm section periodically rises in the kind of crescendo that McCoy Tyner and Elvin Jones employed to push Coltrane to new heights of ecstasy, but here it is followed abruptly by a return of the opening vamp. The effect is wry as the soloists ride over the crescendo, knowing that at its end the background will demand that their passion be chastened rather than released.

"Stuff" is the rhythm section's tour de force. It establishes a pattern that hints at rock, bossa nova, country and western, and even an occasional ballroom glide. Tony Williams plays a rock beat but spaces it out and diminishes its volume. Herbie Hancock does some beautiful work on electric piano, emphasizing its relationship to electric guitar and organ. Ron Carter either plays electric bass on this track or his technique on the conventional bass enables him to simulate the rumbles and slides of the electronic instrument.

Over this pattern Miles and Shorter play a theme that hints at a number of the uptempo conventions of the late '50s, but these phrases, slowed down to a walk, take on the strange grace of a man running under water.

On "Paraphernalia," George Benson's guitar is added, and he successfully captures the mood of the composition, subduing his bright, blues-based conception so he sounds almost like Jimmy Raney. "Country Boy" sums up the album's effect—an attempt by Miles to retain his style while pushing it to its limits. The track begins with Miles in full flight, but his first phrase (the "Summertime" echo) sounds like the middle of something, not a beginning. He ends the track in similar fashion, letting a phrase that seems to demand a resolution stand by itself. It is as if Miles were saying, "I don't need new material. I only have to look at the old in a new way."

This album indicates that, for himself at this time, he is absolutely right.

—Larry Kart

"Stuff"; "Paraphernalia"; "Black Comedy"; "Country Boy."

Personnel: Davis, trumpet; Wayne Shorter, tenor saxophone; Herbie Hancock, piano, electric piano; Ron Carter, bass; Tony Williams, drums.

―――――

May 29, 1969
Miles Davis
Filles de Kilimanjaro
Columbia 9750
★★★★★

I can think of a few of Miles' albums I wouldn't have given five stars, but to make shadowy distinctions among the rest of the beautiful offerings of an authentic genius requires more chutzpah than I can possibly summon up. I think it was Miles who said that every jazz musician ought to get down on his knees once a day and thank God for Duke Ellington. Ditto every jazz listener for Miles.

And the quintet, of course. Five musicians, one mind. Dig Tony, flailing away, then suddenly shimmering pianissimo to allow a horn statement to etch itself into the listener's mind. Dig Ron, humming and buzzing little countermelodies whose dissonances are at once startling and appropriate, and suddenly walking, tall and funky, reminding the listener of the foundation that was there all along. Dig Herbie, gently supplying the right colors for the stark pen-and-ink drawing of the horns. Dig Wayne, who has grown from a good hard-bop tenor into a creative soloist and composer of immense stature.

No. I won't attempt analysis or evaluation. I'll tell you what's slightly different about this record. First, the compositions, all by Davis, are voiced in harmony more than has been his wont recently. "Petits Machins," for example, is a lovely melody based on a G tonal center and a four-note CBAG riff.

Second, Miles and/or his pianists seem to be attracted to the electric piano sound; only "Mademoiselle Mabry" and probably "Frelon Brun" have standard piano. (Hard to tell about the latter, since the upper range sounds electric, the lower acoustic.)

Third, I detect hints of the interest in rock Miles has spoken of lately. "Frelon"'s basic riff has a soupçon of R&B, and "Mabry" has a rock-bluesy kind of tag. This reaching out toward rock seems an undercurrent throughout, and the electric piano reinforces it.

Fourth, Williams is a bit more restrained than usual, though not a bit less effective. His backing for Davis and Shorter on "Tout de Suite" consists chiefly of an evenly accented fast four on ride and hi-hat with generally symmetrical bass–drum counterpoint. When he breaks out of that to underscore crucial phrases by the horns, the dramatic contrast is excruciating.

Fifth are the new members, Corea and Holland. Sounds like they'll fit in just fine. It won't be the same quintet, but it'll be a great quintet. Tony's split leaves a gaping hole, but that will be filled, too.

Sixth is Miles. He's not playing differently; it's just that whatever he plays is always new. His solo on "Mabry"—every note perfectly chosen, each part blending into a perfect whole. Out on a limb. Back to the tonal center. How'd he get there? Wings, child. Angel's wings.

—Alan Heineman

"Frelon Brun"; "Tout de Suite"; "Petits Machins"; "Filles de Kilimanjaro"; "Mademoiselle Mabry."

Personnel: Davis, trumpet; Wayne Shorter, tenor saxophone; Herbie Hancock (tracks 1, 2, 4) or Chick Corea, piano, electric piano; Ron Carter (tracks 1, 2, 4) or Dave Holland, bass; Tony Williams, drums.

Aug. 7, 1969

Caught in the Act: Miles Davis
Plugged Nickel, Chicago
Personnel: Davis, trumpet; Wayne Shorter, soprano and tenor saxophones; Chick Corea, electric piano; Dave Holland, bass; Jack DeJohnette, drums.

Outside of Charlie Parker's best units, I don't think there's ever been a group so at ease at uptempos as Miles Davis' current quintet. Their relaxation at top speed enables them to move at will from the "hotness" uptempo playing usually implies to a serene lyricism in the midst of turmoil.

This "inside-out" quality arises from the nature of human hearing, since, at a certain point, musical speed becomes slow motion or stillness (in the same way the eye reacts to a stroboscope). Yet the group doesn't move into circular rhythms wholesale. They generally stay right on the edge, and, when the rhythm does seem ready to spin endlessly like a Tibetan prayer wheel, one prodding note from Davis or Shorter is enough to send them hurtling into "our" time world, where speed means forward motion.

Recent changes in the group's personnel and instrumentation have had important effects. Chick Corea is playing electric piano, and while this move may have been prompted by the variable nature of club pianos, Corea has made a virtue of necessity, discovering many useful qualities in the instrument. In backing the horns, its ability to sustain notes and produce a wide range of sonorities frees Holland and DeJohnette from these roles. Corea is now the principal pattern maker in the rhythm section, a task to which Ron Carter and Tony Williams had given much attention.

As a soloist, Corea has found a biting, nasal quality in the instrument, which can be very propulsive. I heard a number of first sets, and each time it seemed that the rhythm section really got together for the night during Corea's solo on the first tune.

As mentioned above, Holland and DeJohnette don't often set up the stop-and-go interludes of Carter and Williams. Instead, they burn straightahead, creating a deep, luxurious groove for the soloists.

Holland is as fast as anyone on the instrument, but it is the melodic and harmonic quality of his bass lines one remembers, as cohesive and austere as Lennie Tristano's. Shorter, in particular, responds to this kind of musical thought, since it so closely resembles his own. At times it seems as if he and Holland could improvise in unison if they wished.

Williams had a greater range of timbres and moods under control than DeJohnette does, but the latter is just right for this group. He sounds something like Elvin Jones with a lighter touch, and he really loves to swing in a bashing, exuberant manner.

Shorter's approach to improvisation, in which emotion is simultaneously expressed and "discussed" (i.e., spontaneously found motifs are worked out to their farthest implications with an eyes-open, conscious control), has a great appeal for me. The busyness and efficiency of a man at work can have an abstract beauty apart from the task. Of course, his playing has more overt emotional qualities of tenderness or passion, which can give pleasure to the listener.

The problem with such an approach lies in keeping inspiration open and fresh and maintaining a balance between spontaneity and control. Here, Shorter's recent adoption of the soprano saxophone is interesting. As a master craftsman of the tenor, he already has great technical control of the second instrument, and its newness seems to have opened areas of emotion for him on both horns. Often, while Davis solos, one can see Shorter hesitate between the soprano and tenor before deciding which to play. It's a fruitful kind of indecision. Shorter once referred to his soprano as "the baby," and I think I know what he meant.

There's not much new to say about Davis, except to note that he is to some degree responsible for every virtue of the group's members mentioned above, and that he uses all of them to achieve the effects he wants. He is the leader in the best sense of the term. Playing almost constantly at the limit of his great ability, he inspires the others by his example. There is no shucking in this band, and if Davis occasionally is less than serious in his improvising, as he was one night on "Milestones," mocking the symmetrical grace of his mid-'50s style, one soon realizes that he is serious after all.

With this version of the Miles Davis Quintet, one aspect of jazz has been brought to a degree of ripeness that has few parallels in the history of the music. Now let's hope that Davis and Columbia decide to record the group in person.

—Larry Kart

Oct. 30, 1969
Miles Davis
In a Silent Way
Columbia 9875
★★★½

With the exception of *Miles Smiles* and *Miles in the Sky,* recent years have seen Miles Davis playing one kind of music on record and another kind in person. The majority of his recordings have been concerned with musical color and enforced spontaneity (as on *Kind of Blue*), and the results have been impressionistic and rather tentative. In person the group is something else altogether—an explosive band that tears into the music rather than feeling their way through it.

I prefer the in-person Miles, and I think there is objective reason for that preference. Putting it simply, the frequency of significant musical events on this album and its stylistic predecessors (*Sorcerer, Nefertiti* and *Filles de*

Kilimanjaro) is rather low. When something does happen it is almost always something good, but more good things happen during most in-person tunes by the quintet than on this whole album.

The new musical color this time is an intriguing rhythm section combination of electric piano and organ, but it seems as if half the album is taken up while this color is established and adjusted.

"Shh/Peaceful," which appears to have been spliced together from several takes, is the less successful performance. Miles' solo is a lukewarm elaboration of one of his favorite phrases, and there is a lengthy guitar solo that never quite emerges from the rhythm section's noodling.

Wayne Shorter's turn is brief but beautiful (the personnel listing has him on tenor, but he plays soprano saxophone throughout). He has a remarkable technical command of the instrument (this recording was reportedly the first time he ever played the soprano), and he reveals a touching, blue lyricism that rarely appears in his tenor playing.

The second side begins with Zawinul's "In a Silent Way" (all the other lines are by Miles), and its hymn-like quality fits the electric piano-organ-guitar-bowed bass ensemble quite well. This segues into "It's About That Time," which finds Davis and Shorter in very good form over a striding rock rhythm.

If the performers of this music were merely good musicians the results would probably put anyone to sleep, but the skill and subtlety of the accompanists and the genius of Davis and Shorter make this album worth hearing.

—Larry Kart

"Shh/Peaceful"; "In a Silent Way/It's About That Time."

Personnel: Davis, trumpet; Wayne Shorter, soprano saxophone; John McLaughlin, guitar; Herbie Hancock, Chick Corea, electric piano; Joe Zawinul, electric piano, organ; Dave Holland, bass; Tony Williams, drums.

May 14, 1970

Caught in the Act: Miles Ahead in Rock Country

University of Michigan, Ann Arbor, Mich.

Rock 'n' roll, embodied by the SRC, Stooges, Up and the MC5, walks the streets of Ann Arbor, Mich., while jazz hides behind the record collections of a few pre-Beatles-age graduate students at the University of Michigan.

It's not exactly the place where one would expect to find a jazz festival, but nevertheless Ann Arbor did have one of sorts—a two-night, student-organized program featuring the Miles Davis Quintet, Ron Carter's New York Jazz Sextet, the Cannonball Adderley Quintet, Alvin Batiste and William Fischer.

Having seen Miles Davis last summer while visiting New York, I naturally qualified as the jazz expert among my undergraduate friends, and I was fairly certain they were not going to dig Miles. After all, the Davis Quintet doesn't sound a whole lot like the Stones.

No matter; they and everybody else knew Miles was supposed to be hip—what with his cover story in *Rolling Stone* and all—so how could they lose? Tickets sold fast, and Miles practically filled the 4,000-seat auditorium on the festival's first night.

As for what the quintet (plus added guitarist John McLaughlin) laid down that night, it was typically fantastic. But my peripheral interest was focused on how the crowd would react. I remembered, when I had seen Miles in Central Park, that only a handful of first-row admirers had given the quintet a standing ovation. The vast majority of the audience, like myself, had been left behind.

But in Ann Arbor, Miles' performance received an overwhelming reception—far out, freaky, heavy and every other catch phrase was thrown around. A standing ovation was assured.

It seemed simple: The people had been told that Miles is great, and they did their best to make their minds confirm it. Maybe somebody's got a name for that—like "directed" thinking. But anyway, the fact is that everybody dug it, and with a degree of concentration and sensibility rarely if ever displayed at a rock concert. Mental fatigue!

The Davis Quintet strikes very close to where many whites listeners are at, and I think that has to do mostly with guys in his group—like Chick Corea on electric piano and Dave Holland on electric bass. They're out front, mixing together everything new—spontaneous jazz, rock rhythms and a whole spectrum of sounds. Corea's piano turned on as many people as did Davis' trumpet.

I bet if Miles were to cut a "live" college performance album, he'd find himself in some pretty unlikely company, like the Stones; Crosby, Stills, Nash & Young; Beatles; etc. Who knows what Miles would say to that, but I know rock 'n' rolling Ann Arbor would sure dig it.

—Bert Stratton

June 11, 1970
Miles Davis
Bitches Brew
Columbia GP26
★★★★★

Listening to this double album is, to say the least, an intriguing experience. Trying to describe the music is something else again—mainly an exercise in futility. Though electronic effects are prominent, art, not gimmickry, prevails and the music protrudes mightily.

Music—most of all music like this—cannot be adequately described. I really don't want to count the cracks on this musical sidewalk—I'd rather trip over them. Fissures, peaks, plateaus; anguish, strange beauty—it's all there for a reason, and it can be torn up for a reason.

To be somewhat less ambiguous—but to list only my lasting impressions: Maupin's bass clarinet work generally; the eerie echo effect employed on Miles' various phrases through "Bitches Brew"; the rhythm section's devices during parts of "Brew" (highly reminiscent of Wagner's "Siegfried's Funeral March" from *Goetterdaemmerung*); Shorter's solos on "Spanish Key" and "Voodoo"; the electric piano work on "Key"; Miles' lyricism on "Sanctuary"; and McLaughlin on "John McLaughlin."

Parenthetically, my liking for recorded Miles came to an abrupt halt with *Nefertiti*. I didn't think I could go beyond that with him. I'm still uncertain, but this recording will surely demand more of my attention than the three intervening albums. It must be fully investigated.

You'll have to experience this for yourself—and I strongly advise that you do experience it. Miles has given us the music, and that's all we need.

—Jim Szantor

"Pharaoh's Dance"; "Bitches Brew"; "Spanish Key"; "John McLaughlin"; "Miles Runs the Voodoo Down"; "Sanctuary."

Personnel: Davis, trumpet; Bennie Maupin, bass clarinet; Wayne Shorter, soprano saxophone; John McLaughlin, electric guitar; Chick Corea, Larry Young, Joe Zawinul, electric piano; Dave Holland, bass; Harvey Brooks, Fender bass; Lenny White, Jack DeJohnette, Don Alias, drums; Jim Riley, percussion.

Sept. 16, 1971
Miles Davis
A Tribute to Jack Johnson
Columbia 30455
★★★★

Davis' trumpet work in the *Jack Johnson* documentary film music is cleanly articulated and as lucid in terms of well-connected ideas as any he's done since he went into his new bag. Aha, you say, which new bag? And you have a point, for it seems Miles is into something different every six months or so. But in fact it's easy to hear the steady development of the new, freer Davis approach from the 1965 *E.S.P.* album forward.

The Davis brand of the New Thing may have reached its extreme possibilities in the Fillmore package, which presents a maximum of rhythmic density and a minimum of creative melodic exploration. No recording dates are disclosed by Columbia for the album at hand, nearly 50 minutes of music for the documentary film about the life of the great heavyweight boxer. Whether the LP was done before or after *Fillmore* is beside the point. What is important is that it emphasizes that Davis has not abandoned his lyricism (however far removed it may be from his plaintive lyricism of the 1950s) and has not buried in a mound of rock his genius for constructing melodies. Muted (yes, a return to the Harmon mute) or open, straight or electronically assisted, Miles' playing is brilliant through both sides of the album. He reaches high and moves fast and virtually always makes whatever leap or speed he attempts. This performance will give no support to the old saw that Miles is good but sloppy.

Much of the time when Davis is not playing, the music drops several creative notches to become merely good rock 'n' roll. That is due in large measure to McLaughlin, a guitarist who does not deal in subtlety, and Cobham, an excellent drummer whose role here is limited to rather routine patterns. McLaughlin does deal in broad humor and at one point he combines the low register of the guitar and the wah-wah pedal to get an effect remarkably like a plunger trombone. His fuzz-feedback obbligatos to Davis are for the most part effective, although they occasionally come close to dominating.

In the film, a stunning drum solo accompanies a Charlie Chaplin silent movie boxing routine thrown in as atmosphere, but that solo is missing from the album, as is other incidental music.

Grossman's soprano solos are pretty and graceful.

There's nothing about the electric piano or organ playing that speaks to these ears of Herbie Hancock, but producer Teo Macero's office says Hancock is on the record. (No players are listed on the album jacket.)

This music ends with Miles floating muted over a large ensemble voice, if not by Gil Evans, in the Evans style. Those few seconds add a half star to the rating. Pure beauty, tromped on by Brock Peters doing a speech from the movie.

As background for the film, the music is frequently appropriate. At other times it seems the record session must have been held independently of the film making; the music just doesn't fit. Nonetheless, on balance it is a good deal more successful than the vast majority of movie music.

Apart from considerations of the sound track, don't miss the film when it's released. Producer Jim Jacobs has done a remarkable job of combining old film clips and painstaking research into a cogent statement not only about a black hero's triumph and agony but about the United States of America.

—Doug Ramsey

"Right Off"; "Yesternow."

Personnel: Davis, trumpet; Steve Grossman, soprano sax; Herbie Hancock, electric piano, organ; John McLaughlin, guitar; Mike Henderson, bass; Billy Cobham, drums.

———————

April 13, 1972
Miles Davis
Live-Evil
Columbia 30954
★★½

One should, I suppose, be thankful for any and all recorded scraps that help document the ongoing development of a major musical innovator. On these grounds, this double-LP album might be considered important. Otherwise, it continues the downward spiral that has marked much of Miles' recorded efforts since *In a Silent Way*—which remains the incontestable apogee of this musical direction. *Live-Evil* is in many ways the least interesting or effective of all the Davis albums since that beautiful achievement.

With the exception of the curious *Jack Johnson* soundtrack album, each of the sets since *In a Silent Way* has been a double album that could have benefited immeasurably from a process of careful editing down to a single disc preserving only the most coherent, consistent moments of music-making and sparing us the arid stretches which bracket them. There's an inordinate amount of the latter in this set.

Of course, painstaking editing of the music would add a great deal more production time and cost to the albums. It's far easier just to mix the recorded performances and issue them as is. On the face of it, too, it seems a far more "honest" proposition to present unedited performances, as though the record listener were hearing the group "live" in a club or onstage. And then, isn't the purchaser getting greater value for his money in these two-LP sets?

Well, yes and no. Like the previous Davis double albums, this offers the listener a considerable amount of material. The shortest of the four sides is about 24½ minutes long, as contrasted with the far more usual 15 or 16 minutes per side. So it's true—there is a lot of playing time per album. But equally true (to these ears, at any rate) is the fact that there's really not a lot of playing—that is, genuinely, consistently creative high-level music making.

Despite the ferment of electronic and rhythmic energies, there's quite a bit of musical temporizing throughout the four sides of the set. Or maybe it just seems that way, since there are fewer moments of truly inspired playing by Miles or his compatriots than in either *Bitches Brew* or *Live at the Fillmore*. Still, there are enough of them to have resulted in an impressive single LP.

It's not that this set is a collection of odd performances left over from previous sessions (though there is such a slack air about it) or that there are occasional technical difficulties (loud amplifier buzz, bad piano, soprano saxophone mixed in at a curiously low level from time to time, etc.) that leads me to rate this album as I have. No, the rating is for the music and the music alone, exactly as Miles and/or producer Teo Macero have given it to us: straight, unedited, as played, as though all elements—creative and lesser moments alike—were of equal rate. Were the album composed entirely of "live" recordings, there might be some justification in presenting the tracks as documentaries of spontaneous musical creation. But "controlled" studio cuts are included as well, and they're just as subject to the vagaries of performance, i.e., long dull stretches of water-treading alternating with moments of strength and inspiration—as the live pieces.

"So what?" you ask. Is all the foregoing fussy and academic niggling over a series of small points esthetic matters better left to the discretion of the artist? Then too, since jazz is nothing if not a music of the moment, a music based in and charged with spontaneous creation and, as such, subject to the inevitable ebb and flow of creative energies, should not the recordings reflect this aspect of the music? After all, an artist—let alone a group of interacting musicians—is not always at the very top of his game, so why should one expect his recordings to reflect a perfection that is only rarely present in his club or concert performances? Should one demand of his recording of the music a kind of perfection which even its most gifted practitioners hope to achieve only occasionally? Is every recording to be a deathless, timeless memorial?

Obviously not, of course. Every trip of the jazz artist to the recording studio does not automatically result—as so many current recordings so forcibly remind us—in interesting, let alone classic, performances. Though courted assiduously, inspiration strikes when and where it will and its incidence is certainly no higher in the recording studio than in the club, concert hall or rehearsal studio.

Miles Davis, however, has been a law unto himself. Over the duration of his recording career, he has insisted on the highest standards in his music, and as a consequence his recordings have been distinguished for the extraordinarily high creative levels they have attained. Davis has until now stood aside from the often demanding pressures of the commercial music apparatus and resolutely gone his own clear-sighted way. We have been the beneficiaries of this purposeful integrity, which has been documented in countless albums of superbly realized music through all the phases of his music's development.

And that's why this album, which otherwise might not occasion such attention, is so distressing: It represents a relaxation of the standards we've come to expect of the trumpeter, a relaxation that is as unwelcome as it is unexpected. With perhaps anyone else, the album simply might be dismissed as a record that for some reason or another failed to coalesce into a totally striking expression; but because it is a Miles Davis album one inevitably feels a keen sense of disappointment that's disproportionate to the music's dereliction.

Is this relaxation of standards a sign of sudden, unfortunate (primarily for us) complacency on Davis' part? Or does it reflect disdain for his newly acquired mass audience, his unconscious reaction to indiscriminate adulation? Perhaps, knowing that his music is viewed by many of his new listeners as a kind of strange, weird but essentially pleasantly freaky trip music, is this the form his retaliation has taken—that is, give them what they deserve; they won't know the difference anyway, so why bother? Or is the collection an accommodation to the record company's urgent need for a new Davis record—any record, irrespective of quality—to merchandise? After all, when you're hot, you're hot, the song tells us.

I earnestly hope it's none of these things, any of which would distress me more than I can say. Let's hope it represents some unavoidable, temporary hiatus and that Davis will give us an unequivocally affirmative answer in his next recording. Jazz is not so conspicuously healthy nowadays that it can uncomplainingly suffer the sacrifice of so brilliant a contributor on the altar of commercial success.

—Pete Welding

"Sivad"; "Little Church"; "Medley—Gemini/Double Image"; "What I Say"; "New Um Talvez"; "Selim"; "Funky Tonk"; "Inamorata and Narration."

Personnel: Davis, trumpet, all tracks; tracks 1, 4, 7, 8: Gary Bartz, saxophones; John McLaughlin, guitar; Keith Jarrett, piano; Michael Henderson, bass; Jack DeJohnette, drums; Airto Moreira, percussion; track 2: Steve Grossman, saxophones; McLaughlin, guitar; Hermeto Pascoal, Herbie Hancock, Jarrett, keyboards; Dave Holland, bass; DeJohnette, Moreira, drums; track 3: Wayne Shorter, saxophones; McLaughlin, guitar; Joe Zawinul, Chick Corea, keyboards; Holland, bass; DeJohnette, Moreira, drums; Khalil Balakrishna, sitar; tracks 5, 6: Grossman, saxophones; Hancock, Corea, Jarrett, keyboards; Ron Carter, bass; DeJohnette, Moreira, drums; Pascoal, voice.

Oct. 12, 1972
Miles Davis
Relaxin'/Cookin'
Prestige 24001
★★★★★

But first those classic 1956 Davis quintet sides! The two LPs were formerly *Relaxin'* and *Cookin'*, and derive from two mammoth recording sessions that produced a total of about two dozen issued performances. Apart from Davis, the men involved were just beginning to make names for themselves, largely through this group, and would make numerous recordings together, though never quite sounding as fresh and integrated as they do under Miles' direction.

Miles had been going doggedly along his own path right from the beginning, commanding the respect of, among others, Charlie Parker, even when the outsider can find little justification in the recorded evidence. With the formation and success of this group he had achieved the consistent and slightly perverse aristocratic presence that prevades all his subsequent work.

He has many superb solos on these records. The two Sonny Rollins lines, "Oleo" and "Airegin," for example, have very fine playing. The former has Miles strolling in over Paul Chambers' well-placed underpinning to provide a definitive lesson in the tension/relaxation technique, using his edgy tone to enhance the effect. "Airegin," with its strong percussion support from Philly Joe Jones, recalls the earlier Blue Note sides with Art Blakey and has tough trumpet from the leader, who is in excellent spirits, really reaching out on this piece—particularly when the pianist takes a rest. Philly Joe and John Coltrane are also at the top of their game, making "Airegin" one of the finest complete performances of the period. "My Funny Valentine" and "You're My Everything" have bruised and romantic trumpet solos—there is one remark-able sustained silence in Miles' second solo on "Valentine." And he tells the story chapter by chorus with the necessary conviction on "Blues by Five."

As noted above, I feel that some of the other musicians excelled themselves in this group, certainly pianist Red Garland and bassist Paul Chambers, neither the most innovative. Most of the rhythm work is excellent, though I'm not much enamored with the two-beat style too often employed. Philly Joe is simply one of the most exciting drummers in jazz, and right on the line through Max Roach and Roy Haynes to Tony Williams.

If the rhythm section seems designed to project Miles' personality to best effect, then Coltrane was apparently happy enough to be a contrasting foil. At times he sounds both in and out of place in the group, but this was not entirely the fault of the group structure, because the tenorist had already started out on that self-absorbed quest for his own apotheosis in music. The strangely Puritan esthetics were beginning to appear—that combination of austerity (bleak tone) and hard work (at this time expressed in necessarily playing every possible note on the chord; later it would take the form of emotional and incantatory marathons). While much of his playing with the quintet in 1956 sounds unformed and experimental, there are also some very fine moments. He comes in strong and urgent on "I Could Write a Book," demonstrates his dark blues style in embryonic form on "Blues by Five" (which also has brief vestiges of the Dexter Gordon influence) and jams all the notes he can find into the explorative "Tune Up" solo. But perhaps "Airegin" is as good as anything here.

—Terry Martin

Dec. 21, 1972
Miles Davis
The Complete Birth of the Cool
Capitol 11026
★★★★★

The only set in this release that almost duplicates an available LP is *Miles Davis: The Complete Birth of the Cool*. This is the famous 1949–'50 nine-piece band, and the key word is "complete"—earlier LP issues omit the 12th piece recorded, "Darn That Dream," probably because it has a long vocal by Kenny "Pancho" Hagood.

It's good to have it included, and even better is the other innovation: The album presents the pieces in recording sequence instead of haphazardly.

Too much has been written about this influential music to dwell on it here. To this writer, "Boplicity," "Israel," "Move" and the haunting "Moon Dreams" are the standouts, but the entire output is of a high order.

—Dan Morgenstern

March 29, 1973
Miles Davis
On the Corner
Columbia 31906
★★

The title is apt and maybe a little too close for comfort. In fact, it's almost as though Miles was "on the corner" during much of the recording.

Take some chunka-chunka-chunka rhythm, lots of little background percussion diddle-around sounds, some electronic mutations, add simple tune lines that sound a great deal alike and play some spacy solos. You've got the "groovin'" formula, and you stick with it interminably to create your "magic." But is it magic or just repetitious boredom?

Miles is playing not much differently than he did in the '50s and '60s. The mean, tight little hard-edged lines are still there. The purity and simplicity of approach, the wide-open spaces to create that teasingly beautiful tension—it all remains. Sure, he's added some electronics, but it really doesn't alter his style much. Just thank God he's got more taste in the use of his electronic hookups than Don Ellis.

Pete Welding said it all too well in his review of Miles' last release, *Live-Evil.* He said the music needs editing. Miles' music has suffered from this since *In a Silent Way,* though the first side of the *Jack Johnson* album was smokin' and parts of the other albums since *Way* have been grand.

Anyway, Miles solos here and there, and they're mostly fine solos—if you don't get bored by the supposedly hypnotic but ultimately static rhythm. There really aren't that many solo moments, however.

Garnett has more space than Miles. His soprano, which gets the most time in the spotlight, is reedy and fleet but somehow doesn't convince. On the other hand, his tenor work is strong and distinctive.

Guitarist Creamen is OK in a neo-soul bag. The rest of the group? Chunka-chunka-chunka. There are a few fleeting seconds from the keyboards, but so what.

The personnel information, not included on the album, was provided by Columbia. It would indicate that perhaps both new and old material has been included (Hancock's presence, for example).

The aforementioned Welding review asked for an affirmative answer from Davis' next album. Sorry, Pete. How about next time?

—Will Smith

"On the Corner"; "New York Girl"; "Thinkin' One Thing and Doin' Another"; "Vote for Miles"; "Black Satin"; "One and One"; "Helen Butte"; "Mr. Freedom X."

Personnel: Davis, trumpet; Carlos Garnett, soprano and tenor saxes; Herbie Hancock, electric piano; Harold J. Williams, keyboards; David Creamen, guitar; Colin Walcott, sitar; Mike Henderson, bass; Jack DeJohnette, Billy Hart, drums; Mtume, percussion; Badal Roy, tabla.

Jan. 17, 1974
Miles Davis
Jazz at the Plaza, Vol. 1
Columbia 32470
★★★★½

I've always considered myself a charter member of Rev. Leroy's congregation—I've always, that is, been more interested in "What's happening now" than in "What used to was." But I guess most of us are suckers for some nostalgia trip or other, and when I saw the personnel and date (1958) on this album, I fell out. These are six of the most beautiful musicians of their time—too short a time, for Trane and P.C.—and any addition to their relatively small recorded output is automatically welcome.

But this is not just any addition. This is the sextet at very nearly peak form; why this session went unreleased for 15 years is therefore a mystery. Two small gripes: The title cut is clearly and unmistakably Thelonious Monk's "Straight, No Chaser" and I don't understand why it was retitled and credited to Miles; also, Evans and Chambers are miserably underrecorded.

Apart from that, a stone gas, "Jazz at the Plaza" (i.e., "Chaser") sets the groove. Most of Miles' opening solo is in a straight, lively, show tune bag. Then, there's a marvelous rest followed by some bluesier phrasing. Trane follows, running chords until there's nothing left of them. This solo is a striking example of his moving through first the standard and then the abstract intervals, getting himself into what seems to be a dissonant dead-end, and releasing that tension with an utterly natural slur or a lightning-like phrase that reestablishes the basic progression. Cannonball follows, and as usual, the stylistic contrast is remarkable. Bird's ghost sits on his shoulder, but the influence is usually benign. Evans has a short solo before the out-chorus, to which the "Miles Theme" coda is appended.

"My Funny Valentine" is all Miles. The saxes lay out. The leader's melody statement is typically idiosyncratic, as he performs radical surgery on the opening eight bars and then mostly paraphrases or counterpoints the rest. I can think off-hand of at least four other versions by Miles of this tune, and this may well be the best he ever did with it. Gorgeous!

Miles metamorphoses "If I Were a Bell"'s melody, too, omitting much of the bridge to good effect and closing the solo with one of his patented broad quavers. Trane gets into near-atonality in spots, clearly presaging the later, freer Trane, and there's a hesitancy in the playing that would naturally accompany a venture into unexplored territory. Miles takes the out-chorus, but Chambers and Jones, on brushes, are apparently so stimulating to Miles that he takes another chorus. Here you realize how effective and provocative the rhythm section has been all the way through.

Miles hits his only blatant clinker of the date on the first eight bars of "Oleo." Nice to know he's human—he never did have much luck with the big skips in standard uptempo bop lines. Trane follows with an incredible display of virtuosity, freedom and coherence. Cannonball takes the frenzy down a peg; he's just as fast as Trane, and just as fluid, but he seems rather intimidated by what he's just heard—as who wouldn't be? Evans and Chambers, plus some trumpet–bass tradeoffs, take it out.

I didn't give this five stars because the recording quality is only fair, and because both Cannonball and Evans have been better than they are here. And even Trane sometimes overdoes the chord-running number. But that's a relative assessment. When the music is good here—as it is more often than not—the solar system is too low a rating.

—Alan Heineman

"Jazz at the Plaza"; "My Funny Valentine"; "If I Were a Bell"; "Oleo."

Personnel: Davis, trumpet; John Coltrane, tenor saxophone; Cannonball Adderley, alto saxophone; Bill Evans, piano; Paul Chambers, bass; Philly Joe Jones, drums.

June 20, 1974
Miles Davis
Big Fun
Columbia 32866
★★★★

Somewhere along the way Davis expressed dissatisfaction with Columbia's policy of reissuing a ton of his older material without taking care of the miles and miles of newer, unreleased tape still in the can. The result, or the first effect of a complete rectification, is *Big Fun,* a four-sided LP with new material that spans the years 1969–'72 (from *Bitches Brew* to within a few months of his *Philharmonic in Concert* set.)

Each cut covers a complete side (more than 25 minutes on the average) and represents the band's growth at that particular time period. "Great Expectations," recorded Nov. 19, 1969, is closest in texture, voicing, rhythm and melodic development to *Bitches Brew,* cut Aug. 19–20, 1969. "Go Ahead John," recorded with a sparse quintet, was set down March 3, 1970, and mirrors the *Jack Johnson* session (the only personnel change is Jack DeJohnette on drums in place of Billy Cobham). *Live-Evil,* an amalgam of material done throughout 1970, is here paralleled by the in-studio composition "Lonely Fire" (Jan. 27, 1970); in fact, simply drop Harvey Brooks and add Steve Grossman and John McLaughlin and you've got the personnel of the *Live-Evil* medley, "Gemini/Double Image."

The most recent session, "Ife" (June 12, 1972), shows the Miles band in transition from the *On the Corner* twofer to the Philharmonic concert of September '72. Billy Hart, Bennie Maupin and Harold Williams, all members of Miles' previous band, are heard on their way out the revolving door, while Al Foster has surfaced for the first time. Both Lonnie Liston Smith and Sonny Fortune are transitional replacements, making their first appearances on a Miles recording marathon.

But what about the music which, after all, is the issue here? Like so much of Miles' stuff since *In a Silent Way,* the concept of chordal freedom has allowed musicians to fade in and out of the impressionistic electronic network, so often without resolution or explicit direction. At times the interplay, and tonal empathy, is brilliant with Davis' compact, warpingly forlorn horn—much in evidence here—inferring the path for the multitude of sonic coloring brushes and metric accents.

But it's difficult to sustain attention as the prolonged ruminations offer few handle bars. The music is best appreciated under a set of good headphones where the frequent overdubs and subtle use of volume and voicing will not be missed.

One curious note about the musical content of *Big Fun* is the lack of rhythmic verve that envelops the entire album. Whereas his other albums have moments of high-energy polyrhythms and feverish propulsion, little here manages to break through an often highly provocative, often mirky and dispirited languidness. In a sense, it's the epitome of Miles as a hornman "walking on eggshells."

Ultimately, *Big Fun* is another Miles-stone in the endless unraveling of a genius at play. It's a further crystallization of one of Miles' most crucial developmental periods; and, in historical perspective, it further illuminates Miles as the musical prophet of the '70s, which he certainly is. It also makes a good sampler for those unfamiliar with Miles' contemporary posture, if indeed there are any such reclusives still among us. But the real reward of this album is the raspy, hoarse voice at the conclusion of "Ife," saying, "OK, that's enough. Let's hear some of that, Teo."

—Ray Townley

"Great Expectations"; "Ife"; "Go Ahead John"; "Lonely Fire."

Personnel: Side one—Davis, trumpet; Herbie Hancock, Chick Corea, electric pianos; John McLaughlin, guitar; Steve Grossman, soprano sax; Bennie Maupin, bass clarinet; Ron Carter, bass; Harvey Brooks, Fender bass guitar; Billy Cobham, drums; Airto Moreira, percussion; Khalil Balakrishna, Bihan Sharma, electric sitar, tambura. Side two—Davis, trumpet; Michael Henderson, bass guitar; Carlos Garnett, soprano sax; Lonnie Liston Smith, piano; Harold I. Williams Jr., piano, sitar; Maupin, clarinet, flute; Sonny Fortune, soprano sax, flute; Billy Hart, Al Foster, drums; Mtume, African percussion; Badal Roy, tablas. Side three—Davis, trumpet; Grossman, sax; McLaughlin, guitar; Dave Holland, bass; Jack DeJohnette, drums. Side four—Davis, trumpet; Corea, electric piano; Joe Zawinul, electric piano, Farfisa organ; Wayne Shorter, sax; Maupin, bass clarinet; Brooks, bass guitar; Holland, bass; Cobham, DeJohnette, drums; Airto, Balakrishna, Indian instruments.

Feb. 27, 1975
Miles Davis
Get Up With It
Columbia 33236
★★★★★

Is this the '70s answer to Duke Ellington's jungle band? The rhythms are certainly hot enough; and in some cases (the steaming "Rated X," for example), they tell the whole story of the music. Miles has made innovations in every area of contemporary music: harmonic, melodic, coloristic and now rhythmic. *Get Up With It,* Davis' most diverse, coherent LP statement since 1971's *Live-Evil,* explodes the possibilities of fusion rhythms first suggested as far back as Tony Williams' tenure with the band. By and large, the album is a wailing, boiling, invigorating torrent of body pulse.

As he has for several years now, Miles uses the rock-steady figures of Michael Henderson as the static base around which percussionists Al Foster and Mtume construct an intricate latticework. This is a true dialogue of the drums; each percussionist (and this goes for Badal Roy on two of the earlier recordings here, also) carries countermelodies in his playing, as well as rhythmic figures. These are talking drums in the most basic, African-rooted sense.

Miles' electric piano and organ playing provides color, tone and a limited harmonic direction. As one might expect, his keyboards sound like no one else's; the playing is devoid of pyrotechnics, providing the bare essentials with nothing out of place. One suspects that Miles has been playing keyboards longer than he's been recording them, and his mature, very personal style acutely reflects his own musical mind.

The guitars phrase, bicker, comment and fall back to riff-chants in the background. During the latter part of "Calypso Frelimo," they contribute almost choral sub-textures beneath the trumpet solo. Cosey and Lucas seem to be able to do it all, from abstract blues lines in the quiet spaces to churning rhythm blankets in the wilder ensembles. Cosey, in particular, possesses a thick, ringing sound that works well in the echo-chamber that Miles and Teo Macero seem to favor in places. Lucas is more angular and rambling, but certainly no less accomplished.

Miles plays more horn here than we've heard in a while. He's more into vocalization on the trumpet than ever, the wah-wah now completely incorporated into the way he hears the music. His solos are all variations on blues concepts: lean, economical, always burning fiercely. It's a basic voicing, yet linearly abstract. It exposes the chant-like, field-holler texture of the music. And it speaks from a frankly black perspective.

We can assume that the humor of the rhythm and blues number, "Red China Blues," will be lost on those whose repeated cries of "sell-out" (ringing abrasively for several years now) drown out the funky good-time projections of the Sonny Boy Williamson-styled harmonica and tight brass arrangement. There are the moody, ominous, mournful feelings created by the 30-minute-plus tribute to Duke, "He Loved Him Madly." Particularly beautiful colors by Liebman's flute here. "Maiysha" is a basically dreamy, "island/exotic" soul-chord suspended to form the basis for the piece, sounding like a mutant Earth, Wind & Fire gestated on Saturn. Miles' horn blows a light, sweet melody with little improvisation, before the piece harshly and abruptly ends as a jagged blues in Milesian trumpet frenzy. "Honky Tonk," an earlier recording (one would guess from the *Live-Evil* period), sets the direction for the newer music. It provides both recent history and musical parallels: One discovers Miles' keyboard directions from the experiments of Jarrett; the guitar progression from McLaughlin to Cosey, Lucas and Gaumont; and the colors of Airto predicting the equally unique drum commentary of Mtume.

But as the true statement of this particular phase of Miles music in culmination, "Calypso Frelimo" deserves as much intensive listening as any piece he's done in 25 years. It explores both the roiling, Afro-space, electronic-tribal cauldron of rhythmic fire, and the abstract blues-hollers in one piece of staggering length and sustained drive and fire. Though this review has focused on the individual components, the final strength of this music lies in its total power. For the first time, Miles Davis has forged a music of collective intensity and ensemble unity, rather than stellar individuals in orbit around Miles' sun. It represents yet another new direction; and as one hears the complex, soulful music on *Get Up With It,* one is already aware that Miles is gone, moving in sonic territories that we, as yet, cannot hear.

—Charles Mitchell

"He Loved Him Madly"; "Maiysha"; "Honky Tonk"; "Rated X"; "Calypso Frelimo"; "Red China Blues"; "Mtume"; "Billy Preston."

Personnel: Davis, electric piano, organ, trumpet (all tracks); Michael Henderson, bass (all tracks); Reggie Lucas, guitar (all tracks except 3 and 6); Pete Cosey, guitar (tracks 1, 2, 5 and 6); Dominique Gaumont, guitar (tracks 1 and 2); David Liebman, flute (tracks 1 and 5); Sonny Fortune, soprano sax (track 2); John Stubblefield, soprano sax (track 5); Carlos Garnett, soprano sax (track 8); Cedric Lawson, piano (track 4); Al Foster, drums (all tracks except 3); Mtume, conga drums, African percussion (all tracks except 3); Badal Roy, tabla (tracks 4 and 8). Track 3 only: Keith Jarrett, electric keyboards; Steve Grossman, soprano sax; Airto Moreira, percussion; Jack DeJohnette, drums; Herbie Hancock, electric piano; John McLaughlin, guitar. Track 6 only: Bernard Purdie, drums; Cornell Dupree, guitar; Wally Chambers, harmonica; unidentified horn section.

March 13, 1975
Caught in the Act: Miles Davis
The Troubadour, Los Angeles
Personnel: Miles Davis, trumpet, Yamaha organ; Pete Cosey, guitar; Sonny Fortune, soprano sax, flute; Michael Henderson, bass; Al Foster, drums; Reggie Lucas, rhythm guitar; Mtume, congas.

Who knows what music lurks in the heart of Miles Davis?

The Troubadour audience didn't, that's for sure. The legendary innovator, whose mere presence on stage initially generated excitement and high-voltage sexual energy may again be well "ahead of his time," but the final effect of his opening set, his first L.A. appearance in three years, was one of befuddlement and disappointed boredom.

He looked super-cool with his huge dark glasses, his white silk shirt and pants, his silver belt and his orange scarf, but he shattered it all when he contemptuously spat on the stage and later, sans handkerchief, blatantly blew his nose with all the cool of a Georgia redneck.

After he left the stage the music dribbled off into a series of inconsequential blues clichés, finally faltering to a directionless halt. Most of the people clapped. Some because they felt morally obliged to.

He knew the press was there en masse, and it was almost as if he were spitting on them. I've since heard that he cleaned up his act and his attitude the following evenings and played some dynamic music. But his conduct opening night was infantile, pointless and boring.

What happened musically? Henderson, Foster, Lucas and Mtume laid down a funky, rocking beat at a single tempo, which Miles retained for 45 minutes. The audience could relate to that—no problem. Over the top, however, Miles and lead guitarist Pete Cosey defied all of the "laws," all of the "rules" and all of the customs of what has traditionally constituted a musical experience.

Instead of playing within a recognizable scale, Miles and Cosey for the most part played completely outside. Rather than playing notes, Miles squeaked, whimpered, whooped, mewled and growled. On the electric organ, he sustained great mashes of dissonant and seemingly arbitrary chords.

Instead of building series of melodic phrases within the traditional four-, eight- and 32-bar sections, he and Cosey generally played spurts and jumps of notes, apparently unrelated to each other, apparently coming from nowhere, leading to nowhere.

Occasionally, the mood would shift, and Miles would state an orthodox melody, or saxophonist/flutist Sonny Fortune (whom everybody liked) would take a relatively "inside" solo that tinkled bells of the familiar. On the whole, however, the audience left feeling excluded, confused and unfulfilled.

I, too, left feeling unfulfilled, but at the same time I suspect Miles is trying to take us into a new, dark world of inner experience—a new mood—that jars with our every preconception and with all of our past associations.

Granted, his conduct was offensive, and he may still be searching for the perfect musical means of expressing his diabolical vision, but I personally believe he is leading us into an area that has all of the subjectively frightening urgency, the angry darkness and the screaming jungle ferocity of a sleeping dream. He is leading us into our own broodingly primeval subconsciousness.

In this respect, Miles Davis is becoming profoundly natural, and I think in the future he is once again going to electrify us.

—Lee Underwood

Sept. 11, 1975
Miles Davis and His Tuba Band
Pre-Birth of the Cool
Jazz Live 8003
★★★★★

Here is an LP of enormous significance—something akin to the Dead Sea Scrolls of modern jazz. We all know, and most accept, the classic stature of the Davis Capitol sessions of 1949 and '50. Well, here, in air checks from the Royal Roost, is substantially that same repertoire performed in the group's only public engagement a full four months before the first Capitol date.

If a sense of perfection pervades the Capitols, these "workshop" performances are best characterized by their comparative uncertainty and sense of experimentation and discovery. These are not sloppy, however, only looser and more spontaneous. They will be an absolute treasure to all familiar with the definitive sides. Their somewhat altered personnel and strikingly different solos occupying the now-hallowed spaces in the classic scores are real ear openers!

Davis at this time was seeking an alternative form of expression to that fashioned by master boppers Charlie Parker, Dizzy Gillespie, Fats Navarro, et al. Their virtuosity made it virtually impossible for serious younger musicians to meaningfully extend their work still further. So Davis found a new direction at the confluence of the harmonic essence of bop and the rich ensemble sense Gil Evans and Gerry Mulligan had brought to the bands of Claude

Thornhill and Gene Krupa–Elliot Lawrence, respectively. The results heard on this record are a highly restrained, sometimes introspective, bop line disciplined still further within the framework of sensitive and detailed scoring. This is true chamber jazz.

The appropriateness of the form seems reflected in Davis' playing, which is firm and sure within its technical limitations. This is Miles as a resident of his own house, not a servant in Parker's. It would be arbitrary to say that he's better here than on the Capitols. I don't think he is. Just different. The same goes for Konitz, Mulligan and Lewis. Dig Lee and Gerry on "Hallucinations."

As if all this wasn't enough, we are also treated to two charts never recorded. "Plait" is a contrapuntal Davis chart juxtaposing a somber theme against a bright boppish line. "Why Do I Love You" is a fine Gil Evans scoring of the Jerome Kern tune.

This is an LP of basic importance to any jazz collection, on a level with the recent Charlie Christian/Lester Young and Wichita Parker discoveries. The sound is excellent. An import from Peters.

—John McDonough

"Why Do I Love You"; "Godchild"; "S'il Vous Plait"; "Moon Dreams"; "Hallucinations"; "Darn That Dream"; "Move"; "Moon Dreams"; "Hallucinations."

Personnel: Davis, trumpet; Mike Zwerin, trombone; John Barber, tuba; Junior Collins, French horn; Gerry Mulligan, baritone sax; Lee Konitz, alto sax; John Lewis, piano; Al McKibbon, bass; Ken Hagood, vocal.

───────

May 6, 1976
Miles Davis
Agharta
Columbia 33967
★★★★

For two or three years now, various accounts have filtered through the press about Miles Davis' '70s band, endowing them with a legendary status before they ever found their way into a studio. When Miles finally assembled the young troupe for a recording and conceded to release the results (*Get Up With It*), critics were cool. They weren't sure it was what they heard live, and they were even less sure they liked it. But, mainstream opinions aside, *Get Up With It* was a magnificent testimony to Miles' resourcefulness and determination to

SEPTEMBER 1980 $1.25

the contemporary
muric magazine

MILES DAVIS
Breaking
His Long Silence?

JAMES
BROWN
Seeks
New Stardom

BOB
WILBER
Reshapes His
Image

GLOBE
UNITY
ORCHESTRA
Individuals
Sound Shaping
En Masse

INTEGRATE
JAZZ & LEGIT
Part II

PRO SESSIONS by Brian Eno
and Ornette Coleman

OUR 50th YEAR

July, 1983 $1.75 U.K. £1.50

down beat

For Contemporary Musicians

The Electric
MILES DAVIS

LYLE MAYS
Electro-Jazz
Synthesist

RON CARTER
Basses Covered

ANDY SUMMERS
Guitar Activist

The Sixth Annual
down beat
Student Music Awards
1983

MILES DAVIS
SOLO TRANSCRIPTION

First 50 Years 1934·1984

December, 1984 $1.75   U.K. £1.70

down beat

or Contemporary Musicians

A Conversation With

Miles Davis

49th Annual
Readers Poll

King Sunny Adé
Juju Beat

John Cage
New Music Pioneer

7 4820 08270

12

A MILES TRANSCRIPTION:
So What

For Contemporary Musicians

down beat

October, 1988 $1.75 U.K. £ 2.0

MILES DAVIS
The Enabler: Part 1

GIL EVANS
The Touch Of Svengali

A CONVERSATION WITH

Miles Davis

For Contemporary Musicians

down beat

November, 1988 $1.75 U.K. £ 2.00

MILES
PART II

56th ANNUAL READERS POLL

DOWN BEAT

Jazz, Blues & Beyond

Dec. 1991, $2.50 U.K. £2.25 Can. $3.25

Miles
The final bow

HALL OF FAME

ARTIST OF THE YEAR

TRUMPET UPSET

DIVA SUPREME

GUITAR KING

BASS CHAMP

DOWN BEAT ®

azz, Blues & Beyond

December 1995
$2.95 U.K. £2.50
Can. $3.75

Miles
The '60s Explosion

Chick Corea Blindfolded

Mike Mainieri

Mark Whitfield

1 2>

74851 08270 6

PATRICIA BARBER   moe.   SHERMAN IRBY

DOWN BEAT

Jazz, Blues & Beyond

STEVE SWALLOW
and **CARLA BLEY'S**
Mental Jukebox

Jay McShann on
BIRD AND BEYOND

Joe Lovano
and **Greg Osby**
BLINDFOLDED

Final MILES

Band Members Discuss the Last Years
of the Dark Prince

www.downbeat.com

$3.99US $5.99CAN

05>

0 09281 01493 5

May 2001   U.K. £2.95

survive. And *Agharta* provides the living proof so many have waited to hear. Recorded on a lone winter night last year during a tour of Japan, it captures the demonic band at the peak of their integrative skills and performing ability. It won't change the fact that Miles' genius still has to be disseminated by his disciples and imitators before a general audience will recognize it, but after the sparks settle, one thing remains clear: Miles is inscrutable.

Interestingly, the best moments on *Agharta* occur during "Prelude" and "Interlude," lengthy and propulsive performances that seem to say this band cooked best when the race was on. "Prelude" evolves from one simple motif that Miles states on trumpet, and alludes to time and time again. It sounds like a clock, winding and slipping, ticking off disjunct and exotic rhythms. Miles directs the motion, starting and stopping the band and shifting tempos in an almost capricious manner with frightening, jolting intrusions from his seat behind the Yamaha organ. (More than any other factor, it is Miles' strange, nearly perverse presence on organ that defines the temper of his new music.) The rhythm section aims for a big, unified sound, pushing some passages in a relentless, breakneck drive, until Miles shifts gears and sends them scurrying into a lifting action that pulls the meter up by its roots. "Interlude" flies by like a train ride in a dream, where scenes flash past the window in a fascinating and illusive sequence. Michael Henderson drives the piece with a mammoth, blues-derived bass line that inspires the other musicians to forge their brightest solo statements.

Saxophonist Sonny Fortune is the most lyrical and yet cautious of the soloists on this date. He floats over formidable rhythmic density, taking long and graceful breaks that wing off into a private reverie, and whose substance and structure owe much to John Coltrane's *Love Supreme* period. By contrast, guitarist Pete Cosey throws all caution to the wind. His intense forays achieve a staggering emotional dimension, and freeze every other sound within range. One suspects Miles imposes the sense of stillness to underscore the effect of Cosey's solos, but sometimes it just sounds as if nobody else really knows how to respond to the guitarist's unique ferocity. Indeed, on the slower material, Cosey's work is unseemly and conspicuous, but when the band hits a blues groove, he proudly and justifiably displays his natural disposition.

Oddly, the *Agharta* band's only major failings are its attempts to re-create the recent past. "Maiysha" has none of the charm or humor of the *Get Up With It* version, and "Theme From Jack Johnson" suffers from an inability to come to grips with the relentless and triumphant purpose set forth so memorably in the original recording. Miles' trumpet alone, a plaintive voice speaking gently, poetically and uncompromisingly for its own right to endure, redeems their inclusion. And after all the shock value of Miles' present music fades, the

understated passion of his own musicianship will remain. His brave journey
has become one of the most significant musical odysseys of our time.

— Mikal Gilmore

"Prelude (Part I)"; "Prelude (Part II)"; "Maiysha"; "Interlude"; "Theme From
Jack Johnson."

Personnel: Davis, trumpet and organ; Sonny Fortune, soprano and alto sax,
flute; Michael Henderson, Fender bass; Pete Cosey, guitar, synth, percussion;
Al Foster, drums; Reggie Lucas, guitar; Mtume, conga, percussion, water
drum, rhythm box.

═══════

May 5, 1977
Miles Davis
Water Babies
Columbia 34396
★★★★

Water Babies is the first issue of a long-rumored multivolume collection of
unreleased Miles Davis, from the mid-'60s to the present day, to be released
over the course of the next couple of years. For those who have no active experience of the pre-*Bitches Brew* Miles, *Water Babies* may seem cool and remote;
for those who remember the '60s Quintet, it will prove indispensible.

The first side—featuring the Quintet—bears three Wayne Shorter compositions, an extension of the modal-blues style that graced the earlier *Kind
of Blue* and that was to be shortly resurrected for the pivotal *In a Silent Way*
sessions. Where in the former, Miles was concerned with freeing his melodic
pursuits from a harmonic regimen and in the latter with forging a rock
scheme to a serene, metronomic ambience, these tracks find Miles experimenting with rhythmic space, perhaps the major achievement of his latter-day
career. Miles and Shorter play the straightmen, etching themes in tandem,
blowing so calm that it occasionally borders on dispassion, like pearls passing
through an envelope of viscous oil. Testing the theory that—on grounds of
familiarity alone—the pulse is a given, understood element, Tony Williams
invents continuously shifting rhythms, seemingly capricious spurts, rolls and
flickers that punctuate the proceedings with chaos, and therefore impose a
new order. Conversely, Herbie Hancock is the introspective anchor, gently
dropping even, buoyant chords.

The second side, recorded with the *Silent Way* band (minus Zawinul and
McLaughlin), also aims to redefine musical space, but the two tracks included

vacillate to little good effect. "Two Faced" sounds like an embryo of "Bitches Brew" or "Pharaoh's Dance," with Chick Corea's spiralling thunk-funk chords and Williams' uncharacteristically heavy-handed attempt at pounding out a Latin-imbued rhythm. Here space means a rambling void, a conception Miles has realized becomingly on *Live-Evil* and *Agharta,* but "Two Faced," clearly, was a sketch, not a blueprint. "Dual Mr. Tillman" employs a seesawing funk progression that threatens (for nearly 14 minutes) to jell and soar, but instead spins in place.

Water Babies invites some curious questions about the new Miles Davis archives series: Why not release the albums in a chronological order, or at least arrange them so that each record depicts a narrow period, rather than this scatter-gun approach? Why was no information listed other than personnel? And why—oh why—the lamentable cover art? On the basis of side one alone, *Water Babies* comes highly recommended, a welcome addendum to the Davis library. But after *On the Corner,* Miles recorded volumes that were never released. Where are they? Where are the tapes recorded with Sam Rivers a decade ago? And, more importantly, where is Miles now?

—Mikal Gilmore

"Water Babies"; "Capricorn"; "Sweet Pea"; "Two Faced"; "Dual Mr. Tillman Anthony."

Personnel: Side one—Davis, trumpet; Herbie Hancock, keyboard; Tony Williams, drums; Ron Carter, bass; Wayne Shorter, soprano and tenor sax. Side two—Davis, trumpet; Herbie Hancock, keyboard; Tony Williams, drums; Ron Carter, bass; Wayne Shorter, soprano and tenor sax; Chick Corea, keyboard; Dave Holland, bass.

———

November 1981
Miles Davis
The Man With the Horn
Columbia 36790
★★★

Let's get this out of the way. This record gets three stars because it's Miles Davis. After all, three stars does mean good. Most players would be considered successful if they were judged good on the first throwdown after five years out of the ring. Not Miles Davis. Whether he likes it or not, or chooses to acknowledge it or not, Miles Davis carries the weight—burden, if he chooses to see it that way—of his past achievements. Miles Davis is expected to be great upon his return. His rhythms are expected to dance like butterflies; his melodies to sting like bees. Here, they don't. There are others who are secretly—if not publicly—happy that Davis has produced a record like this over which his detractors can gloat. I don't belong to either camp. This record—parts of it—is pleasant. That's all. No more. No less. But I expect more than pleasantries from Miles Davis.

Certainly it's difficult to review Davis with a supposed critical stance and keep a straight face. Just about everyone's thing with Davis is personal on some level. Davis' music is personal, introspective. For many he is a persona—a male Greta Garbo of jazz. At this point, with 25 years of great and significant music recorded, one wonders why he came out from retirement. His musical capacities are still beyond question. It's his motivation that is puzzling. Granted the man likes money, still one might have thought he was coming back because he had something to say. At least that was the hope. Judging from this record it is more like Davis is back because he felt like "talking" and maybe is figuring out what to say as he goes along.

The album credits list Davis as the arranger/composer for all of the music except "The Man With the Horn" and "Shout." Although it has been suggested in the past that he may be just as much the conductor or lightning rod for innovative ideas as the creator of them, it has never been suggested that he is the willing victim of producers, or that he played any music he didn't personally "hear." Nevertheless it's been a long time since Davis made a record as disjointed as this one.

On one hand we have music—the bulk of the record—that represents the cool funk sound that Davis' current working band—Bill Evans on sax, Mike Stern's guitar, Marcus Miller's bass, Al Foster and Mino Cinelu on drums and percussion—seems to be developing. On the other hand, it seems that the inclusion of "The Man With the Horn" and "Shout" were acts of generosity toward two young artists, Randy Hall and Robert Irving III. This sound—which had me thinking that maybe Davis decided to come back as a Herb Alpert clone and that apparently anticipated Tom Browne's urbane funkiness—may be marketable. But I find it strange to hear Davis play this haunting, reclusive trumpet on a piece that with a few changes in the vocal could be his eulogy.

The Man With the Horn is cool funk à la *On the Corner* but with a more nonchalant, more simplistic attitude. Davis has always been a hipster, a commentator who said volumes with his style and his posture. Over the years his style hasn't changed so much as it has been polished, honed. With Davis the changes have been largely contextual; each rhythm, each chord, each texture, each context, if you extend it, reflects his attitude to place and time. If you don't like or can't relate to the dance music this album reaches for, it is because

you have problems with Davis' attitude and the time and place in which he
has ensconced himself for the moment.

But on the positive side, Davis leaves no doubt that he can still play as
much jazz as he wants to. His flirtation with swing rather than rock on
"Ursula" makes that point. One wonders, however, whether he will overcome
the cult of personality implicit in *The Man With the Horn*. Stay tuned.

—W.A. Brower

"Fat Time"; "Back Seat Betty"; "Shout"; "Aida"; "The Man With the Horn";
"Ursula."

Personnel: Davis, trumpet; Al Foster, drums; Sammy Figueroa, percussion;
Bill Evans, soprano saxophone; Marcus Miller, electric bass; Barry Finnerty,
guitar; Mike Stern, guitar (1); Randy Hall, vocals, guitar, celeste, Minimoog
synthesizer (3, 5); Robert Irving III, acoustic piano, Yamaha CP30 (3, 5);
Felton Crews, electric bass (3, 5); Vincent Wilburn, drums (3, 5).

August 1982
We Want Miles
Columbia 38005
★★★★★

Pangaea
CBS Sony 9697
★★★★★

Directions
Columbia 36472
★★★★

Circle in the Round
Columbia 36278
★★★★

Miles Davis hasn't aged like most men. At 55, he's leading a smart young
gang out on international tours that test their musical techniques, personal
coherence and inspiration by his own high standards. They must be doing
something right: The charisma-struck audience and Davis' adoring record
company cry *We Want Miles,* and the trumpeter has reached the point where
his art and mass popularity have a chance to meet.

It hasn't always been such for Miles, not even recently, though he has
tapped a fountain of youth by attending to the musical tides since 1955,

the earliest track date on *Circle in the Round*. Few improvisers of this late American century have bathed in the waters of fashion so openly, adjusting the temperature to their own boiling point, and attracting so many players to plunge in after them as Miles.

In the beginning, as a prodigy, Miles played it cool beside Bird. By his first re-emergence in the mid-'50s, he had the old strokes down cold. Miles' blues, on side one of *Circle,* are simply bad, and he passes them around infectiously—hear Cannonball Adderley pour his all into a fast "Love for Sale." Trane, Paul Chambers, Bill Evans—they get kind of blue around Miles. The older pros—Hank Mobley, Wynton Kelly, Red Garland, Philly Joe Jones—play their best, as though indebted to Miles for the rejuvenation of their souls. When for a moment they forget what they owe him, he moves on. Gil Evans, by 1960, is suggesting new colors and looser design to Miles through a modern orchestra ("Song of Our Country"); the formerly hard boppers are flaccid on a '61 "'Round Midnight," oblivious as Miles squeezes his favorite Monk feature full of hot red blood. Later, or better yet, never, for clichés—why should Miles burnish his trumpet voice to repeat himself when there are younger cats with whom to get it on?

Miles carries Shorter/Hancock/Carter/Williams through his most fertile and fervid period of experimentation, the late '60s so thoroughly documented in the two Columbia anthologies of previously unreleased material. Miles directs their musical embrace of keyboardists Chick Corea, Keith Jarrett and Joe Zawinul, drummers Jack DeJohnette and Billy Cobham, guitarists Joe Beck, George Benson and John McLaughlin, bassist Dave Holland, and such occasional contributors as Airto Moreira, Bennie Maupin, Steve Grossman, Harvey Brooks and sitarist Khalil Balakrishna.

Like other progressives of that era, Miles wanted a new rhythm—he got it, solid and surging. Miles wanted freedom from changes—he took it, searching the modes that his casual themes opened wide. He wouldn't be constrained by form—he built flexible structures out of ostinatos, vamps and moody tension that might last an entire set, album side or more. He encouraged his sidemen to check out new instrumental gear. He didn't need competition in his horn's range, but let reedmen who would stay out of his way come around.

With these elements in balance, as in '67's *Circle,* the resulting ensemble and Miles' individual statement are wondrous. As naturally as in the Balinese gamelan, *Circle*'s parts are indivisible—from Hancock's ringing celeste and Beck's broad-beamed, rolling guitar figure to Williams' dynamically graceful drums and Shorter's tenor interpretation of the exotic melody. Recorded within the same month's time, "Water on the Pond" and "Fun" (both on *Directions*) are equally delightful, if less ambitious. By November '68, with

Zawinul's tune ("Directions I" and "II") and the multiple pianos of Zawinul, Hancock and Corea replacing the guitar, Miles is charging forth without a glance to the past.

Sometimes, though, he drops back into timeless space, as on *Circle*'s opiated "Sanctuary" and "Guinnevere." Sometimes, too, he tries to pack an abrupt line into too brief a span—despite his band's intelligence, they prove ineffective without room to breathe (as on the two "Sidecars"). A little rhythmic emphasis, though, like the danceable boogaloo "Splash," and they readily get down.

As these points became obvious to Miles, by the early '70s, he concentrated on the dimensions of texture, density and speed. On *Direction*'s "Ascent" he becomes touchingly tender over four restful pianos. He's feisty on "Duran," a slight riff that his sextet doesn't know quite how to engage. But he won't let go of that skeletal format, and on the similar "Willie Nelson," he finds McLaughlin ready for the challenge. There's a steadily held bass pattern, Grossman is allowed to snake along, and DeJohnette is frankly rockish. McLaughlin's guitar expansively catches up Miles, without holding him still. On "Konda" Davis sees how far and freely they can fly, McLaughlin and Jarrett twining harmony and rhythm, while Airto's percussion is mostly for color.

In McLaughlin, Miles discovered a real collaborator, whose imagination and spontaneity could complement his own. Their rapport was apparent by *Jack Johnson* and really comes to fruition on the twofer *Big Fun*. Perhaps Miles was wary of extended partnerships, or McLaughlin so busy with his Mahavishnu band that he wasn't always available. But when the guitarist was gone, Miles tried a project that had no place for him anyway—the ultra-percussive *On the Corner*. And for a working band in mid-decade, Miles chose to use two or more guitarists, and added Mtume to intensify the rhythms.

That's the lineup of *Pangaea,* as well as *Dark Magus* (both on the Japanese CBS-Sony label) as well as Columbia's *Agharta,* from the same '75 tour of the Orient. Pete Cosey and Reggie Lucas provide the advanced psychedelic guitar interplay—Miles, freed by a pickup on his horn, screams from the vortex of their sound. Sonny Fortune offers his own siren-force on alto over the relentless pulse of the disc-long "Zimbabwe." Miles' language, however, is in the manner of the guitarists—whines and wah-wahs, feedback and reverberating cries, smears and stretched staccato runs. Liner notes recommend listening to this aural apocalypse at highest possible volume; even the quieter "Gondwana," with its flute, water-drum and koto moments, is like the calm following the fire storm. Miles haunts its two sides like a specter surveying the scorched earth.

Apparently his dire message was excessive for the kids, though the '70s were heavy metal's heyday. Regrettably, Miles' older fans had long before *Pangaea* thought him mad. So the trumpeter retired while the world caught up. Now it welcomes him back pleading for more. He's kept his concept, refreshing it only by thinning the attack. Miles isn't smashing atoms now; he's twisting nursery taunts like the *We Want Miles'* theme "Jean Pierre" (two versions) into deadly hooks. His new boys take this phase seriously (as they'd better), and their faith adds quite a bit of credibility to Miles' current music. As they believe, so do we.

Tenor saxophonist Bill Evans is increasingly confident on soprano, harmonizing alongside muted Miles, and daring to try his own squeaks, modulations and irregular, off-center gambits; they often pay off. Guitarist Mike Stern can capably comp bop-voiced chords, can even swing Miles lightly. When he steps forward, Stern's tone is as steely as a rocker's, but he tries to rein in his lines, rather than flash all the power at once. Climaxes overtake him, sometimes, though he tries holding back. But that's OK, it happens to all the soloists, Miles, too—suddenly his peak is past—and the rhythm section has learned how to cover and carry on. Al Foster, Miles' one holdover from the mid-'70s, is largely responsible for the solid drum underpinning—he's a puncher. But Marcus Miller's bass is fat in the group mix; "My Man's Gone Now" is recomposed around his lick. Mino Cinelu is less busy than, say, Airto or Mtume, and when you watch him his role seems ritualistic; but his bells and congas sound good in the grooves.

And Miles is Miles; he's unique, and speaks volumes. He's cleared away a lot of clutter, so he doesn't have to cut through the bombastic explosions—now he comes out lean and tough, as on "Fast Track." He lays down some beautiful stuff—you can hear the crowd gasp on "My Man"—and he stirs up "Back Seat Betty" and "Kix." Particularly welcomed is his shifting of gears between solos on a given song—his hardest-rocking splatters seem stronger by contrast with the easy swing feel he's saved from jazz history.

Miles is a father figure to all the brassmen about—Lester Bowie, Wynton Marsalis, Don Cherry as much as Freddie Hubbard and Woody Shaw—whether they like it or not, and even if he himself denies it. But he's impossible to ignore, and his influence is too pervasive to evade. There's subtlety and snarl aplenty left in his lips, and he's got surprises yet in mind. Oh, Miles has aged, his music has changed—but he ain't old, not hardly, nor has he stopped evolving.

—Howard Mandel

August 1983
Miles Davis and John Coltrane
Miles and Coltrane
Columbia 44052
★★★½

Just to try to clear things up in front: This is a collection of tracks previously released on various LPs over the last 30-odd years. It's a discographical mess—like all too much of Miles' vast and often unfindable catalog—but the basics go like this. Four of the first five cuts ("Bye Bye Blackbird" was omitted) appeared on the now-out-of-print *Miles and Monk at Newport;* two of them, "Ah-Leu-Cha" and "Two Bass Hit," were among the four songs Miles had waxed nearly three years earlier at his first-ever Columbia session in October 1955, when he was still technically under contract to Prestige. That earlier session also yielded the versions found here of Jackie McLean's "Little Melonae" (which didn't appear on vinyl until 1973) and "Budo," which has surfaced occasionally on anthologies and compilations since the late '50s. The actual four takes from that 1955 date have never been released in one package, so you have to scratch your head and wonder a bit. Why not take this opportunity, when CBS is going back through the vaults and refurbishing the sound digitally for the Jazz Masterpieces series, to release intact what should have been Miles' first CBS album? Are there more cuts from Newport 1958? Why splice together these two snapshots of the frenetically evolving Miles Davis Sextet/Quintet instead of releasing each separately? And if you have to, why put the earliest tunes at the end of the disc?

Now that I've gotten that out of the way, I've got to add that the music is hard to argue with. Heaven, bebop-style, is surely washed over by something like the sounds these powerhouse units pumped out. That's especially true of the last two tracks, cut when the group was finding its own driving bebopper voice—a quest that would climax a year later, when they recorded Prestige albums like *Cookin'* and *Relaxin'*. The 1958 cuts reveal a band with its own moving-beyond-bebop idiom thoroughly under control. "Ah-Leu-Cha" finds Miles sprinting uncharacteristically but without losing his spatial sense of phrasing to the rush, while Trane's solo on the whimsical "Fran-Dance" bends rhythms and scales in a way that points clearly, if retrospectively, to his near future. "Blackbird" is deft and witty, and "Straight, No Chaser," is a twisted, bluesy delight.

So if the album gets three-and-a-half stars instead of five, it's not because of the music, it's because of the package.

—Gene Santoro

"Ah-Leu-Cha"; "Straight, No Chaser"; "Fran-Dance (Put Your Little Foot Right Out)"; "Two Bass Hit"; "Bye, Bye Blackbird"; "Little Melonae"; "Budo."

Personnel: Davis, trumpet; Coltrane, tenor saxophone; Julian "Cannonball" Adderley, alto saxophone (1–5); Bill Evans, piano (1–5); Red Garland, piano (6, 7); Paul Chambers, bass; Jimmy Cobb, drums (1–5); Philly Joe Jones, drums (6, 7).

August 1983
Miles Davis
On the Corner
Columbia 31906
★★★★★

Static. Electric. Distorted. No Tunes. No real solos. Percussion mixed up front. Most of all, not jazz.

Those are just a few reasons this is one of my favorite Miles albums. What others list as its flaws seem to me its biggest virtues. They result from several different insights that reshaped Miles and collaborator Teo Macero at that time.

For better or worse, those insights were rooted in nothing less revolutionary than a radical restructuring of the way jazz musicians thought of the studio. It was happening in the wake of multitracking—studios at the time were moving up from four- and eight-track technology, and popsters like the Beatles and Jimi Hendrix were redefining what the studio meant. No longer were recordings simply supposed to transcribe or simulate live performances: They were free to become something utterly different, more along the lines Les Paul first imagined decades earlier when he began struggling with several turntables and multiple wax discs to formulate the primitive overdubbing techniques that launched him and then-wife Mary Ford into the million-dollar class.

Not coincidentally, *On the Corner* has become a touchstone for marginal music types from downtown New York to Tokyo.

On the Corner is thousands of tape bits spliced together for your sheer listening discomfitures, a sonic *I Am a Camera* for jazz. Listen, and squirm.

—Gene Santoro

"On the Corner"; "New York Girl"; "Thinkin' One Thing and Doin' Another"; "Vote for Miles"; "Black Satin"; "One and One"; "Helen Butte"; "Mr. Freedom X."

Personnel: Davis, trumpet; Carlos Garnett, soprano and tenor saxes; Herbie Hancock, electric piano; Harold J. Williams, keyboards; David Creamen, guitar; Colin Walcott, sitar; Mike Henderson, bass; Jack DeJohnette, Billy Hart, drums; Mtume, percussion; Badal Roy, tabla.

August 1983
Miles Davis
Star People
Columbia 38657
★★★★½

In *Star People* Miles seeks to assert his mastery of the time-honored blues and demonstrate the maturation of his iconoclastic electric ensemble. Blunt editing and cavalier disregard for the polished studio sound usually preferred by artists of his stature don't dull the excitement or stifle the power of Miles' newly amended band, in which John Scofield shares the growing guitar responsibilities with Mike Stern, electric bassist Tom Barney takes over for Marcus Miller, and Mino Cinelu's percussion, with Al Foster's peculiarly amplified trap drums, transparently veil a mix that simulates an icy, empty hall.

Saxist Bill Evans gets little blowing space, and it's not clear just how Teo Macero and Gil Evans contributed to this project, but no matter. Miles dominates the album. He claims "All Drawing, Color Concepts, and Basic Attitudes," and his keyboard work is increasingly functional, but it's his relentlessly expressive trumpet vocalizing his very own idiom that absorbs all our attention. His organ clusters stir the initial intense activity of "Come Get It," until he darts in, brass at lips, snapping and squeezing ever more pitches into his fast glisses. Stern answers by unreeling an original heavy gauge solo, and from that point on Miles' flinty charges, his mewing vulnerability, his cynical riverboat tricks, his playful sentimentality, his stabbing attack, rhythmic ease and convincing feel for all the material are the prime causes eliciting heightened response most noticeably from the guitarists, but actually from the group as a whole.

One of several strange, brief "interludes"—organ or Oberheim synth, funky plucked bass, stray guitar figures, outlandish clanging—is inserted to cover the segue from "Come Get It" to "It Gets Better," a lazy swinging blues to which Scofield adds fragments that are smart and gut-nudging. Barely audible, Miles murmurs underneath him; they trade half-choruses to a fade. "Speak" is the complex cousin to "Shout" from *Man With the Horn*—a full band surge that glints and throbs, packed densely as a harmolodic rave up.

Side two opens with the title track, an unhurried, 18-minute-plus blues that is also interrupted by a blatant tape cut, setting us adrift just as Miles has effortlessly seduced us, toying with four innocent tones. "U 'n' I" presents more contrast: Miles and Evans alternate playing the jaunty eight-bar melody, to the bass and drums' somewhat ominous bottom. The tune could be from an ancient show score, and no one varies it much, but the light approach is refreshing and unexpected. "Star on Cicely" closes the LP; it's a tightly arranged number, trumpet and soprano led, bass bouncing it and keyboard accents (Miles? While he's blowing, as Leonard Feather's liner notes aver?) kicking it along.

Then you'll want to hear it all again. Despite the roughshod production—at high volume, bass hum and guitar distortion become apparent, and the drums still sound weird to me. *Star People* is an audacious, ambitious advance for Miles in the '80s. As on his last release, the live twofer *We Want Miles*, the trumpeter's technique is commanding, but here's the first album he's made in years that forges a strong band personality. *Star People* couldn't be created by any group other than Miles' young sextet. When his ideas demand all-out elegance, Miles will have these musicians up to that challenge, too.

—Howard Mandel

February 1984
Caught in the Act: Tribute to Miles Davis
Radio City Music Hall, New York

"Miles Ahead: A Tribute to an American Music Legend" was a four-hour-plus program, sponsored by the professional and fraternal Black Music Association, with dozens of jazz artists and a handful of pop stars, pre-taped testimonials, an honorary doctorate in music from Fisk University, speeches and plaques, and good-natured, heartfelt ribbing by Bill Cosby, among others, all celebrating Miles Dewey Davis Jr.—most simply and accurately described by someone as "trumpeter nonpareil."

While the public outpouring of near-peer adulation may have momentarily flustered the founder of the cool blues, and the attempts to link him with some soul-gilded singers seemed somewhat beside the point, the evening's high percentage of inspired improvisation and conceptualization proved that Davis has, indeed, created and affected sounds the whole world's dug during the past four decades. And his stunning septet's short, climactic set this evening announced he's nowhere near done yet.

Pianist Don Shirley began the sold-out show with a sophisticated solo rendition of the "Adagio" from Miles' collaboration with Gil Evans—one figure conspicuously absent from the formal well-wishing, especially as the all-star orchestra conducted by Quincy Jones fleshed out the overture with re-arrangements by Slide Hampton of Evans-arranged Miles hits from *Sketches of Spain, Porgy and Bess,* and *Miles Ahead.* Then came a juicy bop shot from Art Farmer, sultry love notes from singers Shirley Horn and Chris Connor, rousing vocalese from Jon Hendricks & Company and the Whispers' Scott brothers (a credible "Milestones"). Howard Hewett of Shalamar (funkifying Thelonious Monk's "'Round Midnight"), Peabo Bryson, Angela Bofill and George Benson lifted voice, too, but for many Davis devotees, the highlights were mostly to be instrumental.

Here was tap dancer Honi Coles trading accents with traps master Roy Haynes, Herbie Hancock striding firmly through "Footsteps" with Ron Carter and Tony Williams keeping pace, J.J. Johnson interpolating an '80s Davis riff into his unaccompanied trombone version of the '60s "Solar," and flugeler Farmer with trumpeters Jimmy Owens, Lew Soloff, Jon Faddis, Randy Brecker, Wallace Roney and Maynard Ferguson trading choruses and fours before brilliantly harmonizing (Hampton's chart) a blues.

Here were Davis alumni—Jimmy Heath, George Coleman, Jackie McLean, Pepper Adams, Walter Bishop Jr., Buster Williams, Philly Joe Jones, Farmer, Owens, Johnson and Hampton—rolling through "All Blues" and "Freddie Freeloader," with Benson adding a few bars of exceptional guitar. Grover Washington Jr. overcame sound problems with his soprano's pickup in a Coltrane-esque "So What" urged on by pianist Kirk Lightsey and drummer Grady Tate; Cicely (Mrs. M.D.) Tyson, generally credited with revitalizing her husband's spirit, recited a poem; VPs from Columbia Records and Miller beer gave gifts, and Cosby, waving his Groucho cigar, coaxed a croaked "thank you" from the abashed honoree, resplendent in gray velvet suit and cap, very ready to play.

So Miles finally blew his own horn—with John Scofield, Bill Evans, Mino Cinelu, Al Foster, Steinberger-ed bassist Darryl Jones and multikeyboardist Robert Irving III helping the legend live. New directions in music is what Miles makes—either his uncompromising, energized joy or the late hour drove a smattering of listeners more comfortable with his past than his present from the hall—and for once an official acknowledgment of a great musician's career included his work in progress.

—Howard Mandel

April 1984
Miles Davis
Heard 'Round the World
Columbia 38506
★★★★★

Maybe these two discs aren't new to you because you bought the premium-priced Japanese editions long ago. Then you'll know to tell your friends that two of Miles Davis' most exhilarating performances on record have finally been made readily available. Don't forget to mention they feature a band whose fires still warm the jazz world more than 20 years later, along with one tenor saxophonist who burned so brightly maybe his leader didn't dig the heat.

Either trying to impress his Japanese audience or simply feeling grand, Davis opens what has long been known as *Miles in Tokyo* fast and happy—if he were a bell he'd go ding-aling-a-ding-d'dong-riiing. The classy young rhythm trio he'd had for a year immediately ignites—Tony Williams sizzles on his cymbals, Ron Carter so low as to seem subliminal but dependably there, Herbie Hancock chording cautiously as though to tend a small blue flame. Then Sam Rivers' tenor bursts forth, scorching the changes and threatening to flare out of control.

He doesn't. The trio rises to his pitch and, after three quick choruses in which Rivers singes the edge, regroups behind Hancock, who simmers prettily, like Red Garland. They lay back under Miles' second, unhurried turn. As he chooses his dramatic rendition of "My Funny Valentine" as the next tune, there's a sense Davis won't be rushed beyond his own experiments by Rivers or anyone else into the free style becoming a rage in '64. Miles dares much, trying tempo suspensions, extending his personal technique, sense of harmony and intonation throughout both the *Tokyo* and *Miles in Berlin* concerts included in this album. But he insists the second horn, like the rhythm section, underline his directions. While Rivers is masterly, emotional and to the point, there's a hint of friction—at least, sparks are flying. When Shorter takes over (on sides three and four) the quintet still sounds inspired—and, overall, better balanced.

Hancock, Carter and Williams continue to play at top form, adjusting to the immediate needs of the group sound. Hancock displays all the elegance for which he's become justly renowned: two-hands-in-tandem runs, a light, even touch, ease across the keyboard, admirable self-editing. Carter makes the seven-note ostinato of "So What" distinct though he's plucking so fast only three moves seem possible. And Williams makes time elastic.

The Berlin program is similar to the Tokyo one; Miles again flourishes his singular skills, command and direct expressiveness. Shorter gets around his tenor as impressively as Rivers, but his attack is not so startlingly ferocious, his emphasis less exaggerated. At this point in his career, Shorter's still a player of many notes, somewhat under Coltrane's sway; it's a thrill to hear him—all of them—playing their standards. "Autumn Leaves," "Milestones," "So What" and "Walkin'" are the occasions for improvisation, not the polished renditions of a band bored by its repertoire.

Of course, with Shorter, Hancock, Carter and Williams, Miles was about to enter a period of re-evaluation and renewed conceptual quest. This band gave him the cohesion to forge ahead. Rivers came to represent other forces and ideas in jazz; his months with Miles attest that before his Blue Note sessions he could compact his statements and discipline his fervid imagination. Miles was equal to the firebrand, though not necessarily interested in being put to a test by a sideman. In the crucible of performance, he'd long before proved his mettle—and 'round the world, Miles Davis with his great '60s bands blazed trails that still glow in these grooves.

—Howard Mandel

"If I Were a Bell"; "My Funny Valentine"; "So What"; "Walkin'"; "All of You"; "Theme"; "Milestones"; "Autumn Leaves"; "So What"; "Walkin'"; "Theme."

Personnel: Davis, trumpet; Sam Rivers (1–6), Wayne Shorter (7–11), tenor saxophone; Herbie Hancock, piano; Ron Carter, bass; Tony Williams, drums.

August 1984
Miles Davis
Decoy
Columbia 38991
★★★★½

Miles Davis' music often projects mystery and menace, but the mystery of *Decoy* is: What tape tricks will Miles deploy next, and whose ideas are these anyway? The menace, meanwhile, whether provided by Mino Cinelu shaking like a rattler or synthesist Robert Irving III floating dark motifs as a conspirator-in-the-know, is leavened by Davis' own high-spirited playing. From the brilliant brassy blasts, irregular bass stride and rusty-spring sound effects over solid Foster rhythms that Miles darts through on the title track, to the in-sync ensemble energy which closes this fourth LP of experiments with song form, recording techniques, new instrumentations, and new personnel since his '80s emergence from inactivity, Miles is clearly having a fine time.

You can most easily hear his devil-may-care self-assurance and pride in his tough new idiom on this production's second side. John Scofield's nimble figures and octave-divided edge on "What It Is" leads Miles to perform the impossible—duet with himself! "That's Right" is a reprise of *Star People*'s "It Gets Better," the blues everyone raved about, and comprises a twisted soprano solo by Branford Marsalis—his debut with Davis may be hyped as the big news on this LP, but while Marsalis is very good here and on "Decoy," it may take him a moment to define his own voice as distinct from Bill Evans' in relation to the master.

"That's What Happened"—like "What It Is," a treated excerpt from a festival concert in Montreal—is fast, hot fun. It's rumored Gil Evans had more to do with compiling these pieces than his co-production credit for "That's Right" allows, and if so, kudos to him for faithfully selecting Miles' most exalted moments and setting them, each separately, as songs.

Irving, the multikeyboardist and programmer whose work dominates side one, is not nearly as faceless as Gil, though his contributions are equally as fascinating. He dares, in "Decoy," to fade out everything but a triangle about two-thirds through, then bring up Sco's solo. This, after presenting a dense and complicated course for the band to maneuver through, speaks volumes about Irving's creative security. His duet with Miles, the barely a minute long "Robot 415," is somewhat reminiscent of something Bill Laswell's done, but overall Irving sounds like another original artist whose freest thoughts Miles will absorb. Besides "Decoy," Irving is credited with writing and arranging "Code M.D.," my candidate for a single, simply because it's the most conventionally plotted cut here, with the most obvious melody. Not to say the details from the pervasive synth signals and Scofield's quotes of "Jean Pierre," plus Branford's piping and "M.D.'"s coiled attack feints, flurries and slurs building to a piercing point lack subtlety. Not at all—in fact, there's a lot to listen to, and at six minutes it's too long for a single anyway.

Which leaves "Freaky Deaky," the only cut Miles claims with composition and arrangement all on his own. He doesn't play trumpet, only synth, in a style like the late Larry Young's, and Darryl Jones runs the voodoo down while Scofield plucks peculiar patterns. "I definitely want to hear that back," Miles mutters at the end of it, which is how I've felt every time I get through a side of this astonishing album. I can't quite grasp it any one time through, but I know it's there. So it's a *Decoy*—I'll take the good bait.

—Howard Mandel

"Decoy"; "Robot 415"; "Code M.D."; "Freaky Deaky"; "What It Is"; "That's Right"; "That's What Happened."

Personnel: Davis, trumpet, synthesizers; Branford Marsalis (1, 3, 6), Bill Evans (5, 7), soprano saxophone; John Scofield, electric guitar; Robert Irving III, synthesizers, electronic drum programming, synthesizer bass; Darryl Jones, electric bass; Al Foster, drums; Mino Cinelu, percussion.

———————

September 1985
Miles Davis
You're Under Arrest
Columbia 40023
★★

At Last! Miles Davis and the Lighthouse All-Stars
Contemporary 7645
★★★½

Relaxin'
Original Jazz Classics 190
★★★★★

The Complete Amsterdam Concert
Celluloid 6745/46
★★★★

First of all, consider the cover. Miles sits, holding a serious-looking gun (I'm not familiar enough with firearms, fortunately, to be able to tell whether it's real or a toy), dressed in black, peering menacingly through heavy lidded, partially hidden eyes. Given the state of world terrorism and the mindless violence in our streets, such a stance is not hip, not playful, not a joke. Miles Davis, like Bob Dylan's portrait of outlaw John Wesley Hardin, "was never known to make a foolish move," and this is an ominous pose—but Miles is posing inside the album's music as well.

The LP's first cut, "One Phone Call/Street Scenes," opens with the sound of "Sniffing"—then a car squeals up, and we hear the police rousting Miles, seemingly for drugs, driving a fancy car, being seen with a stylish woman. As the voices threaten to handcuff Miles and take him away (in varying languages, the French provided by Sting—a member of The Police, get it?) he responds with high schoolish verbal comebacks. Though he's had his run-ins with the authorities in the past—most probably unprovoked and uncalled for—this rap is silly and childish. The background music is the vamp from *Jack Johnson* (another strong, independently minded black artist who was hassled by the [white] authorities), which segues into "Human Nature."

By now it seems that we have enough clues to determine that *You're Under Arrest* is Miles' concept album. Throughout his career Miles has proven to us that attitude communicates more than instrumental technique—his entire musical esthetic has been based on that philosophy—and here he's out to make a statement. The initial attitude that people have picked up on is Miles' playing pop tunes, but there's nothing new about that. Though the primary trend over the last 20 years has been to primarily compose one's own material, most of jazz history has consisted of improvised interpretations of the current pop hits of the day. And it makes sense—assuring audience recognition while allowing one's own personal variations to register with more clarity and directness. But Miles' playing on Michael Jackson's "Human Nature" and Cyndi Lauper's "Time After Time" fails to do what jazz interpretations of popular material must do—transform the original into something greater than what you began with, not merely to cover (imitate or mimic) the original. Though the arrangements here are well-crafted and polished to a lustrous sheen (probably by keyboardist Robert Irving III, who co-produced the LP with Miles), Miles doesn't really solo on either he basically plays the themes as written (or as sung by Jackson and Lauper, though without the emotional impact of either), with some very minor ornamental doodling (à la his drawings on the inside cover). This is not great ballad playing, of which Miles has always been the paragon.

The closing track on the album is nothing but a kiddie-type melody ("Jean Pierre") over a tape of a day in the park with lots of kids playing, happy baby sounds, followed by a countdown, rocket sounds, explosion—"And Then There Were None." A "serious" statement, which Miles deflates with a joke at the end.

The rest of the album, where the serious music lies, has its moments, but that's all they are—isolated moments. The forthright rhythm track adds some interest to "Something's on Your Mind," but the tight arrangement doesn't seem to inspire Miles; a few chromatic licks at the end of his solo lead to Scofield's sliding chromaticism and fine, albeit brief, outing. Miles on open horn reveals some sturdy and clean upper-register chops, then fluffs a few. "Ms. Morrisine" has a catchy polyrhythmic hook and a nice textural feel, but Miles is simply playing riffs—he sails up, calms down, but there's no continuity, no edge, no shocks. Guest John McLaughlin adds a heavy metal ring to his solo, and his presence on "Katia" (why the 30-second "Prelude" on side one?) gives the music some real potential, but in place of the free-flowing, open-air environment that galvanized *Bitches Brew* and the subsequent '70s electric albums, these cuts sound truncated, insubstantial, unsettling. Just as "Katia" introduces a healthy ensemble interaction (motifs woven between trumpet, guitar and keyboard) and begins to build up a head of steam, the tension is allowed to dissipate, without a true sense of direction. John Scofield's title tune has an actual head—and an intricate one at that—instead of merely a riff to build on, which Miles doesn't play. But in his solo, he plays around. Bob Berg is heard from briefly, and Scofield is finally heard at length—and he sustains interest.

For the most part, though, *You're Under Arrest* is a disappointment, even beside Miles' recent work, lacking the ebullience and bluesy energized spirit of *Star People* and *Decoy*'s soaring melodies and acute invention. The album as a whole takes no risks, and adds nothing to our knowledge or experience of Miles Davis' considerable art. Beyond the questionable extra-musical messages, the music is merely pedestrian, if occasionally, well . . . pleasant. But when we hear music from Miles Davis, we don't want pleasant—we want to be challenged. Miles has created his own standards over the years, and he simply doesn't equal those standards here.

Nor does he reach his highest standards on the newly released 1953 live recording of *At Last!*—but at least he tries. To put this recording into a chronological sequence, at the time of this Sunday afternoon Lighthouse jam Miles had left Charlie Parker's group, cut the soon-to-be-famous *Birth of the Cool* nonet sides, but not yet formed his classic quintet. Max Roach, the drummer on this day, was to put together the Roach/Clifford Brown Quintet within the next two months. Chet Baker (who plays here, wistfully, only on the title tune but doesn't appear with Miles) was on the rise, and casual jamming was the order of the day. The accompanying cast was the Lighthouse All-Stars, a rotating aggregation of mostly ex-Kentonites. Bud Shank particularly shines, with a bluesy fervor that stands out among the procession of soloists on Shorty Rogers' "Infinity Promenade." Roach keeps up a healthy percussive chatter throughout, goosing the laidback soloists when necessary. And Miles, on a borrowed horn without mute, plays with aplomb, alternating cascading arpeggios with sly sidestepping asides. "'Round Midnight" is his best—subtracting notes from the melody in the sparsely lyrical fashion he was soon to turn into gospel, then injecting brash quicksilver runs. Throughout the LP everyone's playing is sloppy but playful, unfocused but spontaneous. It's a jam, after all, and it tries to be nothing more than what it is.

What *Relaxin'* is, is a masterpiece—one of the landmark recordings of modern jazz. Here, too, Miles plays some of the popular tunes of the day, but adds a unique vision to them, revitalizing them in a substantial, meaningful way. The difference lies not in acoustic vs. electric instruments, but in the sensitivity and the concept with which they're used. There is an assurance in

Miles' playing—he sounds incisive, confident, sometimes audacious, always emotionally arresting. The perfect pacing and flow of solos—from cocky Miles to aggressive John Coltrane to comfortable Red Garland—provides a satisfying balance of tension-and-release. This is music that didn't need to strive to be timely—it is timeless.

The *Complete Amsterdam Concert* was recorded in late '57, while Miles was on a solo tour of Europe, just four days after he cut (with basically the same personnel) the soundtrack for the French film *Ascenseur Pour L'Echafaud*. This was one of Miles' peak playing periods, and he sounds bluesy, ballsy and soulful throughout; he's responsible for whatever surprises and shining moments the music contains. The repertory is standard Miles of the period, and the backing band gives solid support if less than outstanding solos. Barney Wilen—an occasionally wily if conservative tenorman in something of a Hank Mobley mold—shows up best here. Kenny Clarke's variegated pulse is on the money throughout. The sound is serviceable, whatever the source, but some liner notes explaining the background of the concert and the origin of the tapes would have been helpful. Further, the song listings on both album cover and label are botched; "Night in Tunisia" (not mentioned anywhere), not "Four," closes side two. "Four" opens side three, which holds three cuts, not two as listed. And with four sides in the 11–15 minute range, all the music could have been put on two sides instead of four, saving everyone a bit of money. Still, the set is a strong sample of where Miles was in 1957—a scintillating and straightforward place to be. No jive.

—Art Lange

You're Under Arrest: "One Phone Call/Street Scenes"; "Human Nature"; "MD1/Something's on Your Mind/MD2"; "Ms. Morrisine"; "Katia Prelude"; "Katia"; "Time After Time"; "You're Under Arrest"; "Medley (Jean Pierre, You're Under Arrest, Then There Were None)."

Personnel: Davis, trumpet, OBXA synthesizer (5, 6), voice (1); Robert Irving III, DX-7, Korg Poly-6, OBXA synthesizers, organ, celeste, clavinet; Bob Berg, soprano (1), tenor saxophone (8, 9); John Scofield (1–3, 7, 9), John McLaughlin (4–6), guitar; Darryl Jones, bass; Al Foster (1, 7–9), Vince Wilburn Jr. (2–6), drums, Simmons drums; Steve Thornton, percussion, voice (1); Sting, Marek Olko, voice (1); James Prindiville, handcuffs (1).

At Last! Miles Davis and the Lighthouse All-Stars: "Infinity Promenade"; "'Round Midnight"; "A Night in Tunisia"; "Drum Conversation"; "At Last."

Personnel: Davis (1–3), Rolf Ericson (1, 3), Chet Baker (5), trumpet; Bud Shank (1–3), alto, baritone saxophone; Bob Cooper (1–3), tenor saxophone; Lorraine Geller (1–3), Russ Freeman (5), piano; Howard Rumsey (1–3, 5), bass; Max Roach, drums.

Relaxin': "If I Were a Bell"; "You're My Everything"; "I Could Write a Book"; "Oleo"; "It Could Happen to You"; "Woody 'n' You."

Personnel: Davis, trumpet; John Coltrane; tenor saxophone; Red Garland, piano; Paul Chambers, bass; Philly Joe Jones, drums.

The Complete Amsterdam Concert: "Woody 'n' You"; "Bag's Groove"; "What's New"; "But Not for Me"; "A Night in Tunisia"; "Four"; "Walkin'"; "Well You Needn't"; "'Round Midnight"; "Lady Bird."

Personnel: Davis, trumpet; Barney Wilen, tenor saxophone; René Urtreger, piano; Pierre Michelot, bass; Kenny Clarke, drums.

October 1985
Miles Davis
Live in Stockholm 1960
Dragon 90/91
★★★★★

It's too bad that this two-record set from Sweden arrived too late to be included in last month's survey of recent Miles Davis releases and reissues, because in many ways it would have helped to both widen that review's perspective and define its focus.

As Jan Lohmann's liner notes suggest, this was a transitional period for Miles. His repertoire contained both modal explorations from the previous year's *Kind of Blue* ("So What," "All Blues") and songs built on conventional chord changes ("On Green Dolphin Street," "Fran-Dance")—though the playing of Miles and John Coltrane is anything but conventional. Miles' approach in the coming few years was to lead increasingly "out"—stretching structural constraints and relying on his keen sense of nuance and intuition to spontaneously determine the direction of his solos—but there are episodes on these discs that reveal his brilliant timing and labyrinth-escaping logic as clearly as anything he ever recorded.

Coltrane, too, is remarkable here, though his solution to escape from the labyrinth was more forceful and direct than Miles' twisting and turning. His solos are a curious blend of expressive strength and exhaustive self-examination, as he painstakingly, obsessively scrutinizes small intervals and arpeggios, prodding and poking at them, then watching almost impassively at times when they erupt into sheets of sound or elsewhere thin out into overtones or harmonics.

Much of the time Coltrane seems surprisingly reserved; his outing on "Green Dolphin Street" initially hovers around a few low notes, working and worrying them over and over again before breaking free to run notes beyond the confines of the rhythm. There's a similar muscularity within constricted material on "Walkin'," though when Wynton Kelly lays out Coltrane turns the blues into a riot of gritty hollers tumbling around each other, and on the second version of "So What," where he takes a "Willow Weep for Me" motif and turns it upside-down and inside-out in a rigorous display of emotion.

Miles, meanwhile, exhibits remarkable confidence and control. On the first "So What" he calmly squeezes out an audacious sequence of half-valved notes right on target, and everywhere his tonal effects and colors are exquisite. His ironic statement of "Green Dolphin Street"'s melody punctures the romantic rubato of Kelly's introduction, and he typically extends that irony into the quirky curves and angles of his phrases, as his lines splinter and are reconstructed with wit and wile. But whether coolly architectonic or artfully abstract, Miles' music is saturated with what is perhaps that most human of emotions—melancholy—which is what endears him to us above all.

The rhythm section, as expected, is supportive, but little more. Kelly was an uncanny accompanist—his thinking along with the soloists in the second "So What" is telepathic—but his concise, gem-like solo ideas sound lightweight and strain for effects at these drawn-out lengths. Paul Chambers is his usual propulsive self, and Jimmy Cobb, though not the variegated pulsemaker Philly Joe Jones is, drops bombs with alacrity to enliven the long solos.

Coltrane left the band within weeks of this concert to put together his own full-time quartet and follow the dictates of his private muse. Miles, never one to look back, took off in a different direction, and, like it or not, continues to do so to this day.

—Art Lange

"So What"; "On Green Dolphin Street;" "All Blues/The Theme"; "Coltrane Interview"; "So What"; "Fran-Dance"; "Walkin'/The Theme."

Personnel: Davis, trumpet; John Coltrane, tenor saxophone; Wynton Kelly, piano; Paul Chambers, bass; Jimmy Cobb, drums.

July 1986
Caught in the Act: B.B. King/Miles Davis
Beacon Theatre, New York

On the surface, it may have seemed an odd pairing: the hip, trendsetting jazz renegade and the conservative gentleman of the blues. Though the two are only a year apart in age (B.B. being the elder), they seem generations apart in the way they present themselves before the public. B.B. takes the traditional route—band uniforms, three-piece suits, ties, shined shoes. He observes all the amenities, thanking the audience after each tune, humbling himself before public scrutiny. Miles, on the other hand, still ignores those show business customs, preferring to stalk the stage like the Grinch Who Stole Christmas in threads that appear jointly inspired by Sun Ra and Norma Kamali.

But despite his outer appearance, his outrageous behavior and nasty disposition, Miles is ultimately tied to the blues, which is, of course, B.B.'s meat. Many of Miles' vamps these days are blues-based and strictly 4/4. His music has perhaps more in common with B.B.'s now than it ever did.

B.B.'s band opened the bill with its usual fare—jump tunes like "Caledonia" and "Rock Me Baby," melancholy moaners like "Darlin' You Know I Love You" and "The Thrill Is Gone." It was a typical set, but the great gentleman of the blues was really on his game this night. Perhaps being on the same bill with Miles and playing before a more discerning audience lit the fuse. But whatever did it, B.B. sang and played Lucille with more fire and fervor than I've seen him display since 1970. And the crowd picked up on it, applauding his falsetto leaps, vocal nuances, and passionate string bends. It was a great performance, totally redeeming the man from the dreadfully slick, overproduced albums he's released in recent years.

Before departing the stage, B.B. thanked the crowd for its encouragement and support, adding, "It's really an honor to be on the same show with the maestro, because this guy has meant so much to the music and has done so much for it . . ." At that point, some over-zealous fan in the balcony screamed out, "So have you!" And the packed house at the Beacon Theatre heartily concurred, breaking into a thunderous two-minute standing ovation that brought tears to B.B.'s eyes. It was a great tribute to a classy man.

This edition of the Miles Davis show is more constrained, controlled and rock-funk oriented than previous lineups since the heralded 1981 "comeback." Guitarist Robben Ford (replacing Mike Stern who returned to briefly replace John Scofield) has sizzling chops; he can burn on a rock vamp, and he's certainly an appealing presence on stage, but he seldom wanders out of the blues scale. Ford's playing has more in common with the electrified blues of Stevie Ray Vaughan than the more oblique bop lines that Scofield and Stern favored. He's a rocker and a blues screamer, which fits in well with Miles' concept these days.

Speaking of comparisons, Vince Wilburn is hardly in the same league with Al Foster, whose versatility and subtlety previously underscored the churning rhythms. Wilburn is strictly a 4/4 groover, as is the current funk bassist in the band. Suffice it to say, much of the new material was funk-oriented and strictly on-the-one; closer in spirit and structure to the Funkadelics than to Miles' more ambitious fusion experiments of the past. These vamps were basically blowing vehicles for Miles, reedman Bob Berg, and occasionally Ford, the tunes were filled with the same cool horn pads by synthesist Robert Irving and marked by those memorable melodic hooks that worked so well for Miles on tunes like "U 'n' I" from *Star People* and "Back Seat Betty" from *Man With the Horn*.

The group came charging out of the gate with a blazing rendition of "Street Scenes" that made the studio version from *You're Under Arrest* seem tame by comparison. That jam highlighted Berg's considerable tenor chops, and neatly segued into "That's What Happened" from *Decoy*—a killer opening. The crowd was excited.

Miles laid into a slow, muted-trumpet blues, followed by more vamps for Berg to blow on. His reading of the Michael Jackson hit "Human Nature" was far more interesting than the studio version on *Arrest,* but an uninspired reading of Cyndi Lauper's "Time After Time" only points out the need to drop this schlock from his set.

—Bill Milkowski

January 1987
Miles Davis
Tutu
Warner Bros. 25490
★★★★

Just as Gil Evans was hailed for his work with Miles on *Sketches of Spain,* so should Marcus Miller be acclaimed for his work with Miles on this album. In fact, the two projects are very similar.

Now, before all you curmudgeons out there begin crying "heresy," consider this: Both projects were basically conceived by other minds and presented to Miles as a foundation on which to add his own individual voice. Both projects were intended to cross over into a more commercial market. Neither project was jazz, per se.

And not only does Marcus lay the groundwork, he plays nearly all the instruments himself as well. Basically, *Tutu* is the finest Marcus Miller to date.

Side one is even a good Miles album, full of the dark, sinister, mysterious qualities that have graced his music all through the years. The brooding title cut may even satisfy old-school Miles fans, as he acquits himself beautifully on muted trumpet on a sparse, spacious arrangement. They may also accept "Portia," a somber, haunting work in the tradition of *Sketches of Spain*. But then in kicks the bombastic funk of "Splatch," with its many sampled sounds, thumb-heavy bass line, and catchy hooks. And forget about side two. Much too poppy for anyone still stuck in a *Milestones* time warp.

I'm not so hot on side two myself, but I admire Marcus' production values. The cat is subtle. Hear how he weaves Count Basie's voice, uttering the classic "one mo' time," from "April in Paris," into the bright fabric of "Perfect Way." Not to mention all the near-subliminal pieces happening in that pop puzzle. And dig all the weird electronic dub sounds in "Don't Lose Your Mind," or his clever use of clarinet to double the bass line on that tune. He makes sure there's plenty happening, both in the pocket and in the fabric, before he summons the maestro to add his voice to the proceedings.

Bass players will like this album. Young fans (those who consider *Bitches Brew* his early period) will dig it. Prince fans may even groove to "Full Nelson." Fellow producers will drool over this album. And big-name pop stars should take note: With *Tutu*, Marcus Miller may have established himself as "the new Nile Rodgers" of production.

As for Miles, who knows what might be next for the man who keeps moving? Since reemerging onto the scene of 1981 with *The Man With the Horn*, his projects have been getting increasingly commercial. And yet all the while he's still playing Miles. Skeptics may dismiss *Tutu* as hip Muzak. But if they would forget about the labels, ease up on the jazz fascism and listen to his horn, they'd hear that the man is still blowing. And more power to him.

—Bill Milkowski

"Tutu"; "Tomaas"; "Portia"; "Splatch"; "Backyard Ritual"; "Perfect Way"; "Don't Lose Your Mind;" "Full Nelson."

Personnel: Davis, trumpet; Marcus Miller, bass, guitar, soprano saxophone, clarinet, synthesizers; Paulinho Da Costa (1, 3–5), Steve Reid (4), percussion; George Duke (5), Bernard Wright (7), Omar Hakim, drums (2); Jason Miles, Adam Holzman, synthesizer programming.

April 1989
Miles Davis
The Columbia Years 1955–1985
Columbia 45000
★★★★½ / ★★

"At record sessions, there still is no question who is in charge and who has the final cut—the final editing." Nat Hentoff's notes about Miles Davis for this five-LP/four-CD box give us the picture of a man "who is in charge." Unfortunately, neither he nor longtime producer Teo Macero had anything to do with this project. A sad irony, because the lingering impression after all this music gets played is one in which Davis is strangely absent.

As with Davis' (sort of) *Greatest Hits* (Columbia 9808), there is no center of gravity here, no sense that an artistic creation has emerged. Rather, a hodge-podge of seemingly random selections in an attempt to chronicle what Miles Davis recorded for one record company over a 30-year span.

OK, every fan of his has their favorites. And so, it would be impossible for Columbia to put together the definitive collection—the assumption being that it's not feasible to release everything, i.e., *The Complete M.D. on Columbia.*

Given such a restriction, what we end up receiving is some of his music broken up into five sections: "Blues," "Standards," "Originals," "Moods" and "Electric." (On the records, it corresponds evenly; I'm not sure how it's done on the four CDs.) The divisions seem interesting until you give a listen. Aside from the apparent arbitrary selections, there is little or no coherence stylistically—*Kind of Blue*'s ('59) "All Blues" followed by *E.S.P.*'s ('65) "Eighty-one" and *Miles Ahead*'s ('57) "Blues for Pablo," for example. What emerges is the consistency of the music in and of itself, particularly Davis' trumpet/flugelhorn from track to track; but the overall effect is sort of like being on a roller coaster—great if your goal is one of amusement, lousy if it has more to do with serious enjoyment of vital art.

There are welcome surprises: the out of print "Love for Sale," "Fran-Dance," "Honky Tonk" and previously unreleased takes of "Pinocchio," "Flamenco Sketches," "Someday My Prince Will Come" and "I Thought About You." All of these versions provide delightful and interesting perspectives to the originals and the time in which they were recorded.

Who is the market for this unique sampler? Jon Pareles of *The New York Times* sees it as an attempt "to finesse the difference between a best-of set, an introductory sampler and a collector's item." Whoever it may appeal to, one thing seems certain: The music matters, but making a buck matters more. What else could account for the manhandling of certain selections to fit the prescribed format? "It's About Time" and "Sivad" are excised from their original settings, thus allowing more time for other songs, but hardly giving these two numbers their rightful place in the listener's understanding of original artistic conceptions. What do the small letters next to the song titles on each disc mean? Typographical errors exist throughout—people are wrongly identified in photos as are the personnel on a number of songs.

And mention should be made of Columbia's generally poor record of digital remixing. Of all the artists to be botched in the transfer from analog to digital, this company's work on Miles Davis leaves little room for rejoicing. Listen (if you must), for instance, to the muddy sound of "Miles Runs the Voodoo Down" as compared with the original. An aside: How is it that Davis' concerts at Carnegie Hall in '61 and Antibes in '63 were so poorly recorded to begin with? The enclosed versions of "So What" and "I Thought About You" speak for each concert, respectively. Finally, besides gearing the music toward a more mellow Miles, I can't help wondering where all that great electric Miles from the '70s went, particularly the material CBS-Sony in Japan released. This period represents, in my opinion, some of the most experimental and intriguing sides to Davis. As Pareles states, this package "offered the perfect opportunity."

It may be that, short of a Miles Davis trunk, any attempt to distill this man's music on Columbia into such a container as this is a thankless and impossible feat. For some, including those relatively unfamiliar with Davis' music, this set may prove educational and enjoyable. After all, except for *Jazz Track*'s three selections, only one cut per LP represented exists here, thus offering lots of variety (and no competition with records currently available). You can't miss with this man's music.

On the other hand, if a solution exists, an ongoing reissue campaign, similar to the one Mosaic has done with its Commodore series, might just be the only one suitable to honoring one of America's artistic treasures. In the meantime, this boxed set—four-and-a-half stars for Davis, two for Columbia—is not definitive. Not by a long shot.

—John Ephland

Tunes taken from more than half of the nearly 50 extant and out-of-print Columbia catalog LPs along with four alternate takes and/or previously unreleased versions.

Personnel: Davis, trumpet, electric trumpet, flugelhorn, keyboards (on "Star on Cicely"); along with, among others, Gil Evans, John Coltrane, Philly Joe Jones, Herbie Hancock, John McLaughlin, Tony Williams, Bill Evans and Kenny Clarke.

September 1989
Miles Davis
Sorcerer
Columbia 9532
★★★★½

All of them recorded for other labels at the time, particularly Blue Note. But when they were with Miles, it was not only different, it was eerie. They played some of the same stuff, their own stuff, elsewhere, like Herbie Hancock's "The Sorcerer." But Miles' mystique and unorthodox and uncanny abilities to lead and arrange their music lifted it beyond "mere" jazz.

Sorcerer, among the crop that this quintet produced in the mid-to-late '60s, isn't necessarily any better than the others. Rather, it reflects yet another chapter in the book of this band carefully yet passionately seeking fusion, or some kind of transcendence of post-hard-bop sensibilities. It was this restlessness combined with genius that gave us the definitive statements on trad acoustic jazz's final hours. This was new music, then. Everything since has been either a copy or an interesting—and sometimes invigorating—variation.

Ballads, uptempo romps—it all coheres here, despite Bob Dorough's hep throwaway at the end. This music isn't nice, tight or swinging. This music is magical, wonderful and scary, style taking a back seat to the chemistry of personal expressions. To quote another LP, there's *E.S.P.* here. It's jazz, but it's something else as well.

—John Ephland

"Prince of Darkness"; "Pee Wee"; "Masqualero"; "The Sorcerer"; "Limbo"; "Vonetta"; "Nothing Like You."

Personnel: Davis, trumpet; Wayne Shorter, tenor saxophone; Herbie Hancock, piano; Ron Carter, bass; Tony Williams, drums. Track 7: Davis, trumpet; Bob Dorough, vocal; others unidentified.

September 1989
Miles Davis
Bitches Brew
Columbia 40577
★★★★★

It was audacious then, and it remains so. *Bitches Brew* has not aged in 20 years because Miles' view of the music was so visionary, and his ambition and adventurousness were matched only by his nerve. But the music remains misunderstood, misinterpreted, misjudged—whether for reasons of ignorance, antogonism or racism—and its origins and subsequent importance have never been fully documented or critically explored.

Critical consensus has it that *Bitches Brew* paved the way for the entire fusion phenomenon of the '70s, but if that's true it was an indirect influence at best. Check the personnel listing and you'll find that nearly all of the participants went on to carve out their own slice of the commercial pie-in-the-sky fusion that was to become; but this was due, if anything, to the experience of working with Miles, and not the music per se. The truth is, this music was too unique, too unusual to be imitated, and didn't influence anyone—except for Miles himself, the originator, who built upon its dizzying maelstrom of sounds and rhythms for another six years, searching out combinations ever more extravagant, until he had left his puzzled audience (old-line fans and critics alike) far in his wake. No, it was the artistic license—the willingness to experiment, the freedom to break with tradition, the exhilaration of discovering a new audience—which Miles offered like the alchemist's stone. It was his followers who turned rock into gold.

In a Silent Way's polite, pastel charms gave no advance clue to the glorious, spicy gumbo of *Bitches Brew*. Bordering on chaos, the communal improvisation was a miracle of intuitive organization and tape editing. Probably no one outside of Miles and Teo Macero knows exactly how the music was constructed—a tape splice here, a spontaneous arrangement there.

With various instruments bubbling up briefly, then submerging into the electronic/percussive flux, timbres and textures are constantly shifting; there are a few real "lead" statements or solos (outside of Miles' masterful commentary) and no recognizable accompaniment. Four drummers, three electric keyboardists and two bassists contribute to the lush detail and rhythmic density, but, remarkably, never overwhelm the often delicate, often devious atmosphere. Electricity allowed the medium-sized ensemble to rival the volume and voicings of Gil Evans' orchestra, with polyphony as rich and intricate as African choirs.

Today, on CD, we could wish for a better mix, cleaner sound, more presence. But the music is still magical—sinister, seductive, dramatic, invigorating, creative: an oasis of possibility, an homage to the other.

—Art Lange

"Pharaoh's Dance"; "Bitches Brew"; "Spanish Key"; "John McLaughlin"; "Miles Runs the Voodoo Down"; "Sanctuary."

Personnel: Davis, trumpet; Bennie Maupin, bass clarinet; Wayne Shorter, soprano saxophone; John McLaughlin, electric guitar; Chick Corea, Larry

Young, Joe Zawinul, electric piano; Dave Holland, bass; Harvey Brooks, Fender bass; Lenny White, Jack DeJohnette, Don Alias, drums; Jim Riley, percussion.

September 1989
Miles Davis
Kind of Blue
Columbia 1355
★★★★★

At the time this album was recorded in March and April 1959, Coltrane and Chambers had been in the Davis group for three-and-a-half years, Adderley for one year, Bill Evans and Jimmy Cobb for about 10 months, while Kelly was just beginning to settle in for his two-year stay, which culminated in the famous *In Person at the Blackhawk* albums of April 1961. This was a most fruitful period for Miles: His playing was the best it ever had been; he had his choice of the most provocative and inventive musicians around; he had just completed recording *Porgy and Bess* with Gil Evans and was about to embark on the similarly conceived *Sketches of Spain;* but, what is even more important, he was at the cutting edge of the then revolutionary modal approach to jazz composition and improvisation.

What a joy it is to listen to these seminal recordings once again, especially with the heightened realism of digital sound and the CD format. But it is a joy somewhat tinged with sadness for lovers of mainstream jazz, for within a few years everything was to change irrevocably. Cannonball was to completely abandon the mind-stretching creativity of this period for a formularized patness geared primarily toward commercial success, Trane was to immerse himself more and more into areas of musical experimentation that were ultimately to prove wearisome to many of his former supporters, and Miles was soon to become the guru and leading light of jazz–rock fusion, the virtual embodiment of everything antithetical to traditional swing-based jazz. But on *Kind of Blue,* as well as many others of his recordings from this period, you can hear what it was all about before the ever-widening generational gap split asunder the world of modern jazz.

—Jack Sohmer

"So What"; "Freddie Freeloader"; "Blue in Green"; "Flamenco Sketches"; "All Blues."

Personnel: Davis, trumpet; Julian Adderley, alto; John Coltrane, tenor; Bill Evans (all tracks except "Freeloader"), Wynton Kelly (2), piano; Paul Chambers, bass; Jimmy Cobb, drums.

———

February 1990
Miles Davis
Ascenseur Pour L'Echafaud (Lift to the Scaffold)
Fontana 836-305
★★★★★

Aura
Columbia 45332
★★½

Miles hits Paris, 1957. Reminds me of the bridge of "Love for Sale": "Love that's fresh and still unspoiled/Love that's only slightly soiled." Miles here is like Jeanne Moreau's screen persona: petulant, alluring, tainted, unattainable. This soundtrack to *Ascenseur* was a happy accident: no plans, uninhibited, fresh, chancy. Perfect: the French formula for cinematic success. I never did get to see the movie, but the music—released in part on Columbia as *Jazz Track* around 1960 and long out of print—burns with the dark thrills of the perfect crime gone awry. Leave it to the French to come up with film blanche!

And here's Miles, in the white heat of it with his Harmon mute poised like a stiletto. He has expatriate brushmaster Kenny Clarke and three hip, dangerous Frenchmen as accomplices: snub-nosed Michelot, sidewinder Wilen, professor Urtreger. Things move circuitously, with perspicacious cool, but occasionally all hell (Sartre's chill variety) breaks loose. OK, so they could have edited the tape; but Columbia's 26-minute version was a little too tidy. And for all its flaws and stretchers, cuts and repeats, this is a period classic, like a '58 Impala. It's smoky, sexy. Great black-and-white backdrop for intimate tête-à-têtes.

Aura captures for a moment flashes of that evanescent yet abiding musical nature that is Miles Davis. However maddening and elusive the man, his music is right there—tactile, electrifying, broody, driven—as it nearly always has been. Miles, still going like 60 at 63, doesn't have to play a lot; when he lays it, it stays laid. But his aura is fuzzy on this big date. He doesn't sound completely in it: arch and echoey on the contempo-vamped "Orange"; quizzical and fretful on the final half of "Violet."

Danish musician Palle Mikkelborg arranged a date for Dexter Gordon (Steeplechase, 1976) that played off Dex's warmth and came out purring positive. Here Mikkelborg's Nordic cool and Miles' own interior chill cancel each other out; the date's on ice. The charts hang in mid-air, irresolute and static. The color-coding doesn't wash: I hear gray, beige and lavender. Miles feints and prances, but never gets a toe-hold. Spots for the composer's ex-bandmates Clausen and NHOP only distract, though McLaughlin lends his spark, a voice untamed. If Gil Evans had lived a little longer, Miles and he might have made that reunion session (they debuted together for Columbia with *Porgy and Bess* in 1959); the rest of us have to live with that.

—Fred Bouchard

Ascenseur Pour L'Echafaud (Lift to the Scaffold): "Nuit sur les Champs-Élysées" (4 takes); "Assassinat" (3); "Motel"; "Final" (3); "Ascenseur"; "Le Petit Bal" (2); "Sequence Voiture" (2); "Generique"; "L'Assassinat de Carala"; "Sur L'Autoroute"; "Julien Dans L'Ascenseur"; "Florence sur les Champs-Élysées"; "Diner au Motel"; "Evasion de Julien"; "Visite du Vigile"; "Au Bar du Petit Bac"; "Chez le Photographe du Motel."

Personnel: Davis, trumpet; Barney Wilen, tenor saxophone; René Urtreger, piano; Pierre Michelot, bass; Kenny Clarke, drums.

Aura: "Intro"; "White"; "Yellow"; "Orange"; "Red"; "Green"; "Blue"; "Electric Red"; "Indigo"; "Violet."

Personnel: Davis, trumpet; 30-piece augmented big band directed by Palle Mikkelborg (trumpet, composer, producer). Soloists: John McLaughlin, guitar (2, 4, 10); Niels-Henning Ørsted Pedersen, bass (6, 9); Bo Steif, fretless bass (6); Thomas Clausen, piano (9).

May 1990
Miles Davis
Big Fun
Columbia 21398
★★★½

I never could figure out Miles' approach to reaching black music listeners during the late '60s and early '70s, when this music was recorded for Columbia. Cries of selling out, of attempts to reach a mass audience with more "contemporary" sounds, always baffled me because, aside from its "pseudo-trance music" qualities, most of *Big Fun*—a CD reissue from '74—comes across as experimental, not calculated. About the only thing reeking of commercialism here is yet another in a series of silly cartoon covers by somebody named Corky McCoy.

OK, maybe most of us could have played bass on a lot of what's here, but simpler in one sense doesn't a best-seller always make. If memory serves, "hits" tend to come in bite-sized, easy-to-swallow doses, with a regular (rock) beat, pervasive electric guitar, vocals—you know, something you can dance to. If Miles was looking for the Top 10, he missed it four-out-of-four on this one by an average of 20 minutes per. Certainly not your typical pop, rock or soul, the man who trumpets had already stopped calling his music "jazz."

As with *In a Silent Way, Bitches Brew* and *On the Corner, Big Fun* takes risks with relatively large (shall we say, bulky?) groups of musicians. Yes, some of it is tedious, repetitive to a fault, lilting one moment, limp the next. "Great Expectations/Mulher Laranja" (the secondary title's a new one on me) rambles on and on, complete with a bass line suggesting the early stages to Henry Mancini's "Peter Gunn"; Michael Henderson's bystander bass lines on "Ife" seem to trip over the equally simple drumming of Al Foster; and "Lonely Fire" runs the risk of losing its flame time and again, thanks to only slight embellishments on a pared-down melody. In a sense, what we've got here is music that wanders with no apparent beginnings, middles or ends.

So what's the big deal on *Big Fun?* Well, in addition to Miles' (sometimes reckless) risk taking, there is indeed a sense of adventure, of taking chances with so much talent, and with such skeletal designs. *Big Fun* reinforces the notion that Miles' primary contributions to music have come via orchestrating, organizing, enabling. How this music was put together proves to be as interesting as any solo or ensemble work. There's intrigue, as Chick and Herbie navigate their ways through "Great Expectations"'s various sonic layers and moods (the second half is Joe Zawinul's "Orange Lady"); mystery, as Wayne Shorter and Miles explore the haunted remains of their music together on "Lonely Fire"; even Miles' funky wah-wah on "Ife" lends itself well to the genre.

Speaking of wah-wahs, John McLaughlin's electric guitar is a signal presence, especially on "Go Ahead John," Miles' most obvious allusion to the Godfather of Soul, James Brown. Conjuring up images of Brown's "I Can't Stand Myself" and "I Got the Feelin'," from '67 and '68, respectively, "Go Ahead John" shuffles, swirls, gets down and runs rampant, with some very creative editing, courtesy of producer Teo Macero. McLaughlin's all-too-brief, blues-drenched solo is the highlight of this collection. As a whole, *Big Fun* makes for some curious and oftentimes rewarding . . . fun.

Incidentally, the digital sound quality is consistently high throughout. Ron Carter's acoustic bass, for example, rings true on "Great Expectations."

—John Ephland

"Great Expectations"; "Ife"; "Go Ahead John"; "Lonely Fire."

Personnel: Davis, trumpet; Herbie Hancock (1), Chick Corea (1, 4), electric piano; Joe Zawinul, electric piano, Farfisa (4); Lonnie Liston Smith, piano (2); Harold I. Williams, piano, sitar (2); John McLaughlin, guitar (1, 3); Ron Carter (1), Michael Henderson (2), Dave Holland (3, 4), bass; Harvey Brooks, Fender bass (1, 4); Steve Grossman (1, 3), Carlos Garnett (2), Wayne Shorter (4), soprano sax; Sonny Fortune, soprano sax, flute (2); Bennie Maupin, bass clarinet (1, 2, 4), flute (2); Billy Cobham (1, 4), Al Foster (2), Billy Hart (2), Jack DeJohnette (3, 4), drums; Airto Moreira (1, 4), Mtume (2), percussion; Khalil Balakrishna (1, 4), Bihari Sharma (1), electric sitar, tambura; Badal Roy, tabla (2).

December 1990
Chase the Miles Down

Reissues on CD of Miles Davis' classic recordings reveal fresh sonorities in the music of a man for whom nuance is the cake, not just the frosting. Perhaps owners of expensive analog equipment already enjoy the sounds provided by the digital format, but for most of us, CDs restore the tweak of Miles' highs, the ache of his lows and the depth of his mid-range. These CDs freshen colors of his most complex orchestrations, and recharge material familiar for years.

Birth of the Cool (Capitol 7 9286 2; 35:57) ★★★★, recorded in 1949 and '50, has long been acclaimed for its nonet arrangements, virtuosic solos and solid but understated swing. The charts by Gil Evans, John Lewis, Gerry Mulligan and John Carisi are among the best in the American repertoire, remaining cliché-free to this day. Twelve tunes—my favorites: Jeru's "Rocker" and George Wallington's "Godchild"—are beautifully played; this project was a labor of love. The original monophonic taping was good, so the blend of tuba, French horn, Mulligan's bari and J.J. Johnson's 'bone swirling beneath soloists' concise and cogent remarks is now audibly richer. Miles, chops up, is in glorious transit from playing with Bird; drumming by Max Roach and Kenny Clarke is more airy, crisp and prounounced than on LP; the bass takes on a virtually physical presence, and the piano comping (by Al Haig or John Lewis) is clearer. The CD reshuffles song order for no apparent reason, and substitutes a perspective by Pete Welding for notes by Simon Korteweg; Mulligan's comments remain. A treasure.

Volumes 1 and 2 of *Miles Davis* (Blue Note 7 81501 2; 58:27) ★★★★★/(81502 2; 39:40) ★★★★½ respectively present the trumpeter's first

('52), third ('54) and second ('53) sessions for the label in "complete recorded order." With a previously unissued alternate take, five great, definitive tracks with Horace Silver, Percy Heath and Art Blakey and nine with pianist Gil Coggins, Oscar Pettiford, Kenny Clarke, plus J.J. and Jackie McLean (these two sat out "Yesterdays" and "How Deep Is the Ocean"), *Volume 1* is the choice. But hear Jimmy Heath replace McLean, and the group's comparable approach to repertoire on *Volume 2*. These discs contain standards of jazz interaction and improvisation, as well as Miles' newly mature, technically accomplished voice: dry and pointed, tough and vulnerable, dramatic and lyrical. Rudy Van Gelder's engineering shines.

Beyond Davis' Prestige era and first albums for CBS to his March '61 music, there's the Teo Macero-produced studio date with Hank Mobley, Wynton Kelly, Paul Chambers, Jimmy Cobb, overdubbed John Coltrane and the uncredited Philly Joe Jones, *Someday My Prince Will Come* (Columbia 40947; 42:03) ★★★★/(Mobile Fidelity 828; 42:19) ★★★★. The consumer can choose sound quality or documentation. Ira Gitler's notes on the Columbia CD are informative; Mobile Fidelity's licensed release sounds somewhat less harsh in the treble range, but is without notes and is mistimed. Still, either's better than worn vinyl.

As its title suggests, *Someday* is among Miles' most romantic, bluesy and intentionally seductive programs. He (and everyone else) selects notes with care, attends to dynamics, allows space for the music to sigh. A star is reserved for ambition. Except for Trane, and Davis' muted musings, the session's a commercial realization rather than an artistic exploration. It's a lovely groove, though, so nice to come home to.

Must have been cool to go out to hear *Miles Davis in Person, Friday Night at the Blackhawk, San Francisco, Volume 1* (Columbia 44257; 53:29) ★★★★½. CD representation of the club sound is predictably superior, especially when one focuses on the rhythm team of Kelly, Chambers and Cobb. Restored in the rereleases are Mobley's tenor solo on "All of You" (on *Volume 1*), a complete sax solo on "Well, You Needn't," edited sax solo on "If I Were a Bell" and complete bass solo on "Fran-Dance" (on *Volume 2*). Ralph Gleason's notes are retained—my LPs don't have any personnel listings. In sleekness this quintet anticipates Miles' next, younger, more harmonically open and rhythmically elastic combo. But these sets are exemplary: Dig tightly wound Miles, mellow Mobley and after-church Kelly on "Bye, Bye Blackbird," "So What," "Oleo," etc.

As *DownBeat* managing editor John Ephland writes in the liner notes, *Nefertiti* (Columbia 46113; 39:12) ★★★★ was "the fourth and final all-acoustic studio installment" from Miles' mid- to late-'60s Hancock/Carter/Williams/ Shorter quintet, as well as "a collection of music composed by others bearing the distinctive sound" of the master. Recorded in the summer of '67, it seems perched on a cusp. The compositions by Wayne, Herbie Hancock and Tony Williams are distinctive, their performances perfectly pitched and Miles' treatments are innovative; the cyclical melodies, subdued in mood and sonically bejeweled, are well-served by CD sound. What's wrong? Miles hasn't yet mastered his trumpet's role within the new style. Loose ensemble passages are effective, but solos revert to regular rhythms. Slated to lift off, the band remains ready on the launch pad.

Not so on *Filles de Kilimanjaro* (Columbia 46116; 56:32) ★★★★★, recorded by the same combo and replacements Chick Corea and Dave Holland one year later. The Fender Rhodes electric piano's sound dates this music as if it were a harpsichord; ostinatos and cycle structures are established, then abandoned; Williams' drums are backbone, punctuation and commentary all in one. Davis' sense of placement is marvelous, but he is far from alone. The CD's digital remixes of "Frelon Brun" and "Mademoiselle Mabry" seem to add something—maybe new richness of tone increases their sumptuous languor.

Pangaea (Columbia 46115; 41:50/46:52) ★★★★★ is the long-delayed first U.S. release of Miles and electrified, percussion-heavy company live in Osaka, Japan, in 1975, his last outing before a five-year retreat from public life. Free of any inhibitions, Miles' trumpet-with-pickup screams, whines and wah-wahs at the vortex of a firestorm provided by guitarists Pete Cosey and Reggie Lucas, bassist Michael Henderson and conguero Mtume. Sonny Fortune is an alto siren over Al Foster's relentless pulse of the disc-long "Zimbabwe"; "Gondwana," with flute, water-drum and koto moments, offers the contrast of dead calm. Miles haunts the now uninterrupted 40-plus-minute takes like a specter surveying scorched earth. Except for details on the bottom, this one production sounds as good loud on imported CBS/Sony pressings as on CD. Kevin Whitehead's exemplary liner notes make up for diminished graphics.

—Howard Mandel

July 1991
Miles Davis
Agharta
Columbia 46799
★★★★★

Agharta, from an afternoon performance on Feb. 1, 1975, at Osaka's Festival Hall, is a groove-oriented, wah-wah-inflected, distortions-laced invocation that would no doubt scare your mother. This landmark electric album (and its companion set, *Pangaea,* culled from evening performances on the same date) unlocked a door for a whole generation of musicians who became intrigued by the possibilities of getting past the notes and dealing more in catharsis than precision on their instruments. Pete Cosey's wild excursions pointed the way, spawning an entire school of "sick" guitar playing. But *Agharta* was hardly just noise for noise's sake. Cosey's sickness is grounded by rock-solid, syncopated grooves created by Foster, former Motown bassist Henderson and Lucas. Their quintessential pocket playing connected Miles to the funk of Sly Stone, James Brown and the Meters.

Sonny Fortune's urgent, angular sax lines on top of these mesmerizing funk vamps predate Steve Coleman and Greg Osby's M-Base experiments by 10 years. Miles himself is in fine, psychedelic form on this set, emulating Jimi Hendrix with wah-wah blasts of his own on trumpet. And notice how he uses the organ as a baton to abruptly change the vibe from ugly and aggressive on "Prelude (Part II)" to smooth and mellow on "Maiysha." Just as that flute-laden buppie ballad threatens to turn saccharine, Cosey steps in to puncture the sweetness and light with another of his sick onslaughts. The band also reaches deep into a blues bag during a segment from the sprawling "Theme From Jack Johnson" jam, producing some of Miles' most inspired playing of the afternoon.

—Bill Milkowski

"Prelude (Part I)"; "Prelude (Part II)"; "Maiysha"; "Interlude"; "Theme From Jack Johnson."

Personnel: Davis, trumpet, organ; Sonny Fortune, soprano sax, alto sax, flute; Michael Henderson, Fender bass; Pete Cosey, guitar, Synthi, percussion; Al Foster, drums; Reggie Lucas, guitar; Mtume, percussion.

October 1991
Miles Davis
'58 Sessions
Columbia/Legacy 47835
★★★★½

Circle in the Round
Columbia/Legacy 46862
★★★½

Both of these collections are just that—collections. Containing previously released material, *'58 Sessions* and *Circle in the Round* represent, among other things, record company shuffling in an attempt to issue loose ends from the amazing recorded legacy of Miles Davis. And of course, Columbia has the lion's share of material (not to mention the reportedly immense supply of unissued Miles in their vaults).

Including the first three tunes from half of the original *L'Ascenseur Pour L'Echafaud*, *'58 Sessions* is the more integrated set, thanks mainly to the unchanging personnel and because the music represents just one year in the life of the then-Miles Davis Sextet. A studio date in May (the initial four tunes) finds Jimmy Cobb and Bill Evans recording their first music with Miles, having replaced Philly Joe Jones and Red Garland in the wake of another album from '58, the legendary *Milestones*.

Despite Evans' softer touch and the shift to cover more ballads, most of the music from *'58 Sessions* is a delightful, swinging romp, with a mostly muted Miles and plenty of blowing from Trane and Cannonball. Cannonball sits out on "Stella by Starlight," the gentle "My Funny Valentine" is a feature for Evans and Davis only, and "Love for Sale" (first issued in 1975!) is less adorned, more freewheeling than the version Davis cut from a Cannonball date just 10 weeks earlier. Digital restoration appears to have saved what was originally an underrecorded Miles on Sonny Rollins' "Oleo," with the then-relatively overrecorded Cobb now more listenable. The live music comes from a late July date done just weeks after Columbia recorded the band at Newport (heard on *Miles and Coltrane*). Initially released in '73 as *Jazz at the Plaza,* the program mistakenly listed Philly Joe Jones as the drummer and included another cut which could have easily been added here, an eight-minute version of "If I Were a Bell." What gives?

Circle in the Round and *'58 Sessions* share the same version of "Love for Sale." That's about all they share. Only two tunes are from the '50s, the rest serving to chronicle the unwanted "scraps" from recording dates from 1961 through 1970. Originally a '79 twofer, *Circle in the Round* helps fill the gaps between albums and offers interesting musical commentary: 1967's "Circle in the Round," a 26-minute number, is a mesmerizing, sometimes tedious piece with Joe Beck providing trippy, drone-like electric guitar; '68's "Teo's Bag," both "Side Cars" and "Splash" all reflect Miles' growing unease with chord changes and bop rhythms in general, and provide a backdrop to the quintet studio albums of the period. "Sanctuary," also from '68, is a less caustic, more serene take on a tune that would later be recorded with fuller ensemble on *Bitches Brew*. As for the 18-minute version of pop star David Crosby's "Guinnevere," complete with sitar, let's just say it's an interesting historical footnote.

—John Ephland

'58 Sessions: "On Green Dolphin Street"; "Fran-Dance"; "Stella by Starlight"; "Love for Sale"; "Straight, No Chaser"; "My Funny Valentine"; "Oleo."

Personnel: Davis, trumpet; John Coltrane, tenor saxophone; Cannonball Adderley, alto saxophone; Bill Evans, piano; Paul Chambers, bass; Jimmy Cobb, drums.

Circle in the Round: "Two Bass Hit"; "Love for Sale"; "Blues No. 2"; "Circle in the Round"; "Teo's Bag"; "Side Car I"; "Side Car II"; "Splash"; "Sanctuary"; "Guinnevere." (48:44/50:07)

Personnel: Davis, trumpet, chimes and bells (cut 4); with, among others, John Coltrane, Wayne Shorter, saxophones; Bill Evans, Herbie Hancock, Chick Corea, Joe Zawinul, keyboards; George Benson, electric guitar; Paul Chambers, Ron Carter, Dave Holland, bass; Philly Joe Jones, Jimmy Cobb, Tony Williams, drums.

January 1992
Miles Davis/Michel Legrand
Dingo
Warner Bros. 26438-4
★★

This soundtrack from the Australian film *Dingo,* co-starring the late Miles Davis, is notable only for the presence of Miles' signature rasp on a few spoken interludes. The music, which was arranged, orchestrated and conducted by Michel Legrand, is undistinguished at best. Suffice to say, Legrand is no Gil Evans, and this is no *Miles Ahead* let alone *Legrand Jazz* (a '58 series of collaborations that included Miles).

From the snatches of dialog here, Miles plays Billy Cross, an iconic American jazz émigré living in Paris. At a concert in Australia, he meets a kid named John Anderson and tells him, "If you ever get to Paris, look me up." Apparently, the kid grows up to be a hot trumpeter Down Under, known to the locals as Dingo Anderson. He takes Billy up on his word, travels to Paris to seek out his hero and ultimately exchanges fours with him on stage.

Legrand weaves in a couple of Miles motifs here and there, making allusions to "Milestones" on "Concert on the Runway" and to "All Blues" on "Trumpet Cleaning." The rest of the album consists of stiff big band fodder and tired-ass vamping on lame funk arrangements, hardly the kind of thing that you would want to remember Miles for. On half the tunes Chuck Findley is the sole featured trumpeter. He's a competent enough West Coast player and provides some evocative moments on "Kimberley Trumpet in Paris," a haunting bit of solo trumpet set against the Paris street ambiance. But this is supposed to be Miles Davis and Michel Legrand, not Chuck Findley and Michel Legrand. Consumer beware. The added disappointment here is that Miles' chops sound shaky, though his muted trumpet sound remains unmistakably Miles.

About the only thing of interest is the scene that Miles acts out with co-star Colin Friels. Shades of Dexter Gordon in Bernard Tavernier's *'Round Midnight*. But then, the music was much better in that film. (reviewed on cassette)

—Bill Milkowski

"Kimberley Trumpet 1"; "The Arrival"; "Concert on the Runway"; "The Departure"; "Dingo Howl"; "Letter as Hero"; "Trumpet Cleaning"; "The Dream"; "Paris Walking 1"; "Paris Walking 2"; "Kimberley Trumpet in Paris"; "The Music Room"; "Club Entrance"; "The Jam Session"; "Going Home"; "Surprise."

Personnel: Davis, Chuck Findley, featured trumpets; Michel Legrand, Kei Akagi, Alan Oldfield, keyboards; Nolan Smith, Ray Brown, George Graham, Oscar Brashear, trumpets; Mark Rivett, guitar; Alphonse Mouzon, Harvey Mason, Ricky Wellman, drums; John Bigham, percussion; Abraham Laboriel, Foley, Benny Rietveld, bass; Buddy Collette, Jackie Kelso, Marty Krystall, Bill Green, Charles Owens, John Stephans, woodwinds; Vince de Rosa, David Duke, Marnie Johnson, Richard Todd, French horns; Jimmy Cleveland, Dick Nash, George Bohanan, Thurman Green, Lew McGreary, trombones; Kenny Garrett, saxophone.

August 1992
Miles Davis
Doo-Bop
Warner Bros. 9 26938
★★★★½

Those who hail Miles for hitting upon something entirely new on these sessions, his last-known recordings, are missing the most exciting part of it all. Some of these tracks could have easily been on *Tutu, Amandla* or maybe even 1974's *Get Up With It* (with Al Foster's hi-hats splashing on a hip-hop groove).

What excites me most about *Doo-Bop,* the joyous teaming up of Miles and young rapper and instrumentalist Easy Mo Bee, is the way Miles was playing in his last days. "Chocolate Chip" is some of his best—clear, darting phrases, punctuated by generous, dramatic space. He scampers like a kitten on the supergroove "High Speed Chase." His muted trumpet is doubled by steel drum for a minute, there's a sax point/counterpoint line at another spot, and he kicks alone with the drum track for a few frenetic measures. Where he has sounded tentative at times on recent recordings, here he starts and ends his ideas crisply. The mute is in most of the time and his sound doesn't change much, but his phrasing and concept adapt sharply from tune to tune.

"Yo chief, blow," raps Easy Mo Bee in a rich baritone. The sounds on these tracks aren't as sophisticated as what the trumpeter was getting in recent years from Jason Miles and Marcus Miller, but they're fresh and closer to the street. Bee throws out a collage of beats and samples that soothes with almost a Barry White vibe, and startles with undefinable sounds from the 'hood, some cries industrial, some human. Keyboardist Deron Johnson adds tasty, spicy sounds, solos and cluster chords to help it work. Miles and Easy really hit it off musically—I just wish he was still around to jam with folks like Ice T, Whodini, Queen Latifah, Public Enemy and Geto Boys.

Miles' embrace and encouragement of the new has made an impact on musicians of all ages. It's a hell of an exit, Chief.

—Robin Tolleson

"Mystery"; "The Doo-Bop Song"; "Chocolate Chip"; "High Speed Chase"; "Blow"; "Sonya"; "Fantasy"; "Duke Booty"; "Mystery (Reprise)"; "Doo-Bop (edit)."

Personnel: Davis, trumpet; Easy Mo Bee, instrumental programming, voice; Deron Johnson, keyboards (2, 5, 6, 8); J.R., A.B. Money, voice (2).

September 1992
Miles' Decade, Part 1

The decade of the '60s was clearly Miles Davis' most inventive, not to mention controversial. The trend-setting trumpeter started things off playing post-cool bop with holdovers from his acclaimed late-'50s band (John Coltrane among them), later mixing it up with a revolving cast of characters—everyone from Buddy Montgomery and Sonny Stitt to Gary Peacock and Sam Rivers. Collaborations with Gil Evans continued, offering up, among others, the contentious, brief yet lovely bossa nova project *Quiet Nights*. Davis' repertoire (standards mixed with dated originals) changed very little until a new quintet was formed and recording in the studio. To be exact, it was January 1965, and the record was *E.S.P.*, a landmark album of all-new material. Herbie Hancock, Ron Carter and Tony Williams (all having joined Davis in '63) saw the problematic saxophone chair suddenly filled by ex-Jazz Messenger/composer extraordinaire Wayne Shorter—who, by the way, had already recorded for Davis in '62.

But before we get on to *E.S.P.* and the other recent reissues that followed, there's still this business of the standards rep, with an occasional original chestnut thrown in for good measure. Behold *Seven Steps to Heaven* and *The Complete Concert: 1964—My Funny Valentine + "Four" & More*, albums that showcased a transitional Miles Davis. In the case of 1963's *Seven Steps to Heaven* (Columbia/Legacy 48827; 46:21) ★★★½, Davis recorded half of this heavily edited album in Hollywood, half in New York. Featured are pianist/composer Victor Feldman and drummer Frank Butler (Hollywood), tenor saxist George Coleman, and the rhythm section of Hancock, Carter and Williams for the first time (N.Y.). Carter and Coleman were the only holdovers for both sessions. The material is played in a style reminiscent of *Someday My Prince Will Come* ('61): smooth, polished, yet without Coltrane's heat. Feldman's lush chordal voicings (e.g., "I Fall in Love Too Easily") contrast with Hancock's bluesier, funkier swing (Davis and Feldman's "Seven Steps to Heaven"). The West Coast band's tendency to double-time the slower tunes gives their music a slightly generic quality (Butler's distracting, repetitive snare clicks leading the charge). Despite this, the band's extended treatments of old favorites "Basin St. Blues" and "Baby, Won't You Please Come Home" are memorable. The East Coast band is clearly the more integrated. Definitive, albeit tame, studio versions of "Seven Steps" and Feldman's "Joshua" are slower, elongated progeny for what was to follow in live settings.

One of those settings was a benefit concert held in New York's Philharmonic Hall at Lincoln Center the following year, chronicled on *My Funny Valentine + "Four" & More* (Columbia/Legacy 48821; 66:11/54:15) ★★★★½. Originally issued as two individual records, one of mostly ballads, the other, cookers, a half star is deducted due to the package's maintained incorrect song order for both discs (an opportunity missed). In any event, Coleman turns in some inspired playing (according to Davis, his best), particularly on "My Funny Valentine" and Miles' "All Blues" (a late-'50s holdover waltz given an uptempo shot of rhythm & blues). Hancock, Carter and Williams all perform with grace, poise and fire. But it's Davis who plays some of his most impassioned trumpet on record. Leading his team up and down, in and out, through slow tempos and fast, stopping everything when the notes demanded it, the soul of a man sounds revealed through crying treatments of "Valentine," "Stella by Starlight" and "I Thought About You." It was this specific music that taught me the meaning of jazz: swing loved and forgotten amidst a musical organism composed of distinct parts, offering at once both vulnerability and assertiveness, improvisation with a thorough immersion and eventual abandonment of technique, all driven by the tension of a fresh, intoxicating rhythm team in Carter and Williams. Stripped-down versions of "Four," "Seven Steps to Heaven," "Walkin'," "So What" and "Joshua" all attest to a band pushing the music at furious, blinding speeds. Compare "Seven Steps" and "Joshua" with the '63 studio versions listed above for a study in rhythmic and harmonic overhaul. Gone is the need for formal statements, adherence to melodic shape and contour. Williams' drum solos remain free of the pulse as he chooses to extend the drums' range as a musical instrument. The ballads (again, there's a tendency to double-time things) showcase Hancock, Coleman and Davis' individual, lyrical expressions as they dispense with rhythm, restate themes, even go it alone at certain points. The '60s avant-garde impinges in subtle, delightful ways, providing clues to this transitional bands' method of deconstruction. Miles Davis' songbook was once again up for grabs.

Turning more than a few heads, *E.S.P.* (Columbia/Legacy 46863; 48:26) ★★★★ was the first example of this massive facelift. Shorter's arrival provides the occasion for a whole new concept to studio recording. (This band continued, with very few exceptions, to play the usual repertoire when performing live.) Davis and Shorter's uptempo "E.S.P." fittingly begins the set, with Shorter's tenor sounding like the perfect blend of Coleman's sweetness with Sam Rivers' tartness/sourness, Davis proudly turning in one blistering line after another. Outright funk enters the Davis canon with the Davis/Ron Carter tune "Eighty-one." Unfortunately, Hancock is given less solo time next to the front line on most of the uptempo pieces. "Agitation" opens the second half of the *E.S.P.* with another classic unmetered solo by Williams (reminiscent of Elvin Jones' intro to side 2 of "Pursuance" on Coltrane's *A Love Supreme* a month earlier). "Agitation" became one of the few originals from this band to be recorded live—without Tony's intro (the studio take was actually a separate drum solo). *E.S.P.* marks the emergence of this band's unabashed impressionism with originals, the lovely, melancholic "Little One," "Iris" and "Mood" taking the balladic treatment to new heights. Producer Irving Townsend's flat sonic glaze persists in the digital transfer.

We skip to 1966 and the even more startling *Miles Smiles* (Columbia/ Legacy 48849; 42:10) ★★★★½, grinning with four originals and one each from composer/saxophonists Eddie Harris and Jimmy Heath. Davis' exquisite waltz, "Circle," showcases his lyrical, muted-trumpet playing laden with sighs, slurs and the occasional high note. Shorter and Hancock follow suit. The rest of the album, however, is more interested in experiments than with *E.S.P.*'s more aggressive, modal side: Hancock lays out during Davis and Shorter's solos, with a solo-piano style more horn-like in conception, forsaking chords for single notes in the treble clef; with scaled-down arrangements, and generally simpler melodies with few or no harmonic references. (However devised, *Miles Smiles* clearly shows Ornette Coleman's invisible hand.) Shorter's "Orbits" and "Dolores" move the band closer to melodic abstraction, with Heath's "Ginger Bread Boy" getting a new arrangement as the closer. With a simpler, drier, more austere (and relatively pianoless) sound, the unrehearsed, rough *Miles Smiles* holds up so well simply because it was more of a jazz record, spontaneous warts and all: e.g., Hancock gets lost in his solo on Shorter's 6/4 vamp "Footprints"; Davis and Shorter weave and bob on the out chorus to "Dolores" like two punch-drunk boxers who aren't sure how, or when, to stop. Regular producer Teo Macero returns (having produced everything else here except *E.S.P.*), bringing with him that more direct Davis band sound. (Digital transfers on all the titles sound very much like their analog counterparts—a blessing, perhaps.)

As *E.S.P.* and *Miles Smiles* clearly showed, Davis' new studio direction meant traditional song forms (e.g., with theme statement, bridge, chorus) were now a thing of the past. Instead, looser sketches became the band's skeleton written primarily for improvisation and the extra-sensory perception that was becoming more and more a hallmark of this quintet.

—John Ephland

October 1992
Miles' Decade, Part 2

For Miles Davis, the '60s provided the setting for the most amazing stylistic metamorphosis of any jazz musician in history. Fresh from the late-'50s successes of *Porgy and Bess* and *Kind of Blue,* Davis went on to stretch and twist his modal bop and blues roots, recombining them every which way with a startling cast of characters, only to end up in the late summer of '69 with the big band of *Bitches Brew,* an album loaded with electronics, percussion, funk . . . and controversy.

Last month, we took a look at some recent Davis reissues from 1963 through '66, a critical period for Davis that witnessed major changes stylistically and otherwise. This month we continue to trek to the end of the decade with two completely different and influential albums: '68's *Filles de*

Kilimanjaro and *Jack Johnson,* an album recorded in early 1970 that points back to the late '60s even as it looks forward to a changed perspective for the '70s. We end our survey in the middle of the decade with the recent arrival of *Complete Live at the Plugged Nickel,* a seven-CD import set of mostly previously unavailable material from 1965.

Filles de Kilimanjaro (Columbia 46116; 56:32) ★★★★½ is notable, in part, for its personnel changes (it was the classic quintet's last record) and the total absence of swing rhythms as well as acoustic keyboards (contrary to the liner-note references). Recorded on the heels of *Miles in the Sky,* and at two different points (June and September), the later recordings of "Frelon Brun" and "Mademoiselle Mabry" introduced many fans to keyboardist Chick Corea and English bassist Dave Holland, replacements for Herbie Hancock and Ron Carter. (The new liner notes also maintain incorrect keyboard and bassist personnel for "Frelon Brun" and "Petits Machins," and wrongly note the presence of acoustic basses.) The stylistic precursor to the ever-popular *In a Silent Way* of 1969, *Filles* is performed (and edited) like a suite, with a sense of flow unlike anything Davis had recorded up to that point. That flow is enhanced by a music played all in one key (F), with only five "tunes," and with a mood and rhythms that change gradually from start to finish. (The uncredited Gil Evans—co-composer, arranger and all-around consultant with Davis for *Filles*—played a crucial role in the album's development.)

As for the classic quintet tracks, "Petits Machins," "Toute de Suite" and "Filles de Kilimanjaro," noted Miles Davis biographer Jack Chambers observed that the band went beyond their usual minimal structures and search for a common mood, asking listeners to "discover the unity of the pieces instead of just locating it, as viewers must discover the unity in a painting with several simultaneous perspectives." You might say these pieces are a fitting climax to four-plus years of growth from Hancock, Carter, Tony Williams and Wayne Shorter under Miles Davis. As for the presence of Holland and Corea, "Frelon Brun" and "Mademoiselle Mabry" today sound more contemporary and rockish, less jazzy in execution, as a stronger pulse combines with a more pronounced melodic framework (as opposed to the relatively freewheeling, jazzy abandon of the now-old band). In passing, *Filles de Kilimanjaro* is a turning-point album unlike any other for Davis: For the first time, his bebop roots were essentially severed, rockier rhythms, electricity and ostinato-driven bass lines now holding sway.

A Tribute to Jack Johnson (Columbia/Legacy 47036; 52:32) ★★★★½, Davis' music for a documentary film on black 1908 world heavyweight boxing champ Jack Johnson, jumps us into the future, or more precisely, April 1970. The first studio album after *Bitches Brew, Jack Johnson*'s cast is much larger than the one listed. On hand throughout this heavily edited mélange of musical forms were (credited) Herbie Hancock on organ (!) and electric piano, electric guitarist John McLaughlin, drummer Billy Cobham, ex-Stevie Wonder electric bassist Michael Henderson, soprano saxist Steve Grossman, and (uncredited, among others) guitarist Sonny Sharrock, Chick Corea, saxist Bennie Maupin, Dave Holland and drummer Jack DeJohnette.

"Right Off" (with "additional music by Teo Macero") actually exists in four parts, edited for maximum impact; and, like "Yesternow," the second half of *Jack Johnson,* "Right Off" fades in and out of territory at times rhythmic, sensual, dreamlike and downright funky. Propelled by Cobham's muscular shuffle beat, the more aggressive "Right Off" swings and/or rocks through slurpy, *Phantom of the Opera*–Hancock Farfisa organ and Grossman's sax squeals (part 3), John McLaughlin's now-famous electric-guitar rave-up (part 4), and a blistering, front-loaded Davis open trumpet.

"Yesternow" combines elements in a surreal pageant of sound. Against a simple bed of funk (notice the almost mechanical role of the electric bass), Davis and producer Macero weave a tapestry that includes a section of "Shhh/ Peaceful" from *In a Silent Way* (along with its musical cast), an unreleased version of something called "Willie Nelson" (more guests), and an excerpt at the end that has Davis playing his mute in the midst of an orchestra (a creation of Macero's?) while actor Brock Peters narrates the saga of the star of our show. *Jack Johnson,* like the times, was trippy stuff. Would anyone dare to try and make a jazz album like this nowadays?

More likely are cheap imitations of the Japanese import *Complete Live at the Plugged Nickel 1965* (Sony 5766-5772; 66:48/75:38/68:18/51:59/64:23/67:05 /36:31) ★★★★½. Recorded at the end of 1965, after the innovative January recording of *E.S.P.,* and following three cancelled engagements at the now-defunct Chicago club due to serious health problems for Davis, the music here has been doled out in parts Stateside, once on a now-out-of-print twofer, *Live at the Plugged Nickel,* and more recently with a CD's worth of more material, *Cookin' at the Plugged Nickel* (Columbia 40645). It's the classic quintet blowing standards and blues similar to the February '64 concert *My Funny Valentine + Four & More,* with one from the new book, *E.S.P.*'s "Agitation."

Space limits discussion of the music with the kind of detail and attention it deserves. For those devoted fans of this quintet, this compact boxed set (the liner notes are in Japanese) is a must-study in contrast, variation and development of one of jazz's most important bands. Instead of reviewing the package on a disc-by-disc basis, with most of the repertoire repeating itself, examples and highlights will be lifted to hopefully give a taste of what went down during this two-day Christmas engagement.

Not surprisingly, there's a fair amount of consistency throughout. The band sounds real loose (Davis sounds loaded more often than not), playing with a club—as opposed to more formal, concert-hall—approach. Of the main soloists, Hancock gets less time, Shorter is the standout. A blues sensibility pervades whether the music is "Stella by Starlight," "All of You" or "All Blues." The recording quality (stereo) is generally very good, with, for example, Williams' deft cymbal and brushwork a marvel, and the occasional off-mike playing of Davis and Shorter adding to the feel of a "you are there" club date. Most everything ends up with a medium-tempo gait, as if the band were on some kind of cruise-control. Except for the surprise, extremely rare appearance of the sadly edited "Yesterdays," a near-nine-minute "'Round About Midnight," a six-minute "Oleo" and shortened versions of "The Theme," the tunes swing and sway for luxuriating lengths (most run well over 10 minutes).

A bluesy, boozy "Stella by Starlight" (disc 1) starts out in a typically slow, balladic manner, with Davis' familiar yearning trumpet siren leading the way, only to speed up after two-and-a-half minutes, only to slow down two minutes later, only to speed up again. Does this kind of treatment suggest a band impatient or uncomfortable with slow tempos? Hardly. By this time, these guys were starting to read each other like maps, and were using this material like clay, to be reshaped in musical conversation; it's as if the actual tunes didn't matter, it was the creme center, the improvising, that tasted best. "Stella" is typical, as the soloists weave in and out with barely a mention of the theme, with little sense of a beginning, middle or end to the solos. Shorter's dancing solo pokes at the melody through soft staccato bursts, oblique thematic references buried in a whirlwind of velvety notes. As he does frequently with the ballads here, Hancock's lovely "Stella" solo eventually goes impressionistic and a capella.

In general, Davis' horn sound is clipped, flinty, less than typically lyrical. The ballads "My Funny Valentine" and "When I Fall in Love" (both disc 2) are played in a style similar to the upbeat numbers, with scant, passing references to the beautiful melodies as Davis basically slides through the changes with a melancholic tone. His "lack of perfection"—slurring notes with imprecise intonation, playing over bar lines en route to who knows what—is ultimately a musical virtue. At times, his horn sounds oddly triumphant as he's led by the rhythm section one moment, leading the next ("Walkin'," disc 1). "All of You" (disc 3) is played as a slow burn, Davis' mute hanging on every beat, suddenly flying off like a bumble bee, all the while tempered.

One of the features of this boxed set is the way you get to hear Davis and Co. experimenting. Hancock's lead into Sonny Rollins' "Oleo" theme (disc 3) comes at the end of the tune, which leads into "I Fall in Love Too Easily" (given four treatments overall, and second only to "The Theme," with seven, most of which are four-minute-and-under tags). The experimenting is possible mainly because of Carter's solid-state bass, freeing everyone up even as he directs traffic, dropping tempo, double-timing, changing meters, maintaining the pulse while Williams' marvelous cymbal work keeps things cozy. Hancock lays out, doesn't even solo on some tunes ("My Funny Valentine," disc 2; "All of You" and "On Green Dolphin Street," disc 5). On the uptempo "So What" (disc 5), Shorter's sustained solo climax leads the rhythm section into a rare free-time free-for-all, Williams' rough-and-tumble solo capping things off. "No Blues/The Theme" (disc 6) runs more than 19 minutes and is a marvel of group cohesion. At a certain point during Shorter's hypnotic solo, I'd swear there were three different tempos going at once. "All Blues" (disc 7) gets funky at times, recalling Davis and Carter's "Eighty-one" (from *E.S.P.*). Here is an excellent example of Carter leading the band through deliciously alternating 3/4 and 4/4 sections.

Overall, the feel to the *Plugged Nickel* engagement is so relaxed, the playing so elevated yet so swinging, any movements toward atonality and abstraction (and there are many) go hardly noticed. The band was, in a sense, creating a new musical syntax, using familiar material to explore the unfamiliar, getting under not only the music's skin but each others' as well. The fact that Davis typically ran tunes together is no accident: The music was seen as one, the mood created, a group mood with simultaneous perspectives. As with all the available live material from this band, the music was always pointing outward, toward the original studio work that was to continue well beyond *E.S.P.* For most listeners, the *Plugged Nickel* sets are too much of a good thing. For Davis, Shorter, Hancock, Williams and Carter fans, it was, and is, a fascinating work in progress. And the stuff legends are made of.

—John Ephland

March 1993
Swedish Miles

The first "So What" of the two extraordinarily fine concerts documented on the four-CD *Miles Davis With John Coltrane and Sonny Stitt in Stockholm 1960 Complete* (Dragon 228; 70:43/62:41/50:02/75:20) ★★★★★ has a brisk clarity that is nothing less than inspired. Miles really leads. Fleet of thought and execution, elegantly and incisively articulating detailed runs and phrases way up over bar lines, the trumpeter demonstrates his mastery as a fact, not for his personal vanity.

Coltrane follows cautiously, as though watching where he puts his feet, but he's soon racing through double-tongued notes to reach something beyond them. Pianist Wynton Kelly comps and stretches with sparkling ideas—sustained tremolos, contrarily moving lines, fresh modulations, a less-is-more philosophy—that gave Herbie Hancock a place to begin. The Paul Chambers/ Jimmy Cobb rhythm team is implacable, unobtrusive and steady as they come. So what! The set continues, rich with Davis' creativity and reflexes, dramatic flourishes, poise and diffidence; Trane's obsessive searching, which is sometimes brushed with melancholy; and a rhythm section that's all taste.

Despite repertorial familiarity (the surprises, "June Night," "Stardust" and "Makin' Whoopee," are features for Kelly and Stitt), the March performance from Coltrane's final tour with Miles and the October show with Stitt on board contain revelations regarding melodic, harmonic and tonal development that have not yet been turned into clichés. For two, there's Trane's outside-from-deep-inside "On Green Dolphin Street," and his extended choruses of uncharacteristic false-fingered(?) bleating on "All Blues," the sound of sax to come.

Stitt, technically slick and sure on both his horns (compare his alto in duo with Kelly on "Dolphin" with his tenor after Miles' solo), can be overly calculating, predictable (at least in hindsight), even corny in his interpretations. Still, he had true rapport with Miles, oil to the trumpeter's vinegar. In their blend the two can combust suddenly—and Miles is encouraged to be expansive, fully brash in one passage, whispering low in another, warm and dulcet as on "All of Me."

Besides informative liner notes and sharp if mislabeled photos (that's Cobb, not Chambers, hitting a cymbal), this repackaging of two Dragon LPs includes eight previously unreleased pieces from the Stitt date and Carl-Erik Lindgren's smarmy radio interview with Trane, who remains dignified and responsive throughout. Sound quality is state-of-the-art (stereo) for a live remote, more distant than studio recording but delivering Kelly's touch, Chamber's attack and Cobb's accents, as well as the horns with honest depth.

—Howard Mandel

November 1993
Ghost of a Chance

It was an ambitious project; maybe too ambitious. The much-celebrated meeting of Miles Davis with Quincy Jones (and the apparent ghost of Gil Evans), documented on *Miles & Quincy Live at Montreux* (Warner Bros. 9 45221; 56:44) ★★★½, gives the impression of too many musicians in over their heads, Davis included. Having said this, it's a wonder the combined forces of Evans' ghost band (eight in all) with the 17-piece George Gruntz Concert Jazz Band (with an additional supporting cast of 22 more musicians) ended up sounding as good as they did, performing Evans' gorgeous, idiosyncratic and multilayered arrangements on top of and around solos by Davis as well as alto saxophonist Kenny Garrett and trumpeter Wallace Roney.

Recorded during the 25th anniversary of the Montreux Jazz Festival (July 8, 1991), Davis was to die just a little more than two months later. His playing reflects his poor health, his tired-but-steady chops handily augmented and/or rescued by Roney and Garrett. (Adding a saxophone for solos to this music was a novel idea, but sounds out of place.) Davis' frail, primarily muted trumpet suggests a quiet voice amidst the busy bombast, his horn occasionally recalling his youthful vigor (e.g., his firm, gently swinging tone on "Miles Ahead," his slurred, flamenco intonation on the set-closer, "Solea," the exchanges with Roney on "Blues for Pablo").

At times, the chorus of horns surrounding the soloists provides just the right cushion and envelope (the *Miles Ahead* medley); elsewhere, doubling up on horns only adds to the confusion on a number like "Solea," where the tricky 6/4 marching groove has Jones and his troops in occasional disarray, with a tacked-on climax to boot.

The accommodation to electric bass, listed along with the less-pronounced "bass," detracts from this essentially acoustic music. "Here Come de Honey Man" is a prime example of electric-bass overstatement. Like the electric bass, the drums have been mixed too far up into the music, and tend to be either too flashy ("Summertime," "Gone, Gone, Gone," *Birth of the Cool*'s "Boplicity") or painful reminders of what once was (Philly Joe Jones' exquisite 1958 romp on "Gone," performed—and misspelled—here as "Orgone"). The generally medium-to-slow tempos only aggravate this problem.

The last time any of this material was recorded live was at Carnegie Hall in 1961, with a Davis quintet fronting an 18-piece Evans orchestra. Then, the music had been a fascinating work-in-progress. This music played in 1991 is at turns amazing and difficult to hear—amazing in historic importance (Davis was going back in time—something totally uncharacteristic of him—and with such rarefied material, in collaboration with a renowned fellow artist in Quincy Jones); difficult, touching and sad, because of Davis' struggles to essentially hold his own, and with such familiar music. And yet, true to form, the Old Man went down swinging.

It's a serious shocker. In this, it merits attention.

—John Ephland

February 1994
Book Review
The Sound of Miles Davis: The Discography 1945–1991
by Jan Lohmann (JazzMedia)

Although it has no publication date in it, I assume that Jan Lohmann's exhaustive *The Sound of Miles Davis: The Discography 1945–1991* (JazzMedia) was actually published a few years ago, since Lohmann took pains to write to me and explain that this book preceded the Miles discography in Tom Lord's *The Jazz Discography,* making Lohmann's the first. "Tom Lord has actually borrowed 99.9 percent of my listing of commercial recording sessions," writes Lohmann. "And that without any credit at all." If this is true, one can understand Lohmann's anger, since the task of laying out all of Miles' work—which in Lohmann's book includes all the known bootleg tapes (what are the ethics of this?), radio and TV broadcasts, interviews and Davis' parts as an actor—must have been a monumental task. A note of caution: This is a hardcore discographer's discography; there's little more than raw data here, with plenty of ways to cross-reference using the index and charts of album equivalents, but nothing useful for the casual Miles Davis fan.

—John Corbett

March 1994
Video Review
Miles Davis & Quincy Jones Live at Montreux
Warner Bros./Reprise

The same title could have served for *Miles Davis & Quincy Jones Live at Montreux* (Warner Bros./Reprise). The music has been much discussed by now; Miles had returned at last to Gil Evans' enduring, cool, orchestral charts. In truth, it's anticlimactic. Davis sounds all right, but for insurance keeps Wallace Roney at his right hand to hit the bold, clear, high notes, and keeps altoist Kenny Garrett near to spell him as soloist. Rehearsal footage and Quincy Jones' comments honestly reveal Miles' limited role in shaping this project, despite lots of fawning commentary from associates. The concert footage comes off jittery, with lots of fades from one POV to another; a camera may zero in on a player doing nothing significant at the time. It's late to complain about excessive hero worship of Miles, but obsession takes a bizarre turn here. As a reverse tracking shot leads Miles from stage door to stage, in slow motion, you half expect Jack Ruby to emerge from the shadows.

—Kevin Whitehead

April 1994
Miles Davis Tribute Band
A Tribute to Miles Davis
Quest/Reprise 45059
★★★

Finally. After all the hoopla of previous tribute albums, this one had the potential to knock 'em all out of the box. Alas, like the self-conscious kid given free reign in a store full of all kinds of goodies, the Tribute Band stays pretty much in the aisles, looking straightahead, only occasionally glancing left and right to grab for something new.

To be fair, these guys are on the money with this stuff. It's beautiful to hear the medley of "R.J."/"Little One" followed by "Pinocchio," all numbers that've pretty much been ignored since Miles' passing. And the funky "Eighty-one" cooks at a nice, slow tempo. Turning the clock back to '59, the band takes the closer "All Blues" at close to its original rolling tempo, Roney's mute sweetly and serenely guiding this classic Davis waltz. Certain liberties are taken along the way as well, most notably Hancock's wayward comping and Shorter's occasional atonal fits. And Williams, true to form, pushes the band like a seasoned rock drummer. The music is presented in a way that wisely downplays the Roney/Davis connection, instead putting the band out front.

Two views predominate. One, that the band is executing this Davis program in a near-flawless manner, providing interesting if not intriguing variations on a theme of Miles, circa '66 (the music they toured with in '92). The other view is that they're coasting, with arrangements that've been tweaked here and there on material that suggests the proper name for this group should be the Miles Davis Trad Band. Apart from Roney, everyone here (the button-downed Ron Carter included) played a significant part in Davis' bridge music, the stuff that led to the well-known *Bitches Brew*-and-beyond material. (The black-hole year for everybody doing tributes, from Joe Henderson to Keith Jarrett to the Lincoln Center Jazz Ork, seems to be 1968.)

Like its VSOP predecessors with Freddie Hubbard and Wynton Marsalis, the Tribute Band is more about convention, the convention of playing out of today's predominantly post-bop bag. In so doing, the more experimental treats they once savored remain untouched.

—John Ephland

"So What"; "R.J."; "Little One"; "Pinocchio"; "Elegy"; "Eighty-one"; "All Blues."

Personnel: Wallace Roney, trumpet; Wayne Shorter, tenor and soprano saxophones; Herbie Hancock, piano; Ron Carter, bass; Tony Williams, drums.

September 1995
Miles Davis
Miles Davis: The Complete Plugged Nickel Sessions
Mosaic 10-158
★★★★★

Scrimp and save where necessary—you're going to want this. During Christmas week 1965, Miles Davis played a Chicago nightclub, with two nights recorded for release.

Breathtaking, bountiful and a bit overwhelming, *Complete Plugged Nickel* emerges from the vaults as a joint venture between the Mosaic and Columbia labels, available in a 10-LP, Q-disc format from Mosaic, and on eight CDs from Columbia.

Where does one start? The leader is in prime form, sounding particularly wired and caustic on "No Blues" (disc 5) and "Agitation" (7). Even on ballads like "When I Fall in Love" (3), his playing is searching and on edge. On tenor sax, Wayne Shorter is amazing throughout—urgent, fluent and unpredictable, bringing new vigor and a taste of Coltrane-ish fire to staples like "Walkin'" (6) and "So What" (8). Tony Williams also seems ready to push the envelope as far as his employer will allow. By contrast, Herbie Hancock's luminous piano is heard to best advantage on medium-tempo tunes and ballads. With bassist Ron Carter, the rhythm section sounds flawless.

How's the sound quality? Significantly cleaner than the original LPs, and more detailed than the original single CD, with Williams sounding crisper and more prominent. Davis and Shorter are tightly miked, with Hancock and Carter at times sounding a little distant. Teo Macero's production captures the "audio verité" of the club, including phones, cash registers and the patrons, both the inattentive and the overly enthusiastic.

The box contains two full nights (seven sets) of music previously available as two LPs, a single CD and a rare seven-CD Japanese import, and is now enhanced by the restoration of additional solos, adding more than 20 minutes. Despite some repetition (e.g., three versions of "Stella by Starlight"), the set is full of variety and the quality of performance is uniformly excellent.

This is not a "historical interest" release that will merely look good on the shelf. Start anywhere, and 30 years quickly melt away. *Complete Plugged Nickel* is still fresh and vital, the definitive document of Miles and company at their collective peak, in concert.

—Jon Andrews

August 1996
Miles Davis
Live Around the World
Warner Bros. 9 46032
★★★★

Miles Davis shrewdly predicted that, after his death, the tape vaults would fly open. His posthumous catalog should soon rival that of Jimi Hendrix or Elvis Presley. *Live Around the World* documents Davis' last working groups from 1988 through 1991, usually a "double quartet" lineup with saxophonist Kenny Garrett and bass guitarist Foley the featured sidemen. Keyboardist/coproducer Adam Holzman complied this "virtual concert," following a representative set list and selected performances from several shows. Performances of tunes from *Tutu, You're Under Arrest* and *Amandla* are often superior to the studio versions, and the band out-performs my memories of frustrating, uneven concerts.

Davis' once-controversial covers of pop tunes benefit from expansions and improvements. "Human Nature" quickly metamorphoses into an eerie, quiet space, where Garrett joins Miles with a long, brooding alto solo that gathers intensity and consumes the tune. Davis stretches out on a long version of "Time After Time," where he's more an interpreter than an improviser, decorating the melody, investing it with new substance.

Three unrecorded Davis originals are included. "New Blues" seems not so new, a variant on the slow blues he favored, but "Wrinkle" suggests a possible result of the abandoned collaboration with Prince, with its whirlwind funk driven by frenzied synthesizers from Davis and Kei Akagi. As a coda, the CD closes with a foreboding "Hannibal" from Miles' final show. His tone is piercing and jagged, and he's followed by another strong, equally scary solo from Garrett. *Live Around the World* also offers an opportunity to hear intriguing players Akagi, bassist Benny Rietveld and percussionist Marilyn Mazur, whose work with Davis is not otherwise documented.

—Jon Andrews

"In a Silent Way"; "Intruder"; "New Blues"; "Human Nature"; "Mr. Pastorius"; "Amandla"; "Wrinkle"; "Tutu"; "Full Nelson"; "Time After Time"; "Hannibal."

Personnel: Davis, trumpet, keyboards; Kenny Garrett, alto saxophone, flute (1–5, 7–11); Rick Margitza, tenor saxophone (6); Foley, Benny Rietveld (1–6, 9–10), Richard Patterson (7–8, 11), bass guitar; Adam Holzman (1–4, 6, 9–10), Joey DeFrancesco (1–2, 4), Robert Irving III (3, 9), John Beasley (5), Deron Johnson (11), keyboards; Ricky Wellman, drums; Marilyn Mazur (1–4, 9), Munyungo Jackson (5–6, 10), Erin Davis (7, 8), percussion.

November 1996
Dreaming of the Re-Master

There are controversies, there are opinions, there certainly is room for measured disagreement and criticism. But let us begin by acknowledging the sheer and unequivocal sublimity of this music. If these sounds do not make you melt, consult your physician. You may need open-heart surgery.

Miles Davis & Gil Evans: The Complete Columbia Studio Recordings (Columbia 67397; 73:49/76:45/74:38/77:27/64:45/77:12) ★★★★ Miles Davis and Gil Evans met in 1948, when Evans was living in a basement apartment that had become a "bebop salon" on Manhattan's West 55th Street. Evans was arranging for Claude Thornhill; Davis was playing on 52nd Street with Charlie Parker. This remarkable friendship, which lasted the rest of their lives, resulted first in the landmark 1949–'50 *Birth of the Cool* recordings for Capitol Records.

The present six-disc compilation picks up the story in 1957, after Miles had signed with Columbia, and takes it to 1968. It is the second installment in a comprehensive program beginning with last year's *Live at the Plugged Nickel,* covering the entire Miles opus on Columbia. (These studio dates with Miles and Gil will be followed by their live recordings.) The heart here is the trio of famous collaborations: the airy and pungent *Miles Ahead* (1957), the more jazzy and brassy *Porgy and Bess* (1958) and the somber Spanish fusion classic *Sketches of Spain* (1960). This package also marks the first authentic stereo remix of *Miles Ahead.* (A fudged one came out in 1987; more on that later.) Also included is the less successful Brazilian project *Quiet Nights* (1964).

Each of the four familiar albums is presented in original program order, on its own disc, followed by bonus tracks. *Sketches of Spain* now includes "Song of Our Country," discovered later. *Quiet Nights* has lost the irrelevant quintet track, "Summer Night," but gained three sextet titles (two with singer Bob Dorough), and two previously unreleased short works, "Time of the Barracudas" (1963) and "Falling Water" (1968). Discs five and six are composed entirely of alternate and rehearsal takes. It's a gold-card package, with 198 pages of discography, annotations, rare photographs, original liner notes and jacket art, some fine essays and a shiny brass binding. (Mosaic has simultaneously released their 11-LP, 180-gram "Q" version.) More than half of this material has never been issued.

Total immersion in such exhilarating musical waters highlights why Davis and Evans got along so well. In music, as in life, they despised the obvious, preferring the inferences of hip. They also shared a passion for pastel colors and pretty melodies, and a fondness for chords that created narrative through their "weight" (like Ravel's). Spiritually, they were fellow suitors of duende, that elusive state of suspended soulfulness, expounded by the poet Federico García Lorca. Their collaboration brought out the best in them, as individuals, as well, particularly Miles' ability to speak. People always talk about his unique tone, but Miles also understood "tone" the way a poet or an actor does: When Evans' music demanded insouciant, uncontained joy on "I Don't Wanna Be Kissed (By Anyone but You)," Miles spoke in a joyful tone. When it called for piercing sadness on "Summertime," he spoke mournfully.

Evans, for his part, had his finest moments with Miles. Fascinated by the possibilities for jazz of European orchestral timbres—oboe, French horn, bassoon, flute, harp—he created dazzling, airy, sometimes ambivalent chords that fluctuated through a seemingly limitless range of colors. Unlike many "Third Stream" composers, Evans used the rhythm section (sans piano) for the actual colors it had to offer, not as add-ons for "jazz feeling." A master of contrary motion—dig the way the flutes and brass wheel in and out of each other as well as Miles on "The Pan Piper"—he advanced the concerto form beyond the figure-and-ground syndrome. Miles' horn and the 19-piece orchestra trade places, echo, weave, bob, even finish each other's sentences.

What a treat it is, on *Miles Ahead,* to listen again to the grainy, exploding brass of "I Don't Wanna Be Kissed," the loping eighth- and two 16th-note phrase of "Miles Ahead," the jaunty Brubeck melody "The Duke" and the elated, cool contours of "Springsville." *Porgy and Bess* brings back pleasant memories, too: Bill Barber's agile tuba solo on "The Buzzard Song," the wild spread in the winds and flugelhorn lead on "There's a Boat That's Leaving Soon for New York" and the oddly independent figure behind Miles' solo on "Summertime."

Sketches of Spain is a model of how successful fusion digs to the intersections of genres to create something new, as Evans found the hook between Gypsy blues (flamenco) and American blues. Listen to the "jazz" cymbal and "Spanish" snare and castanet on "Solea." That's duende. In spite of a valiant effort to restore its reputation, the heavily edited *Quiet Nights* remains an unsatisfying (and incomplete) project, a fact acknowledged by both Miles and Gil at the time it came out. It's not enough to suggest that the failure was due to commercial pressure to capitalize on the bossa nova fad, since *Porgy,* too, was timed to the film release of the musical. Evans seems to have been genuinely defeated by the bossa nova pulse.

"The Time of the Barracudas," 12 minutes-plus of underscoring for a play by Peter Barnes, is far more interesting. Rehearsal shouts and occasionally poor execution suggest that it wasn't ready for release; but nevertheless there are intimations of the tense, open territory Miles would explore in the 1970s, with Tony Williams' clackety snare and Herbie Hancock's polyphonic piano forging a new mood. A telegraphed, long-short-long-short passage would later become "General Assembly"; some devilishly slow, brass-lip trills "Hotel Me Blues." "Falling Water," a four-minute tone poem recorded in 1968, showcases Miles' emerging interest in electric instruments and a more dominant bass line. Listening to it is rather like staring into a fishbowl, watching a lot of beautifully suspended, random activity.

Comparisons of alternate takes is instructive. The master of "Gone" reveals the judicious choice of a slower, more elegant tempo. Miles' solo on take two of "Summertime," on the other hand, is better than the master, but the feeling overall was probably rejected as too "happy." The four solo overdubs of "Springsville" play like a little storybook, showing how a great jazz improviser gradually finds a balance between shapeliness and surprise.

When Teo Macero remastered a stereo version of *Miles Ahead,* it was believed that the mono masters were lost. In fact, the stereo version was created from unissued and incomplete alternate takes. A fraud, most of the takes differed from the original, resulting in the disc being taken off the market and replaced by the currently available and slightly altered original mono version. Phil Schaap was hired to piece together this puzzle. The result is a lovingly reconstructed stereo remix, "as was," of the original takes, plus a breathless concordance of every scrap that did or did not go into the final mix. Was it worth it? Soundwise, absolutely. Schaap's 20-bit stereo remix has decidedly more depth, three-dimensional brilliance and (naturally) stereo separation than the original. The reverb on the mono version has been removed, so the sound is more natural, as well.

Ironically, Schaap's zealous fidelity occasionally has highlighted differences in room ambience between masters and overdubs. (On "I Don't Wanna Be Kissed" you can hear a definite shift.) And while the overall clarity of sound on all the discs has been vastly improved by Schaap and Bob Belden, who produced the 1962–'68 material for this release (the ride cymbal, particularly, has been happily brought up) one has to question the merit, even for aficionados, of issuing all this rejected material, especially takes where Miles or an orchestra member simply turned in a honker. As for the much-vaunted "rehearsal tapes," they are meager; surely it is something of an exaggeration to label 33 seconds of shuffling manuscript paper and mumbling, ending with, "Let's play it at [letter] E," a "studio discussion." And isn't it unfair to ask consumers to pay more than $100 to get a stereo remix of *Miles Ahead*?

As we begin to codify the jazz past into a "classical" heritage, we will no doubt see more of such hagiographic completism. If any artist deserves such careful curation of his canon, it is Miles Davis. However, even zealots may find this brass-bound package contains more than they actually want. Maybe.

Flashback: Jimmy Cleveland, who played trombone on *Miles Ahead* and *Porgy and Bess,* had some insights into Gil Evans' voicings: "What Gil was doing seemed funny to all of us. He would have A's and B-flats close together, and maybe the next horn would have an F-sharp. To get that kind of sound and overtones he was looking for, one part would be marked forte, another mezzo forte and another mezzo piano. The volume that each player would bring to each particular chord is what made it sound right. The atmosphere was quite different from other sessions. We knew that the music was going to be new and fresh and as far, modernwise, as you could go with it. The scene was just so upbeat. I found those sessions to be sheer pleasure."

Lee Konitz, a *Birth of the Cool* veteran who played on the *Miles Ahead* sessions, recalls, "When I heard this music for the first time, I got major goose pimples. It was very, very moving. After a while, though, with the repetition, with that soothing sound, I started to get a little bit sleepy. I recall at one point I could feel myself drifting off. Then a very beautiful, very sexy woman walked into the date and I woke up."

"The session [for 'Falling Water'] started early in the morning," recalls tuba player Howard Johnson. "In the coffee shop across the street I ran into [French horn player] Ray Alonge and Larry Lucie, the studio guitar player. They didn't know who the date was for and they were complaining that it was too early to start recording. Lucie, who had been called to play mandolin, asked, 'What kind of dreck is this going to be? Who's the artist, anyway?' I said, 'Miles Davis and Gil Evans.' You can be sure those two sleepy musicians woke up in a hurry!"

Johnson scoffs at producer Teo Macero's claim that Macero stepped in as conductor to rescue the "Falling Water" session: "I don't remember him conducting anything. Gil's stuff always came together with difficulty. You came in and you didn't know where anything fit. I've listened to all of those takes, and it's amazing how different each one sounds."

—Paul de Barros

July 1997
Miles Beguiles

Rarely has a corpus of music so polarized a star's fans as Miles Davis' electric period did. The trumpeter's incorporation of rock and (much more dominantly) funk in the late '60s was taken by some followers and critics as heresy, as Miles turned his back (literally) on the acoustic jazz audience. His excommunication from certain circles was as severe as the one Bob Dylan earned by strapping on his electric guitar at Newport in 1965. And nearly 30 years later, the grumblers continue to grumble about what critic Stanley Crouch, in a moment of uncharacteristic politeness, called "the mire Miles Davis pushed jazz into."

But like it or not, the records that documented Davis' initial forays into experimental jazz-funk spawned countless new electric bands, inspiring a wave of vanguard fusioneers picking at their Fender Rhodes and peeling off electric bass ostinati like they'd found a new page in the big book of ideas. Take *Going to the Rainbow* by German clarinetist Rolf Kühn, for instance, a 1970 record that featured two keyboardists (one of them Chick Corea) coordinated à la Miles. The concept didn't take long to spread, and soon the pervasive influence of Davis' sprawling collage-form funk-jazz was international in scope.

Until now, the full expanse of the electric music from the early- to mid-'70s was difficult to grasp for American listeners, since many of the key post-*Bitches Brew* releases were never issued on domestic CD. Columbia Legacy is helping to right this by releasing five two-disc sets of live, amplified Miles, remastered (but not remixed) and replete with the freak-out, ghettoid graffiti-art graphics that originally graced their covers and with new liner notes, primarily by former band members. (Note: Though they're being marketed as "first time ever on CD," this music has been available on import CDs.)

Black Beauty (Columbia/Legacy 65138; 45:07/34:16) ★★★½ A gritty recording from the Fillmore West in San Francisco, made at the same time *Bitches Brew* was hitting stores in 1970, *Black Beauty* kicks off with aggressive Miles blowing and Airto Moreira's laughing cuica on "Directions." Other pert themes are taken from *Brew* ("Spanish Key," "Miles Runs the Voodoo Down," "Sanctuary," "Bitches Brew"). Steve Grossman's soprano is featured throughout, and the fascinating rhythm section of Jack DeJohnette on drums and Dave Holland on electric (often wah) bass keeps the grooves honest and open. Corea mans the electric keyboard alone, overdriving it expressively on "Willie Nelson"; but there are no cranked guitars in earshot, so the density dimension is held in check. And there's lots of Miles, including a short, stirring ballad, "I Fall in Love Too Easily."

Live at the Fillmore East (65139; 50:57/50:18) ★★★★ Recorded a few months later, with the same band plus Keith Jarrett on organ (and Holland on acoustic bass, as well as electric), the brush begins to thicken, turn veldt-like. But it still feels like a band, unlike some of Miles' (also wonderful) musique-concrete-ish outings. Basically identical in formula to *Black Beauty,* with many of the same submerged themes, *Fillmore East* consists of scraggly funkified static groove music, each piece seguing into the next, stretching into rambling suites. The interplay and counterpoint between Jarrett and Corea make for especially fascinating listening. And check Miles' acrobatics on "It's About That Time" (from '69's *In a Silent Way*).

Dark Magus (65137; 50:12/50:51) ★★★★ This is about as demonic as the Prince of Darkness can make it. Carnegie Hall '74, primo sorcery with three guitars displacing keyboards, save Davis' own wicked injections of organ—his drone washes (same jams and jellies he would wield on *Agharta* and *Pangaea*) work very differently from his more flamboyant former key punchers. Exceptional guitarist Pete Cosey takes the lion's share of solos, with Azar Lawrence on tenor sax and Dave Liebman on other reeds. The Michael Henderson/Al Foster/Mtume rhythm section is in full flower; Miles proudly recalled that by the time of this band "most of the European sensibilities were gone," replaced by a "deep African thing." Burbling, near frantic congas on "Moja (Part 1)" and "Tatu (Part 2)" presage jungle by 20 years.

In Concert (65140; 46:04/38:26) ★★★★ The original vinyl release of this 1972 recording, made at New York's Philharmonic Hall, was (like the studio album *On the Corner*) typically mysterious, containing no information at all—no personnel, recording date, publishing, song titles. But one listen and you know the rhythm concept is transformed; now it's Al Foster holding down the drum kit, with an ever denser mix of Indian instruments (Badal

Roy on tabla, Khalil Balakrishna on electric sitar . . . man!) and ex-Aretha
Franklin sideman Henderson on menacing, but much straighter, funk bass.
Check out Henderson's relentless four-note/two-pitch riff on the first 14
minutes of "Ife." More superimpositional, heavily layered, still crystal clear,
the electric melange also includes Reggie Lucas on guitar, Cedric Lawson
on electric piano and synth, with the excellent Carlos Garnett on saxes and
Mtume on percussion. Everyone compares their wah skills on "Honky Tonk,"
while the fave blues rave "Theme From Jack Johnson" glide along. Sly Stone
is clearly the pop totem here.

Live-Evil (65135; 49:46/52:13) ★★★★½ Initially recorded in '69 and '70,
when the band was in flux, this palindrome-titled monster was later assembled
out of live and studio tapes by Davis and producer Teo Macero. Davis' amplified wah trumpet strikes like a cobra on "Sivad" (hey, what's the original pre-
electric wah but a brass mute?) that also contains an absolutely lunar guitar
outburst by John McLaughlin, guesting with the band for a night. Reed stars
include Wayne Shorter and Gary Bartz, and combinations of keyboardists:
Corea, Jarrett, Herbie Hancock and Joe Zawinul. As on all these records, this
isn't pyrotechnic techno-dweeb fusion, but an outstandingly creative electric
collage, folding in black pop, Hendrix rock and a very healthy hit of free-jazz.
Today's "post-rock" and trip-hop bands, from Tortoise to the Herbalizer, are
deeply indebted to this sound.

—John Corbett

April 1998
Quintessence, and Then Some

Some records define their time. The tunes create associations and lodge
permanently in the listener's subconscious. Occasionally, a group creates a
convergence of talent that thrills equally both the audiences and the critical
community. For a time, everything clicks. Despite the passage of time, changes
in tastes and departures by personnel, the ideal remains, frozen in time and
preserved on record. For most jazz listeners, the quintet of Miles Davis,
Wayne Shorter, Herbie Hancock, Ron Carter and Tony Williams touched
perfection. This boxed set comprehensively documents their time together.

Miles Davis Quintet 1965–'68: The Complete Columbia Studio Recordings
(Columbia/Legacy 67398; 72:35/73:33/76:35/70:51/74:21/73:26) ★★★★½ This
six-CD collection spans the interval between January 1965 and June 1968,
wherein the Miles Davis Quintet recorded material sufficient for five full LPs
and sides of two others, along with discarded masters to fill out the compila-

tions that followed. Included are the albums *E.S.P., Miles Smiles, Nefertiti, Sorcerer* and *Miles in the Sky* in their entirety, along with sides making up one-half of *Water Babies* and one-half of *Filles de Kilimanjaro*. Numerous other tracks previously appeared in the compilations *Circle in the Round* and *Directions,* the latter of which has yet to be reissued on CD. There are few revelations among the 13 previously unissued tracks, which include several alternate takes, two rehearsals of Hancock tunes that were rejected by Davis, and "Thisness," an intriguing Davis original discovered posthumously in his personal archives.

Unlike Columbia's *Miles Davis and Gil Evans* box, released in 1996, these recordings are presented in a strict, ruthlessly chronological order. This could be disconcerting for listeners who have memorized (and loved) the sequence of the original, classic albums. The bifurcation of *Filles de Kilimanjaro* may also trouble those who cherish that album. (The later sessions with Chick Corea and Dave Holland will appear in a future boxed set.) Painful as it may be for some, this hard logic gives new meaning to orphaned tracks like "Water Babies," "Circle in the Round" and "Sanctuary" that are now given their rightful context within more familiar material.

Most of this music has been available for years in various formats. Who should buy *The Complete Columbia Studio Recordings?* For anyone interested in Miles Davis, in Shorter, in jazz during this period or its impact on the present day, this box contains essential music. Thornier issues exist for die-hard Davis fans who may already have bought these recordings two or three times, particularly in light of the cost of this purchase.

Classic recordings like "Dolores," "Freedom Jazz Dance" and "Prince of Darkness" are plentiful; and set in their appropriate context, displaced tunes like Shorter's "Water Babies" and "Sweet Pea" fit right in. Among the highlights: Shorter's "Footprints" (from *Miles Smiles*), surely one of the most performed of his tunes, shaped by Carter's hypnotic bass vamp and minimalist accompaniment by Hancock; Davis' "Agitation" (*E.S.P.*), ignited by Williams' solo intro, contrasts the fire of Davis' muted trumpet with the ice of Shorter's tenor. Then, there's Shorter's aching, beautiful performance of his "Nefertiti" (*Nefertiti*), followed by a sighing refrain from the horns and complemented by Williams' progressively active, finally triumphal drumming; the graceful acrobatics of "Water Babies" (*Water Babies*) and the eerie atmosphere of "Tout de Suite" (*Filles de Kilimanjaro*).

Shorter's arrival served as the catalyst for this group, which continued until the career aspirations of its members and Davis' "new directions in jazz" led to the departures of Williams and Carter during the sessions for 1968's *Filles de Kilimanjaro*. Confronted with the polar extremes of traditional repertoire (which had occupied Davis' set lists for years), and the sometimes anarchic approach of the free-jazz movement, the trumpeter's quintet found a third path, one that retained the melodicism and structure of the past while selectively embracing elements of the New Thing. In 1965, the first year represented in this collection, Shorter and Williams recorded side projects for Blue Note (*The All Seeing Eye* and *Spring,* respectively) that explored open-ended compositions and turbulent soloing. That same year, former Davis sideman John Coltrane's quest took a new, adventurous turn with daring LPs like *Meditations* and *Ascension,* a development that was not lost on the trumpeter.

Working with a significantly younger crew of musicians wrenched Davis out of a somewhat stagnant situation. As these sessions progress, Davis seems increasingly open to the directions his colleagues are pointing, ultimately adding innovative elements of his own. Here, as on the 1965 *Plugged Nickel* sessions (recorded after *E.S.P.,* but before 1966's *Miles Smiles*), he sounds invigorated by the challenges posed by compositions like "Orbits." He's surprisingly malleable, but his sound, whether a piercing blast or a muted cry, remains instantly recognizable and distinctive. Shorter contributed an amazing 17 compositions during this period, including the aforementioned "Footprints," "Pinocchio," "Nefertiti" and "Water Babies." Aside from quantity, these are among the most beautiful, exotic and memorable tunes Davis ever recorded. Shorter's fecundity is even more remarkable when you realize that he also recorded five albums replete with original compositions for Blue Note during this period, but repeated only "Footprints."

An important transition occurs midway through this set, one that was transparent to listeners of the time. During the December 1967 sessions, Davis started experimenting with strikingly different elements, including electric keyboards and guitars, rock rhythms and use of the studio as a compositional tool. His first forays, "Circle in the Round" and "Water on the Pond," were not released until 1979 and 1980, respectively. Now expanded to its original 33:32 length, Davis' "Circle in the Round" uses repetition. Joe Beck's electric rhythm guitar, Hancock's celeste and a trance-like rhythm to realize a fascinating, if unsuccessful, project. Along with "Water on the Pond," these sessions point to the rock rhythms of *Miles in the Sky,* the studio assemblies, electronic instruments and vamps of the *Bitches Brew* period and beyond. The experiments continued with the additions of guitarists Bucky Pizzarelli and George Benson, and, for the *Miles in the Sky* sessions, the addition of electric keyboard and electric bass. Curiously, the early 1968 sessions seem the most dated, and the least cogent. Davis and his cohorts are clearly anticipating and stalking another New Thing, achieving greater success with the later *Filles de Kilimanjaro* sessions.

With a reissue program of this magnitude, one expects an upgrade in sound quality in keeping with the latest digital innovations. Better sound sometimes justifies repurchasing music; though, as *DownBeat* contributor John Corbett has cautioned, "There's always a better copy." Compared to previous domestic and Japanese CD issues, the sound in this package is noticeably better. Expect to hear improved stereo separation between trumpet and tenor saxophone, and a tighter sound to Carter's bass. Williams' cymbals sound crisper, Hancock's piano seems a bit brighter and Shorter's tenor has more depth and presence. There's added clarity when Davis hits the high notes, and bass and drums seem more prominent in the mix.

Final packaging for the boxed set was not available at press time. Liner notes by Todd Coolman and Bob Belden, along with an overview by Michael Cuscuna, offer detailed and frequently insightful analyses of the quintet's activities, as well as the aural documents. Until now, Coolman was best known for playing the bass, most notably in the company of James Moody. Here, he's responsible for describing the big picture, including the historical context, the backgrounds of the players and the events that shaped the music. Coolman does a commendable job, though his notes sometimes focus on details while ignoring larger issues. For example, Coolman names seven bassists who filled in for Ron Carter on the road, but doesn't discuss Carter's shift to electric bass in the studio, or his eventual departure from the quintet.

Belden, who co-produced this reissue with Cuscuna, offers a track-by-track commentary, including more-than-customary attention to the structure and studio assembly of the pieces. Students of harmony will love Belden's nuts-and-bolts discussion; less technically inclined listeners may feel lost at times. Belden consistently mines interesting nuggets of information, as he explains the construction of "Circle in the Round," or the evolution of Hancock's "Madness." He also provides some color as to what transpired in the studio, observing that *Miles Smiles* is composed entirely of first (and only) takes, and describing Hancock's unsuccessful efforts to rehearse his compositions for Davis' approval.

Without diminishing the quality of the notes, it would have been nice to read more of the firsthand perspectives of participants in these sessions. I wanted to know how it felt to be in the studio with the band when these tracks were recorded. Coolman and Belden's notes prompt, and leave unanswered, a number of tantalizing questions. For example, both writers suggest that Gil Evans was involved in the 1968 sessions, acting as a "prominent collaborator/contributor" by influencing "Stuff" and possibly composing "Petits Machins," but further elaboration is needed. I also wanted to know more about the selection process that determined which tracks were worthy of immediate release. Were the remaining tracks abandoned because of dissatisfaction on the part of the artists? Or, as the pace of innovative recordings accelerated, did Davis simply prefer to release newer material?

The last question is important because an in-depth boxed set like *The Complete Columbia Studio Recordings* invites the listener to second-guess the producers, artists, et al., as to which excised tracks deserved release, which alternate takes are preferable to the masters and how the albums should have been sequenced. Substituting one's own value judgments for those of the professionals is part of the fun, but it helps to know who's been second-guessed. The question also revives issues that have been debated since the reissue craze began. Is it fair to the artists to release work that they may have deemed substandard? Does it diminish the luster of tracks like "Fall" and "Pinocchio" to include rehearsals, second alternates and unsuccessful tracks like "Sidecar II"?

With so much perfection at hand, why only 4½ stars? Although I can't praise the 1965 through 1967 masters enough, *Miles in the Sky* hasn't aged as well. Too few of the numerous archival tracks achieve the same pinnacles as the other five originally issued albums. Clearly, the set is most valuable to the Miles Davis enthusiasts who can glean new insights from the odds and ends, or who must own everything this quintet recorded.

—Jon Andrews

June 1998
Miles Davis & The Modern Jazz Giants
Bags' Groove
JVC 0046
★★★★½

This album comes from two 1954 sessions recorded by Rudy Van Gelder. Davis, Percy Heath and Kenny Clarke play on both. One quintet contains Sonny Rollins and Horace Silver. The other contains Milt Jackson and Thelonious Monk for two takes of the title track. Davis' improvisations have a luminous, almost gentle lyricism, though their symmetry and linearity date them as early Miles. Jackson's two solos are soul from a pure original strain. Rollins makes concise, definitive statements on three of his own standards-to-be: "Airegin," "Oleo" and "Doxy." Van Gelder's fully resurrected 1954 mono sound is so good it's almost supernatural.

—Thomas Conrad

July 1998
Miles Davis
At Carnegie Hall
Columbia/Legacy 65027
★★★★½

It's about time. One of the no-brainers in reissue history has finally been resolved: namely, putting all of the May 19, 1961, Miles Davis Carnegie Hall music together in one package. Why it was sliced and diced in the first place is beyond reason. Another twist: Why the awful sound quality for such a momentous occasion? (The label states "360 Stereo Sound," but what we get sounds like a below-average radio transmission, not unlike the original releases.) An honest account as to why a concert of this stature was recorded so poorly remains to be heard.

This show was the first public performance of anything by the trumpeter and arranger Gil Evans with a 21-piece orchestra, the two having bagged three albums' worth of material by this time. As for Davis' group, it was a transition band, all the players fresh from recordings in March (*Someday My Prince Will Come*) and April (the Blackhawk club dates). Clearly, the Carnegie Hall performances are inspired, one to the next, alternating between quintet and full-ensemble performances, drawing from Davis' distant past ("Oleo," "Walkin'") to more recent band themes ("So What," "Someday My Prince Will Come," "Teo") to selections from two of the three Davis/Evans collaborations ("The Meaning of the Blues/Lament," "New Rhumba," the adagio from "Concierto de Aranjuez" from *Sketches of Spain*) to what ended up being the surprise of the concert, Davis' first public performance of the standard "Spring Is Here."

There are two things that make this recording one for the ages: Davis' playing and the fact that this is the only legit live document we have of the trumpeter with Evans and his orchestra. The fact that they could pull it off in public, playing strong renditions of music recorded in the studio, is enough to silence those critics who carped that their three albums were possible only because they made their music in the haven of a recording studio, practicing, dubbing and remixing takes many times over. In fact, it's unfortunate that there wasn't more of the orchestra on this program, as only about 30 minutes of this 86-and-a-half-minute concert features everyone together.

Evans' somber orchestration of pianist Bill Evans' mood-setting introduction to the original version of "So What" begins the program. What follows is the band's jam on the famous blues. One wishes the orchestra would have been brought back in to conclude the song somehow. As it is, we hear more orchestra in a lovely rendition of "Spring Is Here," complete with pianist Wynton Kelly's beautiful chords at the end. "Teo" and "Walkin'" are straight-out, blowing numbers for the band, as are later tunes "Oleo" and "No Blues," while the ballad "I Thought About You" features Davis in, as critic Bill Coss stated in his *DownBeat* concert review, "an open, emotional experience" (July 6, 1961). Coss went on to say that "all the impressive features of the concert were insignificant in the face of Miles' performance. He soared away from his usual restraint and limited register, playing high-note passages with tremendous fire, building magnificent solos that blazed with drama." He also praised Evans' scores as "perfect complements to Davis' middle-register brooding." Indeed.

For those familiar with the original release (and subsequent CD of additional material), it's a treat to finally hear this music in the order it was performed. As it is, this band with tenor saxophonist Hank Mobley, Kelly, bassist Paul Chambers and drummer Jimmy Cobb can be heard in what was essentially their swan song with Davis.

—John Ephland

"So What"; "Spring Is Here"; "Teo": "Walkin'"; "The Meaning of the Blues/ Lament"; "New Rhumba"; "Someday My Prince Will Come"; "Oleo"; "No Blues"; "I Thought About You"; "En Aranjuez con Tu Amor (Adagio from Concierto de Aranjuez)."

Personnel: Davis, trumpet; Hank Mobley, tenor saxophone; Wynton Kelly, piano; Paul Chambers, bass; Jimmy Cobb, drums; Gil Evans Orchestra.

January 2001
Radical Dudes

Last August, Columbia/Legacy and Epic/Legacy added five important releases to its series of remastered albums from the '70s. Three of the titles revolve around Miles Davis and feature an ever-changing cast of the trumpeter's electric-period all-stars; two others highlight Davis-alum John McLaughlin's Mahavishnu Orchestra and Weather Reporter Jaco Pastorius, respectively. Taken together, these re-releases represent a radical movement in instrumental music and reveal everything from the heights of artistic genius and virtuosity down to the depths of self-indulgence and slop.

Thanks to a combination of positive critical revisionism and excessive hero worship, Davis' early-'70s recordings have benefited from endless praise and lip-service during the past two decades. Their influence on modern music remains undeniable, and quite impressive, to be sure. And the grooves they're built on are hypnotic and sexy, even mind-expanding. But to be brutally honest, it's hard to overlook some of the obvious flaws that have marred the electric-Miles listening experience since day one.

On the Corner (Columbia/Legacy 63980; 54:49) ★★, originally released in 1972, marked a turning point for Davis in terms of rhythmic concept. "Tunes" are defined by ever-shifting (and heavily edited) layers of drums, percussion and bass, a further departure from the horn-melody/keyboard-harmony paradigm he and his celebrated quintet helped shatter during the 1960s. Chord changes gave way to varying degrees of rhythmic density as Miles and producer Teo Macero started using new devices to introduce solos, alter moods and contextualize melody. They completely rearranged song structure and stretched it way out into a thick funk that soloists passed through rather than blew on.

On the Corner is a rough listen, though. When the album starts, it sounds like someone let up the "pause" button right in the middle of a tape loop, as drums and percussion jump out from some arbitrary place. The underlying grooves are tediously repetitive and not especially hip, even if they were unlike anything recorded by jazz musicians up to that point. Sure, the music here can put you into a trance, if that's what you seek. But be prepared for rude awakenings caused by jarring misplaced beats, the product of both over-ambitious and lazy editing. All the while, Davis remains mostly buried in the muck. When he does emerge for a solo, he mostly toys with a wah-wah that makes him sound like a bad electric guitarist.

Out of a similar bag but significantly more refined, 1974's *Big Fun* (63973; 73:56/68:42) ★★★½ comes as a big relief. Davis actually plays, for one; his presence is much stronger here, starting with the long haunting melody of the first track, "Great Expectations." With melodic support from saxist Steve Grossman and bass clarinetist Bennie Maupin, he blows (sans wah-wah) over a more coherently grooving ensemble that breathes and accompanies like a real band. *Big Fun* blows away *On the Corner* in the musicality department, but the grooves and improvs still have a tendency to stretch past the point where they remain interesting.

Collectors will find four new tracks on this expanded, two-CD edition of *Big Fun*—"Recollections," "Trevere," "The Little Blue Frog" and "Yaphet"— all of which appeared on 1999's *The Complete Bitches Brew Sessions.*

Get Up With It (63970; 60:00/64:07) ★★★, also from 1974, was Davis' last studio release before a long absence ('75–'81) from playing and recording. Here, Davis and Macero seem finally to have found the right balance of the elements that distinguish this electric period of their partnership. The album starts with the 32-minute "He Loved Him Madly" (Davis' tribute to the recently deceased Duke Ellington), which threatens to bore but ultimately sucks you in and breaks your heart. Davis, who plays a lot of brooding organ on *Get Up With It,* grieves over Duke with funereal reverence. Dave Liebman's echoing alto flute fills every apse with sweetness and light. The drums/percussion, electric guitars and bass contribute to the sorrow and the joy.

—Ed Enright

Editor's note: Also reviewed in this column were Mahavishnu Orchestra, Birds of Fire *(66081;* ★★★★*) and* Jaco Pastorius *(Epic/Legacy 64977;* ★★★★★*).*

July 2001
The Hot Box

The Hot Box is a column in *DownBeat* where four reviewers each review the same four albums. One writes the full review for each disc. The others write a brief synopsis with their rating. Here are what the four critics thought of *Live at the Fillmore East.*

Miles Davis
Live at the Fillmore East—March 7, 1970: It's About That Time
Columbia 85191
★★★★

After dredging the catalog for as much extant Miles as they could repackage, Columbia is apparently now trolling their holdings for previously unreleased material from the Prince of Darkness' live recordings. Good move. This is supercharged electric modal jazz funk, restlessly creative and at times unrelenting, and it contends with the best of Davis' known discography from the period.

The fact is, however, that contrary to what is suggested in the PR accompanying this two-disc set, this is not at all a badly documented epoch in the trumpeter's history. This particular run of concerts at the Fillmore East in New York were the last of Shorter's tenure with the band, but if you swap Steve Grossman in for him, there's *Black Beauty,* recorded a month later with an otherwise identical band at Fillmore West in San Francisco; if you add Keith Jarrett to this amalgam and flash forward two months you get *At Fillmore,* documented back in New York. In all cases, the repertoire is very similar, consisting mainly of themes debuted on *In a Silent Way* and *Bitches Brew.* At the time, Davis was sometimes featured on bills with rock acts—in this case, with Neil Young and Crazy Horse and the Steve Miller Blues Band—and in his autobiography he describes Miller as a "sorry-ass cat" and "non-playing motherfucker" with whom he was not happy to share the marquee.

If such an ego-clash dynamic sparked the ferocity of this particular performance, we should thank Mr. Miller. The two discs collect two full, scalding, 40-plus minute sets, and though they could almost fit on a single CD it's good to have them separate and complete. Each program is a medley; the two sets share some themes, but they're so stretched as to not feel redundant. The familiar drone-funk rumble of Joe Zawinul's "Directions" starts both sets and culminates each time in a torrid tenor saxophone solo from Shorter, who is thoroughly engrossing here; elsewhere, Shorter's soprano cuts the thick molasses jams like a slashing guitar.

Chick Corea is magnetic and focused, contributing atomic energy to a Rhodes-colored, psychedelic R&B, his acid piano pinned down by the looping electric bass lines of Dave Holland and muscular, shock-absorbing drumming of Jack DeJohnette, spiced by Airto Moreira's gulping and gasping cuica and bone-dry shakers. In the first set's finale, the electric piano and drums relent for a sweet Shorter/Airto duet over bubbling bass, then Corea and Holland break out of tempo into unrestricted abandon, Airto's vibraslap and metal percussion dinging playfully in the rear.

One can sense the presence of Davis everywhere on these recordings, not only in the evil sandpaper tone of his trumpet, but in the shape of the sonic montages, the aggressiveness of the funk, and the swagger and strut so perfectly epitomized on "Miles Runs the Voodoo Down" on the second disc. It's a very welcome addition to the already bulging bag of electric Miles.

—John Corbett

> Disc 1—"Directions"; "Spanish Key"; "Masqualero"; "It's About That Time/The Theme." Disc 2—"Directions"; "Miles Runs the Voodoo Down"; "Bitches Brew"; "Spanish Key"; "It's About That Time/Willie Nelson."
>
> Personnel: Miles Davis, trumpet; Wayne Shorter, soprano and tenor saxophone; Chick Corea, electric piano; Dave Holland, acoustic and electric bass; Jack DeJohnette, drums; Airto Moreira, percussion.

———

Filling in the historical blanks is a hero's gig, so Belden and the Legacy dudes should spend the summer on Mount Olympus for coming up with a legit copy of the Wayne–Chick–Dave–Jack brigade. The bootlegs we've learned from (*Double Image*) haven't lied. Vicious, vicious stuff. No wonder their jazz-rock progeny couldn't live up to it.

—Jim Macnie ★★★★

———

Those who value Davis' work of the 1970s will revel in this new material. Most will find it yet another lamentable early chapter in his descent into sonic savagery and sheer camp. Davis himself is full of fire, fury and fervor. It's stirring at first. But without the emotional controls that turn such natural forces into artistry, it quickly becomes a harangue.

—John McDonough ★

———

The music is ferocious. To think this stuff was sellout stock is laughable, given the difficult terrain these pre-*Bitches Brew* workouts represent. Sadly, the distortion indicates engineers in over their heads, but with a band, especially Miles, playing their hearts out.

—John Ephland ★★★★

═══

September 2001
Miles Davis
Jazz at the Plaza
Columbia/Legacy 85245
★★★★
At Newport 1958
Columbia/Legacy 85202
★★★★

Time has been good to this music and these musicians. Both of these live dates from 1958 present the *Kind of Blue* band at work, playing music more expressionist than impressionist, following the codes of that decade's hard-bop logic, only to upend that fertile terrain in true Milesian fashion.

The release of both discs is to be celebrated for the great shows they were, but hardly for the lack of this material having been available in one form or another over the years. In particular, the Miles and Coltrane connection has spurred ongoing interest with cannibalized releases not available as actual original albums. The *Plaza* material is more obscure, and, in some ways, more interesting. First time on CD in the U.S., *Jazz at the Plaza,* unfortunately, continues to be marred by spotty recording quality, and offers no additional material. The Newport set, on the other hand, adds "Bye, Bye Blackbird" and

"The Theme," 12 minutes of music left off the original releases of this concert. (Issued in the '60s as *Miles and Monk at Newport,* Monk's music on the B side actually came from another year at Newport.)

Recorded in September, *Jazz at the Plaza* was an impromptu concert, performed at a recording company shindig. Soundwise, Davis' trumpet, ironically, is the greatest casualty (the sound, overall, is improved somewhat on this release, and Davis' trumpet is finally heard to good effect by the time the band ends the concert with Monk's "Straight, No Chaser"). The music itself, highlighted by "My Funny Valentine" and featuring Davis and Evans with the saxophonists sitting out, is in some ways more engaging than the Newport material. The tune both releases share in common is "Straight, No Chaser," the *Plaza* version played at a faster, more spirited clip. The intrigue generated from the redefined hard-bop on *Jazz at the Plaza* has everything to do with Davis' ever-growing elliptical phrasings and seeming impatience with the already stuffy tendencies of this latter-day offspring of bebop.

The summer of 1958 was a high point for Davis and his band as they wowed the crowd at Newport. This outdoor show was all about blowing, and the trumpeter plays it hard and fast, especially on "Ah-Leu-Cha" and "Two Bass Hit." The same is true for Coltrane and Adderley, as they build on the newfound energy created earlier in the year with the sextet's first recording, *Milestones.* Jimmy Cobb, playing too busy as usual, is all over his drum set to the point of losing control on the uptempo fare. By way of contrast, bassist Paul Chambers, the consummate pro, provides the necessary anchor for four musical giants with a lot to say.

—John Ephland

Jazz at the Plaza: "If I Were a Bell"; "Oleo"; "My Funny Valentine"; "Straight, No Chaser."

Personnel: Miles Davis, trumpet; John Coltrane, tenor saxophone; Julian "Cannonball" Adderley, alto saxophone; Bill Evans, piano; Paul Chambers, bass; Jimmy Cobb, drums.

At Newport 1958: "Introduction by Willis Conover"; "Ah-Leu-Cha"; "Straight, No Chaser"; "Fran-Dance"; "Two Bass Hit"; "Bye, Bye Blackbird"; "The Theme."

Personnel: Miles Davis, trumpet; John Coltrane, tenor saxophone; Julian "Cannonball" Adderley, alto saxophone; Bill Evans, piano; Paul Chambers, bass; Jimmy Cobb, drums.

January 2003
Swiss Swan

Not since those heady, unsteady days of the early '60s had Miles Davis led a band that was so organized around songs and harmony. You might say the bop was back in some cases. That is, bop with a backbeat. *The Complete Miles Davis at Montreux 1973–1991* (Columbia/Legacy 86824) ★★★½ is the best place to look for what was Davis' last major transition in style and concept. That this 20-CD box set is made up of completely live material makes the point even more valid.

Indeed, the greatest benefit to this set is the link to the trumpeter's live performances. We have had a great deal of material from the 1970s, but the '80s on through to the end of his career and life in 1991 offered relatively little in the way of concert material. Montreux Jazz Festival organizer Claude Nobs is to be commended for releasing this music, designed for "hardcore Miles fans." There are, incidentally, no edits or remixes in this set.

As for the first two discs—which cover Davis' first visit to Montreux in 1973 with his "jungle band" of reedist Dave Liebman, drummer Al Foster, bassist Michael Henderson, percussionist Mtume, and the distinctive two-guitar lineup of Reggie Lucas and Pete Cosey—the music is typically abstracted jazz-rock, with Foster driving everything. Davis' wah-wah works the corners with a program that's generically labeled "Miles in Montreux '73 #1," "#2" and "#3," the only familiar material of the time being a reworked "Calypso Frelimo." Important, but not essential.

While the challenge of a group sound remained the calling card for Davis' '70s-era live bands, the music that was to follow after his retirement in 1975 reflected a kind of demarcation of roles. No longer a band to be reckoned with, it was more Davis the showman with a crack backup band. Gone were the wah-wah, funk and soul elements germane to so much of the preceding decade's experiments. The new sound was characterized more by rock and pop elements, with Davis using his mute on ballads again. Discs 3–18 and 20 offer the best look at this radical transition from James Brown, Sly Stone and all things funky to Michael Jackson, Prince and even Al Jarreau. The music was still black, but with a polish never seen before.

Discs 3–10 featured guitarist John Scofield, saxophonist Bob Berg and bassist Darryl Jones, among others. This was the period where Davis was working out his high-energy rock material, with tight arrangements, bop-like phrases and lots of jamming. Unfortunately, as time went on, one gets the sense that Davis' bands were doing most of the work, and the old man was slowing down, pacing himself. This is true with the bands that follow on discs

11–18 as well, even though the material is less demanding. Apart from other tunes, highlights from Columbia albums *You're Under Arrest, We Want Miles, Star People* (still out of print!) and *Decoy* (discs 3–10) gradually give way to *Tutu* and *Amandla* highlights (the latter two released on Warner Bros.). The soloists included saxophonist Kenny Garrett, guitarist Robben Ford and bassist Foley. Throughout discs 3–18 and 20, the role of the keyboardist remained one of colorist rather than distinct musical voice—one of the downsides to Davis' musical choices that began during 1972's *On the Corner.*

The only previously released material in this set comes from the much-heralded *Miles and Quincy Live at Montreux,* the larger-than-life return-to-roots performance the summer before Davis died in 1991. This interesting document (disc 19) is made up of Gil Evans charts from *Birth of the Cool* on through to *Sketches of Spain* and includes both the Evans orchestra as well as the George Gruntz Concert Jazz Band, conducted by Quincy Jones and also featuring trumpeter Wallace Roney and Garrett. Disc 20, the only non-Montreux material, is a 1990 Nice, France, show (with previously released edits) Davis put on with crew regulars of the time.

—John Ephland

March 2003
Book Review
So What: The Life of Miles Davis
by John Szwed (Simon & Schuster)

At the beginning of *So What: The Life of Miles Davis* (Simon & Schuster), author John Szwed asks a good question: Why yet another book about Miles Davis? There are undoubtedly more books about the trumpeter than any other jazz musician, yet, as Szwed points out, Davis remains a mystery. He is a towering figure in jazz, yet his legend has often obscured his central place in American music.

There are few jazz writers more equipped to say something fresh about Davis than Szwed. His previous book, *Space Is the Place,* was about a figure at least as shadowy—Sun Ra. Yet in some ways that was an easier project since so little is known about Ra. Separating fact from legend is a daunting task when it comes to a figure as mercurial and volatile as Davis.

For the most part, Szwed handles it brilliantly. The book is enormously readable and the story is familiar: the coddled childhood within the upper middle class family, the early years as a musician, his attendance at Juilliard (Szwed makes it clear that Davis spent more time in class there than is generally acknowledged), hooking up with Charlie Parker, his addiction and his journey through the most important musical directions of his time, from bop to fusion. Yet Szwed manages to find details that change our angle on Davis, and puts a precious new perspective on the subject. One example early in the book is the old story about Davis losing a trumpet contest to a white boy who was clearly inferior. Never happened, according to Szwed. This tale has been a key part in Davis' mythology, especially in understanding the lifelong rage he carried with him toward injustice, racial and otherwise.

Szwed states that his book is not truly a definitive biography but rather a "meditation on the life of Miles Davis." Nor does Szwed dwell much in detailed musical interpretation. Szwed most brilliantly succeeds in putting Davis in the context of his times. This too is not an easy thing to accomplish. Davis was both a product of his times as well as a figure who had an enormous effect on culture and society. Szwed understands this and genuinely adds to our understanding of these profound and complex matters.

One of the book's highlights is Szwed's discussion of Davis' relations with women. He had a terrible need for female companionship that went beyond sex, yet he wound up mistreating, often viciously, the women he loved. This might seem to some as nothing more than celebrity gossip, but Davis' relationship with women was so central to his life and psyche it is crucial information.

The book is not without its flaws, some of them serious. For example, there is short shrift given to Davis' musical relationship with John Coltrane, certainly the most important of his life, even more so than that with Charlie Parker. Years after Coltrane's death, Davis remained bitter over the saxophonist's departure from his group. And there is little doubt that Davis was deeply affected when Coltrane overshadowed him in the 1960s, both as a musical and cultural force (Davis claimed to have little use for Trane's quartet of that time). As Szwed himself points out, wherever Davis lived, he kept a photo of Coltrane on his wall.

There are also a number of errors in the book, some more disturbing than others. One (admittedly niggling) example is Szwed's discussion of *Miles Smiles*. He mentions that all the tunes on the album were written by members of the band except one, Eddie Harris' "Freedom Jazz Dance." But the group also plays a stunning version of Jimmy Heath's "Ginger Bread Boy" on the album. Not a big deal but such errors make us less trustful of Szwed's facts.

The chronology is often confusing, and will be particularly so for those not familiar with Davis' life and career. At one point, Szwed discusses the 1955–'57 quintet and uses an anecdote that mentions the group playing "So What." Davis never played that tune until after its initial recording on the *Kind of Blue* session in 1959.

These flaws are distracting, but they do little to interfere with the book. No writer has portrayed the complexity of Davis the man and the connection between that complexity and the music he played as well as Szwed does. That in itself is a towering achievement.

—Eric Nisenson

July 2003
Burnin' by the Bay

Miles Davis, In Person Friday Night at the Blackhawk, Complete (Columbia/ Legacy 87097, 60:20/57:05) ★★★★½; *In Person Saturday Night at the Blackhawk, Complete* (Columbia/Legacy 87100, 65:47/58:04) ★★★★½ Instant classics since their release, the original LP and CD issues of *Live at the Blackhawk,* documenting a two-night engagement by the Miles Davis Quintet at the funky San Francisco club, are part of the lingua franca of contemporary hardcore jazz, desert island picks for numerous musicians and fans. The music is urbane, down-home and flat-out swinging, and Miles is pungent and pithy, complemented by Hank Mobley's effervescent lines and the Rolls-Royce rhythm section of Wynton Kelly, Paul Chambers and Philly Joe Jones. Less fluid and intense than the Adderley–Coltrane–Evans unit that preceded it and less venturesome than the Shorter–Hancock–Carter–Williams freedom quintet of 1964–'69, this short-lived band exemplified the bebop esthetic circa 1961, projecting a grounded, communicative attitude and a deep blues feeling that gave it immense cache among an audience comprised of inner-city African American sophisticates and white hipsters.

So iconic is this music that it's a curious experience to hear the unexpurgated proceedings of both nights, seven sets presented in real time, warts and all. It turns out that the albums were virtual representations of the actual event—the indelible versions of "No Blues," "If I Were a Bell," "All of You" and "Fran Dance" are edits, and both albums are completely resequenced, to the extent that the producers lifted "Fran Dance" and "Oleo" from their Friday provenance to the Saturday night album. To these ears, the real-time Saturday program is more satisfying by a hair; Mobley plays with savoir faire and abandon, his message unimpeded by the occasional squeak, while Kelly, Chambers and Cobb lock into perfect tempos from the jump until the end—a trio romp through a medium-groove "Softly As in a Morning Sunrise" with a discursive prime-time Kelly solo—of a slamming, never-issued wee-small-hours fourth set. Actually, 12 tunes appear for the first time on the complete

Blackhawks, and each of the nine that is not a fragment (*Friday:* "If I Were a Bell," "Neo" and "I Thought About You"; *Saturday:* "Green Dolphin Street," "Walkin'," Autumn Leaves," "Two Bass Hit," "I Thought About You" and "Someday My Prince Will Come") is a worthy addition to the Davis lexicon. In point of fact, Miles operates at an astonishing level of consistency, drawing upon an immense lexicon of moods and sounds both on open-horn and Harmon mute, testifying with unwavering focus, heat and a hard-won sense of proportion. Ever the master of dynamics, he doesn't blow an unnecessary note, and there are no clichés.

The sound is vivid and well-balanced, and Ralph Gleason's (original) and trumpeter Eddie Henderson's (new) liner notes are insightful. After a while, it's as though you are in San Francisco circa 1961, with a front-center seat in the grungy house, having a ball with the free-thinking audience.

—Ted Panken

December 2003
Biopics & More

The Miles Davis Story (Columbia Music Video/Legacy Recordings 54040) ★★★★½ offers a refreshing, European slant, as it was produced for British television. The program's greatest strengths, apart from playing clips, revolve around its sources, coming as they do from all walks of Davis' life. From Irene Cawthorn (a childhood sweetheart who gave birth to his first three children), first wife Francis Davis and daughter Cheryl, to Bob Weinstock, Jimmy Cobb, George Avakian, Ron Carter, John McLaughlin, Joe Zawinul, Clark Terry, Marcus Miller and Shirley Horn, the insights are both illuminating and a confirmation.

—John Ephland

April 2004
The Hot Box

The Hot Box is a column in *DownBeat* where four reviewers each review the same four albums. One writes the full review for each disc. The others write a brief synopsis with their rating. Here are what the four critics thought of *Birdland 1951*.

Miles Davis
Birdland 1951
Blue Note 41779
★★★★½

Let's dispense with any questions about the musical content right away. This is Miles Davis leading two different sextets, slight variations on the ones documented on Prestige studio LPs from the early '50s, post-*Birth of the Cool*. The difference between this and those is that these airchecks were recorded live at Birdland, broadcast on WJZ, on Symphony Sid's show, and hence they've got the potency of the best live bebop. The excitement is immediately palpable; if you can't hear it, check your pacemaker.

Two of these three sessions have been extensively released before, in unauthorized versions appearing illegally on vinyl by shadowy labels like Ozone, Beppo, Kings of Jazz and Session Disc, always with worse sound. There's good reason that they've been bootlegged—the groups include trombonist J.J. Johnson melting his slide, some phenomenally brilliant drumming by Art Blakey, and a 20-year-old tenorman named Sonny Rollins. The excitement for tenor fans isn't limited to Newk, however, as there are three tracks with Eddie "Lockjaw" Davis and George "Big Nick" Nicholas squaring off and explosively trading eights. The biggest surprise, though, will come to those who think of Miles Davis exclusively as the master of mood and 'tude; on these live dates he shows what a fine bebop trumpeter he could be (a corrective to some of his more fumbling dates with Bird), cutting through the hyper tempos like he's sculpting metal with an acetylene torch.

Producer Michael Cuscuna's concept is to bootleg the bootleggers, releasing authorized versions that are designed to supercede any inferior releases. Jazz of this caliber certainly deserves to be part of the official registry—it's canonical American music, and its archiving shouldn't be left in the hands of mobsters and amateur enthusiasts.

Regarding sound quality, there are significant flaws on these recordings (particularly the four previously unreleased tracks), which were made off the radio by a thoughtful jazz fan. Restoration has made them sound much better than the unofficial versions but only so much can be done, and sometimes the clean-up starts to take away the vitality of a recording, rendering it spiffy and lifeless. Engineer Kurt Lundvall has stopped short of that, leaving them sounding very alive, as they should. So, there are a few crunchy spots and some speed problems, but anyone who's overly concerned with that needs simply to imagine the alternative: Would you prefer not to hear this? Listen to Davis and Blakey interacting on "Down," and tell me that, for technical reasons, it should be consigned to the archival wastebasket. This is about outrageously great music, not demonstrating your fantastic hi-fi.

—John Corbett

"Move"; "Half Nelson"; "Down"; "Out of the Blue"; "Half Nelson"; "Tempus Fugit"; "Move"; "Move"; "The Squirrel"; "Lady Bird."

Personnel: Miles Davis, trumpet; J.J. Johnson, trombone (1–7); Sonny Rollins (1–7), Eddie "Lockjaw" Davis (8–10), George "Big Nick" Nicholas (8–10), tenor saxophone; Kenny Drew (1–7), Billy Taylor (8–10), piano; Tommy Potter (1–7), Charles Mingus (8–10), bass; Art Blakey, drums.

———

Two words: Art Blakey. Holy shit! On "Move" Bu takes Denzil Best's title at its word, and drives the whole band. This archival find is an almost irrefutable case for jazz being a soloist's art.

—Jim Macnie ★★★★

———

A live ultrasound of Miles in vitro as a bopper. As Louis Armstrong was conceived in Creole ensembles but grew into a soloist, Miles was born in bebop, proving that everyone is someone else before becoming himself. Lots of flinty, staccato zip in his playing.

—John McDonough ★★★★

———

Beyond making the point that coolster Miles could bebop with the rest of the boys in 1951, I'm not too keen on a disc with three versions of "Move" and two of "Half Nelson," one of which features 20 seconds of noise. Kenny Drew sounds great, though, on this faded sonic document, taken from a private recording of a radio broadcast.

—Paul de Barros ★★★

═════

November 2004
Heaven On—Reissues

Seven Steps: The Complete Columbia Recordings of Miles Davis 1963–1964 (Columbia/Legacy 90840; 54:12/63:24/67:40/71:10/54:19/57:24) ★★★★½ documents trumpeter Davis' ongoing steps away from the studio, as he wrestled with time-tested standards, searched for ideas and tried on different players in the process.

The seventh and largest box in the Davis series, *Seven Steps* includes all of the *Seven Steps to Heaven* sessions as well as the unedited *Miles Davis in Europe* Antibes Festival date, and the full *Miles in Tokyo* and *Miles in Berlin* shows. Perhaps most significant, the New York Philharmonic Hall concert is now issued in its original song sequence. All together, the set amounts to 47 selections, with seven previously unissued performances, three in newly unedited form, all culled from six albums and their rejected offspring.

As with previous Columbia Davis box sets, the songs are presented chronologically, which, in this case, only adversely affects the studio material. It's fascinating to hear the previously unreleased takes from discs one and two, where the new songs "Joshua" and "Seven Steps to Heaven" are still being worked on, less "perfect" than the versions originally released but no less delightful. Likewise, "So Near, So Far" (disc one, released in 1981). These 1963 recordings are the only studio dates in the set and feature tenor saxophonist George Coleman, pianist Victor Feldman, Ron Carter on bass and drummer Frank Butler for disc one, substituting Herbie Hancock for Feldman and Tony Williams for Butler on disc two. Apart from Davis' sound and Feldman's smart and snappy playing, the attitude and energy level found on disc one is more subdued. By contrast, Williams' drive and slightly off-kilter approach sets the pace on disc two and after.

The balance of disc two and all of disc three is the unedited 1963 Antibes Jazz Festival concert, still in mono but no less exciting. With the later release of "I Thought About You" (1988), and previously unreleased takes of "Bye, Bye Blackbird" and "The Theme" we get the full effect as this band with the "second quintet" rhythm section and Coleman dive into the standard fare, Davis' trumpet on fire like never before, the trio section already tight and Coleman applying his bop dexterity with a few surprising twists and turns. Indeed, the risk taking was evident from the start in these live performances, the most obvious sign being the torrid pace given to normally easy-swinging tunes like "Walkin'" and "Milestones."

Discs four and five are dedicated to the remarkable Philharmonic Hall concert, now heard as it was played, no longer broken into ballads and burners across two previous releases. Coleman is at his peak on these recordings, and everyone seems to be either trying to outdo each other or is, paradoxically, incredibly patient, listening for cues and clues. Again, Williams' drumming sets the pace, his kick-ass waltz vamp landing somewhere between jazz, rock and R&B on an energized, uptempo "All Blues." All members swing furiously, and the ballads mine the melodic contours completely. Hancock's introduction to "My Funny Valentine" is a song unto itself.

The *Miles in Tokyo* concert takes up disc six. Featuring tenor saxophonist Sam Rivers, the band sounds like a working unit. Rivers' more aggressive attack and tendencies to throw in atonal gestures are a welcome contrast to Coleman's more conventional approach. Again, the material is standard fare, well-recorded and the last stop en route to the second great quintet. Disc seven is the *Miles in Berlin* show, with Wayne Shorter aboard. He's first heard on "Milestones," and it's clear from the start that his every move is in sync with the band, a deeper simpatico having been reached across to all five members. In the next few years, this band would redefine accepted jazz notions of rhythm, texture and compositional form. For those in attendance at the Berlin Philharmonie in September 1964, this concert was the first indication.

—John Ephland

April 2005
Miles Davis
Miles Electric: A Different Kind of Blue
Eagle Eye Media 39020
★★★★★

Nearly 35 years ago, Academy Award-winning filmmaker Murray Lerner had the foresight to record the entire 1970 Isle of Wight festival, during which legendary artists like Jimi Hendrix, The Who, Joni Mitchell and The Doors performed. The DVD *Miles Electric: A Different Kind of Blue* contains Miles Davis' entire 38-minute performance at the festival in glorious full color and with excellent sound quality, as well as interviews with many of Davis' sidemen during 1968–'75, Carlos Santana and journalist Stanley Crouch.

The only dissenting voice is that of Crouch, who explains how listening to *Bitches Brew* had the effect on him of a man pounding a nail into his hand, over and over again. For years, many lovers of Davis' electric music would have loved to drive nails into Crouch's hands, infuriated that a man who they see as narrow-minded managed to keep the discussion about the validity of Davis' electric music alive. After watching this spectacular DVD, one doubts that even the most ardent electric Davis fan will still want to drive nails into Crouch's hand. Such is the power of this DVD, and such is the degree to which it validates Davis' electric music, that the most likely response is a sense of pity that Crouch doesn't "get it."

The combination of the stunning performance footage and talking heads like Herbie Hancock, Keith Jarrett, Chick Corea, Dave Holland, Jack DeJohnette, Airto Moreira and Gary Bartz conveying with a glint in their eyes and a sense of awe in their voices what working with Davis was like, is a knockout.

Miles Electric leaves electric Davis lovers with nothing to prove and nothing to defend. They will simply cherish and adore this astonishing DVD. As for the skeptics, many of them may find themselves suddenly "getting it" and loving some of the greatest music the 20th century has ever produced.

—Paul Tingen

November 2005
Miles Davis
The Cellar Door Sessions 1970
Columbia/Legacy 93614
★★★★

Whenever Miles Davis changed direction, it was usually in tandem with a sideman's emergence as a force to be reckoned with on their terms—John Coltrane in the mid-1950s; Wayne Shorter in the mid-'60s and, with Joe Zawinul, into the fusion era; John McLaughlin on *Jack Johnson*. It's hard to imagine Davis' quantum leaps without them. Had his thinking been less mercurial in 1970, had he been content to keep a band together for a couple years, Keith Jarrett would perhaps now be on the short list. Much more so than suggested by the original two-LP *Live-Evil,* the pianist was the impact player in Davis' band at the end of one of the more amazing years of the trumpeter's career, which is revealed on the six-CD *The Cellar Door Sessions 1970.*

Davis opened the four-night pre-Christmas stand with a quintet: saxophonist Gary Bartz, drummer Jack DeJohnette, bassist Michael Henderson and Jarrett. Percussionist Airto Moreira came on the second night (discs 2–6), and guitarist John McLaughlin was there only for the last night (discs 5–6), which yielded the material Teo Macero masterfully edited for *Live-Evil.* Night after night, they revisited tunes such as "Directions," "Honky Tonk" and "What I Say." Some of the elements remained rather constant throughout the week—Davis' darting phrases and jabbing runs, roughened by his wah-wah pedal; Bartz's melding of minor-key lines and blues shouts; Henderson's popping riffs; Moreira's tangy accents.

While DeJohnette's Buddy Miles-with-monster-chops approach often triggered seismic rhythmic events and subsequent shifts in feel (takes of "Directions" veer greatly), Jarrett played an even bigger role in shaping the arc of the sets. Jarrett patched a Fender Rhodes piano and electronic organ through a distortion box and wah-wah pedal to create textures that were both gritty and otherworldly. His materials spanned fugal complexity and gutbucket directness. His adept movements through this spectrum (sometimes gracefully, sometimes pugnaciously) are consistently exciting. Yet, the real measure of Jarrett's centrality to the music was the nightly solo spot Davis allotted him. Four are included in this collection, totaling more than 20 minutes. Not only do they run like silver threads through the fabric of Davis' music, these solos now hover like foreshadows of the bracing solo music with which Jarrett would shortly storm the jazz world.

The other question this collection begs revolves around McLaughlin: What if he had made the entire stand? Though his playing is inspired, the chemistry of the band was already in place, and McLaughlin simply adds another solo voice, albeit a compelling one.

—Bill Shoemaker

Disc 1—"Directions"; "Yesternow"; "What I Say"; "Improvisation #1"; "Inamorata." Disc 2—"What I Say"; "Honky Tonk"; "It's About That Time"; "Improvisation #2"; "Inamorata"; "Sanctuary." Disc 3—"Directions"; "Honky Tonk"; "What I Say." Disc 4—"Directions"; "Honky Tonk"; "What I Say"; "Sanctuary"; "Improvisation #3"; "Inamorata." Disc 5—"Directions"; "Honky Tonk"; "What I Say". Disc 6—"Directions"; "Improvisation #4"; "Inamorata"; "Sanctuary"; "It's About That Time."

Personnel: Miles Davis, trumpet; Keith Jarrett, Fender Rhodes electric piano, Fender electric organ; Gary Bartz, soprano and alto saxophones; Jack DeJohnette, drums; Michael Henderson, electric bass; John McLaughlin, guitar (discs 5–6); Airto Moreira, percussion (discs 2–6).

September 2006
Polar Attraction—Reissues

There's a revealing moment as Steve Allen introduces Miles Davis' quintet on a November 1955 *Tonight Show*—the day after the band cut its first album for Prestige—when that jazz-friendly host has to look up the name of the saxophonist. Nowadays we may forget how little-known John Coltrane was when he became Davis' second-choice tenor that September. (He'd wanted Sonny Rollins.) The abbreviated "Max Is Making Wax" the band dives into after Allen's intro is too ferocious to typify the quintet—it's bebop that jumps like 1940s R&B—but shows how ready Coltrane was, and how that two-month-old quintet already sounded like a band, breathing as one, the pure oxygen rising off of Philly Joe Jones' cymbals.

On their esteemed studio recordings, however, collected still yet once again as *The Legendary Prestige Quintet Sessions* (Prestige/Concord Music Group

4444; 62:39/69:35/61:32/38:55) ★★★★★, one can more clearly hear this band that set the modern nightclub style as an amalgam of diverse borrowings and divergent tendencies. Those included: Ahmad Jamal's repertoire, lilting gait and buried-root piano voicings; the trumpeter's still-new exploration of that most iconic of jazz sounds—himself playing through a Harmon mute; Coltrane's emerging vertical chord-scrubs; bassist Paul Chambers' deep groove and occasional neo–Slam Stewart bowing; and Jones' propulsive rimshots on the fourth beat.

On the Harmon-muted quartet ballads, from that first session's "Just Squeeze Me" to a final "My Funny Valentine," the trumpeter's introspection and the Red Garland–led rhythm section's adaptation of Jamal-ian principles bond on the atomic level. (Only Chambers needs a little time to settle in.) But add Coltrane to the mix and the isotope becomes unstable. With his sweeping entrances, sweeps through the chords and five-espresso euphoria, he was an impractical sideman. What leader could compete? He worked best with Davis (and Thelonious Monk) because the boss's less-is-more-ism leaned so far the other way.

Still, the contrast between Davis' cunning feline and Coltrane's overexcited puppy created internal tensions, anticipating the trumpeter's fractious music to come. On their manhandle of bop anthem "Salt Peanuts"—with its boiling drums and open texture—the horns interjected discords (and all the Coltrane that rubbed off on Wayne Shorter) that forecast Davis' 1960s quintet. The music often has a raucous and (to borrow annotator Bob Blumenthal's word for Coltrane's developing technique) unfinished quality that places it in a broader modernist context. Literature and painting had been moving toward fragmentation for a while. Not that the string-of-solos art of jazz didn't know something about discontinuity already, but this band was supercharged by the horns' polar opposition.

No revelations for these ears in the latest (fourth? fifth?) remastering, by Joe Tarantino. The main added value is the rare live stuff on the final disc, which includes that *Tonight Show* "Max" and "It Never Entered My Mind." There are also two good if slightly fuzzy-sounding December 1956 Philadelphia airchecks, and three numbers from Café Bohemia in May '58, where—with the new Davis sextet's Cannonball Adderley off for the night— the old quintet is reunited, save for Bill Evans having replaced Garland on piano. Davis' plaintive open-horn work is especially fetching, a preview of his sound on *Porgy and Bess* two months later. The following week, Jones was out and Jimmy Cobb in. Davis' first classic quintet had slipped into the past.

—Kevin Whitehead

Grateful acknowledgment is made to the following writers for permission to use the material specified, all of which was previously published in *DownBeat* magazine.

Jon Andrews: "*Miles Davis: The Complete Plugged Nickel Sessions*," September 1995; "*Live Around the World*," August 1996; "Quintessence, and Then Some," April 1998. Reprinted by permission.

Bob Belden: "The Digs," May 1993; "Miles . . . 'What Was That Note?'," December 1995. Reprinted by permission.

Fred Bouchard: "*Ascenseur Pour L'Echafaud (Lift to the Scaffold)/Aura*," February 1990. Reprinted by permission.

W.A. Brower: "*The Man With the Horn*," November 1981. Reprinted by permission.

Thomas Conrad: "*Bags' Groove*," June 1988. Reprinted by permission.

John Corbett: "The Sound of Miles Davis: The Discography 1945–1991," February 1994; "Miles Beguiles," July 1997; "The Hot Box: *Live at the Fillmore East—March 7, 1970: It's About That Time*" (with Jim Macnie, John McDonough and John Ephland), July 2001; "The Hot Box: *Birdland 1951*" (with Jim Macnie, John McDonough and Paul de Barros), April 2004. Reprinted by permission.

Paul de Barros: "Dreaming of the Re-Master," November 1996; "The Hot Box: *Birdland 1951*" (with John Corbett, Jim Macnie and John McDonough), April 2004. Reprinted by permission.

Ed Enright: "Radical Dudes," January 2001. Reprinted by permission.

John Ephland: "The Hot Box: *Live at the Fillmore East—March 7, 1970: It's About That Time*" (with John Corbett, Jim Macnie and John McDonough), July 2001; "*Jazz at the Plaza/At Newport 1958*," September 2001; "Swiss Swan," January 2003; "Biopics & More," December 2003; "Heaven On—Reissues," November 2004. Reprinted by permission.

Art Lange: "*Bitches Brew*," September 1989. Reprinted by permission.

Jim Macnie: "The Hot Box: *Live at the Fillmore East—March 7, 1970: It's About That Time*" (with John Corbett, John McDonough and John Ephland), July 2001; "The Hot Box: *Birdland 1951*" (with John Corbett, John McDonough and Paul de Barros), April 2004. Reprinted by permission.

Howard Mandel: "Miles Davis: 'I Don't Mind Talkin' If People Are Listenin'," December 1984; "Miles—A Life," December 1991; "Sketches of Miles," December 1991; *"We Want Miles/Pangaea/Directions/Circle in the Round*," August 1982; *"Star People*," August 1983; "Caught in the Act: Tribute to Miles Davis," February 1984; *"Heard 'Round the World*," April 1984; *"Decoy*," August 1984; "Chase the Miles Down," December 1990; "Swedish Miles," March 1993. Reprinted by permission.

John McDonough: "The Hot Box: *Live at the Fillmore East—March 7, 1970: It's About That Time*" (with John Corbett, Jim Macnie and John Ephland), July 2001; "The Hot Box: *Birdland 1951*" (with John Corbett, Jim Macnie and Paul de Barros), April 2004. Reprinted by permission.

Bill Milkowski: "Miles Plays Gil at Montreux," October 1991; "Caught in the Act: B.B. King/ Miles Davis, Beacon Theatre, New York," July 1986; *"Tutu*," January 1987; *"Agharta*," July 1991; *"Dingo*," January 1992. Reprinted by permission.

Charles Mitchell: "Miles: Resting on Laurels? Changing His Silent Ways?," September 1980. Reprinted by permission.

Dan Ouellette: "Dark Prince in Twilight: Band Members and Close Associates Discuss the Last Years of Miles Davis' Life," May 2001; "Behind the Cellar Door: The Making of the Explosive, Mostly Unheard Live Miles Davis Electric Sessions," October 2005. Reprinted by permission.

Ted Panken: "Burnin' by the Bay," July 2003. Reprinted by permission.

Gene Santoro: "Miles Davis: The Enabler, Part I," October 1988; "Miles Davis: The Enabler, Part II," November 1988; *"Miles and Coltrane*," August 1983; *"On the Corner*," August 1983. Reprinted by permission.

Bill Shoemaker: *"The Cellar Door Sessions 1970*," November 2005. Reprinted by permission.

Paul Tingen: *"Miles Electric: A Different Kind of Blue*," April 2005. Reprinted by permission.

Robin Tolleson: *"Doo-Bop*," August 1992. Reprinted by permission.

Kevin Whitehead: *"Miles Davis and Quincy Jones Live at Montreux*," March 1994; "Polar Attraction—Reissues," September 2006. Reprinted by permission.